FEDERAL APPELLATE PRACTICE AND PROCEDURE

IN A NUTSHELL®

SECOND EDITION

GREGORY A. CASTANIAS
Partner, Jones Day (Washington, DC)
Adjunct Professor of Law
Indiana University Maurer School of Law

ROBERT H. KLONOFF
Jordan D. Schnitzer Professor of Law
Dean of the Law School, 2007–2014
Lewis & Clark Law School

WEST ACADEMIC PUBLISHING

The publisher is not engaged in rendering legal or other professional advice, and this publication is not a substitute for the advice of an attorney. If you require legal or other expert advice, you should seek the services of a competent attorney or other professional.

Nutshell Series, In a Nutshell and the Nutshell Logo are trademarks registered in the U.S. Patent and Trademark Office.

444 Cedar Street, Suite 700
St. Paul, MN 55101
1-877-888-1330

West, West Academic Publishing, and West Academic are trademarks of West Publishing Corporation, used under license.

Printed in the United States of America

ISBN: 978-0-314-28931-5

To Jane, Alex and Ella-Anne.

—G.A.C.

To my Family.

—R.H.K.

To our many mentors, especially George C. Pratt and John R. Brown, the circuit judges we served as law clerks, and for all of the lawyers and law students throughout the country who are attempting to master the art of appellate advocacy.

—G.A.C. and R.H.K

PREFACE TO THE SECOND EDITION

As with the First Edition, this is a dual-purpose text. It is for law students taking courses on appellate procedure or appellate advocacy. It is also meant to serve as a "desk book" for lawyers practicing before appellate courts. In the years since the publication of the First Edition, we (and others) have used this text as the pedagogical center of courses in Appellate Practice and Procedure, supplemented with case law, rules and statutes, and law-review articles. We have also kept it at our desks as a handy reference for when we confront appellate issues in practice.

The Second Edition reflects a number of changes and updates in appellate law. In addition to reflecting important decisional developments that have occurred since 2007, this Second Edition reflects the most recent changes to the Federal Civil, Criminal, and Appellate Rules, and to the Rules of the U.S. Supreme Court, as well as certain proposed and anticipated rule changes that may occur shortly after this text goes to press. Among other changes, the Second Edition also contains an expanded treatment of motion practice, and an entirely new chapter on Ethics and Professionalism.

As with the First Edition, we are grateful for the research assistance we have received. In particular, we wish to recognize Jacob Abbott, Aria Branch, Roberto Castillo, Max Goins, Elizabeth Graves, Nikki

McArthur, and Daniel Walker for their excellent work.

We are also grateful to those who have reviewed the First Edition and suggested improvements that are now reflected in this Second Edition. Among those providing such assistance are Judge Andy Effron, Eleanor Vuono, Jane Castanias, Tom Fisher, and the students of Professor Castanias's courses on Appellate Practice and Procedure, and on Federal Circuit Advocacy, at the Indiana University Maurer School of Law.

In addition, Jackie Ford, who has worked with Professor Castanias for almost 23 years, again deserves special recognition for her efforts in the preparation of this text, and for managing his practice as a lawyer so efficiently that he could devote the time and energy to this text while maintaining a full-time law practice.

As with the First Edition, the statements and conclusions in this text are ours alone. In particular, they do not necessarily represent the views of Jones Day, its clients past, present, or future, any other attorney affiliated with that law firm, or anyone who had input into this text. Likewise, the statements do not necessarily reflect the views of the Federal Advisory Committee on Civil Rules, on which one of the authors currently sits.

GREGORY A. CASTANIAS
ROBERT H. KLONOFF

May 2017

PREFACE TO THE FIRST EDITION

This text is for students taking courses on appellate procedure or appellate advocacy. It is also designed as a concise reference book for attorneys handling cases in the federal appellate system. Its focus is on the federal courts of appeals and the U.S. Supreme Court. It addresses all of the major issues facing an advocate in the federal appellate court system, including the final-judgment rule and its exceptions, preservation of error, standard of review, filing an appeal, briefs, appendices, oral argument, rehearing and rehearing *en banc*, opinions, Supreme Court jurisdiction, writs of certiorari, and Supreme Court briefing and oral argument. In addition to providing information on core principles and cases, as well as "nuts and bolts" information (such as word and page limits on briefs), the text also provides strategic advice, such as how to prepare a persuasive brief or to deliver an effective oral argument.

Professor Castanias is a Partner in the Washington, D.C. office of the Jones Day law firm, and an Adjunct Professor of Law at the Indiana University—Bloomington School of Law (his alma mater), where he teaches appellate practice and procedure. He has been a practicing appellate lawyer for all of his 17-plus years in practice. He has briefed and argued numerous cases in the U.S. Supreme Court, before most of the federal courts of appeals, and in several state appellate courts as well.

In addition to teaching appellate procedure for a number of years, Dean Klonoff has been a practicing appellate lawyer for about 25 years. As an Assistant to the Solicitor General of the United States (and later in private practice at Jones Day), he has briefed and argued numerous cases before the U.S. Supreme Court. He has also briefed and argued appeals before many other federal and state appellate courts throughout the United States.

Professor Castanias counts Dean Klonoff as one of his early mentors in the practice of law, and as one of his great friends.

Throughout the text, we cite and discuss the Federal Rules of Appellate Procedure (FRAP), specifically the version of those rules that became effective on December 1, 2007. Those rules govern procedure in the United States courts of appeals. The text also frequently references the Rules of the Supreme Court of the United States, specifically the version of those rules that became effective on October 1, 2007. Various rules contained in the Federal Rules of Civil Procedure and the Federal Rules of Criminal Procedure (the versions that became effective on December 1, 2007, as well as statutory provisions of the Judicial Code (Title 28, United States Code) also bear directly on important issues that arise on appeal. The use of the terms "he" and "him" in the text are for simplicity, and are not (unless the context plainly indicates otherwise) gender-specific references.

The reader should also be aware that the individual federal circuits have their own local rules, internal operating procedures, and handbooks that govern or inform appellate practice within each particular circuit. Although a discussion of the specifics of these numerous local rules is largely beyond the scope of this book, anyone practicing before a particular federal circuit must become thoroughly familiar with that court's local rules.

We wish to express our appreciation to our research assistants, who helped with researching various topics in the text. These include Ashely Atwell, Miriam Bailey, Gabrielle Beam, Zhijun Gong, Heather Hermosillo, Rory Kane, Andrew Lonard, Jennifer McGrew, Uzo Nwonwu, Erica Perkin, Michael Raine, Valley Renshaw, Jeremy Wikler, and John Witten.

We also wish to thank Professor Ed Brunet, Jane Castanias, Tom Fisher, Professor Arthur Hellman, Scott Medsker, George Patton, Steve Sanders, and Jennifer Swize for their very helpful comments on an earlier draft of this text.

Finally, Jackie Ford, who has worked with Professor Castanias for almost 13 years now, deserves special recognition for her efforts in the preparation of this text, which included everything from managing the boxes of research files to formatting the earlier drafts.

The statements and conclusions in this text are ours alone, however, and do not necessarily represent the views of Jones Day, its clients past, present, or future, any other attorney affiliated with that law firm, or anyone who had input into this text.

GREGORY A. CASTANIAS
ROBERT H. KLONOFF

February 2008

OUTLINE

PART 4. ISSUES OF ETHICS AND PROFESSIONALISM

PART 5. THE FUTURE OF THE FEDERAL APPELLATE COURTS

TABLE OF CASES

References are to Pages

FEDERAL APPELLATE PRACTICE AND PROCEDURE

IN A NUTSHELL®

SECOND EDITION

PART 1

OVERVIEW

CHAPTER 1

OVERVIEW OF THE FEDERAL APPELLATE COURT SYSTEM

§ 1.1 HISTORY

Article III of the U.S. Constitution established the Supreme Court and granted Congress the authority to create lower, or "inferior" courts. Under the Judiciary Act of 1789, Congress established the number of Supreme Court Justices (five Associate Justices and the Chief Justice). Congress also created 13 judicial districts for the eleven states (Massachusetts and Virginia had two districts each). Judiciary Act of 1789, ch. 20, §§ 1–2, 1 Stat. 73. Two more districts (North Carolina and Rhode Island) were created in 1790. Act of June 4, 1790, ch. 17, 1 Stat. 126; Act of June 23, 1790, ch. 21, 1 Stat. 128.

Each district had a trial court and a circuit court (the circuit courts were composed of district judges and Supreme Court Justices, who were assigned to designated circuits). The circuit courts also heard certain types of significant trial-level cases. Judiciary Act of 1789, ch. 20, §§ 4, 11, 1 Stat. 73.

Congress created additional circuit and district courts in 1801. Judiciary Act of 1801, ch. 4, § 21, 2 Stat. 89, and imposed a further restructuring of the courts in 1802. Act of Mar. 8, 1802, ch. 8, §§ 1–2, 2 Stat. 132. Congress did not establish circuit judgeships for circuit courts until 1869. Act of April 10, 1869, ch. 22, § 2, 16 Stat. 44.

In 1891, Congress passed the Judiciary Act of 1891, more commonly known as the Evarts Act. Act of March 3, 1891, ch. 517, 26 Stat. 826. This Act created the U.S. Courts of Appeals. Nine courts of appeals (numbered "First" through "Ninth") were established for the nine existing judicial circuits. The judges on the circuit courts served on these new appellate courts, along with judges whose judgeships were first created under the Evarts Act. Act of March 3, 1891, ch. 517, §§ 1, 3, 26 Stat. 826.

Over the years, the appellate courts grew in size, number, and importance. Eventually, district judges stopped regularly sitting on the courts of appeals. *See* Act of March 3, 1891, ch. 517, § 3, 26 Stat. 826. Several new circuits were created over the years by dividing existing courts of appeals. The Tenth Circuit was created in 1929, when the Eighth Circuit was divided in two. Act of Feb. 28, 1929, ch. 363, 45 Stat. 1346 (Tenth Circuit). The Eleventh Circuit was created in 1980, when the Fifth Circuit was divided in two. Fifth Circuit Court of Appeals Reorganization Act of 1980, Pub. L. No. 96–452, 94 Stat. 1994.

Other of the courts of appeals were created (or evolved) through congressional changes to the status of existing courts. The D.C. Circuit was created in 1893 as the Court of Appeals for the District of Columbia, Act of Feb. 9, 1893, ch. 74, 27 Stat. 434; from its inception until 1948, it had a Chief Justice and Associate Justices (rather than a Chief Judge and Circuit Judges, like the rest of the federal courts of appeals), and, until 1970, when the D.C. Court of Appeals was created to handle local cases, the D.C.

Circuit had hybrid federal and "state" appellate jurisdiction. The Federal Circuit (which handles, among other categories of cases, appeals in patent cases) was established in 1982 by combining the appellate jurisdictions of the former Court of Claims and the former Court of Customs and Patent Appeals, and adding exclusive jurisdiction over appeals from federal district court patent cases. Federal Courts Improvement Act of 1982, Pub. L. No. 97–164, 96 Stat. 25. Currently, there are a total of 179 judgeships on the 13 federal circuit courts.

Circuit judges are said to be appointed for life (though the statutory authority, in parallel with the Constitution, establishes that they hold their office "during good Behavior"). 28 U.S.C. § 44(b); *see also* U.S. Const. Art. III, § 1. Judges in the First through Eleventh Circuits must reside in the circuit of appointment "at the time of [the] appointment and thereafter while in active service." 28 U.S.C. § 44(c). In the Federal Circuit, each judge must reside within 50 miles of the District of Columbia. *Id.* The D.C. Circuit has no similar residency rule. *Id.* In each circuit except for the Federal Circuit, "there shall be at least one circuit judge in regular active service appointed from the residents of each state in that circuit." *Id.* The reference to judges "in regular active service" is meant to distinguish "active," full-time judges from "senior" judges. Upon reaching a combined 80 years of age and federal judicial service ("the rule of eighty"), an active judge may elect a semi-retired status as a "senior judge," retaining his salary, entitling the judge to handle a reduced caseload, and providing the President and Senate the opportunity to nominate and confirm, respectively, a new "active" judge to take the senior judge's seat on the court. 28 U.S.C. § 371. By electing senior status, however, a judge loses the opportunity to be part of the court sitting *en banc*, unless he or she was a member of the panel initially deciding the case. *See* § 1.4, *infra*.

Parties have an automatic right to appeal to the federal court of appeals from a final judgment of the U.S. district court (and from certain non-final judgments, *see* § 4.1, *infra*). By contrast, review at the Supreme Court level is almost entirely discretionary. *See* § 22.4, *infra*.

Decisions of the federal appellate courts are published in the *Federal Reporter*, which is produced by Thomson West Publishing Company. Not all federal appellate decisions are published in the *Federal Reporter*, but "unpublished" decisions are often also published in Thomson West's *Federal Appendix* or can be obtained through on-line research services (*e.g.*, Westlaw, LexisNexis, Bloomberg Law, Findlaw). Decisions of the U.S. Supreme Court are published in a government publication, the *United States Reports*, as well as in two private publications (Thomson West's *Supreme Court Reporter* and LexisNexis/Michie's *United States Supreme Court Reports, Lawyers' Edition*). In addition, the e-Government Act of 2002 requires that all decisions (published and not published) of the federal courts of appeals be made available on the federal courts' websites.

§ 1.2 CURRENT STRUCTURE OF THE FEDERAL APPELLATE COURTS

The federal court system comprises 94 judicial districts. Every state has at least one district; some states have several. For instance, New Jersey has only one federal district, but New York has four (the Eastern, Northern, Southern, and Western Districts). Each judicial district has both a federal district court (the trial level court, which hears both civil and criminal cases) and a bankruptcy court. Three U.S. territories—Guam, the Northern Mariana Islands, and the Virgin Islands—also have federal district courts that hear civil, criminal, and bankruptcy cases.

The 94 judicial districts are organized into 12 regional appellate courts:

- First Circuit: Maine, Massachusetts, New Hampshire, Puerto Rico, and Rhode Island.
- Second Circuit: Connecticut, New York, and Vermont.
- Third Circuit: Delaware, New Jersey, Pennsylvania, and the Virgin Islands
- Fourth Circuit: Maryland, North Carolina, South Carolina, Virginia, and West Virginia.
- Fifth Circuit: Louisiana, Mississippi, and Texas.
- Sixth Circuit: Kentucky, Michigan, Ohio, and Tennessee.

- Seventh Circuit: Illinois, Indiana, and Wisconsin.
- Eighth Circuit: Arkansas, Iowa, Minnesota, Missouri, Nebraska, North Dakota, and South Dakota.
- Ninth Circuit: Alaska, Arizona, California, Hawaii, Idaho, Montana, Nevada, Oregon, Washington, Guam, and the Northern Mariana Islands.
- Tenth Circuit: Colorado, Kansas, New Mexico, Oklahoma, Utah, and Wyoming.
- Eleventh Circuit: Alabama, Florida, and Georgia.
- D.C. Circuit: District of Columbia.

28 U.S.C. § 41. All of these circuits hear appeals from the district courts located within them. All circuits also have jurisdiction over certain "petitions for review" from federal administrative agencies; the D.C. Circuit is the locus of a majority of these cases, which involve direct appellate review of agency action without the requirement of a district court challenge.

History has shown that because of population shifts and other factors, some circuits can eventually get so large that they become, arguably, too unwieldy to function as a single circuit. As a consequence, as noted above, some of the original circuits have been divided by Congress. Prior to 1929, the current Eighth and Tenth Circuits constituted a single circuit (the Eighth). *See* 45 Stat. 1346. More recently, the current Fifth and Eleventh Circuits constituted a single circuit (the Fifth) until Congress in 1981 split them into two. *See* 94 Stat. 1994. Fifth Circuit law as of the date of the split became binding precedent in the new Eleventh Circuit. *See Bonner v. City of Prichard, Ala.*, 661 F.2d 1206, 1209–11 (11th Cir. 1981).

The Ninth Circuit is now (by far) the largest circuit, both in terms of the number of states and overall caseload. *See* Diarmuid O'Scannlain, *Ten Reasons Why the Ninth Circuit Should Be Split*, Engage (Oct. 2005); Mary M. Schroeder *et al.*, *A Court United: A Statement of a Number of Ninth Circuit Judges*, Engage (March 2006). In 1998, Congress appointed a commission, chaired by retired Supreme Court Justice Byron White, to study the federal appellate courts and their structure, most notably whether the Ninth Circuit should be split. The Commission recommended against such a split, instead proposing that the Ninth Circuit adopt three administration divisions in order to ease its burdens. *See* Commission on Structural Alternatives for the Federal Courts of Appeals, Final Report at 29–30 (1998).

Despite that Report, several proposals have been introduced in the Congress that would split the Ninth Circuit—for instance, to redesignate a Ninth Circuit limited to California, Hawaii, Guam, and the Northern Mariana Islands, and to add a Twelfth Circuit (Arizona, Idaho, Montana, and Nevada), and a Thirteenth Circuit (Alaska, Oregon, and Washington). Most recently, citing the Ninth

Circuit's high caseload and long disposition times, Arizona's Governor, junior Senator, and one of its representatives has proposed severing Arizona from the Ninth Circuit, either by moving it to the Tenth Circuit, or by creating a new Twelfth Circuit that would likely include Idaho, Montana, and Nevada. *See* Matt Ford, *Arizona v. Ninth Circuit Court of Appeals*, The Atlantic (Feb. 9, 2016). Such proposals have generated enormous controversy and debate, on both political and practical grounds, and to date none of them has come close to legislative enactment.

In addition to the eleven numbered circuits and the D.C. Circuit, there is one other circuit: the Federal Circuit in Washington, D.C. Unlike the other twelve circuits, whose appellate jurisdiction is based mostly or entirely on the geographic origin of the cases before it (*e.g.*, cases determined in New York's district courts are appealed to the Second Circuit), the Federal Circuit has nationwide jurisdiction in particular *types* of cases, including patent cases, as well as appeals from specialized courts (such as the Court of International Trade, which hears cases involving international trade and customs, and the Court of Federal Claims, which hears cases involving monetary claims and various other types of disputes against the United States) and particular federal agencies (such as the International Trade Commission, which determines disputes involving alleged unfair trade practices, or the Merit Systems Protection Board, which determines personnel actions under the federal government's merit-based employment system). 28 U.S.C. § 1295.

The United States Supreme Court is at the top of this pyramid. The Supreme Court hears important cases arising under the Federal Constitution, federal statutes, federal common law, and treaties. U.S. Const. Art. III, § 2. The Supreme Court's jurisdiction is almost entirely discretionary (the Court decides whether to grant certiorari). In a small number of cases, the Supreme Court has non-discretionary appellate jurisdiction, 28 U.S.C. § 1253, or original jurisdiction, 28 U.S.C. § 1251; even then, the Supreme Court's "mandatory" jurisdiction has a great measure of discretion to it. The jurisdiction of the Supreme Court is discussed in greater detail at §§ 22.3–22.6, *infra*.

§ 1.3 APPOINTMENT OF CIRCUIT JUDGES AND SUPREME COURT JUSTICES

Federal court of appeals judges and Supreme Court Justices, as well as federal district court judges, are nominated by the President and subject to confirmation by the Senate. U.S. Const. Art. II, § 2. They are appointed for life ("good Behaviour"). U.S. Const. Art. III, § 1.

At the Supreme Court level, the selection of the Chief Justice (whose title is "Chief Justice of the United States," not "Chief Justice of the Supreme Court") follows the same "advice and consent" process as the appointment of an Associate Justice—nomination by the President, followed by Senate confirmation. For instance, even though William Rehnquist was nominated by President Nixon as an Associate Justice and confirmed by the Senate in

1972, when President Reagan decided to elevate Justice Rehnquist to be Chief Justice in 1986, he had to send a formal nomination to the Senate, and the Senate had to vote to confirm him for that new position.

At the circuit level, by contrast, the designation of Chief Judge is not subject to a separate nomination and confirmation process. Instead, the position is determined through seniority—the seniormost active judge (*i.e.*, not in senior status, *see* § 1.4, *infra*) who is 64 years of age or younger, has served at least one year as a circuit judge, and has not previously served as the Chief Judge. 28 U.S.C. § 45. If no judge meets those criteria, then the acting chief judge shall be "the youngest circuit judge in regular active service who is sixty-five years of age or over and who has served as circuit judge for one year or more." 28 U.S.C. § 45(a)(2)(A). The chief judge serves a maximum of seven years or until age 70, unless no one else meets the statutory requirements. 28 U.S.C. § 45(a)(3)(A), (C).

§ 1.4 RETIREMENT OF CIRCUIT JUDGES AND SUPREME COURT JUSTICES

A circuit judge may (but need not) retire or assume senior status subject to the requirements of 28 U.S.C. § 371(c). Specifically, starting at age 65, retirement or senior status is permitted under the following circumstances:

Age	Years of Service
65	15
66	14
67	13
68	12
69	11
70	10

28 U.S.C. § 373(b). This is known colloquially as "the rule of eighty," because it is that sum of age and service that entitles an active judge to elect senior status.

A judge who chooses senior status is allowed to participate as a judge, but (typically) under a significantly reduced workload. 28 U.S.C. § 371(b)(1). A senior judge may not vote to determine whether the court should rehear (or hear) a case *en banc*; however, if a senior judge is a member of a panel whose decision is subject to an *en banc* rehearing, that senior judge may participate in the *en banc* rehearing itself. *See United States v. Hudspeth*, 42 F.3d 1013 (7th Cir. 1994); 28 U.S.C. § 46(c). That practice is not without controversy, however, as some judges have read the statutes differently. *See Igartua de la Rosa v. United States*, 407 F.3d 30, 31–32 (1st Cir. 2005) (per curiam) and *id.* at 32–34 (Torruella, J., dissenting).

When Justices of the U.S. Supreme Court retire, there is no similar provision allowing them to continue to participate in the decisions of the U.S. Supreme Court. Instead, they take on the title of

"Associate Justice (Retired)" (or "Chief Justice (Retired)") and may be designated by the Chief Justice of the United States to perform certain duties, including sitting as a member of the panels hearing cases in the courts of appeals. 28 U.S.C. § 294(a). For instance, Justice Powell sat with the Fourth and Eleventh Circuits after his retirement from the Supreme Court; Justice Brennan sat with the D.C. Circuit; Justice Thurgood Marshall sat with the Second Circuit (he had once been a Second Circuit judge) and the Federal Circuit; Justice White sat with the Eighth, Ninth, and Tenth Circuits; Justice O'Connor has sat with the Second, Third, Fourth, Eighth, Ninth and Eleventh Circuits; and Justice Souter has sat with the First Circuit (where he served prior to his confirmation to the Supreme Court).

§ 1.5 A NOTE ON SPECIALIZED APPELLATE COURTS

Although this text focuses on the federal courts of appeals and the U.S. Supreme Court, there are also various specialized courts (in addition to the Federal Circuit) that hear certain types of agency or other appeals. These courts—the U.S. Court of Appeals for Veterans Claims, the U.S. Court of International Trade, the U.S. Court of Appeals for the Armed Forces, and the U.S. Tax Court—are discussed briefly below.

A. U.S. COURT OF APPEALS FOR VETERANS CLAIMS

The U.S. Court of Appeals for Veterans Claims, created in 1988 as the U.S. Court of Veterans Appeals, reviews final judgments from the Board of Veterans' Appeals, an administrative agency. Only the veteran (not the government) may seek judicial review of an adverse decision of the Board. The court decides most (but not all) cases without oral argument. Either party may appeal the court's decision to the Federal Circuit (and, ultimately, to the U.S. Supreme Court). The seven judges who sit on this Article I court are appointed by the President and confirmed by the Senate and serve 15-year terms. The court hears cases in panels of three or *en banc*. 38 U.S.C. § 7254(b).

B. U.S. COURT OF INTERNATIONAL TRADE

The U.S. Court of International Trade, created by the Customs Courts Act of 1980, reviews cases involving customs, trade, and imports. The court, which is an Article III court, is composed of nine judges, each appointed for life by the President and confirmed by the Senate. It is essentially a trial court, although its trials typically involve "contests" or "reviews" of various executive trade-related decisions. 28 U.S.C. § 1581. The judges typically review cases individually, although the chief judge, at his or her discretion, may designate a panel of three judges to review a case when the case involves the constitutionality of an act of Congress, a Presidential proclamation, or an executive order, or otherwise has broad and significant implications. 28 U.S.C. § 255. Appeals from final decisions of the Court of International Trade are taken to the Federal Circuit.

C. U.S. COURT OF APPEALS FOR THE ARMED FORCES

The U.S. Court of Appeals for the Armed Forces—which was established in 1951 as the Court of Military Appeals, renamed in 1968 as the U.S. Court of Military Appeals, and given its current name in 1994—reviews cases involving members of the armed forces on active duty and others subject to the Uniform Code of Military Justice. The court, which is an Article I court, has jurisdiction over cases (typically court-martials) involving national security, criminal law, constitutional law, and ethics. The court has both mandatory and discretionary jurisdiction over court-martials.

Cases arrive at the Court of Appeals for the Armed Forces through a specialized military structure. In particular, each branch of the armed forces (Army, Navy-Marine, Air Force, and Coast Guard) has authority over its members. After a case is heard by one of these branches, it may be appealed to an intermediary court, the Court of Criminal Appeals. Each branch has its own Court of Criminal Appeals. After review by the relevant Court of Criminal Appeals, the case may be appealed to the U.S. Court of Appeals for the Armed Forces. The latter court has mandatory jurisdiction over cases involving a death sentence and cases sent to the court by the judge advocate general for review. The court has discretionary jurisdiction over all other petitions. Review requires the consent of two of the five judges. The court also has jurisdiction to grant petitions for extraordinary relief. Cases from the court may be taken to the U.S. Supreme Court through certiorari review. 28 U.S.C. § 1259.

The court consists of five civilian judges, appointed by the President and confirmed by the Senate, who serve terms of 15 years. The court sits *en banc* when reviewing cases and decides cases with or without oral argument.

D. U.S. TAX COURT

The U.S. Tax Court hears cases involving disputes over taxes due prior to payment of the disputed amounts. (Refund suits must be filed in federal district courts.) Tax Court judgments are appealable to the regional court of appeals for the taxpayer's residence or principal place of business. 26 U.S.C. § 7482(b). The Tax Court, an Article I court, was established by Congress in 1924 as the Board of Tax Appeals (it was given its current name in 1943) and consists of 19 judges, who are appointed by the President. Each judge serves a 15-year term. 26 U.S.C. § 7443.

Cases come to the Tax Court by taxpayers challenging a finding by the Commissioner of Internal Revenue. The Tax Court is essentially a trial court, but it has an "appellate" function in that it reviews these administrative determinations. The case may be filed only after a taxpayer has received either a notice of deficiency or a notice of determination by the Commissioner.

A taxpayer whose case involves a disputed amount of $50,000 or less has the option of having the case heard through the small tax case procedure, a simplified, informal procedure. Such decisions, however, are not appealable. All cases with a disputed amount over $50,000 (or in which the taxpayer does not elect the small tax case option) are heard as regular proceedings.

Where a taxpayer decides to pay the tax first and then sue for a refund, such a case can be brought in any federal district court (where a taxpayer may obtain a jury trial) or in the U.S. Court of Federal Claims (where no jury is allowed). Appeals from those trial courts go to the relevant regional court of appeals (in the case of district-court proceedings) or to the Federal Circuit (where the case originates in the Court of Federal Claims).

The Tax Court hears cases throughout the United States. When a taxpayer files his or her petition with the court, he or she is able to choose where the case will be heard.

§ 1.6 GOVERNING RULES

It is crucial to know the full panoply of rules that govern procedure in the federal courts of appeals. The Federal Rules of Appellate Procedure are essential reading, but each circuit has its own special gloss on certain rules, which are promulgated as local rules, individual circuit internal operating procedures, and in some cases, unwritten practices.

A. FEDERAL RULES OF APPELLATE PROCEDURE

The Federal Rules of Appellate Procedure (FRAP) "govern procedure in the United States courts of appeals," except that, where the FRAP "provide for filing a motion or other document in the district court, the procedure must comply with the practice of the district court." FRAP 1(a)(1), (a)(2). The rules and amendments thereto are promulgated by the Supreme Court, and become effective after being sent to Congress under the provisions of the Rules Enabling Act, 28 U.S.C. §§ 2071–2077.

The FRAP concludes with a series of forms that may be helpful to practitioners. Among the approved forms are various kinds of notices of appeal and petitions for review, an affidavit to accompany a motion to appeal *in forma pauperis*, and a suggested form of the type-volume certification required by FRAP 32(a).

B. LOCAL APPELLATE RULES

FRAP 47 empowers the various courts of appeals to "make and amend rules governing its practice." The individual circuits are afforded wide discretion to make their own rules of procedure under this rule; the only limitations are (i) "[a] local rule must be consistent with—but not duplicative of—Acts of Congress and rules adopted under [the Rules Enabling Act]"; (ii) the local rules "must conform to any uniform numbering system prescribed by the Judicial Conference of the United States"; and (iii) "[a] local rule imposing a requirement of form must not be enforced in a manner that causes a party to lose rights because of a nonwillful failure to comply with the requirement." FRAP 47(a)(1), (a)(2).

Local rules allow a certain amount of variability among the individual circuits' practices, making it crucial to know the local rules in addition to the FRAP. For example, D.C. Circuit Rule 28 imposes several additional requirements for the content of appellate briefs that are not found in the FRAP. The Seventh Circuit has a special practice, embodied in its Rule 36, requiring reassignment to a different district judge in most cases where a case is remanded for a new trial. The Federal Circuit's Rule 30 has special rules governing the preparation of the Joint Appendix; in fact, that Court's rulebook (available at www.cafc.uscourts.gov) shows several portions of FRAP 30 struck through because they do not apply to cases in that court (*e.g.*, FRAP 30(b)(1) and 30(c)(2), which are struck out in their entirety in the Federal Circuit's rules).

Most circuits also provide "practice notes" to their rules, indicating, for example, how they will be enforced in particular cases. And most circuits also publish Internal Operating Procedures, or I.O.P.s, which set forth certain operating standards, such as when briefs will be distributed to the judges' chambers, how judges will be assigned to panels, and the like. (The Ninth Circuit's version of I.O.P.s are called "General Orders.") The Third Circuit's I.O.P.s are an excellent example: They are available on that court's website, www.ca3.uscourts.gov, and they cover everything from panel composition, to procedures when visiting judges sit with the court, to the expected timetable for the drafting and circulation of opinions. *See* §§ 21.1, 21.2, *infra*. In addition, many courts of appeals have handbooks for practitioners that are available on the courts' websites; the Seventh Circuit's version is a particularly useful guide for practice within that court.

C. FEDERAL RULES OF CIVIL AND CRIMINAL PROCEDURE

In addition to the Federal Rules of Appellate Procedure, provisions of the Federal Rules of Civil and Criminal Procedure play an important role in the federal appellate process. In particular, Rules 50, 52, 54, 59, 60, and 62 of the Federal Rules of Civil Procedure are all crucial with respect to questions of appealability and timing of appeals. *See* §§ 3.2(E), 5.3(D), *infra*.

D. SUSPENSION OF THE RULES UNDER FRAP 2

FRAP 2 permits a court, in order "to expedite its decision or for other good cause," to "suspend any provision of these rules in a particular case and order proceedings as it directs." Rule 2 empowers courts of appeals to, for example, summarily affirm (or reverse) a judgment without full briefing and oral argument, *Joshua v. United States*, 17 F.3d 378 (Fed.

Cir. 1994); *Groendyke Transport, Inc. v. Davis*, 406 F.2d 1158 (5th Cir. 1969); to issue a mandate forthwith instead of following the prescribed procedures and time periods of FRAP 41, *Gitter v. Gitter*, 396 F.3d 124, 136 (2d Cir. 2005); to suspend the rules concerning oral argument, *United States ex rel. Townsend v. Twomey*, 493 F.2d 1325, 1326 (7th Cir. 1974); or to overlook waiver of arguments where manifest injustice would result, *United States v. Allen*, 127 F.3d 260, 264 (2d Cir. 1997); *Nikitine v. Wilmington Trust Co.*, 715 F.3d 388, 389 n. 2 (1st Cir. 2013).

A court may not, however, use FRAP 2 to alter the time periods for filing a notice of appeal in a way that would affect the jurisdictional requirements of FRAP 3 or 4. *See* FRAP 26(b)(1), (b)(2); *Torres v. Oakland Scavenger Co.*, 487 U.S. 312, 317 (1988).

PART 2
FEDERAL CIRCUIT COURTS

CHAPTER 2

THE WORK OF THE FEDERAL APPELLATE COURTS

Workloads. Over time, the total number of appeals filed in the federal appeals courts has been increasing, though there have been some meaningful decreases—followed, often, by meaningful increases—in year-to-year statistics. Statistics compiled by the federal judiciary (and available at www.uscourts.gov) bear this out. For example, for the 12-month period ending in September 2001, 57,464 appeals were filed; for the most recent 12-month period—ending 15 years later, in September 2016, that number was 60,357. But that number has been as high as 68,473 (in September 2005), and as low as 52,698—in the year ending September 2015. Roughly 25 percent of the appeals filed in a given year are prisoner cases (*e.g.*, habeas corpus cases and civil rights cases filed by prisoners), with criminal cases also amounting to about 20 percent. Slightly more than half of the appeals are terminated on the merits, with the remaining numbers consolidated with other appeals or dismissed on procedural grounds. (For instance, for the year ending September 2016, 13,551 new prisoner cases were filed, but only 8,010 prisoner cases were decided on the merits.)

The appeals backlog remains considerable, although the overall numbers have declined over the past 10 years. As of September 30, 2006, there were 56,486 appeals pending; for the year ending ten years later, in September 2016, there were 43,275 appeals pending—a number that has stayed steadily between 40,806 and 43,633 since September 2011. The number of pending cases varies dramatically by circuit, in part because of the courts' respective caseloads and differences in the types of cases on their dockets. For instance, as of September 30, 2016, the Ninth Circuit had 13,334 pending appeals, whereas the D.C. Circuit had only 1,418 pending appeals.

Pro Se Appeals. Every circuit has a considerable number of pro se cases. According to statistics compiled by the Administrative Office of the U.S. Courts, appeals by pro se litigants constituted 51 percent of all appeals filed in the year ending September 30, 2015, and 46 percent of those pro se filings were prisoner filings. Some circuits are particular magnets for pro se cases, likely owing to the number of prisoner inmates located within those particular circuits. Thus, out of the 26,883 pro se cases filed in the year ending in September 2015, 5,855 were filed in the Ninth Circuit, 3,406 in the Eleventh Circuit, 3,288 in the Fifth Circuit, and 1,896 in the Second Circuit. By contrast, only 368 pro se cases were filed in the D.C. Circuit.

Dispositions. The Administrative Office's statistics also reveal the average number of cases each circuit judge participated in resolving. For the 12 months ending on September 30, 2016, the average judge was responsible for 565 terminations on the merits. Each judge wrote, on average, 187 opinions, of which 51 were "signed" opinions (*i.e.*, opinions attributable to an individual authoring judge rather than "per curiam," or "by the court").

There is considerable variation by circuit in the number of signed and unsigned opinions per judge. For instance, in the D.C. Circuit, for the one-year period ending September 30, 2016, the average judge wrote 14 signed and 25 unsigned opinions. For the same period, the average Third Circuit judge wrote 95 signed and 31 unsigned opinions, the average Fourth Circuit judge wrote 36 signed and 266 unsigned opinions, the average Ninth Circuit judge wrote 13 signed and 111 unsigned opinions, and the average Tenth Circuit judge wrote 87 signed and 30 unsigned opinions.

Oral Argument. Circuits differ dramatically in their practices with respect to oral argument. In some circuits, most cases adjudicated on the merits (those not dismissed for procedural or technical reasons) are decided only after oral argument, whereas in other circuits a relatively small number of cases are orally argued. For example, until approximately ten years ago, the Second Circuit prided itself for offering oral argument in all cases except those involving a pro se incarcerated person; even so, the argument time offered in cases before that court has diminished over the years; whereas in the early 1990s, litigants in appeals brought by pro se appellants could expect to receive five minutes of argument time per side, today a pro se case in the Second Circuit is likely to wind up on that court's Non-Argument Calendar. The Fifth Circuit, on the other hand, has long maintained a significant "non argument" docket—*i.e.*, a docket of cases that are not calendared for oral argument, but instead decided on the briefs submitted. "Overall fewer than 20% of the cases briefed actually receive oral argument," and "[c]riminal cases have the least, and private civil cases the greatest probability for argument" in the Fifth Circuit. Practitioner's Guide to the U.S. Court of Appeals for the Fifth Circuit at 60 (2016), *available at* www.ca5.uscourts.gov.

Number of Judges. As noted earlier, the circuits vary widely in size, with the Ninth Circuit being the largest and the First Circuit being the smallest by number of judges in regular active service:

NUMBER OF JUDGES BY CIRCUIT

Circuit	Number of Judges
DC	12
1st	6
2d	13
3d	14
4th	15
5th	17
6th	16
7th	11
8th	11
9th	28
10th	12
11th	12
Federal	12
Total	179

28 U.S.C. § 44(a).

Assignment of Judges to Cases. Except for cases decided *en banc*, and with the further and rarely utilized exception that allows the U.S. Court of Appeals for the Federal Circuit to sit in panels of more than three judges (28 U.S.C. § 46(c)), cases are ordinarily decided by panels of three judges. 28 U.S.C. § 46(b). Congress has left the method of selecting the judges for particular cases up to the individual circuits, and most circuits follow the process of assigning judges at random to appellate panels.

Even so, only a few of these courts have rules that explicitly require random assignment, and some only require random assignment by rule in particular types of cases (*e.g.*, the Third Circuit requires random assignment in death penalty cases, and the Ninth Circuit requires the Clerk to make panel assignments—in both instances, from those judges willing to serve on death-penalty cases—*see* 3d Cir. I.O.P. 16.2; 9th Cir. R. 22–1). In other courts, the duty of panel assignment belongs to the Chief Judge, the court clerk, or the circuit executive. *See* J. Robert Brown & Allison Herren Lee, *The Neutral Assignment of Judges at the Court of Appeals*, 78 Tex. L. Rev. 1037 (2000). The "fundamental academic assumption" that appellate panels are selected at random has been challenged by empirical scholars. *See, e.g.*, Adam S. Chilton & Marin K. Levy, *Challenging the Randomness of Panel Assignment in the Federal Courts of Appeals*, 101 Cornell L. Rev. 1, 2 (2015).

The methods of selecting panel members has, on more than one occasion, led to great controversy in high-profile matters. In 1963, a judge of the U.S. Court of Appeals for the Fifth Circuit accused four of his colleagues of engineering their disproportionate presence on panels deciding civil rights cases. *See Armstrong v. Bd. of Educ.*, 323 F.2d 333, 352–61 (5th Cir. 1963) (Cameron, J., dissenting from the denial of rehearing en banc). The unusual and public allegations made by Judge Cameron led to an extraordinary conference of all of the Fifth Circuit's judges, convened by the Chief Judge. See Jonathan L. Entin, *The Sign of "The Four": Judicial Assignment and the Rule of Law*, 68 Miss. L. J. 369, 372 (1998). A similar issue cropped up again in connection with the University of Michigan affirmative action cases that eventually wound up in the Supreme Court: In 2002, Judge Boggs of the Sixth Circuit leveled similar charges against Chief Judge Martin of his circuit. *See Grutter v. Bollinger*, 288 F.3d 732, 810–14 (6th Cir. 2002) (en banc) (Boggs, J., dissenting).

Locations of Court Sessions. By statute, Congress has designated locations for each circuit to conduct court sessions:

Circuit	Location(s)
DC	Washington, D.C.
1st	Boston
2d	New York
3d	Philadelphia
4th	Richmond (VA), Asheville (NC)

5th	New Orleans, Fort Worth, Jackson (MS)
6th	Cincinnati
7th	Chicago
8th	St. Louis, Kansas City, Omaha, St. Paul (MN)
9th	San Francisco, Los Angeles, Portland (OR), Seattle
10th	Denver, Wichita (KS), Oklahoma City
11th	Atlanta, Jacksonville, Montgomery (AL)
Federal	Washington, D.C., any city above, or as prescribed by court rule.

28 U.S.C. § 48(a). In addition, each federal court of appeals "may hold special sessions at any place within its circuit as the nature of the business may require, and upon such notice as the court orders." 28 U.S.C. § 48(b). For example, several courts of appeals occasionally hold argument sessions at law schools and in district courtrooms within their circuits, even though those locations are not in the cities specified in 28 U.S.C. § 48(a). Additionally, after Hurricane Katrina devastated the New Orleans area and other parts of Louisiana in 2005, the Fifth Circuit temporarily moved its oral arguments from New Orleans to various other cities within the Fifth Circuit, including Houston and Dallas. The courts of appeals may also hold sessions *outside* the geographic boundaries of the circuit in extraordinary

circumstances, such as "emergency conditions." 28 U.S.C. § 48(e).

Appeal Timeline. For the 12-month period ended September 30, 2016, the median length of the federal court of appeals process (from filing the notice of appeal to final disposition) was 7.4 months, a length that has been steadily falling—from over a year in 2006, to 11.0 months in 2011, to 8.5 months in 2015. The longest median period from notice of appeal to disposition was in the Ninth Circuit (15.2 months), while the shortest period was in the Fourth Circuit (4.0 months).

Statistics on Disposition. The conventional wisdom that most cases appealed to the federal courts of appeals are affirmed is confirmed by government statistics. Thus, out of 31,622 appeals terminated on the merits by the federal courts of appeals in the 12-month period ending September 30, 2015, only 8.3 percent of the cases were reversed. Again, there is wide variation among the circuits:

Circuit	Percent of Cases Reversed
DC	14.8
1st	10.2
2d	7.4
3d	6.9
4th	4.5
5th	6.0
6th	9.2
7th	17.3

8th	5.8
9th	10.9
10th	3.7
11th	8.6
Federal	10.0

Backlog. Circuits differ dramatically in the number of cases undecided after extensive periods of time. For example, on September 30, 2015, the D.C., Fourth, Fifth, and Eighth Circuits had no cases pending for a year or more after submission (either after oral argument or submission on briefs without oral argument). By contrast, the Second Circuit had 86 such cases, the Ninth Circuit had 13 such cases, and the Eleventh Circuit had 10 such cases. In fact, the D.C., Fourth, and Eighth Circuits have such an up-to-date docket that each had fewer than 10 cases pending for more than three months after argument (2, 2, and 6 cases, respectively).

Caseload Variety. The caseload of the federal circuits reflects a wide variety. Thus, for the 12-month period ending September 30, 2016, just under a fifth of the appeals commenced—11,536 of the 60,357—were criminal cases. The remaining number were civil cases. Based on statistics for the year ending September 30, 2015, the United States was involved as a plaintiff in 342 of the civil cases and as a defendant in 6,593 of the civil cases (almost two-thirds of the U.S. defendant civil cases were prisoner, habeas, or motion-to-vacate-sentence cases, and thus related to the criminal justice system even though technically deemed civil cases). Of the 21,615 private civil appeals commenced during that 12-month period, 18,624 raised federal questions, and 2,991 involved diversity. The civil federal-question cases involved a broad spectrum, including (among others) employment civil rights (1,238), other civil rights (3,714), antitrust (129), labor (754), copyright, patent, and trademark (334, excluding the Court of Appeals for the Federal Circuit, which contributed another 597 patent-infringement appeals and 411 cases appealed from the U.S. Patent and Trademark Office), securities (127), and contract actions (423).

Origin of Appeals. Out of 52,698 appeals commenced during the 12 months ending on September 30, 2015, 39,930 were from district courts, 841 were from bankruptcy courts, 7,141 were from administrative agencies (5,901 of which were from the Board of Immigration Appeals), and 4,786 were "original proceedings," such as second or successive habeas corpus petitions, mandamus petitions, and other actions initiated in a federal appeals court.

CHAPTER 3

PRESERVATION OF ERROR

§ 3.1 GENERAL RULE REQUIRING PRESERVATION

Appellate courts are courts of "review"—the antithesis of an "original" action. *See, e.g., Osborne v. Bank of the U.S.*, 22 U.S. (9 Wheat.) 738, 820 (1824). Because of the institutional limitations on their proper role—limitations that stem from being a court of second resort—the ordinary rule is that, absent exceptional circumstances, a party may not raise on appeal an error that it did not first ask the trial court to correct. *See, e.g., United States v. Turner*, 474 F.3d 1265, 1276–77 (11th Cir. 2007). This is sometimes referred to as the "contemporaneous-objection" requirement, *see United States v. Gagnon*, 470 U.S. 522, 527–30 (1985) (per curiam), although the requirement applies not just in the context of objections, but also to motions and other ways of bringing trial-court errors to the trial judge's attention.

This general rule is crystallized in Fed.R.Civ.P. 46, which simultaneously abolished the common-law requirement of the "formal exception" to a ruling, but provides, in relevant part: "A formal exception to a ruling or order is unnecessary. When the ruling or order is requested or made, a party need only state the action that it wants the court to take or objects to, along with the grounds for the request or objection. Failing to object does not prejudice a party who had no opportunity to do so when the ruling or order was made."

As most trial lawyers know, it is usually not an effective trial strategy to overload the judge or the jury with objections. Still, strategic choices to avoid objections at trial are not a valid excuse for failing to object. *Henry v. Mississippi*, 379 U.S. 443, 450 (1965). Of course, in extraordinary cases, an appellate court may excuse a failure to object, but the exceptions to the contemporaneous-objection requirement are narrow, and the success rate is low. As such, to ensure that an issue may be raised on appeal and decided by the appellate court, the better practice is the one advocated by the late Judge Aldisert of the Third Circuit: "Preserve the issue at all costs." Ruggero J. Aldisert, *Winning on Appeal: Better Briefs and Oral Argument* 55 (2d ed. 2003).

§ 3.2 TERMINOLOGY—"WAIVER" VERSUS "ABANDONMENT"

Strictly speaking, when courts and lawyers speak of appellate "waiver," they are usually speaking not of waiver, but of appellate "forfeiture." For a "waiver" to occur, there must be an "intentional relinquishment or abandonment of a known right." *Johnson v. Zerbst*, 304 U.S. 458, 464 (1938); *see also, e.g.*, *Freytag v. Commissioner*, 501 U.S. 868, 894, n. 2 (1991) (Scalia, J., concurring in part and concurring in judgment) (explaining that waiver "is merely one means by which a forfeiture may occur"). Forfeiture, by contrast, requires less affirmative conduct than "waiver"—it is defined as "the failure to make the timely assertion of a right," such as the failure to make a contemporaneous objection. *United States v. Olano*, 507 U.S. 725, 733 (1993).

Notwithstanding this distinction, the terminology surrounding issues of error-preservation is often imprecise, even though, in some error-preservation contexts, precision matters greatly. The distinction is particularly important in the context of criminal law. "The difference between waiver and forfeiture is that waiver precludes review, whereas forfeiture permits us to correct an error under a plain error standard. Forfeiture occurs by accident, neglect, or inadvertent failure to timely assert a right. Waiver occurs when a defendant or his attorney manifests an intention, or expressly declines, to assert a right." *United States v. Doyle*, 693 F.3d 769, 771 (7th Cir. 2012). *See also* § 3.4, *infra*.

In the civil context, by contrast, this distinction is less critical, because plain-error review is not categorically unavailable to otherwise "waived" claims of error on appeal. *See, e.g.*, Fed.R.Evid. 103(e). However, the inadvertence with which an available objection is not pressed may affect the equitable determination of whether an error may be reviewed as "plain." The Seventh Circuit's decision in *Williams v. Dieball*, 724 F.3d 957, 961–63 (7th Cir. 2013), contains a useful and extended exploration of these distinctions.

Having identified this issue of terminology, we nonetheless reflect the usage of the case law in this book, using "waiver" and "abandonment" largely interchangeably, except in those areas where the distinction makes a meaningful difference.

§ 3.3 SPECIFIC PRESERVATION ISSUES AT TRIAL

A. PRE-TRIAL MOTIONS

In most cases, denied pre-trial motions—such as motions to dismiss for failure to state a claim under Fed.R.Civ.P. 12, and summary judgment motions under Rule 56—do not preserve errors for appeal. The reason behind this general rule is straightforward: If a pre-trial motion is denied, that simply means that the case proceeds toward trial, and the trial will allow the development of a factual record against which the legal issues presented in these motions can be better tested. *See Arbaugh v. Y & H Corp.*, 546 U.S. 500, 507 (2006) ("[T]he objection that a complaint 'fail[s] to state a claim upon which relief can be granted' may not be asserted post trial. Under Rule 12(h)(2), that objection endures up to, but not beyond, trial on the merits.") (citation omitted).

Making a denied summary judgment motion, without more, is not enough to preserve an error for appeal; the ordinary rule is that the issue must be re-raised at trial or in a post-trial motion under Fed.R.Civ.P. 50. *Watson v. Amedco Steel, Inc.*, 29 F.3d 274, 277–79 (7th Cir. 1994). One prominent exception to this rule lies in the unique area of denials of summary judgment based on qualified immunity, or motions to dismiss on other immunity-from-suit grounds (such as under the Foreign

Sovereign Immunities Act), but that is because such denied motions are immediately appealable under the "collateral order" doctrine. *See Mitchell v. Forsyth*, 472 U.S. 511, 526 (1985); § 4.5, *infra*. Even then, however, a defendant may not appeal an order denying summary judgment on qualified immunity grounds after a full trial on the merits, because, "[o]nce the case proceeds to trial, the full record developed in court supersedes the record existing at the time of the summary judgment motion." *Ortiz v. Jordan*, 562 U.S. 180, 184 (2011).

B. RULINGS ON EVIDENCE

Federal Rule of Evidence 103 governs error based on evidentiary rulings. Rule 103(a) provides that "[a] party may claim error in a ruling to admit or exclude evidence only if the error affects a substantial right of the party," and in addition, one of the following occurs:

- For rulings admitting evidence, a party "timely objects or moves to strike" on the record, and "states the specific ground" for the objection, unless [the specific ground] was apparent from the context"; or
- For rulings excluding evidence, "a party informs the court of its substance by an offer of proof," "unless the substance [of the excluded evidence] was apparent from the context."

Prior to the 2000 amendments to the Federal Rules of Evidence, courts were divided over whether, after a definitive adverse ruling at or prior to trial (*e.g.*, on a motion *in limine*), the adversely affected party was required to make a further objection or offer of proof when the evidence was offered at trial (or would have been offered, but for the adverse ruling). *See, e.g.*, *Wilson v. Williams*, 182 F.3d 562, 565–66 (7th Cir. 1999) (en banc). The amended rule makes clear that "[o]nce the court rules definitely on the record—either before or at trial—a party need not renew an objection or offer of proof to preserve a claim of error for appeal." Fed.R.Evid. 103(b).

The Committee Notes to amended Rule 103 point out that, when a ruling is definitive, requiring an objection would be "more a formalism than a necessity." By contrast, "when the trial court appears to have reserved its ruling or to have indicated that the ruling is provisional, it makes sense to require the party to bring the issue to the court's attention subsequently." According to the Committee, "[t]he amendment imposes the obligation on counsel to clarify whether an *in limine* or other evidentiary ruling is definitive when there is doubt on that point." Moreover, the Committee Notes point out that "[i]f the court changes its initial ruling, or if the opposing party violates the terms of the initial ruling, objection must be made when the evidence is offered to preserve the claim of error for appeal." And if the ruling admitting evidence is conditioned on an adequate foundation being established, and no such foundation is established, "the opponent cannot claim error based on the failure to establish the foundation unless the opponent calls that failure to the court's attention by a timely motion to strike or other suitable motion."

Rule 103(a)(1)(A), sets forth the requirement of a timely objection or motion to strike, and is followed by Rule 103(a)(1)(B), which requires "the specific ground" of objection to be stated, unless the specific ground is "apparent from the context." An obvious corollary to this rule is that, where a specific ground of objection is stated, counsel will not be allowed to urge a different ground as error on appeal. *See, e.g.*, *United States v. Gomez-Norena*, 908 F.2d 497, 500 (9th Cir. 1990).

There has been some controversy regarding whether a party who loses a motion *in limine* seeking to exclude a category of evidence (*e.g.*, evidence of a criminal defendant's prior convictions) waives appellate objection by pre-emptively introducing evidence on that subject in order to "remove the sting." Some lower courts held that such a strategic response to an *in limine* ruling did not waive the issue for appellate review. *See, e.g., Judd v. Rodman*, 105 F.3d 1339, 1342 (11th Cir. 1997); *United States v. Fisher*, 106 F.3d 622, 629–30 (5th Cir. 1997). But in 2000, the Supreme Court seemed to settle the issue on the side of waiver. In *Ohler v. United States*, the Court held that "a defendant who preemptively introduces evidence of a prior conviction on direct examination may not on appeal claim that the admission of such evidence was error." 529 U.S. 753, 760 (2000). The Court explained that "[t]he defendant must choose whether to introduce the conviction on direct examination and remove the sting or to take her chances with the prosecutor's possible elicitation of the conviction on cross-examination." *Id.* at 758.

C. ARGUMENTS OF COUNSEL

Additionally, a party can waive an argument for appeal through an affirmative statement by its counsel in opening statements. Such a waiver can take place through a clear affirmative statement that a party is abandoning or relinquishing a particular claim, theory, or argument. Some courts have granted defense motions for judgment as a matter of law under Fed.R.Civ.P. 50 after a party's opening statement, "where that statement establishes that the plaintiff has no right to recover." *Best v. District of Columbia*, 291 U.S. 411, 415 (1934). This is a narrow rule, based as it is on the theory that a trial court has the same power to act upon "facts conceded by counsel" as "upon evidence produced" at trial. *Id.* This procedure is supported by the timing language of Fed.R.Civ.P. 50(a)(2), which provides that "motion[s] for judgment as a matter of law may be made *at any time* before the case is submitted to the jury." (Emphasis added.)

However, other courts have read the 1991 Advisory Committee Notes to Fed.R.Civ.P. 50 as prohibiting this practice. Those Notes say that the purpose of the rule is "to assure the responding party an opportunity to cure any deficiency in that party's proof that may have been overlooked until called to the party's attention." *See McSherry v. City of Long Beach*, 423 F.3d 1015, 1020 (9th Cir. 2005). Other courts rely upon Rule 50's requirement that a party have been "fully heard" on an issue before judgment as a matter of law may be granted against it. *See, e.g., Echeverria v. Chevron USA Inc.*, 391 F.3d 607, 611–12 (5th Cir. 2004); *Teneyck v. Omni Shoreham Hotel*, 365 F.3d 1139, 1149 (D.C. Cir. 2004). Still, in certain "extraordinary case[s]," an opening statement can constitute a waiver of an issue. *Moore v. Jas. H. Matthews & Co.*, 473 F.2d 328, 329 n.2 (9th Cir. 1972).

Conversely, the fact that an issue *was* mentioned in opening statements (as well as in the answer to the complaint and the pre-trial order) does not by itself preserve the issue for appeal; the issue must actually be pressed at trial. *Cavic v. Pioneer Astro Indus., Inc.*, 825 F.2d 1421, 1425 (10th Cir. 1987).

D. JURY TRIALS—FED.R.CIV.P. 51

Rule 51(d) of the Federal Rules of Civil Procedure provides that a party may assign as error either "an error in an instruction actually given, if that party properly objected," or "a failure to give an instruction, if that party properly requested it and—unless the court rejected the request in a definitive ruling on the record—also properly objected."

Rule 51(c) of those Rules sets forth the requirements for an adequate objection to jury instructions: Rule 51(c)(1) requires the form of an objection to be "on the record, stating distinctly the matter objected to and the grounds for the objection"; Rule 51(c)(2) provides that an objection is timely (i) if made at the opportunity for objection provided for in

Rule 51(b)(2) (before the jury is charged), or (ii) if the opportunity required by Rule 51(b)(2) is not provided, if made "promptly after learning that the instruction or request will be, or has been, given or refused." This rule, too, can be seen as a specific application of the general rule of objections: Make the objection known at the earliest possible time, and give the court the opportunity to correct the claimed error.

If a party does not properly and timely object to an instruction (or failure to give an instruction), then a court "may" (but not "must") "consider a plain error in the instructions that has not been preserved as required by Rule 51(d)(1) if the error affects substantial rights." Fed.R.Civ.P. 51(d)(2). That is a narrow exception, as the Advisory Committee Notes to the 2003 Amendments to Rule 51 make clear: To be a "plain error" warranting reversal, the error must not only be "plain" (in the sense of "obvious"), but must affect "substantial rights" and "seriously affect the fairness, integrity, or public reputation of judicial proceedings." *Id.* (citations omitted).

Even if a jury instruction is not objected to, a properly framed motion for judgment as a matter of law under Fed.R.Civ.P. 50 can serve as a vehicle for challenging the legal rulings in those instructions. *Boyle v. United Technologies Corp.*, 487 U.S. 500, 513–14 (1988); *Ebker v. Tan Jay Int'l Ltd.*, 739 F.2d 812, 825 n.17 (2d Cir. 1984) (Friendly, J.). The principles behind this rule are twofold: One, that legal rulings made in jury instructions are not considered to be "law of the case" for further proceedings in that same case; and two, that it is the duty of the court in ruling on Rule 50 motions to apply the correct law. As then-Judge Blackmun explained, "A proper motion for judgment under Rule 50(b) and its allowance will . . . preserve for review the question whether, in granting that motion, correct legal principles were applied by the trial court." *Hanson v. Ford Motor Co.*, 278 F.2d 586, 593 (8th Cir. 1960). This rule does not excuse a party from failing to raise the issue in *either* an objection to a jury instruction *or* a Rule 50 motion, however. *See Action Marine, Inc. v. Cont'l Carbon Inc.*, 481 F.3d 1302, 1313 & n.10 (11th Cir. 2007).

The same rule has been applied to sufficiency-of-the-evidence challenges in criminal cases: "[W]here a statutory element of an offense is included in the indictment but erroneously omitted from instructions to the jury, and the evidence is insufficient to establish the unobjected-to element used instead, the conviction may be affirmed against a sufficiency challenge where the evidence is so overwhelming or incontrovertible that there is no reasonable doubt that any rational jury would have found that the government proved the statutory element." *United States v. Inman*, 558 F.3d 742, 748–49 (8th Cir. 2009) (relying on the Second Circuit's decision in *Ebker*, *supra*, and the Eighth Circuit's prior decision in *Coca-Cola Bottling Co. of Black Hills v. Hubbard*, 203 F.2d 859 (8th Cir. 1953), both civil cases).

E. POST-TRIAL MOTIONS

As the discussion in the previous subsection illustrates, properly framing arguments in post-trial motions can be crucial for preserving those arguments for appellate review.

Rule 50 Motions. Rule 50 of the Federal Rules of Civil Procedure governs the procedural requirements for motions for judgment as a matter of law (JMOL). The rule requires at least two motions for JMOL to be made in order to preserve the denial of JMOL as an issue for appeal.

The first motion is governed by Rule 50(a). Formerly known (before 1991) as a motion for directed verdict, the first JMOL motion is to be made when the non-movant "has been fully heard on an issue during a jury trial," and requires the court to "fin[d] that a reasonable jury would not have a legally sufficient evidentiary basis to find for the party on that issue." If the trial court so finds, it "may" (not "must") "resolve the issue against the [non-moving] party" and grant JMOL against the party on a claim or defense. Fed.R.Civ.P. 50(a).

The second motion (known before 1991 as a motion for *j.n.o.v.*, or *judgment non obstante veredicto*—judgment notwithstanding the verdict) is governed by Rule 50(b). The change in terminology adopted in 1991, which labeled both types of motions as motions for JMOL, was mainly designed to underscore the fact that Rule 50(b) motions are "renewals" of the same motions brought pre-verdict under Rule 50(a), and to more closely parallel the language of the summary-judgment rule, Fed.R.Civ.P. 56(c)—which, like Rule 50, requires that the moving party be entitled to "judgment as a matter of law." A motion brought under Rule 50(b) must be made "[no] later than 28 days after the entry of judgment—or if the motion addresses a jury issue not decided by a verdict, no later than 28 days after the jury was discharged."

One of the purposes behind the pre-verdict Rule 50(a) motion is to alert the court and the opposing party to an ostensible failure of proof, and allow the non-moving party to fill the evidentiary gap in the record, if that is possible. *Cone v. W. Va. Pulp & Paper Co.*, 330 U.S. 212, 217 (1947). For that reason, it is not fair game for a post-verdict Rule 50(b) motion to expand the grounds on which JMOL is sought.

At the same time, Rule 50 does not require mathematical precision in matching up the pre-verdict and renewed motions. Indeed, some appellate courts approach Rule 50 with such a "liberal spirit" that a "general, all encompassing" motion under Rule 50(a) seeking JMOL dismissing "all counts of the allegation of the complaint" has been deemed sufficient to support a renewed Rule 50(b) motion going into greater detail on the grounds for granting the motion. *Logan v. Burgers Ozark Country Cured Hams Inc.*, 263 F.3d 447, 457 (5th Cir. 2001).

Under Rule 50(b), the court in ruling on the renewed JMOL motion has the option of ordering JMOL for the moving party or, if a new trial is a more appropriate remedy, ordering that remedy in lieu of directing the entry of judgment. In addition, Rule

50(c) gives the trial court the power to grant JMOL and at the same time order a conditional new trial in the event that the appellate court reverses the grant of JMOL; the grant of a conditional new trial does not make the ensuing judgment non-final, however.

Rule 50(d) allows a party against whom JMOL is granted an additional 28 days after the entry of such judgment to request a new trial from the district court.

Similarly, the appellate court may, in ruling on a denied Rule 50(b) motion, reverse the denial of that motion and order judgment for the moving party on appeal. The grant of such relief on appeal, in appropriate cases, parallels the power of the trial court to grant such relief; it does not run afoul of the Seventh Amendment's reexamination clause—which generally prohibits the reexamination of facts found by a jury, but does not impede an appellate court's power to test the legal sufficiency of the evidence supporting a verdict. *Neely v. Martin K. Eby Constr. Co.*, 386 U.S. 317, 320–25 (1967); *Weisgram v. Marley Co.*, 528 U.S. 440, 454 n.10 (2000). Rule 50(e) makes clear that the appellate court may order JMOL, order a new trial, or direct the district court to consider whether a new trial should be ordered.

The failure to file any sort of Rule 50(b) motion, however, can have severe consequences going to the very power of the court of appeals to accord any relief on appeal. It has long been settled law that the failure to file a post-verdict motion under Rule 50(b) deprives the appellate court of the power to order JMOL on appeal. "In the absence of such a motion," an "appellate court [is] without power to direct the District Court to enter judgment contrary to the one it had permitted to stand." *Cone*, 330 U.S. at 218.

In 2006, the Supreme Court extended this long-settled principle to restrict the power of an appellate court to grant a new trial (rather than JMOL) in the absence of a Rule 50(b) motion. In *Unitherm Food Sys., Inc. v. Swift-Eckrich, Inc.*, 546 U.S. 394 (2006), a party in a patent suit "filed a Rule 50(a) motion before the verdict, but did not file a Rule 50(b) motion after the verdict," nor did it "request a new trial under Rule 59." *Id.* at 396. The Court of Appeals, on finding the evidence insufficient to support the verdict, remanded for a new trial. The Supreme Court, however, reversed. Reasoning that the rationale of cases like *Cone* "appl[ies] with equal force whether a party is seeking judgment as a matter of law or simply a new trial," *id.* at 402, the Court held that a party's "failure to comply with Rule 50(b) forecloses its challenge to the sufficiency of the evidence." *Id.* at 404.

Rule 52 Motions. Rule 52 governs the requirements of findings of fact and conclusions of law in cases tried by the court without a jury (or with an advisory jury). Although the ordinary practice in federal district courts is to request that the parties provide proposed findings and conclusions to the court, the rule itself imposes no such requirement; indeed, Rule 52(a), as it existed prior to the December 1, 2007 amendments to the Federal Rules of Civil Procedure, affirmatively stated: "Requests for findings are not necessary for purposes of review."

The 2007 amendments to Rule 52, according to the Advisory Committee Notes, "are intended to be stylistic only"; however, the new version of the rule is silent as to whether or when *requests* are necessary. Instead, the new version speaks only to when *the court* is required to state findings or conclusions. *See* Fed.R.Civ.P. 52(a)(3) ("The court is not required to state findings or conclusions when ruling on a motion under Rule 12 or 56 or, unless these rules provide otherwise, on any other motion.").

In parallel with the timing requirements of JMOL motions under Rule 50(b) (and new-trial motions under Rule 59), Rule 52(b) provides that, on a motion made by a party no later than 28 days after entry of judgment, "the court may amend its findings—or make additional findings—and may amend the judgment accordingly."

Some litigants had read the statement in former Rule 52(a), that "[r]equests for findings are not necessary for purposes of review," to mean that objections to findings are not required for appellate review. That approach can prove to be a trap for the unwary, as courts have not always read this provision so broadly. In *Miller v. Bittner*, 985 F.2d 935 (8th Cir. 1993), the Eighth Circuit held that a party had waived an objection to a district court's alleged "fail[ure] to specifically address" an issue raised by that party at trial. The court held that "by failing to raise this proposition in the trial court, [the party] deprived the trial judge of an opportunity to address the alleged error and make further findings." *Id.* at 940. Thus, while sufficiency-of-the-evidence challenges are preserved without further objection or exception, challenges to the completeness of factual findings may not be preserved for appeal without a further motion under Rule 52(b), or some other analogous kind of request for relief.

Rule 59 Motions. Rule 59(a)(1) is the general authority for new-trial motions. It provides: "The court may, on motion, grant a new trial on all or some of the issues—and to any party—[either] (A) after a jury trial, for any reason for which a new trial has heretofore been granted in an action at law in federal court; or (B) after a nonjury trial, for any reason for which a rehearing has heretofore been granted in a suit in equity in federal court." Rule 59(a)(2) goes on to explain that, "[a]fter a nonjury trial, the court may, on motion for a new trial, open the judgment if one has been entered, take additional testimony, amend findings of fact and conclusions of law or make new ones, and direct the entry of a new judgment."

Similarly, Rule 59(e) allows motions to "alter or amend a judgment" (including, most commonly, motions for reconsideration). In either case, such a motion must be made within 28 days of entry of the judgment, Fed.R.Civ.P. 59(b), 59(e), and that time may not be extended by the court. Fed.R.Civ.P. 6(b)(2).

A new-trial motion is not a prerequisite for seeking a new trial on appeal based on errors that occurred prior to the entry of judgment (and were properly pointed out to the trial court in other fashions), such as errors in the admission of evidence, improper and prejudicial statements by counsel, erroneous jury charges, and the like. As discussed earlier, each of these sorts of errors can be preserved by objection, either to the evidence or conduct, or to the jury charge. A further Rule 59 new-trial motion is not required.

A Rule 59 motion will be required to preserve an issue for appellate review, however, where the motion presents the first opportunity to raise the issue with the trial court. Areas where a Rule 59 motion is required to save the issue for appellate review include challenges to the sufficiency of the evidence supporting a verdict, as well as challenges to the excessiveness of a verdict. (In *Gasperini v. Center for Humanities, Inc.*, 518 U.S. 415 (1996), the Supreme Court upheld the power of federal appellate courts to review the amount of damages verdicts for excessiveness without violating the Seventh Amendment's reexamination clause.)

Rule 60 Motions. Rule 60 of the Federal Rules of Civil Procedure provides broader grounds for relief from judgments or orders than Rules 50, 52, and 59 provide. It has substantial roots in equity practice, where the equity courts could, in extraordinary circumstances, provide relief from improper or unconscionable judgments issued by the law courts.

Rule 60(a) merely gives the courts the power, at any time, to correct mistakes of a clerical nature. Because these errors may be corrected at any time, including while the case is on appeal, and because the subject matter of such motions is so frequently uncontroversial, that portion of the rule typically presents no issues with respect to appellate review.

The only appellate limitation contained in Rule 60(a) is that correction of such an error "after an appeal has been docketed in the appellate court and while it is pending" may only occur "with the appellate court's leave."

Rule 60(b) is the more frequently litigated portion of the rule; it allows relief from a judgment or order, and in appropriate cases a new trial, on such grounds as (1) "mistake, inadvertence, surprise, or excusable neglect"; (2) newly discovered evidence that with reasonable diligence could not have been discovered in time for a new-trial motion under Rule 59(b); (3) fraud; (4) "the judgment is void" (*e.g.*, because it was rendered by a court lacking jurisdiction); (5) satisfaction, release, or discharge; or (6) "any other reason that justifies relief." Motions premised on grounds (1), (2), or (3) must be brought within a year after the judgment or order in question; motions grounded in the other subdivisions of Rule 60(b) must be brought "within a reasonable time," although there is some question whether any time limit should apply to subdivision (4). Obviously, there is no requirement in any case that a party bring such a Rule 60 motion, for the extraordinary grounds meriting such post-judgment relief may not exist.

An important rule that applies to all of these kinds of post-trial motions is found in Fed.R.Civ.P. 6(b)(2). That rule provides that the trial court "must not extend the time to act under Rules 50(b) and (d), 52(b), 59(b), (d) and (e), and 60(b)." If one of the enumerated rules on its face allows for no extensions, then the time cannot be extended—even if the district court purports to exercise the power of granting an extension.

§ 3.4 FORFEITURE OF ARGUMENTS ON APPEAL

The general rule is that " 'an issue not raised in the district court and raised for the first time in an appeal will not be considered by [the federal appellate] court.' " *Walker v. Jones*, 10 F.3d 1569, 1572 (11th Cir. 1994) (citation omitted). This prohibition, however, is not "jurisdictional," *i.e.*, some courts have considered issues raised for the first time on appeal if the issue "involves a pure question of law, and if refusal to consider it would result in a miscarriage of justice." *Wright v. Hanna Steel Corp.*, 270 F.3d 1336, 1342 (11th Cir. 2001) (citation omitted). Likewise, the prohibition "may be relaxed where the appellant raises an objection to an order which he had no opportunity to raise at the district court level." *Id.* Also, the prohibition does not apply if "the proper resolution [of the issue] is beyond any doubt," or if the issue is one of "general impact or of great public concern." *Id.* Finally, some courts retain broad flexibility to consider newly raised issues "where the interest of substantial justice is at stake." *Id.*

Arguments raised below but not in the court of appeals are "deemed abandoned and [their] merits will not be addressed." *Access Now, Inc. v. Southwest Airlines Co.*, 385 F.3d 1324, 1330 (11th Cir. 2004). Nor will a court normally consider an argument raised for the first time in a reply brief. *See, e.g.*,

Enercon v. Int'l Trade Comm'n, 151 F.3d 1376, 1385 (Fed. Cir. 1998) (citing cases). In addition, an argument made in an appellate brief must be sufficiently developed to allow the opponent to answer it, and the court to consider it. *Williams v. Woodford*, 384 F.3d 567, 587 n.5 (9th Cir. 2004). Many courts have applied this rule in the specific context of footnotes and held that an argument made only in a footnote of an appellate brief is waived. *See, e.g.*, *SmithKline Beecham Corp. v. Apotex Corp.*, 439 F.3d 1312, 1320 (Fed. Cir. 2006); *United States v. Restrepo*, 986 F.2d 1462, 1463 (2d Cir. 1993) ("We do not consider an argument mentioned only in a footnote to be adequately raised or preserved for appellate review."). *See* FRAP 28(a)(10); § 13.2(B), *infra*.

§ 3.5 EXTRA-RECORD FACTS

Although the federal courts of appeals normally will not consider facts outside the record, the Federal Rules of Evidence allow a court to take judicial notice—"at any stage of the proceeding"—of a "fact . . . not subject to reasonable dispute" if such fact is either (1) "generally known within the trial court's territorial jurisdiction," or (2) "can be accurately and readily determined from sources whose accuracy cannot reasonably be questioned." Fed.R.Evid. 201(b), (d). A court has discretion to take judicial notice unless "a party requests it and the court is supplied with the necessary information," in which case the court is *required* to take judicial notice if the requirements of Rule 201 are met. Fed.R.Evid. 201(c). Parties have a right (upon timely request) to be heard on the propriety of the court's decision to take judicial notice. Fed.R.Evid. 201(e). The facts subject to judicial notice are "adjudicative" facts (*i.e.*, those related to the specific case), not "legislative" facts (*i.e.*, those facts that help to explain a law's rationality). Fed.R.Evid. 201(a).

In narrow circumstances, the appellate court can expand the trial court record. *See* § 9.5, *infra*. The Third Circuit has outlined three considerations for determining whether "exceptional circumstances" exist that merit supplementation of the record: "(1) whether the proffered addition would establish beyond any doubt the proper resolution of the pending issue; (2) whether remanding the case to the district court for consideration of the additional material would be contrary to the interests of justice and the efficient use of judicial resources; and (3) whether the appeal arose in the context of a habeas corpus action." *Burton v. Teleflex Inc.*, 707 F.3d 417, 435–36 (3d Cir. 2013) (citation omitted).

These exceptional circumstances may include record omissions caused by "error or accident," FRAP 10(e)(2), "when developments render a controversy moot and thus divest [the court] of jurisdiction," *Lowry v. Barnhart*, 329 F.3d 1019, 1024–25 (9th Cir. 2003), and in other "extraordinary cases," *id.*, such as a habeas case where the court of appeals requested the state-court record, *see Dickerson v. Alabama*, 667 F.2d 1364, 1366–68 & n.5 (11th Cir. 1982), or where a district judge refused to allow a party's motions to be filed, *see Int'l Bus. Mach. Corp. v. Edelstein*, 526 F.2d 37, 44–46 (2d Cir. 1975). "Only the court can supplement the record," and parties seeking to do so "should proceed by motion or formal request so that the court and opposing counsel are properly apprised of the status of the documents in question." *Lowry*, 329 F.3d at 1024–25.

By contrast, a party's effort to supplement the appellate record (after a panel decision and an *en banc* decision) with newspaper articles regarding the defendant's admitted conduct was properly denied, where the plaintiff had the opportunity to take discovery on the conduct in question but did not. *Shahar v. Bowers*, 120 F.3d 211, 213–14 (11th Cir. 1997) (en banc).

The power to supplement an appellate record is "rarely exercised." *Ross v. Kemp*, 785 F.2d 1467, 1474 (11th Cir. 1986). This rule is a corollary to the principle that appellate courts are courts of review. *See Shahar*, 120 F.3d at 212 ("The reason for this rule is that the district courts are the courts in which cases are to be litigated and decided initially."). It will be only the most unusual cases where the "review" of whether a trial court's actions are correct will be affected by a matter that was not presented to the trial court in the first instance. *See United States v. Muriel-Cruz*, 412 F.3d 9, 12 (1st Cir. 2005).

The record on appeal comprises only the filings, the transcript, and a certified copy of the docket entries prepared by the district court's clerk. FRAP 10(a). Issues occasionally arise regarding the inclusion of materials that were presented in the trial court but not made a part of the trial court's record. These issues typically arise in the context of demonstrative exhibits used in the trial court or shown to the jury but not filed in the district court under FRAP 10(a). The general rule is that such materials are outside the record on appeal, although some courts, again in unusual circumstances, have allowed such demonstrative exhibits to be added to the appellate record after the fact. *See Waldorf v. Shuta*, 142 F.3d 601, 620 (3d Cir. 1998) (permitting inclusion of two videotapes, which depicted plaintiff undertaking various rehabilitation regimens directly relevant to the merits of his personal-injury lawsuit); *United States v. Burke*, 781 F.2d 1234, 1246 (7th Cir. 1985) (permitting inclusion of three audiotape transcripts, where the audiotapes themselves were played for the jury and placed in the record); *Townsend v. Columbia Operations*, 667 F.2d 844, 847–49 (9th Cir. 1982) (permitting inclusion of four documents containing the "misrepresentations . . . or omissions" underlying the plaintiffs' fraud claims and on which the district court relied in ruling on dispositive motions in the case).

§ 3.6 EXCEPTIONS TO THE GENERAL RULE

A. ERRORS NOT WAIVABLE

The most prominent sort of error that cannot be waived or abandoned by failing to raise it in the trial court is an error going to the trial court's subject-matter jurisdiction. *Arbaugh v. Y & H Corp.*, 546 U.S. 500, 514 (2006); Fed.R.Civ.P. 12(h)(3) ("If the court determines at any time that it lacks subject-matter jurisdiction, the court must dismiss the action."). The reason behind this rule is that "subject-matter jurisdiction, because it involves the court's power to hear a case, can never be forfeited or waived." *United States v. Cotton*, 535 U.S. 625, 630 (2002).

B. PLAIN ERROR

"A rigid and undeviating judicially declared practice under which courts of review would invariably and under all circumstances decline to consider all questions which had not previously been specifically urged would be out of harmony with . . . the rules of fundamental justice." *Hormel v. Helvering*, 312 U.S. 552, 557 (1941). As an equitable tempering of the rules of preservation and waiver, the "plain error" rule allows for appellate review (in limited circumstances) of especially important errors.

Rule 52(b) of the Federal Rules of Criminal Procedure provides that "[a] plain error that affects substantial rights may be considered even though it was not brought to the court's attention." Similarly, Rule 51(d)(2) of the Federal Rules of Civil Procedure, added in 2003 and revised in 2007, provides that "[a] court may consider a plain error in the [jury] instructions that has not been preserved as required by Rule 51(d)(1) if the error affects substantial rights." The Civil Rules' version of plain error, which the Advisory Committee Notes say "is borrowed from Criminal Rule 52," did not exist before 2003. Until then, the Civil Rules' silence on the issue had been read by a few courts as forbidding plain error review in all civil cases, though most of the federal courts of appeals recognized plain-error review as an inherent equitable power.

The Supreme Court's opinion in *United States v. Olano*, 507 U.S. 725, 732–37 (1993), serves as a useful guide to plain-error doctrine. There, the Court provided an explication of the requirements of plain error—that there be an "error," and that the error be "plain"—and the further requirement that the plain error "affect substantial rights."

With respect to the question of whether there is an "error," the Court drew an important distinction between "waiver" and "forfeiture." As the Court explained, there are some rights—such as the right to a jury trial—that can be affirmatively waived, such as by entering into a plea agreement with the government. A defendant could not then appeal his conviction and assert "plain error," because the "waiver" of a known right is not an "error" at all. By contrast, plain-error doctrine deals with cases of "forfeiture"—defined by the Court as "the failure to make the timely assertion of a right." *Id.* at 733–34.

With respect to whether an error is "plain," the Court defined that part of the term as meaning "clear" or "obvious." *Id.* at 734. Putting aside the "special case of where the error was unclear at the time of trial but becomes clear on appeal because the applicable law has been clarified," the Court explained that "[a]t a minimum, the court of appeals cannot correct an error pursuant to Rule 52(b) unless the error is clear under current law." *Id.*

Finally, with respect to whether an error is one that affects substantial rights, the Court explained that "in most cases," that requirement simply means "prejudicial." *Id.* The Court left open the possibility that "affecting substantial rights" might allow for reversal of plain "structural" errors (*i.e.*, the sort that can never be considered harmless error) that are not otherwise prejudicial. *Id.* at 734–35.

An appellate court is almost never obligated to correct a plain error; the language of both the Criminal Rule and the Civil Rule is permissive ("may"), not mandatory ("shall"). But the appellate courts' discretion in correcting plain errors is guided by the principles laid down in *United States v. Atkinson*, 297 U.S. 157 (1936): "The Court of Appeals should correct a plain forfeited error affecting substantial rights if the error 'seriously affect[s] the fairness, integrity or public reputation of judicial proceedings.'" *Olano*, 507 U.S. at 736 (quoting *Atkinson*, 297 U.S. at 160). Indeed, in some cases at the margins, the courts' range of discretion may not be great at all. Almost a century ago, the Supreme Court described the courts' "power *and duty*" to correct egregious, unobjected-to errors, in a case where the defense lawyers had made overt appeals to prejudice in their closing arguments (suggesting, in a train-accident case, that the plaintiff had syphilis): "The public interest *requires* that the court of its own motion, as is its power and duty, protect suitors in their right to a verdict uninfluenced by the appeals of counsel to passion or prejudice." *N.Y. Cent. R.R. Co. v. Johnson,* 279 U.S. 310, 318 (1929) (emphasis added; citation omitted).

The Advisory Committee Notes to Federal Rule of Civil Procedure 51 capture many of these considerations, which recall the plain-error doctrine's equitable roots: "The court's duty to give correct jury instructions in a civil action is shaped by at least four factors. The factor most directly implied by a 'plain' error rule is the obviousness of the mistake. The importance of the error is a second major factor. The costs of correcting an error reflect a third factor that is affected by a variety of circumstances. In a case that seems close to the fundamental error line, account also may be taken of the impact a verdict may have on nonparties."

C. *SUA SPONTE* REVIEW

Courts have an "independent obligation to determine whether subject-matter jurisdiction exists, even in the absence of a challenge from any party." *Arbaugh v. Y & H Corp.*, 546 U.S. 500, 514 (citing *Ruhrgas AG v. Marathon Oil Co.*, 526 U.S. 574, 583 (1999)). But beyond the area of subject-matter jurisdiction, where the court's *sua sponte* power is obligatory, an appellate court's discretion to consider an error not raised by one of the parties is virtually unlimited by any legal principle, even though it is sparingly used. *See United Bhd. of Carpenters v. United States*, 330 U.S. 395, 412 (1947).

Sua sponte error correction is best understood as another species of plain-error review, for the considerations and guidelines to the exercise of discretion are largely the same. *Sua sponte* error-correction power is reserved, as a matter of equity, for exceptional circumstances, especially in criminal cases. The Supreme Court has said that "appellate courts, in the public interest, may, of their own motion, notice errors to which no exception has been taken, if the errors are obvious, or if they otherwise seriously affect the fairness, integrity, or public reputation of judicial proceedings." *United States v. Atkinson*, 297 U.S. 157, 160 (1936) (citations omitted). *See generally United States v. Carter*, 481 F.3d 601, 608 & n.5 (8th Cir. 2007) ("The government did object to this error at sentencing, but did not appeal the issue. Because this error seriously affects substantial rights and the fairness, integrity, and public reputation of judicial proceedings and because we think it is judicially efficient for us to address the error, we exercise our discretion under Fed.R.Crim.P. 52(b) and find the district court plainly erred in excluding the statutory mandatory sentence under Count 10.").

D. HARMLESS ERROR

A fundamental rule of federal appellate procedure is that courts will not reverse the judgment below based on errors that did not affect the outcome. Thus, Fed.R.Civ.P. 61 provides: "Unless justice requires otherwise, no error in admitting or excluding evidence—or any other error by the court or a party—is ground for granting a new trial, for setting aside a verdict, or for vacating, modifying, or otherwise disturbing a judgment or order. At every stage of the proceeding, the court must disregard all errors and defects that do not affect any party's substantial rights." Likewise, Fed.R.Crim.P. 52(a) provides that "[a]ny error, defect, irregularity, or variance that does not affect substantial rights must be disregarded." In addition, 28 U.S.C. § 2111 provides that in any appeal or adjudication on a writ of certiorari, the court shall not reverse based on "errors or defects which do not affect the substantial rights of the parties."

Some errors are so serious, so difficult to evaluate for harmlessness, or so harmful *per se* that they can never be deemed harmless. Examples of such errors include denial of the Sixth Amendment's right to counsel of choice, *United States v. Gonzalez-Lopez*, 548 U.S. 140, 148–51 (2006); the denial of the right of confrontation guaranteed by the Sixth Amendment, *Crawford v. Washington*, 541 U.S. 36, 68–69 (2004); denial of the right to trial by jury by giving a defective reasonable-doubt instruction, *Sullivan v. Louisiana*, 508 U.S. 275 (1993); denial of the right to a public trial, *Waller v. Georgia*, 467 U.S. 39, 49 n.9 (1984); denial of the right to represent oneself, *McKaskle v. Wiggins*, 465 U.S. 168, 177–78 n.8 (1984); and the denial of counsel, *Gideon v. Wainwright*, 372 U.S. 335 (1963). In most cases, the question of whether an error is harmful *per se* depends on whether the error is mere trial error (which is subject to harmless-error analysis) or a "structural defect" (which generally defies harmless-error analysis). *See Gonzalez-Lopez*, 548 U.S. at 148–49 & n.4.

Per se prejudicial errors are rare; the Supreme Court has recognized that "most constitutional errors can be harmless." *Arizona v. Fulminante*, 499 U.S. 279, 306 (1991). If a purported error does not fit in the category of *per se* prejudicial error but nonetheless raises constitutional issues, the error can be ignored only if it is "harmless beyond a reasonable doubt." *Chapman v. California*, 386 U.S. 18, 24 (1967). Some recent examples of constitutional errors that *may* be deemed harmless in an individual case include prosecutorial overreaching in jury summations, *Chapman, supra* at 24–26; omitting an element of an offense from the jury instructions, *Neder v. United States*, 527 U.S. 1, 9–10 (1999) (citing cases); erroneously admitting testimony in contravention of the Sixth Amendment's right to counsel, *Satterwhite v. Texas*, 486 U.S. 249, 257–60 (1988); giving a jury charge that shifts some aspect of the burden of proof to the defendant, *Burger v. Kemp*, 483 U.S. 776, 782 n.5 (1987); or a prosecutor's failure to turn over exculpatory evidence, *Pennsylvania v. Ritchie*, 480 U.S. 39, 58 (1987).

In habeas corpus appeals, and in federal criminal appeals involving nonconstitutional errors, harmless error is evaluated using a different and more forgiving standard. That standard asks whether the error had a "substantial and injurious effect or influence in determining the jury's verdict." *Kotteakos v. United States*, 328 U.S. 750, 776 (1946) (direct federal criminal appeal); *Brecht v. Abrahamson*, 507 U.S. 619, 631 (1993) (state habeas corpus under 28 U.S.C. § 2254). The standard for habeas cases remains the same "substantial and injurious effect" standard even where the state court on direct review entirely fails to perform the *Chapman* harmless-error analysis. *Fry v. Pliler*, 551 U.S. 112, 117–20 (2007). For errors that do not raise constitutional issues, courts should ignore such errors if they are deemed harmless by a preponderance of the evidence. Thus, for example, nonconstitutional procedural errors such as defective verdict forms are subject to the preponderance standard. *United States v. Stiger*, 413 F.3d 1185, 1190 (10th Cir. 2005). As with constitutional error, the party asserting the harmlessness of the error—in criminal cases, the government—bears the burden of showing the harmlessness. *Id.*

Some courts and commentators have indicated that, in the context of harmless error, a bright line should be drawn between criminal and civil cases because of the lower burden of proof generally in civil cases. "Just as the verdict in a civil case need only be more probably than not true, so an error in a civil trial need only be more probably than not harmless." *Haddad v. Lockheed Cal. Corp.*, 720 F.2d 1454, 1459 (9th Cir. 1983) (citation omitted). The reason behind this suggested distinction is based on the "differing degrees of certainty owed to civil and criminal litigants." *Id.* Because the preponderance standard that governs in civil cases reflects a societal judgment that a greater margin of error will be tolerated there than in criminal cases (where the beyond-a-reasonable-doubt standard of proof prevails), so too the harmless-error test should allow more errors to be harmless in civil cases. *Id.* (citing Stephen A. Saltzburg, *The Harm of Harmless Error*, 59 Va. L. Rev. 988 (1973)). This approach is controversial and not uniformly followed in all circuits. *Compare McIlroy v. Dittmer*, 732 F.2d 98, 105–06 (8th Cir. 1984) (following this approach) *with McQueeney v.*

Wilmington Trust Co., 779 F.2d 916, 923–28 (3d Cir. 1985) (disagreeing, *inter alia*, with the notion that civil jury verdicts are less worthy of respect than criminal verdicts).

E. THE "SOLID WALL OF PRECEDENT" EXCEPTION

What are the preservation requirements when the law changes after the trial-court proceedings but before the appeal is decided? As mentioned earlier, the Supreme Court in *United States v. Olano*, 507 U.S. 725 (1993), in its explication of the plain-error doctrine, set aside the "special case where the error was unclear at the time of trial but becomes clear on appeal because the applicable law has been clarified." *Id.* at 734.

Some circuits have recognized an exception to the preservation requirement where a "solid wall of circuit authority" would have rendered an objection at trial futile. *See, e.g., United States v. Viola*, 35 F.3d 37, 42 (2d Cir. 1994); *Phillips v. Cameron Tool Corp.*, 950 F.2d 488, 491 (7th Cir. 1991) ("Rule 51 of the Federal Rules of Civil Procedure does not require a party to be clairvoyant; parties need not state numerous objections to settled law in hopes that something may change while an appeal is pending.").

A few years after *Olano*, however, the Court decided *Johnson v. United States*, 520 U.S. 461 (1997), a direct appeal from a criminal conviction in federal court in which the law had changed between the time of the district court proceedings and appellate review. Applying Rule 52(b) as outlined in

Olano, the Court held that "before an appellate court can correct an error not raised at trial, there must be (1) 'error,' (2) that is 'plain,' and (3) that 'affect[s] substantial rights.' If all three conditions are met, an appellate court may then exercise its discretion to notice a forfeited error, but only if (4) the error 'seriously affect[s] the fairness, integrity, or public reputation of judicial proceedings." *Id.* at 466–67 (citations omitted; alterations in original). In the circumstances of the case before it, the *Johnson* Court held that, on the second prong, "where the law at the time of trial was settled and clearly contrary to the law at the time of appeal . . . it is enough that an error be 'plain' at the time of appellate consideration." *Id.* at 468.

In *Henderson v. United States* 133 S.Ct. 1121 (2013), the Court addressed the standard of review in a case where a legal issue was unsettled at the time of trial but settled by the time of appellate review. The Court held that, in such a case, "as long as the error was plain as of . . . the time of appellate review," the error is "plain" within the meaning of Fed.R.Crim.P. 52(b). *Id.* at 1124–25. The *Henderson* Court explained, *inter alia*, that its decision was supported by "the general rule . . . that an appellate court must apply the law in effect at the time it reaches its decision." *Id.* at 1126.

In sum, following *Johnson* and *Henderson*, it seems clear that, although an intervening change in the law can excuse counsel's failure to object in the trial court, appellate review will be under the demanding "plain error" test (which places the burden on the party claiming error), rather than the "harmless error" test (which puts the burden on the party opposing the claim of error).

CHAPTER 4

THE FINAL-JUDGMENT RULE

§ 4.1 GENERAL RULE

The final-judgment rule governs the question of whether a judgment or order is appealable to the United States Courts of Appeals in the lion's share of instances. That rule is expressed in 28 U.S.C. § 1291, which provides: "The courts of appeals . . . shall have jurisdiction of appeals from all final decisions of the district courts of the United States. . . ." The requirement that there be a "final decision"—*i.e.*, that all of the issues in a case have been resolved by the trial court—applies as a precondition to review by the federal appellate courts, unless the decision falls into one of the exceptional categories (discussed below) allowing for immediate appellate review.

At the outset, it is important to note that there are narrow classes of district-court final judgments that are directly appealable to the U.S. Supreme Court. The most frequent sort is a case heard by a three-judge district court, *see* 28 U.S.C. § 2284, whose decisions "granting or denying . . . an interlocutory or permanent injunction" may be appealed directly to the Supreme Court. 28 U.S.C. § 1253. Many voting-rights cases (such as challenges to redistricting) fall into this category.

Because the federal courts' appellate jurisdiction is defined by Congress, Congress can provide by statute that a final decision rendered by a district court—even a one-judge district court—may be directly appealed to the Supreme Court: In 1989, for example, Congress passed the Flag Protection Act of 1989, 103 Stat. 777, 18 U.S.C. § 700, as a response to the Supreme Court's decision in *Texas v. Johnson,* 491 U.S. 397 (1989). The Act criminalized desecration of the flag, and further provided that "[a]n appeal may be taken directly to the Supreme Court of the United States" in any case ruling upon the Act's constitutionality, and that "[t]he Supreme Court shall, if it has not previously ruled on the question, accept jurisdiction over the appeal and advance on the docket and expedite to the greatest extent possible." 18 U.S.C. § 700(d)(1) & (2). Two one-judge district courts struck down the Act on March 5 and 21, 1990, respectively; the Supreme Court noted "probable jurisdiction" over both appeals on March 30, 1990; heard argument on May 14, 1990; and decided the case (striking down the federal statute as violative of the First Amendment) on June 11, 1990. *United States v. Eichman*, 496 U.S. 310 (1990). The same kind of direct-appeal provision was included as part of the McCain-Feingold Bipartisan Campaign Act of 2002, 116 Stat. 81, 2 U.S.C. § 431 *et seq.*, which provided for a three-judge district court. *See McConnell v. Fed. Elec. Comm'n*, 540 U.S. 93, 133 (2003) (citing 2 U.S.C. § 437h note).

Still, the ordinary case is an appeal from a final decision of a federal district court to a federal court of appeals. And in those cases, the final-judgment rule of 28 U.S.C. § 1291 is the standard for an appealable decision. The rule is frequently described in these terms: "A 'final decision' generally is one which ends the litigation on the merits and leaves nothing for the court to do but execute the judgment." *Caitlin v. United States*, 324 U.S. 229, 233 (1945). The requirement that the decision be one that "ends the litigation on the merits" distinguishes orders that are "final" from those that only resolve some but not all of the issues or claims in the case. Nonetheless, the fact that a collateral matter (most commonly, an application for attorneys' fees) remains to be addressed by the trial court does not destroy finality. *Budinich v. Becton Dickinson & Co.*, 486 U.S. 196, 199–202 (1988); *Ray Haluch Gravel v. Central Pension Fund*, 134 S.Ct. 773, 780–83 (2014). Nor does the district court's retention of jurisdiction to police or enforce obedience to an injunction destroy finality. *See, e.g.*, *United States v. Pauley*, 321 F.3d 578, 581 (6th Cir. 2003).

As the Supreme Court has stressed, the final-judgment rule serves several salutary purposes:

> It emphasizes the deference that appellate courts owe to the trial judge as the individual initially called upon to decide the many questions of law and fact that occur in the course of a trial. Permitting piecemeal appeals would undermine the independence of the district judge, as well as the special role that individual plays in our judicial system. In addition, the rule is in accordance with the sensible policy of "avoid[ing] the obstruction to just claims that would come from permitting the harassment and cost of a succession of separate appeals from the various rulings to which a litigation may give rise, from its initiation to entry of

judgment." The rule also serves the important purpose of promoting efficient judicial administration.

Firestone Tire & Rubber Co. v. Risjord, 449 U.S. 368, 374 (1981) (citations omitted) (quoting *Cobbledick v. United States*, 309 U.S. 323, 325 (1940)).

Thus, a case where summary judgment has been granted in the district court on the plaintiff's claims, but not on one of the defendant's counterclaims, is not appealable. *Miller v. Special Weapons, L.L.C.*, 369 F.3d 1033, 1034–35 (8th Cir. 2004). Similarly, where one claim has been dismissed but another remains pending in the trial court, courts have frowned upon efforts to make a non-final judgment final by dismissing the pending claim "without prejudice" to reinstating it later. *See, e.g.*, *Union Oil Co. of Cal. v. John Brown E & C*, 121 F.3d 305, 309 (7th Cir. 1997). In that situation, courts have reasoned, the judgment does not "end the litigation on the merits," but only resolves it on a contingent basis. Other courts, by contrast, allow for the dismissal of unadjudicated claims "without prejudice" in order to create a final, appealable judgment. *See, e.g.*, *Nystrom v. TREX Co., Inc.* 339 F.3d 1347, 1350–51 (Fed. Cir. 2003) ("the district court could have dismissed the counterclaim without prejudice" to create an "avenu[e] of appeal as a matter of right").

In addition, a judgment holding a defendant liable, but not ascertaining the amount of damages, is not sufficiently final to be appealable, *SEC v. Carrillo*, 325 F.3d 1268, 1272–73 (11th Cir. 2003), except that, "a judgment in a civil action for patent infringement which . . . is final except for an accounting," *see* 28 U.S.C. § 1292(c)(2), may be immediately appealed. *See, e.g.*, *Robert Bosch, LLC v. Pylon Mfg. Corp.*, 719 F.3d 1305, 1320 (Fed. Cir. 2013) (en banc). Civil contempt orders, likewise, are not appealable as final judgments, because they are intended to coerce compliance with court orders, not punish for past behavior. *McAlpin v. Lexington 76 Auto Truck Stop, Inc.*, 229 F.3d 491, 500 (6th Cir. 2000).

Finally, the Supreme Court has clarified that, in a case that has been consolidated for pretrial proceedings in a multidistrict litigation under 28 U.S.C. § 1407, a party's or parties' right to appeal "ripen[s] when the District Court dismisse[s] their case, not upon eventual completion of multidistrict proceedings in all of the consolidated cases." *Gelboim v. Bank of Am. Corp.*, 135 S.Ct. 897, 902 (2015).

§ 4.2 APPEAL BY PERMISSION

Despite the absence of a final judgment, a party may obtain interlocutory review of "an order not otherwise appealable" with the permission of both the trial court and the court of appeals. 28 U.S.C. § 1292(b); *see also* 28 U.S.C. § 1292(c)(1) (providing that the U.S. Court of Appeals for the Federal Circuit has the same sort of jurisdiction); § 4.4, *infra*. Likewise, Rule 23(f) of the Federal Rules of Civil Procedure allows for interlocutory review of certain class-certification decisions with the permission of the court of appeals. *See* § 4.8, *infra*.

Rule 5 of the Federal Rules of Appellate Procedure sets forth the procedures that govern appeals by permission in all such cases. The party seeking an appeal must file a "petition for permission to appeal" with the court of appeals, FRAP 5(a), either "within the time specified by the statute or rule authorizing the appeal or, if no such time is specified, within the time provided by Rule 4(a) for filing a notice of appeal." The petition must contain a statement of facts "necessary to understand the question presented"; the question itself; the relief being sought; the reasons why an appeal should be allowed (and the rule or statute authorizing the request); and copies of the decision or decisions at issue, as well as, where applicable, any district court ruling authorizing the interlocutory appeal. FRAP 5(b). If the court of appeals grants permission to appeal, the appellant must pay all required fees to the court of appeals' clerk, and file a cost bond if required. FRAP 5(d). There is no requirement that a separate notice of appeal then be filed. *Id.*

§ 4.3 RULE 54(b)

Fed.R.Civ.P. 54(b) provides:

When an action presents more than one claim for relief—whether as a claim, counterclaim, cross-claim, or third-party claim—or when multiple parties are involved, the court may direct entry of a final judgment as to one or more, but fewer than all, claims or parties only if the court expressly determines that there is no just reason for delay. Otherwise, any order or

> other decision, however designated, that adjudicates fewer than all of the claims or the rights and liabilities of fewer than all of the parties does not end the action as to any of the claims or parties and may be revised at any time before the entry of a judgment adjudicating all the claims and all the parties' rights and liabilities.

Rule 54(b) allows for the entry of a final judgment on fewer than all claims in a case, or on all claims against one or more but fewer than all parties in the case, thus permitting the appeal of a portion of the case without the necessity of waiting for a final judgment as to all claims and parties. It is important to note that a judgment entered under Rule 54(b) is a species of final judgment; strictly speaking, Rule 54(b) allows the entry of a partial final judgment, so an appeal from such a properly entered judgment is an appeal from a "final decision" under 28 U.S.C. § 1291.

The principal purpose of the rule is to mitigate the unfairness of delaying an appeal that might otherwise occur except for the modern liberal joinder rules that allow multiple claims and multiple parties to be joined in a single civil action. *Dickinson v. Petroleum Conversion Corp.*, 338 U.S. 507, 511–12 (1950).

The mere fact that a court has entered a partial final judgment under Rule 54(b), however, does not automatically make the judgment appealable. The appellate court must determine that the certification was proper, and must do so even if the appellee does not contest the finality of the order. As the Supreme Court has noted, "[n]ot all final judgments on individual claims [are] immediately appealable, even if they are in some sense separable from the remaining unresolved claims." *Curtiss-Wright Corp. v. Gen. Elec. Co.*, 446 U.S. 1, 8 (1980). If an appellate court concludes that a district court has abused its discretion by entering a Rule 54(b) order, it will dismiss the appeal for lack of appellate jurisdiction. *See, e.g., Hogan v. Consol. Rail Corp.*, 961 F.2d 1021, 1025–26 (2d Cir. 1992).

As Rule 54(b) makes clear, three requirements must be met before a court can enter an order under that rule: (1) the action must dispose of one or more but fewer than all claims or parties; (2) a judgment must have been entered that completely disposes of at least one claim, or one party's entire set of claims; and (3) the district court must find that there is no just reason for delay. These requirements are discussed below.

A. MULTIPLE CLAIMS OR PARTIES

Whether multiple parties are involved in an action is, obviously, quite easy to ascertain from the caption of the complaint. Likewise, it usually does not pose much of a challenge to determine whether all of the rights or liabilities of one or more of those parties has been adjudicated. Still, it is not enough to qualify for a Rule 54(b) appeal if an order (for example) leaves a portion of a single claim open as to all defendants. *See, e.g., Alonzi v. Budget Constr. Co.*, 55 F.3d 331

(7th Cir. 1995) (leaving open the question of punitive damages against all defendants).

The harder cases usually involve adjudication of one or more, but fewer than all *claims*. A difficult threshold question is whether the order constitutes " 'an ultimate disposition of an individual claim entered in the course of a multiple claims action.' " *Curtiss-Wright*, 446 U.S. at 7 (quoting *Sears, Roebuck & Co. v. Mackey*, 351 U.S. 427, 436 (1956)). If the order disposes of particular legal issues but not an entire claim, it does not qualify for Rule 54(b) treatment. In determining whether particular claims are separate, the court should consider " '(1) the factual overlap (or lack thereof) between the claims disposed of and the remaining claims, and (2) whether the claims disposed of and the remaining claims seek separate relief.' " *Jordan v. Pugh*, 425 F.3d 820, 827 (10th Cir. 2005) (citation omitted).

The term "claim" is not necessarily synonymous with the "counts" set forth in the complaint; it is much closer to "cause of action" or "legal right." *See Olympia Hotels Corp. v. Johnson Wax Dev. Corp.*, 908 F.2d 1363 (7th Cir. 1990). Consistent with the reason behind Rule 54(b) of mitigating the delays that would otherwise be associated with the liberal joinder of parties and claims, the proper inquiry is "whether the underlying factual bases for recovery state a number of different claims which could have been separately enforced." *Rieser v. Baltimore & Ohio R.R. Co.*, 224 F.2d 198, 199 (2d Cir. 1955). The possible recoveries should be multiple and not mutually exclusive for the claims to be separate. *See Samaad v. City of Dallas*,

940 F.2d 925, 932 (5th Cir. 1991) (takings and equal protection claims were separate because the grounds of recovery were not "mutually exclusive").

B. FINAL DECISION FOR AT LEAST ONE CLAIM OR PARTY

The notion of finality that applies under Fed.R.Civ.P. 54(b) is in most relevant respects the same as the general rule of finality under 28 U.S.C. § 1291. Rule 54(b) "does not relax the finality required of each decision, as an individual claim, to render it appealable, but it does provide a practical means of permitting an appeal to be taken from one or more final decisions on individual claims, in multiple claims actions, without waiting for final decisions to be rendered on all the claims in the case." *Sears, Roebuck & Co. v. Mackey*, 351 U.S. 427, 435 (1956).

C. NO JUST REASON FOR DELAY

The rule states that the district court must determine, expressly, that there is no just reason for delay. This prerequisite to entry of a partial final judgment requires a court to analyze "judicial administrative interests as well as the equities involved." *Curtiss-Wright*, 446 U.S. at 8. As one court has explained, the district court must "determine whether 'the needs of the parties' outweigh the efficiency of having one appeal at the conclusion of the case in its entirety, and it must spell out its reasons for concluding that prompt review is preferable." *GenCorp, Inc. v. Olin Corp.*, 390 F.3d 433, 442 (6th Cir. 2004) (citation omitted).

Generally speaking, the "no just reason for delay" inquiry, which is addressed to the district court's equitable discretion, is not susceptible to bright-line rules. *See Curtiss-Wright*, 446 U.S. at 10–11 ("because the number of possible situations is large, we are reluctant either to fix or sanction narrow guidelines for the district court to follow"). However, a major factor in the decided cases seems to involve the interrelationship between the adjudicated claims and those that would be left behind for adjudication in the district court. Although the Supreme Court long ago rejected the requirement that adjudicated and non-adjudicated claims must be "separate and independent" for Rule 54(b) treatment, *Cold Metal Process Co. v. United Eng'g & Foundry Co.*, 351 U.S. 445 (1956), concerns over duplication of effort and advisory opinions have led courts to seize on the factual overlap of different claims as a reason to deny Rule 54(b) treatment. *See Campbell v. Westmoreland Farm, Inc.*, 403 F.2d 939, 943 (2d Cir. 1968). Thus, by way of example, a claim for severance pay was viewed as sufficiently severable from claims related to wrongful discharge, *see Ginett v. Computer Task Group, Inc.*, 962 F.2d 1085, 1096–97 (2d Cir. 1992) (Pratt, J.), whereas claims for breach of contract and misrepresentation were not sufficiently severable from the remaining claims, all of which were commonly grounded in a university's denial of tenure to a faculty member. *Spiegel v. Trustees of Tufts Coll.*, 843 F.2d 38, 44–46 & n.6 (1st Cir. 1988). The question of overlap is a pragmatic one, asking whether the claims "can be decided independently of one another," *Sears, Roebuck*, 351 U.S. at 436, or whether they are "inextricably intertwined." *Brunswick Corp. v. Sheridan*, 582 F.2d 175, 183–84 (2d Cir. 1978) (Friendly, J.).

Courts may also consider numerous other equitable factors in making a Rule 54(b) determination, such as the preclusive effect of a judgment, *see Cont'l Airlines, Inc. v. Goodyear Tire & Rubber Co.*, 819 F.2d 1519, 1525 (9th Cir. 1987), the hardship of not allowing the plaintiff to execute on or collect his judgment immediately, *see Bank of Lincolnwood v. Fed. Leasing, Inc.*, 622 F.2d 944, 949 n.7 (7th Cir. 1980), the prejudice (or benefits) of an appellate ruling upon the trial of the unadjudicated claims, *see Santa Maria v. Owens-Ill., Inc.*, 808 F.2d 848, 855 (1st Cir. 1986), and even the novelty of the issue to be appealed. *See International Union of Elec., Radio & Mach. Workers v. Westinghouse Elec. Corp.*, 631 F.2d 1094, 1099 (3d Cir. 1980).

D. NEED FOR DISTRICT COURT FINDINGS

Rule 54(b) empowers the district court to "direct entry of a final judgment" as to fewer than all claims or parties, but only if it "expressly determines that there is no just reason for delay." Without the express direction that judgment be entered, there will be no final judgment from which an appeal can be noticed. And without an express determination of "no just reason for delay," the essential and ultimate precondition to Rule 54(b) treatment is unmet, and such an appeal will ordinarily be dismissed for lack of appellate jurisdiction. Still, where the latter certificate is not explicitly made by the trial court, some courts have allowed an appeal to proceed if the judge clearly intended to allow an immediate appeal, and if the reasons for allowing an immediate appeal are "obvious." *See, e.g., Hudson River Sloop Clearwater, Inc. v. Dep't of the Navy*, 891 F.2d 414, 419 (2d Cir. 1989). Other courts may, when faced with the absence of a Rule 54(b) certificate, hold the appeal on their docket and order a limited remand so that the parties may return to the district court to obtain the certificate. *See, e.g., Nat'l Ass'n of Home Builders v. Norton*, 325 F.3d 1165, 1168 (9th Cir. 2003).

Most circuits require more than a mere recitation that there is "no just reason for delay," but instead require (or at least prefer) some sort of reasoned explanation from the district court in order to facilitate appellate review of that determination. *Gumer v. Shearson, Hammill & Co., Inc.*, 516 F.2d 283, 286 (2d Cir. 1974); *Justice v. Pendleton Place Apts.*, 40 F.3d 139, 141 (6th Cir. 1994); *Braswell Shipyards, Inc. v. Beazer East, Inc.*, 2 F.3d 1331, 1336 (4th Cir. 1993) (all requiring reasoned explanation); *Old Republic Ins. Co. v. Durango Air Serv., Inc.*, 283 F.3d 1222, 1225 n.5 (10th Cir. 2002); *Hayden v. McDonald*, 719 F.2d 266, 269 (8th Cir. 1983); *Explosives Supply Co. v. Columbia Nitrogen Corp.*, 691 F.2d 486, 486 (11th Cir. 1982) (all preferring reasoned explanation); *but see Fuller v. M.G. Jewelry*, 950 F.2d 1437, 1441 (9th Cir. 1991) (no need to provide reasons).

E. RESULT OF FAILURE TO APPEAL

"[A] district court's proper certification of an order under Rule 54(b) ordinarily starts the clock running for purposes of filing a notice of appeal." *In re Integra Realty Resources, Inc.*, 262 F.3d 1089, 1107 (10th Cir. 2001). Because the consequence of a Rule 54(b) order is the direction of a partial final judgment, which can be executed upon, the failure to file and pursue a timely appeal from that partial final judgment means that such a judgment cannot be later appealed. *See, e.g., Gross v. Pirtle*, 116 Fed. Appx. 189, 195 (10th Cir. 2004) (unpublished decision) (where district court certified partial judgment, but appellant did not appeal that aspect of the judgment until all claims were resolved, the failure to appeal the earlier judgment "deprive[d] [the court] of jurisdiction," and required dismissal of the appeal as to that earlier judgment).

§ 4.4 INTERLOCUTORY APPEALS UNDER 28 U.S.C. § 1292(b)

A. CRITERIA UNDER 28 U.S.C. § 1292(b)

SECTION 1292(b) provides:

> When a district judge, in making in a civil action an order not otherwise appealable under [section 1292], shall be of the opinion that such order involves a controlling question of law as to which there is a substantial ground for difference of opinion and that an immediate appeal from the order may materially advance the ultimate termination of the litigation, he

> shall so state in writing in such order. The court of appeals . . . may thereupon, in its discretion, permit an appeal to be taken from such order, if application is made to it within ten days after the entry of the order.

As the text of the statute makes clear, certification of an order for interlocutory appeal involves several inquiries.

Question of Law. The district court must first find that the order involves a question of law; questions of fact do not qualify for Section 1292(b) review. A question of law, as used in Section 1292(b), "has reference to a question of the meaning of a statutory or constitutional provision, regulation, or common law doctrine." *Ahrenholz v. Board of Trustees*, 219 F.3d 674, 676 (7th Cir. 2000). It refers to " 'pure' question[s] of law rather than merely to an issue that might be free from a factual contest." *Id.* at 676–77. "A legal question of the type envisioned in § 1292(b) . . . generally does not include matters within the discretion of the trial court." *West Tenn. Chapter of Assoc. Builders and Contractors, Inc. v. City of Memphis*, 293 F.3d 345, 351 (6th Cir. 2002) (holding that a ruling on the admissibility of evidence reviewable under an abuse of discretion standard does not create a controlling question of law). That test generally excludes from Section 1292(b) certification such orders as discovery rulings, denials of motions to change venue, and sanctions orders. *See, e.g.*, *White v. Nix*, 43 F.3d 374, 377–78 (8th Cir. 1994); *Standard v. Stoll Packing Corp.*, 315 F.2d 626 (3d Cir. 1963). All that said, some courts *have* used

Section 1292(b) to review and reverse discretionary decisions. *See, e.g.*, *Harrington v. Cleburne Cty. Bd. of Educ.*, 251 F.3d 935, 936 & n.1 (11th Cir. 2001) (pretrial order); *McClelland Engrs., Inc. v. Munusamy*, 784 F.2d 1313, 1316 (5th Cir. 1986) (*forum non conveniens* ruling).

Controlling Question. The district court must next find that the question of law is a "controlling" one. A legal question is controlling "if reversal of the district court's order would terminate the action." *Klinghoffer v. S.N.C. Achille Lauro Ed Altri-Gestione Motonave Achille Lauro in Amministrazione Straordinaria,* 921 F.2d 21, 24 (2d Cir. 1990). Proof that the resolution of the issue would necessarily result in termination of the litigation is not essential, however. Rather, a question is controlling "if its resolution is quite *likely* to affect the further course of the litigation, even if not certain to do so." *Sokaogon Gaming Enter. Corp. v Tushie-Montgomery Assocs., Inc.,* 86 F.3d 656, 659 (7th Cir. 1996) (emphasis added). Moreover, the issue need not "have precedential value for a number of pending cases" to qualify as controlling. *Klinghoffer,* 921 F.2d at 24. "A legal issue is controlling if it could materially affect the outcome of the case." *West Tenn. Chapter of Assoc. Builders & Contractors*, 293 F.3d at 351.

Substantial Ground for Disagreement. The district court must find that the issue is contestable—namely, that "there is substantial ground for difference of opinion" with respect to the proper resolution of the issue. 28 U.S.C. § 1292(b). This criterion may be satisfied if other court decisions addressing the issue are in conflict, or if the issue is complicated or difficult, even if there is no precedent squarely on point. At the same time, however, even a question of first impression within a circuit may be so clear that it does not present a substantial ground for disagreement. *Singh v. Daimler-Benz, AG*, 800 F.Supp. 260, 263 (E.D.Pa. 1992).

Resolution of Issue Will Materially Advance the Case. The district court must find that the resolution of the issue "may materially advance the ultimate termination of the litigation." 28 U.S.C. § 1292(b). Although this requirement in many ways dovetails with the "controlling question of law" inquiry, the focus here is on efficiency in the particular case—whether interlocutory review would ultimately result in a savings of time and expense for the judiciary and the parties. According to the Eleventh Circuit, the "materially advance" requirement "is not a difficult one to understand. It means that resolution of a controlling legal question would serve to avoid a trial or otherwise substantially shorten the litigation." *McFarlin v. Conseco Servs., LLC*, 381 F.3d 1251, 1259 (11th Cir. 2004) (declining certification because the question of whether some defendants were "strangers" to the contracts at issue would not speed up or streamline the case).

B. DISCRETIONARY DECISIONS

The question whether to grant Section 1292(b) review is within the discretion of the district court in the first instance, and the appellate court's decision whether to accept jurisdiction is also discretionary. *Moorman v. UnumProvident Corp.*, 464 F.3d 1260, 1272 (11th Cir. 2006). A district court's discretionary decision not to certify a case for appeal under Section 1292(b) is not itself appealable. Thus, if the district court refuses to grant certification, the court of appeals has no authority to accept Section 1292(b) review.

Some courts have indicated that Section 1292(b) review should be allowed only under exceptional circumstances, while other courts have eschewed such a rigid approach and have urged flexibility based on the circumstances of the particular case. *See, e.g., Hadjipateras v. Pacifica, S.A.*, 290 F.2d 697, 702–03 (5th Cir. 1961) (Brown, J.). In addition, a court of appeals may exercise its discretion by deferring its decision whether or not to accept review to the hearing on the merits, so that the court can receive briefing and argument to better inform its decision. *See Lukenas v. Bryce's Mountain Resort, Inc.*, 538 F.2d 594, 595 (4th Cir. 1976). Moreover, courts of appeals maintain the discretion to revisit their certification at any time before decision, and can, "with the benefit of hindsight, . . . admit [their] error" and withdraw the certification. *Caraballo-Seda v. Municipality of Hormigueros*, 395 F.3d 7, 9 (1st Cir. 2005); *McFarlin*, 381 F.3d at 1256.

C. TIMING OF SECTION 1292(b) REQUESTS

If the district court agrees to certify the issue for interlocutory review, Section 1292(b) makes clear that the application to the court of appeals must be made "within ten days after the entry of the [district court's] order." Section 1292(b) provides no specific deadline, however, for requesting certification from the district court after the order in question is handed down. Nonetheless, courts have held that such requests must be filed within a reasonable amount of time. *See, e.g., Ahrenholz v. Board of Trustees of Univ. of Ill.*, 219 F.3d 674, 676 (7th Cir. 2000). Because the application to the appellate court must be made within ten days, filing a certification request with the district court within ten days is likely to be deemed reasonable. *Cf. Richardson Elecs., Ltd. v. Panache Broadcasting of Pa., Inc.*, 202 F.3d 957, 958 (7th Cir. 2000) (unexplained delay of two months in seeking certification led to court of appeals declining to accept appeal).

D. SCOPE OF APPELLATE COURT JURISDICTION

When a court of appeals accepts certification under Section 1292(b), "appellate jurisdiction applies to the order certified to the court of appeals, and is not tied to the particular question formulated by the district court." *Yamaha Motor Corp., U.S.A. v. Calhoun*, 516 U.S. 199, 205 (1996). Thus, the appellate court has power to "review an entire order, either to consider a question different from the one certified as controlling or to decide the case despite the lack of any identified controlling question." *Id.*

However, "[t]he court of appeals may not reach beyond the certified order to address other orders made in the case." *Id.*; *see also United States v.*

Stanley, 483 U.S. 669, 676–77 (1987). This is so because the statute specifies that the appeal is "taken from such order." 28 U.S.C. § 1292(b). Thus, a court of appeals reviewing an order regarding notice to potential class members about opting into the class could not expand the review to encompass a second order declining to void consents already given by other plaintiffs. *Sperling v. Hoffman-La Roche, Inc.*, 862 F.2d 439, 440 (3d Cir. 1988), *aff'd*, 493 U.S. 165 (1989).

§ 4.5 COLLATERAL ORDER

As noted in § 4.1, *supra*, under 28 U.S.C. § 1291, appellate courts have "jurisdiction over 'all final decisions' of district courts" that are not directly appealable to the U.S. Supreme Court. The so-called *Cohen* "collateral order" doctrine—which stems from *Cohen v. Beneficial Industrial Loan Corp.*, 337 U.S. 541 (1949)—"accommodates a 'small class' of rulings, not concluding the litigation, but conclusively resolving claims of right separable from, and collateral to, rights asserted in the action." *Will v. Hallock*, 546 U.S. 345, 349 (2006) (quoting *Behrens v. Pelletier*, 516 U.S. 299, 305 (1996)). Such "claims are 'too important to be denied review and too independent of the cause itself to require that appellate consideration be deferred until the whole case is adjudicated.' " *Id.* at 349 (quoting *Cohen*, 337 U.S. at 546). A collateral order under this doctrine is a species of a final judgment; the doctrine "is best understood not as an exception to the final decision rule laid down by Congress in § 1291, but as a 'practical construction' of it." *Id.* Importantly, however, the Court has emphasized that "*Cohen*'s collateral order doctrine . . . must never be allowed to swallow the general rule that a party is entitled to a single appeal, to be deferred until final judgment has been entered." *Mohawk Indus., Inc. v. Carpenter*, 558 U.S. 100, 106 (2009) (citations omitted). Therefore, "stringent" conditions must be placed on the doctrine's application so that it will not "overpower the substantial finality interests § 1291 is meant to further." *Will*, 546 U.S. at 350. The doctrine thus embraces only a "small class" of collaterally appealable orders, with a "modest scope" and a "narrow and selective . . . membership." *Id.*

A. CRITERIA

The Supreme Court has identified three conditions that must be met before a district court's ruling can be considered an appealable collateral order. Specifically, the order must "[1] 'conclusively determine the disputed question, [2] resolve an important issue completely separate from the merits of the action, and [3] be effectively unreviewable on appeal from a final judgment.' " *Puerto Rico Aqueduct & Sewer Auth. v. Metcalf & Eddy, Inc.*, 506 U.S. 139, 144 (1993) (quoting *Coopers & Lybrand v. Livesay*, 437 U.S. 463, 468 (1978)). Each requirement must be satisfied for the order to be appealable.

For a question to be "conclusively determined," it must not be a tentative ruling that is likely to be subject to later reconsideration. Prior to the advent of Rule 23(f) of the Federal Rules of Civil Procedure, allowing interlocutory review of class-action determinations in certain situations, class-certification orders were held to fall into this category of a mere tentative ruling. Similarly, orders declining to appoint counsel for a plaintiff are not "conclusively determined," because they may be reconsidered as the trial-court proceeding continues. *See, e.g., Henry v. City of Detroit Manpower Dept.*, 763 F.2d 757, 761–62 (6th Cir. 1985). At the same time, though, the requirement that a matter be conclusively determined should be evaluated from a practical, or pragmatic standpoint, not a rigid one. That is because Fed.R.Civ.P. 54(b) provides that "any order or other decision," absent the entry of a Rule 54(b) partial final judgment, "may be revised at any time before the entry of a judgment," and so every collateral order entered by a district court is, in the most rigid sense, not "conclusive." *See Moses H. Cone Mem. Hosp. v. Mercury Constr. Corp.*, 460 U.S. 1, 12–13 (1983) (holding that a district court's stay order was appealable and that the contrary argument, that the order did not "conclusively determine" the subject matter, was "true only in the technical sense that every order short of a final decree is subject to reopening at the discretion of the district judge").

The "important issue completely separate from the merits" language embodies the requirement that the order address a "collateral" issue. Because the general rule is that all non-final orders merge into the final judgment and may be brought up on appeal from that judgment, this requirement filters out matters that may be affected or mooted by the proceedings leading to the final judgment. The textbook case of a "collateral" issue is a defense of immunity from suit, whether qualified, absolute, state, or foreign sovereign immunity. Because immunity is said to be not just immunity from an adverse judgment, but immunity from the burdens of suit in the first place, this explains why an order denying immunity is sufficiently "collateral" from the merits, whereas a denial of a Rule 12(b)(6) motion or a summary-judgment motion is typically not. *See, e.g., Mitchell v. Forsyth*, 472 U.S. 511, 527–29 (1985). Also collateral or separate are orders involving security or attachments. Indeed, the seminal collateral-order case, *Cohen v. Beneficial Indus. Loan Corp.*, 337 U.S. 541 (1949), involved the validity and applicability of a law requiring plaintiffs to post security as a condition to suit. *See also Swift & Co. Packers v. Compania Colombiana del Caribe*, 339 U.S. 684, 688 (1950) (finding question regarding attachment of a ship "fairly severable from the context of the larger litigious process").

Finally, the requirement that the question be "effectively unreviewable on appeal from a final judgment" ensures that only matters that are in truly urgent need of immediate review fall into the "collateral order" category. For example, shortly after deciding the seminal *Cohen* case in 1949, the Supreme Court also held that orders denying *in forma pauperis* status or orders denying bail were likewise "effectively unreviewable" on an appeal from a final judgment. *Roberts v. United States Dist. Ct.*, 339 U.S. 844 (1950); *Stack v. Boyle*, 342 U.S. 1 (1951). Similarly, because immunity is said to involve a right not to be subjected to a trial, it would make little sense to require a party to go through a trial in order to appeal the denial of that right. *Mitchell v. Forsyth, supra.*

In *Mohawk Indus., Inc. v. Carpenter*, 558 U.S. 100 (2009), the Court focused on the "effective unreviewability" prong of *Cohen* to hold that disclosure orders adverse to the attorney-client privilege do not qualify for immediate appeal under the collateral order doctrine. *Id.* at 108. While "readily acknowledg[ing] the importance of the attorney-client privilege," the Court nonetheless found that "[p]ermitting parties to undertake successive, piecemeal appeals of all adverse attorney-client rulings would unduly delay the resolution of district court litigation and needlessly burden the Courts of Appeals." *Id.* at 112 (citations omitted). Moreover, the Court noted that a party wishing to challenge an adverse privilege ruling still had a number of options: "standard postjudgment appeals, § 1292(b) appeals, mandamus, and contempt appeals." *Id.* at 114.

Some circuits have applied a fourth factor—the existence of a serious and unsettled question. *See, e.g.*, *Gill v. Gulfstream Park Racing Ass'n, Inc.*, 399 F.3d 391, 397–98 (1st Cir. 2005); *Kensington Int'l Ltd. v. Republic of Congo*, 461 F.3d 238, 241 (2d Cir. 2006); *In re UAL Corp.*, 408 F.3d 847, 850 (7th Cir. 2005). The great weight of authority, however, holds that the *Cohen* test involves only three factors and that this purported fourth factor is not part of the test, even though it may have relevance to the second factor, which requires an "important issue." *See Under Seal v. Under Seal*, 326 F.3d 479, 481–84 (4th

Cir. 2003); *Wiwa v. Royal Dutch Petroleum Co.*, 392 F.3d 812, 816 (5th Cir. 2004); *United States v. Young*, 424 F.3d 499, 503 (6th Cir. 2005); *Kilburn v. Socialist People's Libyan Arab Jamahiriya*, 376 F.3d 1123 (D.C. Cir. 2004).

In attempting to articulate a line between cases involving collateral orders and those that do not, the Supreme Court has stated: "[I]t is not mere avoidance of a trial, but avoidance of a trial that would imperil a substantial public interest, that counts when asking whether an order is 'effectively' unreviewable if review is to be left until later." *Will*, 546 U.S. at 352 (quoting *Coopers & Lybrand*, 437 U.S. at 468). Put another way, in asserting that a collateral order is involved because of a right not to go to trial, the party seeking review must identify "some particular value of high order . . . in avoiding trial," such as "honoring the separation of powers, preserving the efficiency of government and the initiative of its officials, respecting a State's dignitary interests, and mitigating the government's advantage over the individual." *Will*, 546 U.S. at 352.

B. TYPES OF ORDERS THAT QUALIFY AND THAT DO NOT QUALIFY

Orders found within the collateral-order doctrine include orders denying absolute immunity, *Nixon v. Fitzgerald*, 457 U.S. 731, 742 (1982), orders denying qualified immunity, *Mitchell v. Forsyth*, 472 U.S. 511, 530 (1985), orders denying state sovereign immunity, *Puerto Rico Aqueduct & Sewer Auth. v. Metcalf & Eddy, Inc.*, 506 U.S. 139, 144–45 (1993), orders denying immunity under the Foreign Sovereign Immunities Act, *Federal Ins. Co. v. Richard I. Rubin & Co., Inc.*, 12 F.3d 1270, 1281 (3d Cir. 1993), orders adverse to a criminal defendant on the defense of double jeopardy, *Abney v. United States*, 431 U.S. 651, 660 (1977), orders denying an attorney's motion to withdraw, *Whiting v. Lacara*, 187 F.3d 317 (2d Cir. 1999); *Fid. Nat. Title Ins. Co. of N.Y. v. Intercounty Nat. Title Ins. Co.*, 310 F.3d 537, 539–40 (7th Cir. 2002), and orders compelling the disclosure of documents that are claimed to be privileged or protected by the work-product doctrine, *In re Cendant Corp. Sec. Litig.*, 343 F.3d 658, 662 & n.5 (3d Cir. 2003). Legal issues that otherwise fall within the collateral-order doctrine, such as qualified immunity, may continue to do so "even if the underlying facts are disputed—indeed, even if . . . the district court denied summary judgment due to the presence of material facts." *Moore v. Hartman*, 388 F.3d 871, 875 (D.C. Cir. 2004); *see Behrens v. Pelletier*, 516 U.S. 299, 312–13 (1996).

Orders held not to be immediately appealable include orders requiring the disclosure of purportedly privileged documents, *Mohawk Indus., Inc. v. Carpenter*, 558 U.S. 100, 103 (2009), orders rescinding settlement agreements, *Digital Equip. Corp. v. Desktop Direct, Inc.*, 511 U.S. 863, 869 (1994), sanctions orders, *Cunningham v. Hamilton Cty.*, 527 U.S. 198 (1999), orders declining to dismiss a case on *forum non conveniens* grounds, *Van Cauwenberghe v. Biard*, 486 U.S. 517, 527–30 (1988), orders denying class certification, *Coopers & Lybrand v. Livesay*, 437 U.S. 463, 470 (1978), orders requiring the posting of security for the release of an impounded ship, *Seguros Banvenez S.A. v. S/S Oliver Drescher*, 715 F.2d 54 (2d Cir. 1983), orders appointing a guardian *ad litem* for an ERISA plan, *In re Pressman-Gutman Co., Inc.*, 459 F.3d 383, 392–93 (3d Cir. 2006), orders disqualifying counsel because of a conflict of interest, *Cole v. U.S. Dist. Ct. for Dist. of Idaho*, 366 F.3d 813, 817 (9th Cir. 2004), orders denying motions to dismiss based on a contractual forum-selection clause, *Lauro Lines S.R.L. v. Chasser*, 490 U.S. 495, 497–501 (1989), and orders denying a so-called *Rooker-Feldman* defense (*i.e.*, that the Supreme Court is the only federal court that can review a state-court judgment), *Bryant v. Sylvester*, 57 F.3d 308, 310 (3d Cir. 1995), *vacated and remanded*, 516 U.S. 1105 (1996). At bottom, orders are collateral only when they do not "involve[ ] considerations that are 'enmeshed in the factual and legal issues comprising the plaintiff's cause of action.'" *Coopers & Lybrand*, 437 U.S. at 469 (citation omitted).

C. DISCOVERY ORDERS

"[D]iscovery orders are generally characterized as interlocutory and review may be sought only through the contempt process or by waiting for the entry of a final judgment in the underlying action." *United States v. Columbia Broad. Sys., Inc.*, 666 F.2d 364, 369 (9th Cir. 1982). Nonetheless, some discovery-related rulings have been held to present collateral orders, such as whether a trial court abused its discretion in denying reimbursement of costs to several nonparty witnesses who produced substantial discovery under subpoena. *Id.* at 370. *See also* § 6.3, *infra* (discussing appeals by non-parties). Additionally, as noted above, discovery orders compelling the production of material claimed to be privileged may be appealed under the collateral-order doctrine, or, in rare cases typically involving privilege issues, review may be available via mandamus, *See* § 4.7, *infra.*

§ 4.6 OTHER STATUTORY AND RULE EXCEPTIONS TO THE FINAL-JUDGMENT RULE

A. APPEALS FROM INJUNCTIONS

Under 28 U.S.C. § 1292(a)(1), courts of appeals have jurisdiction over appeals from "[i]nterlocutory orders . . . granting, continuing, modifying, refusing or dissolving injunctions . . . except where a direct review may be had in the Supreme Court."

Because the statute authorizing appeals from orders involving injunctions is in derogation of the ordinary rule that appeals lie only from final judgments, and contrary to the overall federal policy against piecemeal appeals, it has been said that the statute is "a limited exception to the final judgment rule, [to be] construed . . . narrowly to ensure that appeal as of right under § 1292(a)(1) will be available only in circumstances where an appeal will further the statutory purpose of 'permit[ting] litigants to effectually challenge interlocutory orders of serious, perhaps irreparable, consequence.'" *Carson v. Am. Brands, Inc.*, 450 U.S. 79, 84 (1981) (quoting

Baltimore Contractors, Inc. v. Bodinger, 348 U.S. 176, 181 (1955)). This section is a far more common source of appealable orders than the rule of narrow construction would suggest, however.

Whether or not an order qualifies as an "injunction" can sometimes be difficult to ascertain. For purposes of Section 1292(a)(1), an injunction is an order "[1] directed to a party, [2] enforceable by contempt, and [3] designed to accord or protect 'some or all of the substantive relief sought by the complaint' in more than a [temporary] fashion." *Cohen v. Board of Trustees*, 867 F.2d 1455, 1465 n.9 (3d Cir. 1989) (en banc) (quoting secondary authority). Under this definition, both preliminary and permanent injunctions are appealable under Section 1292(a)(1).

However, temporary restraining orders are not appealable under Section 1292(a)(1). Despite their seeming similarity to injunctions, there are "practical reasons" why they are not treated as such under the appeal statute: "(1) they are usually effective for only brief periods of time, far less than the time required for appeal . . . and are then generally supplanted by appealable [preliminary] or permanent injunctions, (2) they are generally issued without notice to the adverse party and thus the trial judge has had opportunity to hear only one side of the case, and (3) the trial court should have ample opportunity to have a full presentation of the facts and law before entering an order that is appealable to the appellate courts." *Connell v. Dulien Steel Prods., Inc.*, 240 F.2d 414, 418 (5th Cir. 1957). Put another way, because of the inherently temporary nature of such an order, a party ordinarily may gain adequate "review" of such an order from the trial court itself, without engaging the cumbersome and sometimes time-consuming machinery of an appeal.

Of course, the trial court's denomination of an order as a "temporary restraining order" is not controlling; orders so denominated but being of excessive duration, or otherwise having the effect of an injunction, will be held appealable. *See, e.g., Romer v. Green Point Sav. Bank*, 27 F.3d 12, 15 (2d Cir. 1994).

Likewise, procedural orders issued by a district court—even though their violation may be punished by contempt—may not qualify as injunctions under Section 1292(a)(1). "[T]he mere presence of words of restraint or direction in an order that is only a step in an action does not make § 1292(a)(1) applicable." *International Prods. Corp. v. Koons*, 325 F.2d 403, 406 (2d Cir. 1963) (Friendly, J.) (citing cases). The dividing line between appealable injunctions and nonappealable procedural orders is frequently stated as Judge Friendly did in *International Products*: "We think it better, in line with our prior decisions, to continue to read § 1292(a)(1) as relating to injunctions which give or aid in giving some or all of the substantive relief sought by a complaint . . . and not as including restraints or directions in orders concerning the conduct of parties or their counsel, unrelated to the substantive issues in the action, while awaiting trial." *Id.*

An order sometimes qualifies under 28 U.S.C. § 1292(a)(1) even when it does not directly refuse to grant injunctive relief directly but does so only indirectly. For example, in *Carson v. American Brands, Inc.*, 450 U.S. 79 (1981), the Court held that an interlocutory order denying a joint motion of the class and the defendant to enter a consent decree containing injunctive relief was appealable under Section 1292(a)(1). The Court reasoned that "in refusing to approve the parties' negotiated consent decree, the District Court denied petitioners the opportunity to compromise their claim and to obtain the injunctive benefits of the settlement agreement they negotiated." *Id.* at 89. The Court viewed these "serious, perhaps irreparable, consequences" as being subject to effective challenge "only by an immediate appeal." *Id.* at 90 (citation omitted).

By contrast, the Court held that the denial of class certification in a sex discrimination case seeking injunctive relief was not immediately appealable under Section 1292(a)(1) because the district court's order had "no direct or irreparable impact on the merits of the controversy." *Gardner v. Westinghouse Broad. Co.*, 437 U.S. 478, 480 (1978). Similarly, the denial of a motion for summary judgment that had sought a permanent injunction was not appealable because "the denial of a motion for summary judgment because of unresolved issues of fact does not settle or even tentatively decide anything about the merits of the claim." *Switzerland Cheese Assoc., Inc. v. E. Horne's Market, Inc.*, 385 U.S. 23, 25 (1966).

An order not denominated as an injunction, then, may be appealable as an injunction where "the interlocutory order: (1) has the effect of an injunction; (2) has serious, perhaps irreparable consequence; and (3) is effectively unreviewable on appeal." *United States v. Bowman*, 341 F.3d 1228, 1236 (11th Cir. 2003). In this respect, the Third Circuit has distinguished between orders *granting* injunctions and orders *denying* injunctions, holding that it has only required an appellant to demonstrate "serious, perhaps irreparable consequences" "in the context of determining the appealability of an order *denying* injunctive relief." *Saudi Basic Indus. Corp. v. Exxon Corp.*, 364 F.3d 106, 111 (3d Cir. 2004).

As noted above, Section 1292(a)(1) is strictly construed by courts. Thus, courts have consistently held that "[a]lthough orders that *modify* injunctions may be appealable under section 1292(a)(1), orders that merely *clarify* previously entered injunctions are not." *Morales Feliciano v. Rullan*, 303 F.3d 1, 7 (1st Cir. 2002). To ascertain whether a modification of an injunction has occurred, the court examines "whether the ruling complained of can be said to have altered the underlying decree in a jurisdictionally significant way," with "[d]oubts as to the applicability of Section 1292(a)(1) . . . resolved against immediate appealability." *Id.*

There is no requirement that a party appeal from an order granting or denying an injunction. If a party chooses not to appeal an adverse decision on a preliminary injunction, it may raise the issue on appeal from a final judgment. *Retired Chicago Police*

Ass'n v. City of Chicago, 7 F.3d 584, 608 (7th Cir. 1993). Still, there is always a risk that the issues presented by the grant or denial of an injunction will become moot or otherwise obviated by the final judgment or by the passage of time. And, if a party does appeal from an injunction order, the general rule is that the appeal does not limit the appellate court to just review of the injunction order itself, but rather opens up "the entire case" to the court. *Aerojet-General Corp. v. Am. Arbitration Ass'n*, 478 F.2d 248, 252 (9th Cir. 1973).

B. APPEALS FROM APPOINTMENT OF A RECEIVER

Under 28 U.S.C. § 1292(a)(2), appeal is permitted from "[i]nterlocutory orders appointing receivers, or refusing orders to wind up receiverships or to take steps to accomplish the purposes thereof, such as directing sales or other disposals of property." Section 1292(a)(2) "is interpreted narrowly to permit appeals only from the three discrete categories of receivership orders specified in the statute, namely, [1] orders appointing a receiver, [2] orders refusing to wind up a receivership, and [3] orders refusing to take steps to accomplish the purposes of winding up a receivership." *SEC v. Black*, 163 F.3d 188, 195 (3d Cir. 1998).

The reason why receivership orders are appealable is similar in nature to the rationale for immediate appealability of injunctions—receiverships can have drastic and immediate consequences with respect to property rights. A receiver "take[s] possession of and preserves, pendente lite, and for the benefit of the party ultimately entitled to it, the fund or property in litigation." *FTC v. World Wide Factors, Ltd.*, 882 F.2d 344, 348 (9th Cir. 1989) (internal quotation marks and citation omitted).

Because of the rule of strict construction, Section 1292(a)(2) has been held not to allow appeals that do not strictly fall within the letter of that rule. Thus, while the statute allows appeal from interlocutory orders "appointing receivers," it allows no appeal from an order refusing to appoint one, *United States v. View Crest Garden Apts., Inc.* 265 F.2d 205 (9th Cir. 1958), nor from a decision refusing to vacate an appointment. *Illinois ex rel. Hartigan v. Peters*, 861 F.2d 164 (7th Cir. 1989).

As with injunctions, the terminology or characterization contained in a district court's orders regarding receiverships is not dispositive. "A receiver by any other name, or by no name, is still a receiver." *United States v. Sylacauga Props., Inc.*, 323 F.2d 487, 490 (5th Cir. 1963). Still, the rule of narrow construction will limit the class of orders that are considered appealable under this provision. Even a court-appointed guardian *ad litem* for an ERISA plan was not considered to be the appointment of a "receiver" under this section, since "the functions of the guardian ad litem in this case fell far short of those of a receiver for in each of its several orders the district court expressly limited the role of the guardian ad litem and otherwise did not disturb the [roles of the] fiduciaries and administrators of the plan." *In re Pressman-Gutman Co., Inc.*, 459 F.3d 383, 394 (3d Cir. 2006).

C. CLASSIFIED INFORMATION PROCEDURES ACT

An example of a statutory basis for interlocutory appeal is the Classified Information Procedures Act (CIPA), 18 U.S.C. App. 3 §§ 1–16. Under CIPA, a criminal defendant intending to rely on classified information at trial must inform the trial court prior to trial. 18 U.S.C. App. 3 § 5(a). The government may seek a hearing to obtain a ruling whether the information in question is in fact admissible and relevant. 18 U.S.C. App. 3 § 6(a). If the court rules in favor of the defendant, thus permitting public disclosure of the information at trial, the government is authorized by CIPA to pursue an interlocutory appeal. 18 U.S.C. App. 3 § 7(a). If, however, the court has not definitively resolved the issue of disclosure, but rather has only rejected one of several grounds for inadmissibility of the evidence, or allowed the defendant to take discovery, an interlocutory appeal will not lie. *United States v. Giffen*, 473 F.3d 30, 37–38 (2d Cir. 2006); *United States v. Moussaoui*, 333 F.3d 509, 514–15 (4th Cir. 2003).

D. FEDERAL ARBITRATION ACT

The Federal Arbitration Act permits interlocutory review of an order denying a motion to compel arbitration or "granting, continuing, or modifying an injunction against an arbitration." 9 U.S.C. §§ 16(a)(1)(A)–(C), 16(a)(2). *See, e.g., Sandvik AB v.*

Advent Int'l Corp., 220 F.3d 99 (3d Cir. 2000). Unless otherwise authorized by 28 U.S.C. § 1292(b), however, interlocutory orders that require or permit arbitrations to proceed are not immediately appealable. 9 U.S.C. § 16(b). The reason behind this statutory distinction—between orders stopping arbitrations (which are appealable) and orders allowing arbitrations (which are generally not)—is found in the pro-arbitration policy of the Federal Arbitration Act, of "enforcing binding arbitration agreements." *Sandvik*, 220 F.3d at 104; *see Palcko v. Airborne Express, Inc.*, 372 F.3d 588, 591–92 (3d Cir. 2004).

Further complexity arises from a circuit split over the meaning of 9 U.S.C. § 3, which provides:

> If any suit or proceeding be brought in any of the courts of the United States upon any issue referable to arbitration under an agreement in writing for such arbitration, the court in which such suit is pending, upon being satisfied that the issue involved in such suit or proceeding is referable to arbitration under such an agreement, *shall on application of one of the parties stay the trial of the action* until such arbitration has been had in accordance with the terms of the agreement, providing the applicant for the stay is not in default in proceeding with such arbitration.

Id. (emphasis added). The Second, Third, Seventh, Tenth, and Eleventh Circuits have held that, when all issues in the case are subject to arbitration, the district court is required to grant a stay. *See, e.g.*,

Katz v. Cellco Partnership, 794 F.3d 341 (2d Cir. 2015), *cert. denied*, 136 S.Ct. 596 (2015). By contrast, the First, Fifth, and Ninth Circuits have held that the district court has discretion to dismiss the action in such circumstances. *See, e.g.*, *Bercovitch v. Baldwin School, Inc.*, 133 F.3d 141 (1st Cir. 1998); *see generally* Alessandra Rose Johnson, Note, *Oh, Won't You Stay With Me?: Determining Whether § 3 of the FAA Requires a Stay in Light of* Katz v. Cellco Partnership, 84 Fordham L. Rev. 2261, 2271–83 (2016) (discussing circuit split). The split is significant because, if an action is *stayed* pending arbitration, a party resisting arbitration will not have an opportunity for interlocutory review. On the other hand, if the action is *dismissed*, the judgment becomes "final" and thus immediately appealable.

§ 4.7 REVIEW BY EXTRAORDINARY WRIT

Under 28 U.S.C. § 1651(a), the All Writs Act, an appellate court may issue a writ of mandamus in "extraordinary" or "drastic" circumstances involving a usurpation of power or a clear abuse of discretion by the lower court. *Kerr v. United States Dist. Ct. for Northern Dist.*, 426 U.S. 394, 402 (1976). Mandamus may not serve as a substitute for appeal. *See, e.g.*, *Kerr v. United States*, 426 U.S. 394, 403 (1976); *In re Pressman-Gutman Co.,* 459 F.3d 383, 398–99 (3d Cir. 2006). To obtain mandamus, the movant must show that (1) there is no other adequate way to secure the relief, *Roche v. Evaporated Milk Ass'n,* 319 U.S. 21, 26 (1943), (2) the right to relief is clear and not subject to dispute, *Bankers Life & Cas. Co. v. Holland*, 346 U.S. 379, 384 (1953), and (3) such relief is appropriate under the circumstances, as a matter of the court's discretion. *Kerr v. United States Dist. Ct.*, 426 U.S. 394, 403 (1976); *In re Sch. Asbestos Litig.*, 977 F.2d 764, 772 (3d Cir. 1992). Mandamus will generally be denied when another method is available for seeking interlocutory review, such as 28 U.S.C. § 1292(b).

Courts have granted mandamus when a district court wrongfully permitted the discovery of privileged documents, *see, e.g., In re Avantel, S.A.*, 343 F.3d 311, 317 (5th Cir. 2003), when a district judge erroneously ruled that the plaintiff had no Seventh Amendment right to a jury trial, *Beacon Theatres, Inc. v. Westover*, 359 U.S. 500, 511 (1959); *Dairy Queen, Inc. v. Wood*, 369 U.S. 469, 472 (1962), or when a district judge wrongfully refused to recuse himself, *see, e.g., In re Kensington Int'l Ltd.*, 353 F.3d 211, 219–20 (3d Cir. 2003). Indeed, "[v]irtually every court of appeals has recognized the necessity and propriety of interlocutory review of disqualification issues on petitions for mandamus 'to ensure that judges do not adjudicate cases that they have no statutory power to hear.'" *Alexander v. Primerica Holdings, Inc.*, 10 F.3d 155, 163 (3d Cir. 1993) (citation omitted).

The district court is no longer the respondent in a mandamus action. FRAP 21. This change was made in the 1996 amendments to the FRAP, out of a recognition that, "[i]n most instances, a writ of mandamus or prohibition is not actually directed to a judge in any more personal way than is an order reversing a court's judgment." Advisory Committee

Notes to 1996 Amendments to FRAP 21. Thus, a petition for mandamus is now properly styled as "In re [name of petitioner]." FRAP 21(a)(2)(A). The respondents in a mandamus action (defined as "[a]ll parties to the proceeding in the trial court other than the petitioner," FRAP 21(a)(1)) need not respond unless directed to by the court. FRAP 21(b)(1).

§ 4.8 INTERLOCUTORY REVIEW OF CLASS-CERTIFICATION DECISIONS

This section addresses appellate review considerations applicable to orders granting or denying class certification. In 1998, Rule 23(f) was added to Federal Rule of Civil Procedure 23, providing, as revised in 2007, that "[a] court of appeals may permit an appeal from an order granting or denying class-action certification under this rule if a petition for permission to appeal is filed with the circuit clerk within 14 days after the order is entered." As discussed below, this rule has changed the legal landscape with respect to interlocutory appeals of class certification orders.

As this edition of the Nutshell was going to press, the Judicial Conference Advisory Committee on Civil Rules had proposed an amendment to Rule 23(f) that would extend the time to file a petition for review of a class certification order to 45 days whenever a party is "the United States, a United States agency, or a United States officer or employee sued for an act or omission occurring in connection with duties performed on the United States' behalf." Preliminary Draft of Proposed Amendments to the Federal Rules of Appellate, Bankruptcy, Civil, and Criminal Procedure, Aug. 2016, *available at* http://www.uscourts.gov/sites/default/files/2016-08-preliminary_draft_of_rules_forms_published_for_public_comment_0.pdf.

A. APPEAL WHEN CLASS REPRESENTATIVE FAILS TO PROSECUTE INDIVIDUAL CLAIM

The circuits are split on whether a litigant may seek an immediate appeal of the denial of class status if the putative class member is willing to waive his or her individual claims (effectively creating a final judgment). Some courts have held that appellants may not evade the policy against piecemeal review by failing to prosecute their individual claims. *Huey v. Teledyne, Inc.*, 608 F.2d 1234, 1240 (9th Cir. 1979); *Bowe v. First of Denver Mtge. Investors*, 613 F.2d 798 (10th Cir. 1980). Other courts, however, have held that an order denying a motion for class certification merges into the final judgment that results from the class representative's failure to prosecute his or her individual claims, allowing for immediate appeal. *See, e.g.*, *Allied Air Freight, Inc. v. Pan Am. World Airways, Inc.*, 393 F.2d 441 (2d Cir. 1968); *Gary Plastic Pkg. Co. v. Merrill Lynch, Pierce, Fenner & Smith, Inc.*, 903 F.2d 176, 179 (2d Cir. 1990). Because those potentially meritorious individual claims are forfeited, these courts reason that reviewing the merits of the class-certification order will not substantially undermine the policy against piecemeal review.

As of this writing, the Supreme Court is scheduled to decide "whether a federal court of appeal has jurisdiction under both Article III and 28 U.S.C. § 1291 to review an order denying class certification after the named plaintiffs voluntarily dismiss their individual claims with prejudice." *Microsoft Corp. v. Baker*, 136 S.Ct. 890 (2016). Oral argument in *Baker* took place on March 21, 2017.

B. APPEALABILITY UNDER 28 U.S.C. § 1291

As previously noted, *see* § 4.5, *supra*, 28 U.S.C. § 1291 provides that federal courts of appeals have jurisdiction over appeals from all "final decisions" of federal district courts. In *Coopers & Lybrand v. Livesay*, 437 U.S. 463 (1978), the Supreme Court held that a trial court's order denying class certification or decertifying a class is not a "final decision" within the meaning of 28 U.S.C. § 1291 and, therefore, is not appealable as a matter of right. The Court rejected appellants' arguments that the certification order was appealable under either of two appellate doctrines.

First, the Court found that, with respect to a class-certification ruling, the three *Cohen* criteria are not satisfied because certification is subject to revision by the trial court, the class issues are intertwined with the merits, and the certification ruling can be reviewed on appeal from a final judgment. 437 U.S. at 468–69.

Appellants' second argument in *Coopers & Lybrand* relied upon the "death knell" exception that had been judicially adopted in several circuits. That doctrine assumed that a lawsuit was effectively over when the district court denied class certification in cases in which the individual plaintiffs would not find it economically prudent to pursue their claims in the absence of a class. In *Coopers & Lybrand,* the Court rejected the "death knell" exception, finding that it was based on policy considerations more appropriately left for Congress and that it unfairly facilitated early appeals only by plaintiffs and not by defendants. *Id.* at 469–77.

C. APPEALABILITY UNDER FEDERAL RULE 54(b)

As previously noted, *see* § 4.3, *supra*, Rule 54(b) of the Federal Rules of Civil Procedure provides for "the entry of a final judgment as to one or more, but fewer than all, claims or parties" in a lawsuit when the court determines that "there is no just reason for delay." This rule is not a fertile ground for appealability of class-action rulings, however, because class-action allegations are not "claims" as that term is traditionally understood. Moreover, even if one were to view class-action allegations as "claims," they are likely to suffer from the factual overlap with other claims that is usually fatal to Rule 54(b) treatment. *See Minority Police Officers Ass'n of S. Bend v. City of S. Bend, Ind.*, 721 F.2d 197, 201 (7th Cir. 1983).

D. APPEALABILITY UNDER 28 U.S.C. § 1292(a)(1)

As earlier noted, *see* § 4.6(A), *supra*, Section 1292(a)(1) grants appellate courts jurisdiction over interlocutory orders of the district courts "granting, continuing, modifying, refusing or dissolving injunctions, or refusing to dissolve or modify injunctions." In *Gardner v. Westinghouse Broad. Co.*, 437 U.S. 478 (1978), the Supreme Court narrowly interpreted Section 1292(a)(1) in the context of orders denying class certification. Even though plaintiff's complaint sought equitable relief for the entire class, the Court reasoned that the order denying class certification did not entirely dispose of the relief sought, but merely limited its scope. *Id.* at 480–81. Accordingly, the order was not appealable under Section 1292(a)(1).

E. APPEALABILITY UNDER 28 U.S.C. § 1292(b)

As noted earlier, *see* § 4.4, *supra*, Section 1292(b) permits a district court to certify an otherwise nonappealable order for appellate review when certain criteria are met. For the most part, district courts and appellate courts alike have been reluctant to certify class-action rulings for Section 1292(b) appeal, finding that one or more of the criteria have not been met. Important exceptions exist, however. In *Castano v. American Tobacco Co.*, 84 F.3d 734 (5th Cir. 1996), the district court certified, and the court of appeals accepted, an appeal under Section 1292(b) in what the Fifth Circuit called perhaps "the largest class action ever attempted in federal court." *Id.* at

737. Again, however, with the advent of Rule 23(f), which allows an interlocutory appeal under a provision similar to Section 1292(b)—except that district court certification in the first instance is unnecessary—the importance and availability of a Section 1292(b) appeal for class-certification rulings may have diminished to a vanishing point.

F. MANDAMUS REVIEW OF CLASS-CERTIFICATION RULING

As discussed earlier, *see* § 4.7, *supra*, the All Writs Act, 28 U.S.C. § 1651, permits an appellate court to grant a petition for mandamus in extraordinary circumstances. Under this mandamus power, the courts of appeals may take jurisdiction and intervene to prevent or correct fundamental injustices by a district court. Litigants have petitioned the appellate courts to exercise this power to intervene when district courts have granted or refused to grant class certification. Although most efforts have not been successful, courts have occasionally granted mandamus to review and overturn class-certification rulings. *See, e.g., Matter of Rhone-Poulenc Rorer, Inc.*, 51 F.3d 1293 (7th Cir. 1995) (granting a writ of mandamus and ordering the district court to decertify plaintiff class of HIV-positive hemophiliacs); *In re Am. Med. Sys., Inc.*, 75 F.3d 1069 (6th Cir. 1996) (finding mandamus warranted where district court certified class of individuals alleging injuries from penile prosthesis); *In re Fibreboard Corp.*, 893 F.2d 706 (5th Cir. 1990) (granting mandamus to order district court to vacate phased-trial order in asbestos-exposure class action).

Notwithstanding isolated cases such as these, however, most courts have refused to grant mandamus in the context of class certification rulings.

G. APPEAL UNDER FEDERAL RULE 23(f)

Overview of Criteria. As discussed above, the patchwork of potential appellate vehicles has posed difficulties for parties seeking immediate appeal of class-certification rulings. As a result, a class-certification ruling often operated, as a practical matter, as a final resolution in the case. Plaintiffs whose individual claims could not justify the costs of litigation were effectively barred from continuing their case if they could not obtain immediate review of an order denying class certification. On the other hand, if a class was certified, defendants often felt compelled to settle because the risks of an adverse class verdict were too substantial to justify going forward.

To address some of these concerns, Rule 23(f) was added in 1998. That rule, as revised in 2007, provides:

> A court of appeals may permit an appeal from an order granting or denying class-action certification under this rule if a petition for permission to appeal is filed with the circuit clerk within 14 days after the order is entered. An appeal does not stay proceedings in the district court unless the district judge or the court of appeals so orders.

No specific criteria or limitations are contained in the text of Rule 23(f), and the Committee Notes state that the courts of appeals have "unfettered discretion whether to permit the appeal, akin to the discretion exercised by the Supreme Court in acting on a petition for certiorari." The Notes suggest that "[p]ermission is most likely to be granted when the certification decision turns on a novel or unsettled question of law, or when, as a practical matter, the decision on certification is likely dispositive of the litigation."

In summarizing the reach of Rule 23(f), the Seventh Circuit has stated that "the more fundamental the question and the greater the likelihood that it will escape effective disposition at the end of the case, the more appropriate is an appeal under Rule 23(f)." *Blair v. Equifax Check Servs., Inc.*, 181 F.3d 832, 835 (7th Cir. 1999). The court noted that "it would be a mistake for us to draw up a list that determines how the power under Rule 23(f) will be exercised." *Id.* at 834.

Rule 23(f) has resulted in a significant number of appellate decisions. In those decisions, the circuit courts have devoted considerable attention to the criteria for granting Rule 23(f) review. These decisions differ somewhat in nuance, and a litigant faced with a Rule 23(f) issue should consult the law of the applicable federal circuit.

By way of illustration, one circuit has identified five guideposts for deciding whether to grant Rule 23(f) review: (1) "whether the district court's ruling is likely dispositive of the litigation by creating a 'death knell' for either plaintiff or defendant"; (2) whether the district court ruling contains "a *substantial* weakness"; (3) "whether the appeal will permit the resolution of an unsettled legal issue that is 'important to the particular litigation as well as important in itself' "; (4) "the nature and status of the litigation," such as "the status of discovery, the pendency of relevant motions, and the length of time the matter already has been pending"; and (5) "the likelihood that future events"—such as the possibility of settlement, bankruptcy of one of the parties, or modification of the class-certification ruling—"may make immediate appellate review more or less appropriate." *Prado-Steiman ex rel. Prado v. Bush,* 221 F.3d 1266, 1274–76 (11th Cir. 2000).

One issue that has divided the federal circuits is the weight to be given to the correctness of the decision. Some circuits have held that Rule 23(f) review may be proper to correct a manifestly erroneous decision. *See, e.g., Prado-Steiman*, 221 F.3d at 1275; *Chamberlan v. Ford Motor Co.,* 402 F.3d 952, 959 (9th Cir. 2005). Other circuits, however, have held that even a seriously erroneous decision is not subject to Rule 23(f) review unless the decision would likely be the death knell of the litigation or resolve an important class action legal issue that otherwise would evade review. *See, e.g., Blair v. Equifax Check Servs., Inc.*, 181 F.3d 832, 835 (7th Cir. 1999); *Waste Mgmt. Holdings v. Mowbray*, 208 F.3d 288, 294 (1st Cir. 2000).

A thorough discussion of the various circuit court approaches to Rule 23(f) is contained in the Ninth Circuit's decision in *Chamberlan*, 402 F.3d at 957–60.

Scope. Rule 23(f) applies only to a district court order "granting or denying class-action certification under this rule." As the Committee Notes make clear, "[n]o other type of Rule 23 order is covered by this provision." Thus, for example, an order relating to the scope or content of a class notice, an order restricting communications with class members, or an order allowing or barring certain class discovery would not be reviewable under Rule 23(f) unless such an order was inextricably intertwined with an order granting or denying class certification.

In *In re Nat'l Football League Players Concussion Injury Litig.*, 775 F.3d 570 (3d Cir. 2014), the Third Circuit held that it lacked appellate jurisdiction under Rule 23(f) to review a district court's "preliminary" approval of a class settlement. The court explained: "an interlocutory appeal pursuant to Rule 23(f) permits the court of appeals to review only an 'order granting or denying class-action certification' issued pursuant to Rule 23(c)(1)." *Id.* at 584. By contrast, "[a]n order issued under some other subdivision of Rule 23, such as a case management order issued pursuant to Rule 23(e) that 'preliminarily' or 'conditionally' addresses class certification but reserves the class certification determination for a later time, does not qualify as an 'order granting or denying class-action certification' that is subject to interlocutory review under Rule

23(f).” *Id.* In the case before it, the Third Circuit concluded that the district court’s order was a proper exercise of its case management authority under Rule 23(e), and that the lower court’s ‘preliminary approval’ of the proposed class settlement was for purposes of providing notice to the putative class. *Id.* at 585. Consequently, there was “simply nothing for a court of appeals to review under Rule 23(f) before the district court issues a certification order under Rule 23(c).” *Id.* at 588.

A proposed amendment to Rule 23(f) would essentially incorporate the ruling in *In re Nat’l Football League* into the Rule. The amendment would add the following italicized language to 23(f): “A court of appeals may permit an appeal from an order granting or denying class certification under this rule, *but not from an order under Rule 23(e)(1).*” Preliminary Draft of Proposed Amendments to the Federal Rules of Appellate, Bankruptcy, Civil, and Criminal Procedure, Aug. 2016, at 217, *available at* http://www.uscourts.gov/sites/default/files/2016-08-preliminary_draft_of_rules_forms_published_for_public_comment_0.pdf (emphasis added). The Committee Note to the proposed amendment states that this amendment “makes it clear that an appeal under [Rule 23(f)] is not permitted until the district court decides whether to certify the class.” *Id.* at 231.

Views of the District Court. Unlike review under 28 U.S.C. § 1292(b), review under Rule 23(f) does not require the approval of the district court. Nonetheless, the Committee Notes point out that the district court “often will be able to provide cogent advice on the factors that bear on the decision whether to permit appeal." According to the Notes, "[t]his advice can be particularly valuable if the certification decision is tentative," but it can be helpful "[e]ven as to a firm certification decision" by "focus[ing] the court of appeals" on the critical issues and possibly "persuad[ing] the disappointed party" not to seek Rule 23(f) review.

Timing of Filing and Responding. Rule 23(f) requires that the petition for permission to appeal from a certification order (granting or denying certification) be "filed with the circuit clerk within 14 days after the order is entered."

Although Rule 23(f) does not set a time period for responding to a Rule 23(f) petition, FRAP 5, which more generally governs appeals by permission, addresses the issue: "A party may file an answer in opposition or a cross-petition within 10 days after the petition is served." FRAP 5(b)(2).

When a motion for reconsideration of the district court's certification decision has been timely filed, courts have held that the Rule 23(f) clock does not begin to run until the district court has ruled on the motion for reconsideration. *See, e.g.*, *Jenkins v. BellSouth Corp.*, 491 F.3d 1288, 1290 (11th Cir. 2007).

As this edition of the Nutshell was going to press, the Judicial Conference Advisory Committee on Civil Rules had proposed an amendment to Rule 23(f) that would extend the time to file a petition for review of a class certification order to 45 days whenever a party is "the United States, a United States agency, or a United States officer or employee sued for an act or omission occurring in connection with duties performed on the United States' behalf." Preliminary Draft of Proposed Amendments to the Federal Rules of Appellate, Bankruptcy, Civil, and Criminal Procedure, Aug. 2016, *available at* http://www.uscourts.gov/sites/default/files/2016-08-preliminary_draft_of_rules_forms_published_for_public_comment_0.pdf.

§ 4.9 INTERLOCUTORY REVIEW OF REMAND ORDERS

Under 28 U.S.C. § 1447(d), and subject to certain statutory or case law exceptions—*e.g.*, remands in certain civil rights cases, remands in which removal was sought under the Class Action Fairness Act, 28 U.S.C. § 1453(c), and remands not based on procedural defects in removal or the lack of subject-matter jurisdiction—"an order remanding a case to the State court from which it was removed is not reviewable on appeal or otherwise."

No exception exists under 28 U.S.C. § 1292(b). Courts have consistently held that, even though Congress enacted Section 1292(b) after Section 1447(d), the former did not amend or repeal the latter. As one court has stated, "the jurisdictional bar of section 1447(d) trumps the power to grant leave to appeal in section 1292(b)." *Feidt v. Owens Corning Fiberglass Corp.*, 153 F.3d 124, 130 (3d Cir. 1998). Likewise, courts have consistently held that Section 1447(d)—which uses the language "on appeal or otherwise"—prohibits review of remand orders by way of mandamus. *E.g.*, *Blackwater Secur. Consulting, LLC v. McQuown,* 460 F.3d 576, 593–95 (4th Cir. 2006).

Section 1447(d) prohibits appellate review of remands for lack of subject-matter jurisdiction and for defects in removal procedure. *Quackenbush v. Allstate Ins. Co.*, 517 U.S. 706, 711–12 (1996). Under the removal statute, a case may be removed to federal court using entirely proper procedures, yet the federal district court may still lack subject-matter jurisdiction (*e.g.*, because suit is barred under the Foreign Sovereign Immunities Act). In such cases, the Supreme Court has held, so long as the district court's remand was based on a "colorable" ground of lack of subject-matter jurisdiction, appellate review is barred. *Powerex Corp. v. Reliant Energy Servs., Inc.*, 127 S.Ct. 2411, 2418 (2007).

The Supreme Court's decision in *Thermtron Products, Inc. v. Hermansdorfer*, 423 U.S. 336 (1976), held that the Section 1447(d) bar on appellate review only bars review of certain remand orders issued pursuant to Section 1447(c). *Id.* at 343–44. That decision has been the subject of much criticism, and one member of the Supreme Court has called for its overruling, either judicially or legislatively. *See, e.g.*, *Kakarala v. Wells Fargo Bank, N.A.*, 136 S.Ct. 1153 (2016) (Thomas, J., dissenting from denial of certiorari).

§ 4.10 INTERLOCUTORY REVIEW OF ATTORNEYS' FEES

In 1988, the Supreme Court held that the pendency of an attorneys' fee application did not impair the finality of a judgment on the merits. *Budinich v. Becton Dickinson and Co.*, 486 U.S. 196, 202–03 (1988) ("Courts and litigants are best served by the bright-line rule, which accords with traditional understanding, that a decision on the merits is 'final decision' for purposes of § 1291 whether or not there remains for adjudication a request for attorney's fees attributable to the case."). The consequences of this ruling were severe to the petitioner (Budinich): He had not filed his notice of appeal until after the fee application had been decided, and so the Supreme Court's holding that the merits decision had become final meant that petitioner had filed his notice of appeal two-and-a-half months too late, thus forfeiting his right to appeal. *See id.* at 198, 203.

Two later sets of amendments to the Federal Rules of Civil Procedure have attempted to ameliorate some of the surprise and harsh consequences of this ruling. In 1993, Rule 54(d) was amended to provide a new procedure for presenting claims for attorneys' fees, including a deadline for such motions of 14 days after final judgment (unless otherwise specified by the court or by statute). Fed.R.Civ.P. 54(d)(2)(B)(i).

Also in 1993, Rule 58 of the Federal Rules of Civil Procedure—now entitled "Entering Judgment"—was amended to clarify the effect of a timely attorneys' fees motion on the time for filing a notice of appeal.

Rule 58(e) now provides, in relevant part, that "[i]f a timely motion for attorneys' fees is made under Rule 54(d)(2), the court may act before a notice of appeal has been filed and become effective to order that the motion have the same effect under Federal Rule of Appellate Procedure 4(a)(4) as a timely motion under Rule 59." The basic thrust of this rule is (in the words of the Advisory Committee's Notes) to "permi[t], but . . . not require, the court to delay the finality of the judgment for appellate purposes under revised [FRAP] 4(a)(4) until the fee dispute is decided." But importantly, unlike a timely Rule 59 motion, a timely attorneys' fee motion does not *automatically* have that effect; the district court must enter an order informing the parties that that is its intent. *See Stephanie-Cardona LLC v. Smith's Food & Drug Centers, Inc.*, 476 F.3d 701, 705 (9th Cir. 2007). And, of course, the fee motion itself must be timely; otherwise, the district court will be without authority to delay the appeal. *Robinson v. City of Harvey*, 489 F.3d 864, 868–69 (7th Cir. 2007).

While the order granting or denying attorneys' fees is separately appealable, an order that merely establishes a party's entitlement to attorneys' fees, but does not reduce the fee award to a specific amount, is not sufficiently final to be appealable. *See, e.g.*, *Special Devices, Inc. v. OEA, Inc.*, 269 F.3d 1340, 1345 (Fed. Cir. 2001) ("a decision to award unquantified attorneys fees . . . is not final").

§ 4.11 PENDENT APPELLATE REVIEW

When a party has a proper route to seek appellate review of a specific issue, that party may seek to obtain review over another issue in the case (one otherwise not appealable) by asserting "pendent appellate jurisdiction" over the latter issue. Although the Supreme Court has not foreclosed entirely the reliance on pendent appellate jurisdiction, it has narrowly construed that doctrine.

In *Swint v. Chambers Cty. Comm'n*, 514 U.S. 35 (1995), the owners, employee, and customer of a nightclub sued a county commission, municipality, and three police officers claiming that police raids on the club constituted civil rights violations. Prior to trial, the trial court rejected the officers' qualified immunity arguments and also rejected a summary-judgment motion by the county commission raising a separate theory for the county's nonliability. In a pretrial appeal, the Eleventh Circuit permitted not only the qualified immunity challenge by the officers (which was a collateral order, *see* § 4.5, *supra*), but also the county commission's appeal on the theory of "pendent appellate jurisdiction." After the Supreme Court granted certiorari, both sides urged the Court to reach the merits of the county commission's summary judgment issue, arguing that the Eleventh Circuit correctly applied the pendent jurisdiction doctrine. The Supreme Court disagreed and made clear that, if it existed at all, the doctrine of pendent appellate jurisdiction was very narrow:

> We need not definitively or preemptively settle here whether or when it may be proper for a

> court of appeals, with jurisdiction over one ruling, to review, conjunctively, related rulings that are not themselves independently appealable. . . . The parties do not contend that the District Court's decision to deny Chambers County Commission's summary judgment motion was inextricably intertwined with that court's decision to deny the individual defendants' qualified immunity motions, or that review of the former decision was necessary to ensure meaningful review of the latter.

Id. at 50–51.

The Seventh Circuit has referred to *Swint* as reflecting "profound skepticism concerning judge-made doctrines of appellate jurisdiction" of any kind, and as leaving the doctrine "hang[ing] by a thread." *In re Rimsat, Ltd.*, 98 F.3d 956, 964 (7th Cir. 1996). Yet the doctrine remains today, even if in narrowed form, with the Supreme Court continuing to apply it in appropriate cases. *See Clinton v. Jones*, 520 U.S. 681, 707 n.41 (1997) (it is appropriate for an appellate court to exercise pendent jurisdiction where the issue is "inextricably intertwined" with another issue over which the appellate court does have jurisdiction, such that it is necessary to review both "to ensure meaningful review"); *Johnson v. Jones*, 515 U.S. 304, 318 (1995) ("assuming, for the sake of argument, that it may sometimes be appropriate to exercise 'pendent appellate jurisdiction' "); *see also Vt. Agency of Nat. Res. v. United States ex rel. Stevens*, 529 U.S. 765, 770 n.2, 778–87 (2000) (Supreme Court decided a statutory question after observing that "[t]he Second Circuit exercised pendent appellate jurisdiction over th[at] statutory question").

In post-*Swint* case law, courts have been exceedingly cautious in finding pendent appellate jurisdiction. For instance, in *Poulos v. Caesars World, Inc.*, 379 F.3d 654 (9th Cir. 2004), the court granted review under Fed.R.Civ.P. 23(f) to review a decision denying class certification. The court upheld that ruling and then addressed defendants' request to decide various other issues, including abstention, primary jurisdiction, and personal jurisdiction over various defendants. In declining to address these issues, the court noted that *Swint*'s "inextricably intertwined" prong should be "narrowly construed" and is not satisfied if the court "must apply different legal standards on each issue." *Id.* at 669 (citation and internal quotation marks omitted). The prong is satisfied only if the issues are "either (a) . . . so intertwined that [the court] must decide the pendent issue in order to review the claims properly raised on interlocutory appeal, or (b) the resolution of the issue properly raised on interlocutory appeal necessarily resolves the pendent issues." *Id.* (citation and internal quotation marks omitted). The court further noted that *Swint*'s second prong ("necessary to ensure meaningful review") is "similarly restrictive": "[i]t requires that the pendent decision have much more than a tangential relationship to the decision properly before [the court] on interlocutory appeal." Post-*Swint*, courts that have permitted pendent appellate jurisdiction have done so only in unusual circumstances. *Id.* at 669 (discussing a prior Ninth

Circuit decision authorizing pendent appellate jurisdiction and characterizing it as "extremely narrow and fact-specific"); *CTF Hotel Holdings, Inc. v. Marriott Int'l, Inc.*, 381 F.3d 131, 136 (3d Cir. 2004) (permitting pendent appellate jurisdiction because case was "rife with special circumstances"); *National R.R. Passenger Corp. v. ExpressTrak, L.L.C.*, 330 F.3d 523, 527–28 (D.C. Cir. 2003) (noting, in finding pendent appellate jurisdiction over arbitrability issue in case involving review of an injunction, that "[t]his court does not exercise pendent jurisdiction frequently or liberally"). Still, courts on occasion exercise pendent appellate jurisdiction without expressly saying so. *See, e.g., FreeEats.com, Inc. v. Indiana*, 502 F.3d 590, 595 (7th Cir. 2007) (on appeal from denial of a preliminary injunction, court of appeals also reviewed the district court's separate refusal to dismiss the case on *Younger* abstention grounds).

CHAPTER 5
NOTICE OF APPEAL

§ 5.1 GENERAL REQUIREMENTS FOR APPELLATE JURISDICTION

FRAP 3 and 4 establish the basic notice of appeal requirements for seeking appellate review. More specifically, FRAP 3 sets forth what the notice must contain, while FRAP 4 addresses the requisite timing of the notice. There is a wide body of case law interpreting and applying these rules. Although satisfying the notice of appeal requirements is jurisdictional, courts have sometimes been flexible to avoid making the rules a trap for those attempting in good faith to satisfy them.

There is only one step necessary for taking an appeal as of right, and that is to file a notice of appeal with the district court. FRAP 3(a)(1). Any other failure of an appellant, *e.g.*, the failure to file required papers in the court of appeals, "does not affect the validity of the appeal, but is ground only for the court of appeals to act as it considers appropriate, including dismissing the appeal." FRAP 3(a)(2).

§ 5.2 CONTENTS OF NOTICE

FRAP 3(c)(1) sets forth the required contents of a notice of appeal. It must provide three basic pieces of information:

- it must "specify the party or parties taking the appeal by naming each one in the caption or body of the notice" (if the same attorney represents multiple parties, the attorney may describe them with terms like "all plaintiffs," "all plaintiffs except John Doe," or "defendants John Doe, Susan Smith, and Oliver Brown");

- it must "designate the judgment, order, or part thereof being appealed"; and
- it must "name the court to which the appeal is taken."

FRAP 3(c)(1)(A)–(C).

The Federal Rules of Appellate Procedure conclude with a series of forms. Form 1 is a model for a notice of appeal from a district court decision, and, aside from the case caption and signature block, the content is simple and straightforward, and satisfies all three of the requirements of FRAP 3(c)(1): "Notice is hereby given that _____ (here name all parties taking the appeal) _____, (plaintiffs) (defendants) in the above named case, hereby appeal to the United States Court of Appeals for the ___ Circuit (from the final judgment) (from an order (describing it)) entered in this action on the ___ day of ___, 20___." The rules indicate that this form is a "suggested" one. FRAP 3(c)(5).

FRAP 3(c) also contains some more specific provisions governing notices of appeal in particular cases. Under FRAP 3(c)(2), a notice of appeal filed *pro se* is considered to have been filed on behalf of the signer as well as his spouse and minor children (if they are parties to the case), unless the notice indicates a contrary intent; the purpose of this rule is to avoid technical defaults by unrepresented parties who are less skilled in the law than lawyers. FRAP 3(c)(3) applies to class actions and provides that a notice of appeal filed by a qualified representative of the class will be treated as an appeal on behalf of the class and need not name all of the class members, even if the class certification motion has been denied. The Advisory Committee Notes indicate that this rule avoids the burden of having to name all of the potential class members in the case where class certification has been denied (and, thus, the class representatives technically have not been allowed to represent the putative class members).

Finally, FRAP 3(c)(4) states the rule of liberal interpretation that applies to notices of appeal: "An appeal must not be dismissed for informality of form or title of the notice of appeal, or for failure to name a party whose intent to appeal is otherwise clear from the notice." In that event, according to the Advisory Committee Notes, "neither administrative concerns nor fairness concerns . . . should prevent the appeal from going forward."

Consistent with this rule of liberal construction, FRAP 3(c)(1)(B)'s requirement that the notice of appeal must "designate the judgment, order, or part thereof being appealed" is a requirement that, as the Supreme Court has said, "should be liberally construed," and " 'mere technicalities' should not stand in the way of consideration of a case on its merits." *Torres v. Oakland Scavenger Co.*, 487 U.S. 312, 316 (1988) (citation omitted).

The notice of appeal requirements of FRAP 3(c) are indeed "notice" provisions: They are designed to inform both the court and the opposing parties of who is appealing what order or judgment, and to what court. FRAP 3(c)(4) makes clear that these requirements should be construed to require reasonable rather than perfect efforts. An appeal "must not be dismissed for informality of form or title," or "for failure to name a party whose intent to appeal is otherwise clear from the notice." *Id. See also Becker v. Montgomery*, 532 U.S. 757, 767 (2001) ("Imperfections in noticing an appeal should not be fatal where no genuine doubt exists about who is appealing, from what judgment, to which appellate court.").

Nonetheless, when a court finds, even after applying the rule of liberal construction, that the appellant has failed to comply with Rule 3, the court must dismiss the appeal. Thus, "liberal construction" does not justify "noncompliance," and the lack of compliance is "fatal to [the] appeal." *Smith v. Barry*, 502 U.S. 244, 248 (1992). Put another way, allowing "substantial compliance" with the rule does not mean "waiving the requirement" entirely. *Torres*, 487 U.S. at 315–16.

Torres, for example, held that the omission of one out of 16 appellants' names from the notice of appeal, even though the list of parties concluded with "et al.," was not enough to satisfy the rule's requirement that the notice "must specify the party or parties taking the appeal." *Id.* at 315–16. To counteract this harsh result, Rule 3(c) was amended (with the italicized language) to add that an appeal shall "not be dismissed for informality of form or title of the notice of appeal, *or for failure to name a party whose intent to appeal is otherwise clear from the notice.*" FRAP 3(c)(4) (emphasis added).

Since the 1993 amendments to FRAP 3, few notices of appeal have been found defective for failure to satisfy the requirements of the rule; indeed, documents that are not, on their face, "notices of appeal" may be deemed sufficient. In *Smith*, the Court held that a *pro se* appellant's merits brief indicating an intent to appeal satisfied FRAP 3. 502 U.S. at 248. *See also Taylor v. Johnson*, 257 F.3d 470, 474–75 (5th Cir. 2001) (a brief, if filed within the time frame prescribed by FRAP 4, sufficed as a notice of appeal); *Becker*, 532 U.S. at 767 (unsigned notice of appeal satisfied FRAP 3); *Madej v. Briley*, 371 F.3d 898, 899 (7th Cir. 2004) (document styled as a petition for mandamus was treated as a notice of appeal where it contained the requirements of FRAP 3).

There are exceptions, however. *See, e.g., United States v. Glover*, 242 F.3d 333 (6th Cir. 2001) (where government gave "notice that the United States, Plaintiff in the above referenced case, hereby request [sic] a Protective Notice of Appeal in this Matter," without more, that did not satisfy FRAP 3(c)(1)(B)'s requirement that the notice "designate the judgment, order, or part thereof being appealed," and the appeal was dismissed). Additionally, an oral statement of intent to appeal has been held not to satisfy the requirement that a notice of appeal be "filed" in the district court. *See, e.g., Smith v. United States*, 425 F.2d 173, 174 (9th Cir. 1970); *United States v. Isabella*, 251 F.2d 223, 226 (2d Cir. 1958).

With regard to the requirement that the notice "designate the judgment, order, or part thereof being appealed," it is important to keep in mind the rules of merger—specifically, the general rule that all interlocutory orders that precede the entry of final judgment are said to "merge" into the final judgment, such that an appeal from a final judgment generally brings all of the earlier interlocutory orders before the appellate court for review. *See* § 5.6, *infra*.

FRAP 3(b) allows multiple parties to join in a single notice of appeal, FRAP 3(b)(1), and grants the courts of appeals the power to join or consolidate separate appeals filed by different parties. FRAP 3(b)(2).

Unlike virtually every other paper that is filed by a litigant in a district court, it is not the responsibility of the appellant to serve the notice of appeal on all of the other parties. FRAP 3(d) makes that the duty of "[t]he district clerk." The appellant's duty in this regard is simply to "furnish the clerk with enough copies of the notice to enable the clerk to comply with Rule 3(d)." FRAP 3(a)(1).

§ 5.3 TIMING OF THE NOTICE OF APPEAL

A. LATE NOTICE

The rule of "liberal construction" that applies to the mechanics of a notice of appeal under FRAP 3 should not be mistaken for a *laissez faire* attitude toward the timeliness of a notice of appeal. *See* § 11.1, *infra* (explaining that notices of appeal are filed when received by the clerk, not when mailed). Finality is a crucial value in the law, and having a clear date by which time an appeal is no longer a risk is important to settling the expectations of litigants. Thus, the requirement of a timely notice of appeal is considered jurisdictional. As such, the requirement cannot be waived; indeed, a court must ensure its jurisdiction even if the appellee raises no timeliness challenge.

Two exceptions to the timing requirements exist under FRAP 4, however.

First Exception. A district court may, upon a finding of "excusable neglect or good cause," before or during the 30 days after the time for appeal has expired, extend the time for filing a notice of appeal if "a party so moves no later than 30 days after the time prescribed by this Rule 4(a) expires." FRAP 4(a)(5). This power is the district court's alone; the court of appeals has no power to grant such relief. FRAP 26(b).

According to the Seventh Circuit, writing in 1990, "there are no reported decisions on the meaning of 'good cause' in Rule 4(a)(5)." *Lorenzen v. Employees*

Ret. Plan of the Sperry & Hutchison Co., 896 F.2d 228, 232 (7th Cir. 1990). However, the Advisory Committee Notes accompanying the 2002 amendments to FRAP 4 offered some explanation of the difference between the "excusable neglect" and "good cause" requirements: "The excusable neglect standard applies in situations in which there is fault; in such situations, the need for an extension is usually occasioned by something within the control of the movant. The good cause standard applies in situations in which there is no fault—excusable or otherwise. In such situations, the need for an extension is usually occasioned by something that is not within the control of the movant."

In *Pioneer Invest. Servs. Co. v. Brunswick Assoc. Ltd. P'ship,* 507 U.S. 380 (1993), the Supreme Court adopted what it called a "flexible" view of "excusable neglect" (contained in a similar deadline provision of the Bankruptcy Rules), ruling that "Congress plainly contemplated that the courts would be permitted, where appropriate, to accept late filings caused by inadvertence, mistake, or carelessness, as well as by intervening circumstances beyond the party's control." *Id.* at 388. The Court reasoned that the decision is "an equitable one, taking account of all relevant circumstances surrounding the party's omission." *Id.* at 395. Those circumstances include:

> [T]he danger of prejudice to the [non-moving party], the length of the delay and its potential impact on judicial proceedings, the reason for the delay, including whether it was within the

> reasonable control of the movant, and whether the movant acted in good faith.

Id. There is no doubt that *Pioneer*'s holding, despite being rendered in connection with a Bankruptcy Rule, applies with full force to FRAP 4(a)'s "excusable neglect" standard, as the Court in *Pioneer* identified the preexisting split in the courts of appeals on the meaning of "excusable neglect" in FRAP 4(a) as a reason for granting review in that case. *See id.* at 387 & n.3; *Graphic Comms. Int'l Union Local 12-N v. Quebecor Printing Providence, Inc.*, 270 F.3d 1, 5 (1st Cir. 2001) (discussing case law from various circuits).

Several courts have indicated that these factors are not given equal weight; the reason for delay is the most significant factor. Thus, courts have refused to find excusable neglect when "counsel's failure to comply with a rule that is 'mandatory and jurisdictional' was the result of ignorance of the law and inattention to detail," even where there was no prejudice to the opposing party. *Graphic Comm. Union*, 270 F.3d at 6 (quoting district court opinion; citation omitted). Similarly, in *Two-Way Media LLC v. AT&T, Inc.* 782 F.3d 1311 (Fed. Cir. 2015), a divided panel of the Federal Circuit rejected AT&T's claim of excusable neglect, based on its lawyers' failure to read the substance of the district court's order, which denied AT&T's post-trial motions (and thus started the clock for filing a notice of appeal), even though the emailed notice of electronic filing—which contained a hyperlink to the relevant orders—was labeled only "ORDER GRANTING . . . Motion For Leave to File Sealed Document." *Id.* at 1315–17.

Yet, despite the fact that "a lawyer's failure to read an applicable rule is one of the least compelling excuses that can be offered" for failing to file a timely notice of appeal, "the nature of the contextual analysis and the balancing of the factors adopted in *Pioneer* counsel against the creation of any rigid rule." *Pincay v. Andrews*, 389 F.3d 853, 859 (9th Cir. 2004) (en banc) (upholding extension despite attorney ignorance).

At the same time, though, one can see a degree of tension between *Pioneer* and the 2002 Advisory Committee's definition of "excusable neglect"—particularly in its observation that "excusable neglect" is "usually occasioned by something within the control of the movant," whereas *Pioneer* held that excusable neglect could be found even in the case of "intervening circumstances beyond the party's control." The Advisory Committee's Notes suggest that the "circumstances beyond the party's control" are better viewed as a ground for a "good cause" extension. Still, the Advisory Committee Notes appear to capture the majority of the cases decided under this rule.

Although the rule is written as allowing "excusable neglect" or "good cause" to be a ground for extensions sought before or after the prescribed time period has run, it is generally the case that the "excusable neglect" standard will only come into play with respect to motions made after expiration of the rule's deadlines. But that is not to say that a post-expiration motion must meet the "excusable neglect" standard; the 2002 amendments to FRAP 4(a)(5) clarified that the two grounds for an extension may apply "regardless" of whether the motion is brought before or after the expiration of the prescribed time. The Advisory Committee Notes to that amendment further confirm that understanding of the rule.

Moreover, the Advisory Committee Notes explain that the "excusable neglect" and "good cause" grounds "are not interchangeable, and one is not inclusive of the other." To explain the difference in the standards, the notes give the examples of (a) a deadline missed because the U.S. Postal Service failed to deliver a timely mailed notice of appeal to the court (that would not in any way be "neglect" on the part of the appellant, so the "good cause" standard would be the more applicable one); and (b) a not yet missed deadline that is nonetheless unlikely to be met because of "excusable neglect" on the part of the attorney.

Second Exception. The district court may "reopen the time to file an appeal for a period of 14 days after the date when its order to reopen is entered," but only if three conditions are met: (1) "the motion [to reopen] is filed within 180 days after the judgment or order is entered or within 7 days after the moving party receives notice of entry, whichever is earlier," (2) the court determines that "the moving party was entitled to notice of the entry of the judgment or order sought to be appealed but did not receive the notice from the district court or any party within 21 days after entry," and (3) "the court finds that no party would be prejudiced." FRAP 4(a)(6).

Avolio v. Cty. of Suffolk, 29 F.3d 50 (2d Cir. 1994), provides a good example of this rule in application. Counsel for plaintiffs (the losers in the district court) submitted an affidavit informing the court that his office had never received a copy of the judgment, which had been entered on January 19, 1993. In March 1993, his client called the court and was informed that a judgment had been entered; counsel then (on or about March 18, 1993) obtained a copy of that judgment. The attorney then (on March 26, 1993) made a motion under FRAP 4(a)(6) to reopen the time for filing an appeal. The district court denied the motion on the ground that the lawyer had not shown excusable neglect; the Second Circuit held that the district court had erred because excusable neglect is not the standard set forth in FRAP 4(a)(6). The court of appeals held that the motion met the 180-day and seven day timeliness requirement, because the motion was made within 180 days of the judgment and seven days (excluding weekends and holidays) of the actual notice of the judgment that the lawyer obtained. And, although noting that the factual issues of absence of notice of the judgment and lack of prejudice were basically uncontroverted, the court of appeals remanded to the district court for further proceedings, so that the court could exercise its discretion under a correct understanding of the rule. *Id.* at 51–53.

The court in *Avolio* also noted that the winning party could have avoided this problem by itself sending the plaintiffs' counsel notice of the entry of judgment. Underscoring that FRAP 4(a)(6)'s time limits are triggered by "notice under Federal Rule of

Civil Procedure 77(d) of the entry" of judgment, FRAP 4(a)(6)(B), and that Fed.R.Civ.P. 77(d) allows a "party" to serve notice of entry of judgment, the court recommended (quoting the Advisory Committee Note to the Rule) that "[w]inning parties are encouraged to send their own notice in order to lessen the chance that a judge will accept a claim of non-receipt in the face of evidence that notices were sent by both the clerk and the winning party." 29 F.3d at 53 (quoting Advisory Committee Note); *see also* David S. Siegel, *The Recent (Dec. 1, 1991) Changes in the Federal Rules of Civil Procedure*, 142 F.R.D. 359, 378 (1992).

Likewise, in *Two-Way Media*, discussed above, the Federal Circuit rejected the claim that an arguably misleading Electronic Case Filing notice was inadequate to "constitute notice of the entry of that judgment within the meaning of Rule 4(a)(6)(A)." 782 F.3d at 1318. That rule, the court emphasized, "only applies when a party received *no notice* of that [appealable] order." *Id.* (emphasis in original).

Once the 180 days have run, however, the district court is without power to reopen the time for appeal, no matter how compelling the facts might be. *See, e.g., Zimmer St. Louis, Inc. v. Zimmer Co.*, 32 F.3d 357, 360 (8th Cir. 1994) (although litigant vigilantly checked the court's case file in the clerk's office, that file did not disclose that the post-judgment motions had been denied and those denials entered on the official civil docket). Nor can a district court respond to such situations by vacating its prior judgment and reentering it so that the appeal clock starts anew. *See* id.; *see also Marcangelo v. Boardwalk Regency*, 47 F.3d 88, 90 (3d Cir. 1995) (citing cases).

Both FRAP 4(a)(5) and 4(a)(6) provide that a court "may extend" and "may reopen" the time for filing a notice of appeal. As the cases illustrate, the rules' use of "may" in this respect means that they accord discretionary relief—*i.e.*, the court is permitted, but not required, to order relief if the requirements are met.

Courts have held that the additional three-day period after service provided under FRAP 26(c) is inapplicable to notices of appeal sent to the court by mail. "[T]he additional three calendar days after service by mail as permitted by [FRAP] 26(c) is unavailable because the time for filing notice of appeal commences to run from the entry of judgment and not 'after a paper is served on that party' as provided in Rule 26(c)." *Ludgood v. Apex Marine Corp. Ship Mgmt.*, 311 F.3d 364, 367–68 (5th Cir. 2002).

What if the court clerk erroneously tells a litigant that the time for appeal expires on "April 13, 2001," when under the rules the time for appeal actually expires on April 11, 2001? Under prior law, a litigant in that situation might have attempted to rely on the "unique circumstances" doctrine. Under that doctrine, where a judicial officer assures a litigant that he or she has timely and properly done an act, the litigant's "justifiable reliance" on that assurance will be protected. *See Osterneck v. Ernst & Whinney*, 489 U.S. 169, 179 (1989); *Thompson v. INS*, 375 U.S. 384, 387 (1964). But in *Bowles v. Russell*, 551 U.S.

205 (2007), the Supreme Court abolished the "unique circumstances" doctrine, holding instead that "this Court has no authority to create equitable exceptions to jurisdictional requirements." *Id.* at 206. This ruling underscores the severe consequences of missing the notice of appeal deadline.

One final note. Under FRAP 4(a)(5)(C), "no extension under this Rule 4(a)(5) may exceed 30 days after the prescribed time or 14 days after the date when the order granting the motion is entered, whichever is later." As this manuscript was going to press, the Supreme Court granted certiorari on the question whether an appeal that is untimely under FRAP 4(a)(5)(C) deprives the appellate court of jurisdiction, even where the appellant relied on an extended deadline set by the district court pursuant to a federal statute, 28 U.S.C. § 2107(c). *See Hamer v. Neighborhood Housing Svcs.*, 137 S.Ct. 1203 (2016). The case will be briefed and argued during the Court's October 2017 term.

B. PREMATURE NOTICE

What happens if a party files a notice of appeal too early rather than too late—*i.e.*, before the entry of a final judgment or order? FRAP 4(a)(2) provides that a "notice of appeal filed after the court announces a decision or order—but before entry of the judgment or order—is treated as filed on the date of and after the entry." The Supreme Court has made clear that the reach of this rule is limited; it applies "only when a district court announces a decision that would be appealable if immediately followed by the entry of judgment." *FirsTier Mortgage Co. v. Investors Mortgage Ins. Co.*, 498 U.S. 269, 276 (1991). The rule is designed to "protect the unskilled litigant who files a notice of appeal from a decision that he reasonably but mistakenly believes to be a final judgment, while failing to file a notice of appeal from the actual final judgment." *Id.* If, however, the order as entered would not be appealable, a notice of appeal from the announcement of a decision (but before entry of the decision) would not be a valid notice.

In *FirsTier*, the Court held that under FRAP 4(a)(2), a notice of appeal from the district court's announcement that it was granting summary judgment for defendant on all of the claims was sufficient. The Court reasoned that the entry of the summary judgment order would be a final judgment, so the assumption that the oral ruling was final was not unreasonable: "Rule 4(a)(2) permits a notice of appeal from a nonfinal decision to operate as a notice of appeal from the final judgment only when a district court announces a decision that would be appealable if immediately followed by the entry of judgment. In these instances, a litigant's confusion is understandable, and permitting the notice of appeal to become effective when judgment is entered does not catch the appellee by surprise. Little would be accomplished by prohibiting the court of appeals from reaching the merits of such an appeal." *Id.* at 276.

By contrast, a notice of appeal from a clearly interlocutory decision will not ripen into a proper appeal from a final judgment; the Court in *FirsTier* said as much. *Id.* ("This is not to say that Rule 4(a)(2) permits a notice of appeal from a clearly interlocutory decision—such as a discovery ruling or a sanction order under Rule 11 of the Federal Rules of Civil Procedure—to serve as a notice of appeal from the final judgment. A belief that such a decision is a final judgment would not be reasonable.").

C. MULTIPLE APPEALS AND TIMING

Under FRAP 4(a)(3), "[i]f one party timely files a notice of appeal, any other party may file a notice of appeal within 14 days after the date when the first notice was filed, or within the time otherwise prescribed by . . . Rule 4(a), whichever period ends later." This rule is most commonly—but not exclusively—relevant to cross-appeals. The purpose of the rule is to avoid the prejudice and gamesmanship that might otherwise result if all appeals by all parties had to be noticed within the 30-day period prescribed by the rule; without the additional 14-day period, a party might, by waiting to notice his appeal until the last possible moment, "lull" his opponents (or co-parties) into forfeiting their own right to appeal on the assumption that no other parties would be appealing. The 14-day period of FRAP 4(a)(3) thus allows a potential cross-appellant (for example) an additional period of time to take into account whether another party will appeal and make the determination whether to cross-appeal only after knowing that his adversary will be pursuing an appeal.

D. EFFECT OF POST-TRIAL MOTIONS ON TIMING

FRAP 4(a)(4) provides that if a party makes a timely post-judgment motion under one or more of six specified Federal Rules of Civil Procedure, the time to file an appeal does not commence until "the entry of the order disposing of the last such remaining motion[.]" FRAP 4(a)(4). The six motions are:

(i) for judgment under Rule 50(b);

(ii) to amend or make additional factual findings under Rule 52(b), whether or not granting the motion would alter the judgment;

(iii) for attorney's fees under Rule 54 if the district court extends the time to appeal under Rule 58;

(iv) to alter or amend the judgment under Rule 59;

(v) for a new trial under Rule 59; or

(vi) for relief under Rule 60 if the motion is filed no later than 28 days after the judgment is entered.

FRAP 4(a)(4)(A)(i)–(vi).

A notice of appeal filed early—that is, before the time specified in FRAP 4(a)(4)—is valid. However, the notice does not take effect until the denial of the last one of the specified motions. FRAP (a)(4)(B)(i). Importantly, however, to challenge a ruling made in one of the motions listed in FRAP 4(A)(i)–(vi), *e.g.*, where the post-trial motion alters or amends the judgment or awards attorneys' fees, a new timely notice of appeal (or amended notice of appeal) must be filed. FRAP 4(a)(4)(B)(ii).

The Supreme Court's decision in *Stone v. INS*, 514 U.S. 386 (1995), while not directly involving the appellate rules, provides some useful insights into the operation of these provisions. In *Stone*, which dealt with the interpretation of the judicial review portions of the Immigration and Naturalization Act (specifically, the ability of a party to pursue judicial review while a motion for reconsideration is pending before the agency), the Court also "consider[ed] the analogous practice of appellate court review of district court judgments," and concluded that that practice "confirms the correctness of our construction of Congress' language." *Id.* at 401. The Court noted that a Fed.R.Civ.P. 60(b) motion made after the ten-day period following entry of judgment "does not toll the running of the time for taking an appeal . . . does not affect the continuity of a prior taken appeal . . . [a]nd . . . does not affect the district court's power to grant Rule 60 relief." *Id.* The Court concluded its discussion with an important summary of the rules governing post-judgment motions and appealability: "Motions that do toll the time for taking an appeal give rise to only one appeal in which all matters are reviewed; motions that do not toll the time for taking an appeal give rise to two separate appellate proceedings that can be consolidated." *Id.* at 403.

E. MISTAKEN FILING IN THE COURT OF APPEALS

Under FRAP 4(d), if a party mistakenly files a notice of appeal in the court of appeals rather than in the district court, the clerk is to note the date of the filing on the notice and transmit it to the district court clerk; if the notice was otherwise timely when filed in the court of appeals, it is deemed to have been timely filed in the district court.

§ 5.4 WHEN A CROSS-APPEAL IS APPROPRIATE

It is well settled that "absent a cross-appeal, a party 'may not use his opponent's appeal as a vehicle for attacking a final judgment in an effort to diminish the appealing party's rights thereunder.'" *Neverson v. Farquharson*, 366 F.3d 32, 39 (1st Cir. 2004) (citation omitted). On the other hand, a cross-appeal is not necessary to argue that the judgment is correct but not for the reasons stated by the district court. As one court noted in rejecting an argument that a cross-appeal should have been filed, "[h]ere, respondents merely seek to defend the dismissal of [appellant's] petition on an alternate legal ground that is manifest in the record. This they are entitled to do, even if it means attacking the reasoning of the district court, and even if they lost on the same argument below." *Id.* at 39 (citations omitted). *See also Omnipoint Comm. Ents., L.P. v. Zoning Hearing Bd. of Easttown Twp.*, 331 F.3d 386, 395 (3d Cir. 2003) ("Appellee is free to assert any alternative theory in support of the District Court's decision, even without a formal cross-appeal."); *Lloyd v. Hardin Cty., Ia.*, 207 F.3d 1080, 1082 n.2 (8th Cir. 2000) ("Because Hardin County merely asserts in its cross-appeal additional grounds upon which the district court order arguably could be affirmed, those arguments are responsive to Lloyd appeal and should not have been styled as a separate cross-appeal.").

Increasingly, appellate courts are policing observance of this rule, particularly since the Federal Rules of Appellate Procedure were amended to allow a cross-appellant additional words in its opening brief (as well as an additional reply brief limited to the issues on the cross-appeal). *See* FRAP 28.1(c)(4), (e)(1), (e)(2); *see also In re Violation of Rule 28(c)*, 388 F.3d 1383, 1385 (Fed. Cir. 2004) (per curiam) (discussing (but not imposing) sanctions for violation of earlier version of cross-appeal rule).

§ 5.5 WHEN A JUDGMENT OR ORDER IS "ENTERED" UNDER FRAP 4(a)

Under FRAP 4(a)(1), a notice of appeal "must be filed with the district clerk within 30 days after the judgment or order appealed from is entered." (The time limit is 60 days if "the United States or its officer or agency is a party," FRAP 4(a)(1)(B).) FRAP 4(a)(7) defines "entry" of a judgment or order, depending on whether Fed.R.Civ.P. 58(a)(1) requires a separate document or not. If it does not, then the judgment or order is "entered" when it is entered in the district court's docket under Fed.R.Civ.P. 79(a). *See, e.g.*, *Local Union No. 1992 of Int'l Bhd. of Elec. Wkrs. v. Okonite Co.*, 358 F.3d 278, 286 (3d Cir. 2004) (noting that the rules do not require that "the resolution of each issue or motion have a separate judgment").

If Rule 58(a) does require a separate document, then "entry" requires two conditions: one, entry in the district court's docket; and two, either the date on which "the judgment or order is set forth on a separate document," or, in the case where the district court fails to meet its obligation to enter that judgment or order on a separate document, the date on which "150 days have run" from entry in the docket.

This latter provision, providing for "constructive" entry of a judgment or order after a lapse of 150 days, was added in 2002 to address the problems created by courts and attorneys ignoring the "separate document" requirement. *See, e.g., Armstrong v. Ahitow*, 36 F.3d 574, 575 (7th Cir. 1994) (per curiam) (urging that "district courts and their clerks must strive to more faithfully observe the requirements of Rule 58 because the failure to do so only causes additional work for this court in untangling jurisdictional snarls such as this one"). Before the amendment, however, otherwise-appealable orders could languish on the docket for years without ripening into an appealable order, due simply to the district court's failure to follow the separate-document requirement. *See, e.g., Abdulwali v. Washington Metro. Transit Auth.*, 315 F.3d 302, 304 (D.C. Cir. 2003) ("The court's failure to [set forth the order in a separate document] means that the Transit Authority's allotted time for filing an appeal never began to run, much less expire.").

§ 5.6 SCOPE OF RULINGS COVERED BY NOTICE OF APPEAL

"[A] notice of appeal which names the final judgment is sufficient to support review of all earlier orders that merge in the final judgment." *McBride v. CITGO Petroleum Corp.*, 281 F.3d 1099, 1104 (10th Cir. 2002). The "general rule," as that court explained, is that "all earlier interlocutory orders merge into final orders and judgments except when the final order is a dismissal for failure to prosecute." *Id.* (citation omitted). Thus, an appeal from a final judgment of a district court need specify no more than that the party "appeals from the final judgment of the district court, entered on [date]," and that specification will ordinarily be sufficient to put into play all of the underlying nonfinal orders that led to that judgment.

However, there is a split of authority that may create a trap for an unwary litigant. If the district court enters judgment, and then receives timely post-judgment motions under Federal Rules of Civil Procedure 50, 52, or 59 (any of which, if timely made, tolls the time for appeal), will a notice of appeal "from the final judgment" be sufficient to also bring up the rulings on the post-judgment motions for appeal? The Seventh Circuit has said "yes." *See Librizzi v. Children's Mem. Med. Ctr.*, 134 F.3d 1302, 1305–06 (7th Cir. 1998) ("It is never necessary—and may be hazardous—to specify in the notice of appeal the date of an order denying a motion under Fed.R.Civ.P. 50 or 59. Identifying the final decision entered under Rule 58 as 'the judgment, order, or part thereof appealed from' ([FRAP] 3(c)) brings up all of the issues in the case.").

Other circuits have issued rulings that might seem to say "no," but those rulings involve notices of appeal that are filed after the final judgment is entered, but before the post-judgment motions are ruled upon. *See, e.g., United States v. McGlory*, 202 F.3d 664, 668 (3d Cir. 2000) (en banc). In the case of such a premature notice of appeal, which is discussed in greater detail below, the safer course should be to file a second notice of appeal directed to the rulings on the post-trial motions. *See* FRAP 4(a)(4)(B)(ii).

Because of the merger rule, moreover, there are risks to being too specific in a notice of appeal. Where a party specifies in the notice of appeal that it is appealing certain issues or certain specific rulings, the court of appeals may well draw the conclusion that only the specified rulings, and no other rulings, have been appropriately noticed for appeal; even a rule of "liberal construction" will not save such a notice. *See, e.g., Minnesota Mining & Mfg. Co. v. Chemque, Inc.*, 303 F.3d 1294, 1309 (Fed. Cir. 2002) (holding that "even a liberal construction of the notice requirement" would not allow the notice of cross-appeal to be read as embracing patent invalidity issues, where the notice of appeal "included only the issues of inducement, infringement, and claim construction"); *C.A. May Marine Supply Co. v. Brunswick Corp.*, 649 F.2d 1049, 1056 (5th Cir. 1981) ("Where the appellant notices the appeal of a specified judgment only or a part thereof, however, this court has no jurisdiction to review other judgments or issues which are not expressly referred to and which are not impliedly intended for appeal.").

§ 5.7 EFFECT OF NOTICE OF APPEAL ON DISTRICT COURT JURISDICTION

The general rule is that a federal district court loses jurisdiction over a case when the appellant files a notice of appeal. *See Griggs v. Provident Consumer Disc. Co.*, 459 U.S. 56, 58 (1982) (per curiam) ("The filing of a notice of appeal is an event of jurisdictional significance—it confers jurisdiction on the court of appeals and divests the district court of its control over those aspects of the case involved in the appeal." (citations omitted)). The purposes of this general rule are practical ones: judicial economy, as well as limiting the occasions that the parties will have to engage in a "two front war." *Shewchun v. United States*, 797 F.2d 941, 943 (11th Cir. 1986). But the rule is not a technical one, nor is it an absolute one; rather, it is a "creature of judicial prudence," *Masalosalo v. Stonewall Ins. Co.*, 718 F.2d 955, 956 (9th Cir. 1983).

As a result, the general rule is subject to several exceptions:

- Under Fed.R.Civ.P. 60(a), the district court "may correct a clerical mistake . . . [b]ut after an appeal has been docketed in the appellate court and while it is pending, such a mistake may be corrected only with the appellate court's leave."

- Under Fed.R.Civ.P. 60(b), the district court "may relieve a party or its legal representative from a final judgment, order, or proceeding" because of "mistake," "newly discovered evidence," "fraud," a void judgment, a judgment that has been "satisfied, released, or discharged," or "any other reason that justifies relief." The motion must be made "within a reasonable time," and for mistake, newly discovered evidence, and fraud, must be made within one year from the date of judgment. Fed.R.Civ.P. 60(c). If such a motion is brought while a judgment is on appeal, the district court may deny the motion, or, if it is inclined to grant it, the district court can indicate that inclination and allow the moving party to apply to the court of appeals for a remand order. *See, e.g., Mahone v. Ray*, 326 F.3d 1176, 1180 (11th Cir. 2003).

- Moreover, if a Rule 60(b) motion is brought after a case has been decided on appeal, the district court may entertain that motion without leave of the court of appeals. Fed.R.Civ.P. 60(d). *See, e.g., Standard Oil Co. of Cal. v. United States*, 429 U.S. 17, 18–19 (1976) (per curiam).

- "A district court may retain jurisdiction when it has a duty to supervise the status quo during the pendency of an appeal or in aid of execution of a judgment that has not been superseded." *Stein v. Wood*, 127 F.3d 1187, 1189 (9th Cir. 1997) (citations omitted).

- Similarly, a district court may entertain contempt proceedings for violation of an injunction while an appeal is pending. *See, e.g., Farmhand, Inc. v. Anel Eng'g Indus., Inc.*, 693 F.2d 1140, 1146 (5th Cir. 1982).
- A district court may award attorneys' fees or impose sanctions on a party while an appeal is pending. *See, e.g., Budinich v. Becton Dickinson & Co.*, 486 U.S. 196 (1988); *Apostol v. Gallion*, 870 F.2d 1335, 1337–40 (7th Cir. 1989).
- FRAP 23 "gives the district court jurisdiction concurrent with the appeals court over the custody of a habeas petitioner." *Stein*, 127 F.3d at 1190.

For those motions that a district court cannot grant because of a pending appeal, Rule 62.1 of the Federal Rules of Civil Procedure—adopted in 2009—provides a mechanism for seeking and securing an "indicative ruling." If a timely motion is made for relief that would otherwise be barred by the pendency of an appeal, the district court may defer consideration of the motion, deny it outright, or indicate either that it would grant the motion if the court of appeals were to remand, or that the motion "raises a substantial issue." Fed.R.Civ.P. 62.1(a). If the district court indicates that it would grant the motion—or that it raises a substantial issue—the movant must promptly notify the court of appeals under FRAP 12.1. Fed.R.Civ.P. 62.1(b). The district court may then decide the motion if the court of appeals remands for that purpose. Fed.R.Civ.P. 62.1(c).

CHAPTER 6

PARTIES ON APPEAL

§ 6.1 IN GENERAL

In general, only parties to a proceeding in a trial court may be parties to an appeal. *See* FRAP 3(c) ("The notice of appeal must specify the *party or parties* taking the appeal.") (emphasis added). Also, generally speaking, only a party who has lost some portion of the *judgment* in the trial court may be an appellant; parties who only disagree with the reasoning of a trial court's ruling, or who seek to have the same judgment upheld on different grounds, may ordinarily not be appellants (or cross-appellants). These rules—and the various exceptions thereto—are discussed in the following sections.

§ 6.2 AGGRIEVED PARTIES

Who may appeal from a judgment? "Ordinarily, only a party aggrieved by a judgment or order of a district court may exercise the statutory right to appeal therefrom. A party who receives all that he has sought generally is not aggrieved by the judgment affording the relief and cannot appeal from it." *Deposit Guar. Nat'l Bank v. Roper*, 445 U.S. 326, 333 (1980) (citations omitted). This rule is sometimes stated as the principle that appellate courts "review judgments, not statements in opinions." *California v. Rooney*, 483 U.S. 307, 311 (1987) (citations omitted). Although this principle is often stated as the requirement of "standing to appeal" (and indeed might be understood as a specific application of the constitutional case-or-controversy requirement), the Supreme Court has said that this rule "does not have its source in the jurisdictional limitations of Art. III," but rather "is one of federal appellate practice . . . derived from the statutes granting appellate jurisdiction and the historic practices of the appellate courts." *Roper*, 445 U.S. at 333–34.

A useful survey of the limited grounds for allowing a successful party in the trial court to nonetheless appeal can be found in *Envtl. Prot. Info. Ctr. v. Pac. Lumber Co.*, 257 F.3d 1071 (9th Cir. 2001). The court there noted "three established prudential routes . . . by which a winning party may be deemed 'aggrieved' by a favorable judgment, and thus be deemed to have standing on appeal." *Id.* at 1075.

First, "a party may seek reformation of a favorable decree—but not review of its merits—that contains discussion of 'issues immaterial to the disposition of the cause.'" *Id.* (quoting Elec. Fittings Corp. v. Thomas & Betts Co., 307 U.S. 241, 242 (1939)). The term "decree" here is crucial—it means "judgment," not opinion. *United States v. Good Samaritan Church*, 29 F.3d 487, 488 (9th Cir. 1994) (dismissing appeal where appellant won the judgment below but wanted to challenge a subsidiary issue adjudicated against it, and noting that, if the language adjudicating this issue "had found its way into the judgment then review might be appropriate to 'direct reformation of the decree'") (quoting Elec. Fittings, 307 U.S. at 242).

Second, "a winning party will be considered aggrieved by a favorable judgment if future economic loss will result to the party on account of adverse collateral rulings," such as the denial of class certification. *Envtl. Prot. Info. Ctr.*, 257 F.3d at 1076 (citing *Roper*, 445 U.S. at 334 & n.6). However, because "[f]ederal appellate jurisdiction is limited by the appellant's personal stake in the appeal," *Roper*, 445 U.S. at 336, if—as was the case in *Roper*—the appellants are only aggrieved by the adverse collateral ruling, then the only issues they can present on appeal are those related to the collateral ruling. *Id.* (holding "that the Court of Appeals had jurisdiction to entertain the appeal only to review the asserted procedural error, not for the purpose of passing on the merits of the substantive controversy"). Moreover, "future economic loss" does not include the cost of relitigating the issue in the future. *See, e.g., Sea-Land Serv., Inc. v. Department of Transp.*, 137 F.3d 640, 648 (D.C. Cir. 1998).

Third, "a prevailing party will meet the prudential standing requirement 'if the adverse [collateral] ruling can serve as the basis for collateral estoppel in subsequent litigation.'" *Envtl. Prot. Info. Ctr.*, 257 F.3d at 1076 (quoting *Ruvalcaba v. City of Los Angeles*, 167 F.3d 514, 520 (9th Cir. 1999)). Such arguments succeed only rarely, *see, e.g., TrustHouse Forte, Inc. v. 795 Fifth Ave. Corp.*, 756 F.2d 255, 258–59 (2d Cir. 1985) (allowing appeal of intermediate ruling rejecting successful defendant's waiver defense on the ground that the district court intended the rejection to be binding in later litigation); they are difficult to win in most cases, because preclusion doctrines generally require that, for a prior resolution of an issue to be binding in later litigation, the resolution of the issue must be "essential to the judgment," *see id.* at 258, and it would be rare that an issue decided against an ultimately winning party in the trial court would be "essential" to that winning judgment.

§ 6.3 APPEAL BY NON-PARTIES

As noted, FRAP 3(c) provides that "[t]he notice of appeal must specify the *party or parties* taking the appeal." (Emphasis added.) The Supreme Court has called it "well settled" that, in general, only a party to an action may file an appeal. *Marino v. Ortiz*, 484 U.S. 301, 304 (1988). "Parties" includes original parties as well as those who have attained party status through intervention, substitution, or third-party practice. *See, e.g., United States v. LTV Corp.*, 746 F.2d 51, 53 (D.C. Cir. 1984) (per curiam). Thus, for example, a non-party will not be allowed to appeal a judgment that does not bind him, even if the decision sets a precedent unfavorable to the would-be appellant. *Cf. Boston Tow Boat Co. v. United States*, 321 U.S. 632, 633 (1944) (rejecting such an effort by an intervenor, who *was* a "party").

Although some courts have sought to create exceptions to the rule limiting appeals to parties, "the Supreme Court has been inhospitable to these endeavors." *Microsystems Software, Inc. v. Scandinavia Online AB*, 226 F.3d 35, 40 (1st Cir. 2000). Indeed, some courts have held that when a party fails to exercise its option to seek intervention, it cannot appeal even if it has an interest in the district court's judgment, and even if it participated in the district court proceedings. *See, e.g., id.*

The Supreme Court has, however, carved out an exception to the rule limiting appeals to parties—namely, for certain unnamed class members in a class action. In *Devlin v. Scardelletti*, 536 U.S. 1 (2002), the Court held that unnamed class members could appeal a class action settlement even if they did not formally intervene, provided that they "objected in a timely manner to approval of the settlement at the fairness hearing." *Id.* at 14. The Court reasoned that unnamed class members are in fact treated as parties for many purposes, including the fact that they are "bound by the settlement." *Id.* at 10. Thus, it is arguable that *Devlin* can be read as recognition that unnamed class members are, for all intents and purposes, parties to a class-action settlement.

A number of other (often conflicting) rules have arisen with respect to appeals by non-parties.

First, there is an exception to the general rule that discovery orders are not immediately appealable where the discovery order is directed at a disinterested non-party. The general rule is that the entity ordered to comply with discovery must refuse to comply, be held in contempt, and then appeal from the contempt order. *See, e.g., United States v. Ryan*, 402 U.S. 530, 532–33 (1971); *Church of Scientology of Cal. v. United States*, 506 U.S. 9, 18 n.11 (1992). But where the discovery order is "directed at a disinterested third party," *id.*, such as a third party holding privileged documents where the privilege belongs to a party, *the party holding the privilege* may immediately appeal, since the third party is not likely to have any incentive to risk contempt to protect someone else's privilege. *Id.* (citing *Perlman v. United States*, 247 U.S. 7 (1918)).

There is, however, some division among the appellate courts concerning the ability of a *non-party* to appeal a discovery order entered against it. In *In re Grand Jury Subpoenas*, 123 F.3d 695 (1st Cir. 1997), the court discusses the conflicting case law and holds that there is no right of immediate appeal by a non-party client whose lawyer has been ordered to turn over privileged documents. *Id.* at 698. By contrast, *Burden-Meeks v. Welch*, 319 F.3d 897 (7th Cir. 2003), holds (based on prior precedent) that "non-parties always may appeal immediately when they contest discovery orders." *Id.* at 900. The court, however, expressed concern regarding the correctness of that prior precedent.

Second, some courts have allowed non-parties to appeal injunctions where those decrees bind or constrain them. *See, e.g.*, *United States v. Kirschenbaum*, 156 F.3d 784, 794 (7th Cir. 1998) ("[N]on-parties who are bound by a court's equitable decrees have a right to move to have the order dissolved, and other circuits have held that where a non-party is purportedly bound by an injunction, the non-party may bring an appeal rather than face the possibility of a contempt proceeding.") (citation omitted). As a practical matter, this exception is likely to be narrow, because Fed.R.Civ.P. 65(d) limits the binding scope of injunctions to parties, non-parties who are the parties' "officers, agents, servants, employees, and attorneys," and "persons in active concert or participation with [them]," and then only if they "receive actual notice of [the order] by personal service or otherwise."

Third, and more generally, some circuits have adopted flexible tests—to be applied on a case-by-case basis—for determining whether a non-party may appeal. For instance, the Fifth Circuit looks at three factors: (1) whether the putative appellant "participated in the proceedings in the district court to the extent their interests were involved"; (2) whether "the equities weigh in favor of hearing the appeal"; and (3) whether the putative appellant has a "personal stake in the outcome" of the appeal. *SEC v. Forex Asset Mgmt.*, 242 F.3d 325, 329 (5th Cir. 2001). This three-factor test is largely consistent with the two-factor articulation of the test adopted by the Ninth Circuit, which inquires whether: (1) "the appellant participated in the district court proceedings even though not a party"; and (2) "the equities of the case weigh in favor of hearing the appeal." *Keith v. Volpe*, 118 F.3d 1386, 1391 (9th Cir. 1997) (citation omitted) (quoting *United States v. Badger*, 930 F.2d 754, 756 (9th Cir. 1991)).

§ 6.4 INTERVENTION

When a non-party is granted intervention at the trial-court level under Fed.R.Civ.P. 24, that non-party becomes a party and is thereby entitled to appeal an adverse ruling, subject to the usual requirements of a final judgment or applicable exception, *Int'l Union of Mine Workers v. Eagle-Picher Mining & Smelting Co.*, 325 U.S. 335, 338 (1945), and further subject to the intervenor's showing—if the party on whose side he or she intervened is not appealing—that the intervenor himself satisfies the standing requirements of Article III of the Constitution. *See, e.g.*, *Diamond v. Charles*, 476 U.S. 54, 68 (1986).

An intervenor may seek to intervene after judgment is entered, and for the specific purpose of mounting an appeal from the judgment. *See, e.g.*, *Bryant v. Yellen*, 447 U.S. 352, 366–68 (1980); *United States v. Perry*, 360 F.3d 519, 526 (6th Cir. 2004). If the intervenor would not be directly affected by the judgment—*e.g.*, he or she would only find that the precedent would affect him or her in a later case—then the intervenor is not sufficiently aggrieved by the judgment to appeal. *Boston Tow Boat Co.*, 321 U.S. at 633; *Tachiona v. United States*, 386 F.3d 205, 211 (2d Cir. 2004).

When a non-party is denied intervention, that non-party is entitled to take an immediate appeal of that ruling, because such a ruling is final as to the putative intervenor. *Marino v. Ortiz*, 484 U.S. at 304 ("denials of such motions are, of course, appealable"); *United States v. Peoples Benefit Life Ins. Co.*, 271 F.3d 411, 413 (2d Cir. 2001) (describing the appealability of denied intervention rulings as "well-established"). Indeed, such an appeal may be combined with an appeal going to the merits of the district court's decision, but the court's ability to reach the issues presented by the latter appeal would be contingent upon the intervention ruling being reversed. *See, e.g., Crawford v. Equifax Payment Servs., Inc.*, 201 F.3d 877, 879 (7th Cir. 2000).

No provision of the Federal Rules of Appellate Procedure allows for intervention while a case is on appeal, except in proceedings to review agency action. FRAP 15(d). Nonetheless, "the policies underlying intervention may be applicable in appellate courts," and the Supreme Court has implicitly endorsed the practice. *Int'l Union, United Auto., Aerospace and Agr. Implement Workers of Am. Local 283 v. Scofield*, 382 U.S. 205, 217 n.10 (1965). Thus, the courts of appeals have developed their own standards for appellate intervention, which in general "allow intervention at the appellate stage where none was sought in the district court 'only in an exceptional case for imperative reasons.'" *Amalgamated Transit Union Int'l v. Donovan*, 771 F.2d 1551, 1552–53 (D.C. Cir. 1985) (citation omitted).

Such "exceptional cases" and "imperative reasons" have been found where an intervenor would present arguments going to subject-matter jurisdiction that no party would present, *see Elliott Indus. Ltd. P'ship v. BP Am. Prod. Co.*, 407 F.3d 1091, 1104 (10th Cir. 2005); where an attorney sought to contest the district court's finding of misconduct, made as part of its reasoning for dismissing a complaint for discovery abuses, *see Penthouse Int'l, Ltd. v. Playboy Ents., Inc.*, 663 F.2d 371, 385–86, 392 (2d Cir. 1981); and where a member of the press seeks to defend or invoke the right of public access to documents or other information. *See, e.g.*, *United States v. Moussaoui*, 65 Fed. Appx. 881, 884 (4th Cir. 2003).

Where the constitutionality of a federal or state statute "affecting the public interest is drawn in question," 28 U.S.C. § 2403(a) & (b) grant the United States or the affected state, respectively, an unqualified right to "intervene for presentation of evidence, if evidence is otherwise admissible in the case, and for argument on the question of constitutionality." This statute has been held to give the United States and the states a right to intervene on appeal. *See, e.g.*, *Mississippi River Revival, Inc. v. City of Minneapolis*, 319 F.3d 1013, 1014 (8th Cir. 2003) (United States); *United States v. Wunsch*, 84 F.3d 1110, 1113 (9th Cir. 1996) (State of California).

§ 6.5 ATTORNEY APPEALS AND SANCTIONS

When a sanctions order is directed against an attorney, the attorney may appeal that order. An attorney, however, does not have standing to appeal an order directed solely against his client. *See, e.g.*, *Uselton v. Commercial Lovelace Motor Freight, Inc.*, 9 F.3d 849, 854–55 (10th Cir. 1993). Nor may the attorney appeal such a sanctions order prior to the entry of final judgment, even if the attorney no longer represents a party in the case. *Cunningham v. Hamilton Cty.*, 527 U.S. 198, 204 & n.4 (1999).

§ 6.6 SUBSTITUTION OF PARTIES

FRAP 43 provides procedures for the substitution of parties in an appeal, whether for reason of the death of a party (FRAP 43(a)), for "any reason other than death" (FRAP 43(b)), or because of a change in the identity of a public officeholder (FRAP 43(c)). The Federal Rules govern the procedure for substitution of a party, even where a court must apply state substantive law. *Servidone Constr. Corp. v. Levine*, 156 F.3d 414, 416 (2d Cir. 1998).

One reason why a party may need to be substituted is death. If the death occurs before the filing of the notice of appeal, "the decedent's personal representative—or, if there is no personal representative, the decedent's attorney of record—may file a notice of appeal." FRAP 43(a)(2). (The "personal representative" is usually the executor or administrator of the decedent's estate. *Anderson v. Romero*, 42 F.3d 1121, 1122–23 (7th Cir. 1994).) If death occurs after the notice of appeal, then the personal representative may be substituted by motion. FRAP 43(a)(1). If there is no personal representative, any party may then file a "suggestion of death" to notify the appellate court of this fact so that it may direct appropriate further proceedings.

FRAP 43 does not expressly provide for the dismissal of an appeal on the death of one party if no substitution is made. However, the court has the power to dismiss such an appeal, based on its inherent authority to manage and control its own docket. *Crowder v. Housing Auth. of Atlanta*, 908 F.2d 843, 846 n.1 (11th Cir. 1990). In one case, the court of appeals dismissed the appeal of the decedent when the death of the party was not put on the record and no personal representative came forward on the decedent's behalf. The appeal was dismissed without prejudice to the right of the decedent's personal representative to seek reinstatement of the appeal. *Johnson v. Morgenthau*, 160 F.3d 897, 898–99 (2d Cir. 1998).

FRAP 43(b) allows substitution in other circumstances when "necessary." This means that substitution is permitted when—analogous to death, FRAP 43(a), or departure from public office, FRAP 43(c)—a party is unable to litigate. FRAP 43(b) does not allow for substitution, however, just because one of the parties to the case voluntarily chooses to stop litigating. *Alabama Power Co. v. ICC*, 852 F.2d 1361, 1366 (D.C. Cir. 1988) (denying substitution of Conrail, which was never a party to administrative proceedings, in place of two railroad trade associations).

§ 6.7 *AMICUS CURIAE*

An *amicus curiae* is not a party. *See, e.g.*, *Newark Branch, N.A.A.C.P. v. Town of Harrison*, 940 F.2d 792, 808 (3d Cir. 1991). Thus, absent intervention or other actions making an *amicus* a party, an *amicus*—even if granted that status in the district court—has no right to appeal, and no right to seek relief from the appellate court. *Id.* Indeed, an *amicus* that is granted leave to file a brief in the district court is not automatically allowed to appear as *amicus curiae* in the court of appeals.

In *Eldred v. Ashcroft*, 255 F.3d 849 (D.C. Cir. 2001), the court set forth, at some length, the reasons why it had previously found it "particularly inappropriate" to entertain a constitutional argument pressed by an *amicus* but not by the parties. *Id.* at 850. *See also Eldred v. Reno,* 239 F.3d 372, 378 (D.C. Cir. 2001). For one, the party being supported by the *amicus* took a "diametrically opposed" position in its briefs and argument before the court of appeals. 255 F.3d at 851. For another, because the appellant did not take the position advanced by *amicus*, the appellee did not answer it in its brief. *Id.* (citing cases). *See generally* § 13.6, *infra.*

§ 6.8 CONSTITUTIONAL STANDING

As noted in §§ 6.1–6.2 above, the answer to the question of who is a proper party to an appeal depends upon a number of factors developed by the courts that are rooted in common-law principles, not in Article III standing doctrine. Still, Article III standing plays an important role on appeal: A party's standing must exist at all times, and it can be evaluated by the court of appeals *sua sponte*, or raised by any party at any time, even on appeal. Moreover, standing plays a particularly important role in evaluating whether an intervenor can pursue an appeal without the presence of the original party as a co-appellant. *See* § 6.4, *supra.*

The requirement that parties to litigation have standing stems both from Article III of the Constitution and from prudential considerations. For Article III standing, a plaintiff must allege an "injury in fact"—"an invasion of a legally protected interest in which is (a) concrete and particularized and (b) actual or imminent, not conjectural or hypothetical. . . .” *Lujan v. Defenders of Wildlife*, 504 U.S. 555, 560–61 (1992) (citation omitted). Moreover, “there must be a causal connection between the injury and the conduct complained of,” and there must be a likelihood “that the injury will be redressed by a favorable decision.” *Id.* As a prudential matter, in addition to the Article III requirements, a plaintiff “generally must assert his own legal rights and interests,” as opposed to those of third parties; he or she must not be raising a mere “generalized grievance[ ]” (*i.e.*, an “abstract question[ ] of wide public significance” that should be addressed by the legislature), and his or her “complaint [must] fall within the zone of interests to be protected or regulated by the statute or constitutional guarantee in question.” *Valley Forge Christian Coll. v. Americans United for Separation of Church and State, Inc.*, 454 U.S. 464, 474–75 (1982).

The requirement of standing applies fully at the appellate level. Article III standing is jurisdictional, cannot be waived, and must be addressed by the court even if no party raises it. *See, e.g.*, *AT & T Mobility, LLC v. Nat'l Ass'n for Stock Car Auto Racing, Inc.*, 494 F.3d 1356, 1359–60 (11th Cir. 2007). The prudential criteria, by contrast, are more flexible, and are not always strictly applied. Fundamentally, the focus at the appellate level is whether the appellant has alleged a cognizable injury from the district court's ruling.

The question of standing is potentially dispositive: “if the putative appellants lack standing to appeal, the only role for the appellate court is to memorialize that fact and simultaneously terminate the proceeding." *Microsystems Software, Inc. v. Scandinavia Online AB*, 226 F.3d 35, 39 (1st Cir. 2000).

Courts have broadened standing by permitting "associational" standing in certain circumstances—*e.g.*, permitting associations to sue, and to appeal, on behalf of their members. *See, e.g.*, *Pennsylvania Psychiatric Soc. v. Green Spring Health Serv.*, 280 F.3d 278 (3d Cir. 2002). Courts have also sometimes permitted "third-party" standing, *e.g.*, allowing doctors to sue and appeal on behalf of their patients. *See, e.g.*, *id.*

§ 6.9 MOOTNESS

Just as Article III's case-or-controversy requirement makes it crucial that standing exist at all stages of a case, including appeal, so too Article III prohibits an appellate court's decision in a dispute that has become moot. Thus, "it is not enough that a dispute was very much alive when suit was filed, or when review was obtained in the Court of Appeals." *Lewis v. Cont'l Bank Corp.*, 494 U.S. 472, 477 (1990). Instead, "[the] case-or-controversy requirement subsists though all stages of federal judicial proceedings, trial and appellate." *Id.*

There are three major exceptions to mootness doctrine: (1) where a dispute is "capable of repetition but evading review," *see, e.g., Federal Election Comm'n v. Wis. Right to Life, Inc.*, 551 U.S. 449 (2007); (2) where a party's unilateral cessation of activity (which might be restarted) is the act making the dispute moot, *see, e.g., Friends of the Earth v. Laidlaw Env. Servs., Inc.*, 528 U.S. 167, 189 (2000); and (3) where the named plaintiff in a class action ceases to belong to the class seeking a remedy, *see, e.g., Sosna v. Iowa*, 419 U.S. 393, 398–99 & n.7 (1975) (plaintiff challenging Iowa's one-year residency requirement for divorce successfully divorced in another state).

§ 6.10 VACATING JUDGMENT WHEN CASE BECOMES MOOT WHILE ON APPEAL (INCLUDING BY SETTLEMENT)

In some instances, a case will become moot after an appeal or petition for a writ of certiorari is filed. Perhaps this mootness arises because a criminal defendant has died, or because an enjoined book has been published, or—most commonly—because the parties reached a settlement.

The Supreme Court's decisions are replete with statements to the effect that "[o]ur ordinary practice in disposing of a case that has become moot on appeal is to vacate the judgment with directions to dismiss." *Lewis v. Cont'l Bank Corp.*, 494 U.S. at 482; *Deakins v. Monaghan*, 484 U.S. 193, 204 (1988); *United States v. Munsingwear, Inc.*, 340 U.S. 36, 39–40 (1950). Thus, in the case of a settlement, the party who suffered an adverse ruling in the lower court may seek, as part of the settlement, the opponent's consent to ask the court where the appeal is pending to vacate the lower court's adverse ruling as moot.

However, the Supreme Court's broad statements regarding vacatur as an "ordinary" consequence of mootness do not apply to what may be the most common way that a case becomes moot while on appeal—through settlement. In *U.S. Bancorp Mortgage Co. v. Bonner Mall P'ship*, 513 U.S. 18 (1994), the Supreme Court addressed the propriety of vacatur in these circumstances. The Court held that the "ordinary practice" of automatic vacatur referred to in its prior cases applied only in cases of mootness by "happenstance," or where the party seeking vacatur was otherwise blameless in causing the mootness. *Id.* at 25. A settlement, however, represents the losing party's "voluntar[y] forfeit[ure]" of appellate review, thus "surrendering his claim to the equitable remedy of vacatur." *Id.* Therefore, the Court concluded that "mootness by reason of settlement does not justify vacatur of a judgment under review." *Id.* at 29.

The Court rejected the argument that the availability of vacatur would encourage settlement. It further rejected the argument that vacatur was sensible because it permitted the legal issue in question to be debated further in future cases. The Court emphasized, however, that the determination is an equitable one, and, therefore, in "exceptional circumstances" a court should have authority to vacate a lower court judgment—but such circumstances "do not include the mere fact that the settlement agreement provides for vacatur." *Id.*

This rule can cause difficulties when the parties wish to settle a case on appeal, but the losing party in the district court wishes to obtain a vacatur of the district court's judgment (to avoid the collateral estoppel effect of that judgment in other litigation, for example). Some courts, in fact, have found that exceptional circumstances existed where the parties' settlement agreement was conditioned upon obtaining an order of vacatur. *See, e.g.*, *Hartford Cas. Ins. Co. v. Crum & Forster Specialty Ins. Co.*, 828 F.3d 1331, 1336–37 (11th Cir. 2016) (holding that district court abused its discretion in denying vacatur after settlement, where court of appeals had ordered parties to mediation that resulted in settlement, and because "public interest" also included the freeing of judicial resources to consider other matters); *Keller v. Mobil Corp.*, 55 F.3d 94, 98–100 (2d Cir. 1995) (explaining, in some detail, how vacatur was necessary in that case to consummate an effective settlement); *Major League Baseball Props., Inc. v. Pacific Trading Cards, Inc.*, 150 F.3d 149, 151–52 (2d Cir. 1998) (similar); *Motta v. District Dir. of INS*, 61 F.3d 117, 118–19 (1st Cir. 1995) (similar; noting that parties engaged in settlement discussions at the exhortation of the First Circuit). There is certainly no requirement that a court vacate its own prior opinion even where all parties request such action.

There is a split in the circuits regarding whether a district court has greater discretion to vacate its own prior judgments without a finding of "exceptional circumstances." The Ninth Circuit has held that a district court need not make the same finding of "exceptional circumstances" to vacate its own prior judgments when a case has been rendered moot on appeal. *American Games, Inc. v. Trade Prods., Inc.*,

142 F.3d 1164, 1169–70 (9th Cir. 1998). The Seventh Circuit agrees with the Ninth Circuit. *Marseilles Hydro Power, LLC v. Marseilles Land & Water Co.*, 481 F.3d 1002, 1003 (7th Cir. 2007). But the Fourth Circuit has held otherwise. *Valero Terrestrial Corp. v. Paige*, 211 F.3d 112, 118–19 & n.3 (4th Cir. 2000).

§ 6.11 APPELLATE ALTERNATIVE DISPUTE RESOLUTION

Issues of mootness often arise in the context of proposed settlements coming out of court of appeals-ordered mediation, for when a case is settled, the dispute becomes moot.

FRAP 33 provides that "[t]he court may direct the attorneys—and, when appropriate, the parties—to participate in one or more conferences to address any matter that may aid in disposing of the proceedings, including simplifying the issues and discussing settlement." Pursuant to the authority of FRAP 33, every one of the thirteen federal courts of appeals has established a mediation program.

The Second Circuit's Civil Appeals Management Plan, or "CAMP," was established in 1974. The remaining circuits established programs in the 1980s or 1990s, with the exception of the Federal Circuit, which did not establish its mediation program until 2005. These programs uniformly apply only to civil cases, not to criminal cases. The purpose of each program is to help facilitate settlements at the appellate level and thereby reduce the number of cases that must be heard and decided by the appellate court. Mediation sessions are typically held before briefing and almost always before any oral argument has taken place. "[O]ccasionally," however, appeal conferences are held after oral argument, which is why FRAP 33 was recaptioned from "Prehearing Conference" to "Appeal Conferences" in 1994. Advisory Committee Notes to 1994 Amendment to FRAP 33.

The mediation programs differ widely from circuit to circuit. Some include all or virtually all civil cases, while others are more selective (*e.g.*, some do not include cases where a government agency is a party). In some circuits, the mediations are conducted by telephone, whereas in others they are held in person. Some circuits require parties to mediate, whereas others allow parties to elect participation. In most circuits, the mediators are employees of that court (sometimes retired judges), but some circuits rely on attorney volunteers. The mediations are confidential; mediators are not permitted to discuss the mediations with the judges who are assigned to hear the case in the event that no settlement is reached.

A comprehensive discussion of the mediation programs in each of the 13 circuits is contained in a Federal Judicial Center publication: Robert J. Niemic, *Mediation & Conference Programs in the Federal Courts of Appeals: A Sourcebook for Judges and Lawyers* (Fed. Jud. Center 2d ed. 2006) (available at the Federal Judicial Center's website, www.fjc.gov).

CHAPTER 7

RELIEF PENDING REVIEW

§ 7.1 IN GENERAL

The rules governing relief pending appellate review reflect the fact that "[n]o court can make time stand still while it considers an appeal, and if a court takes the time it needs, the court's decision may in some cases come too late for the party seeking review." *Nken v. Holder*, 556 U.S. 418, 421 (2009) (citation omitted). The authority to grant relief pending review addresses the dilemma facing a court "when there is insufficient time to resolve the merits and irreparable harm [to the parties or the public] may result from delay." *Id.* at 432.

The availability of interim relief allows a party to preserve the status quo while pressing its case on appeal. For example, a losing defendant may want to stay the execution of a money judgment so that the winning plaintiff cannot force execution proceedings on his property in order to satisfy the judgment. Likewise, a trial court's injunction may have such negative and irreversible effects on the enjoined party that an appeal, even if likely to be successful, would not occur soon enough to counteract those negative effects. In such cases, the losing party may be entitled to interim relief. In civil cases, such relief is governed chiefly by Fed.R.Civ.P. 62 in the district courts, and by FRAP 8 in the courts of appeals. *See Hilton v. Braunskill*, 481 U.S. 770, 776 (1987) (noting that, while "[d]ifferent Rules of Procedure govern the power of district courts and courts of appeals to stay an order pending appeal," "the factors regulating the issuance of a stay are generally the same" under both rules).

Rule 62 sets forth specific procedures governing stays and other relief pending appeal, but those provisions are not in derogation of the general inherent power of federal courts to grant equitable relief pending an appeal, or to impose certain conditions on the granting of equitable relief. Indeed, the Supreme Court has described the power to grant stays pending review as being "as old as the judicial system of the nation." *Scripps-Howard Radio, Inc. v. FCC*, 316 U.S. 4, 17 (1942). Accordingly, Fed.R.Civ.P. 62(g) provides that nothing in Rule 62 "limit[s] the power of the appellate court or one of its judges or justices: (1) to stay proceedings—or suspend, modify, restore, or grant an injunction—while an appeal is pending; or (2) to issue an order to preserve the status quo or the effectiveness of the judgment to be entered."

An important consideration in determining a party's entitlement to relief pending appeal is whether the court order from which relief is sought is an injunction or, instead, a money judgment. *See, e.g., Acevedo-Garcia v. Vera-Monroig*, 296 F.3d 13, 16–17 (1st Cir. 2002) (per curiam) (explaining that "[s]tays of monetary judgments are ordinarily sought under either Fed.R.Civ.P. 62(d) or 62(f)," whereas "[s]tays of injunctive orders . . . are evaluated under the traditional four-part standard applied to injunctions"). Sections 7.2 and 7.3, *infra*, deal with issues related to relief from execution of money judgments, while § 7.4 considers stays of injunctive relief pending appeal. Sections 7.5 and 7.6 discuss the specific provisions of FRAP 8 (which applies to both monetary and injunctive relief). Finally, § 7.7 provides a brief discussion of relief pending appellate review in the federal criminal context.

§ 7.2 AUTOMATIC STAY OF EXECUTION OF JUDGMENT

Fed.R.Civ.P. 62(a) provides (subject to certain exceptions discussed below) that "no execution may issue on a judgment, nor may proceedings be taken to enforce it, until 14 days have passed after its entry." This 14-day stay is self-executing—*i.e.*, the losing party is not required to file a motion or take any other steps. The reason for this rule is to allow the losing party a limited amount of time to evaluate and implement his options (including the securing of a supersedeas bond) before allowing the judgment winner to take the powerful steps of enlisting the aid of government authorities to execute upon that judgment.

Rule 62(a) exempts from the 14-day stay, "unless the court orders otherwise . . . (1) an interlocutory or final judgment in an action for an injunction or a receivership; or (2) a judgment or order that directs an accounting in an action for patent infringement." The reason for these exceptions can be seen in 28 U.S.C. § 1292(a) and (c)(2), which allow for immediate appeal of these otherwise interlocutory orders, and in the fact that none of these exceptional circumstances will involve a money judgment requiring the securing of a supersedeas bond as a condition for appeal without risk of execution on the money judgment. The "unless the court orders otherwise" exception retains the courts' inherent powers to grant stays in other cases where appropriate. *See, e.g., Landis v. N. Am. Co.*, 299 U.S. 248, 254–55 (1936) ("The power to stay proceedings is incidental to the power inherent in every court to control the disposition of the causes on its docket with economy of time and effort for itself, for counsel, and for litigants.").

Rule 62 also empowers (but does not require) the district court to stay execution of a judgment pending the court's disposition of any of the types of motions listed in Fed.R.Civ.P. 62(b)(1)–(4). The filing of a timely post-judgment motion under Fed.R.Civ.P. 50, 52(b), 59, or 60 will not extend the automatic stay as a matter of course. Where such motions are filed, however, the district court has discretion to "stay the execution of a judgment—or any proceedings to enforce it—pending disposition of" those four types of post-judgment motions, "[o]n appropriate terms for the opposing party's security." *See* Fed.R.Civ.P. 62(b).

As this book went to press, the Judicial Conference Advisory Committee on Civil Rules had proposed amendments to Fed.R.Civ.P. 62(a) that would extend the automatic stay to 30 days. Preliminary Draft of Proposed Amendments to the Federal Rules of Appellate, Bankruptcy, Civil, and Criminal Procedure, Aug. 2016, *available at* http://www.uscourts.gov/sites/default/files/2016-08-preliminary_draft_of_rules_forms_published_for_public_comment_0.pdf. The Committee Note regarding this proposed change explains, in part: "Setting the period at 30 days coincides with the time for filing most appeals in civil actions, providing a would-be appellant the full period of appeal time to arrange a stay by other means." *Id.* at 237.

§ 7.3 SUPERSEDEAS BONDS

Beyond Rule 62(a)'s automatic 14-day stay of execution, Rule 62(d) allows an appellant to obtain a stay on appeal by posting a supersedeas bond (except for the actions covered by Rule 62(a)(1) or (2)). "The bond may be given upon or after filing the notice of appeal or after obtaining the order allowing the appeal." Fed.R.Civ.P. 62(d). The stay takes effect "when the court approves the bond." *Id.*

Posting of the bond thus prevents the creditor from executing on a money judgment while the appeal is pending. At the same time, the bond protects the creditor in the event that the appeal is unsuccessful. "The philosophy underlying Rule 62(d) is that a plaintiff who has won in the trial court should not be put to the expense of defending his judgment on appeal unless the defendant takes reasonable steps to assure that the judgment will be paid if it is affirmed." *Lightfoot v. Walker*, 797 F.2d 505, 506–07 (7th Cir. 1986).

For that reason, courts typically require that the bond be in a sufficient amount to secure the amount of the money judgment as well as the anticipated post-judgment interest that will accrue while the case is pending on appeal. *See, e.g., SEC v. O'Hagan*, 901 F.Supp. 1476, 1480 (D. Minn. 1995); *see generally Am. Manufacturers Mut. Ins. Co. v. Am. Broad.-Paramount Theatres, Inc.*, 87 S.Ct. 1, 3 (1966) (Harlan, J., in chambers) (explaining the practice before the advent of Rule 62(d)). In many districts, the appropriate amount of a supersedeas bond is set by local rule. *See, e.g.*, N.D. Ill. L.R. 62.1 (requiring amount of bond to include the amount of the judgment, plus "costs, interest, and damages for delay," plus "one year's interest at the rate provided in 28 U.S.C. § 1961, plus $500 to cover costs").

Absent a bond, once the automatic 14-day stay (and any additional periods granted by the district court) expires, the judgment creditor can institute execution proceedings on the judgment even while the appeal is pending.

In certain circumstances, a bond is not required to stay execution of a money judgment. For example, when the United States or agency thereof takes an appeal, and the judgment is stayed, "[t]he court must not require a bond, obligation, or other security." *See* Fed.R.Civ.P. 62(e). Also, members of the military may be entitled to a stay without security under 50 App. U.S.C. § 522.

Likewise, courts have the discretion, under Rule 62, to allow a stay of a money judgment on less than full security—or on no security at all—in exceptional circumstances. In general, courts have held that the bond requirement may be waived when either (1) the judgment debtor's ability to pay the judgment is so plain that posting a bond would be a waste of money, or conversely, (2) requiring a bond would put the judgment debtor's ability to pay its other creditors in "undue jeopardy." *Olympia Equipment Leasing Co. v. Western Union Telegraph Co.*, 786 F.2d 794, 796 (7th Cir. 1986). For examples of the first type of case, *see, e.g., Arban v. West Pub. Corp.*, 345 F.3d 390, 409 (6th Cir. 2003) (district court did not abuse its discretion in allowing a stay without requiring a bond in light of the "vast disparity" between the judgment amount and the annual revenues of the group of which defendant/appellee was a part); *Federal Prescription Serv., Inc. v. American Pharm. Ass'n*, 636 F.2d 755, 761 (D.C. Cir. 1980) (no bond required where defendant's net worth was 47 times the amount of judgment and it was a long-time resident of the judicial district). For examples of the second scenario, *see, e.g., Olympia Equipment, supra*, at 799–800; *Trans World Airlines, Inc. v. Hughes*, 314 F.Supp. 94, 98 (S.D.N.Y. 1970) (court exercised discretion to allow a bond of only $75 million to secure a $161 million judgment where defendant assured the court that it would maintain a net worth of triple the balance of the judgment).

If a supersedeas bond is unattainable, the judgment debtor may file for protection under the Bankruptcy Code. In that event, the act of filing a petition in bankruptcy will trigger the automatic stay of the Bankruptcy Code, which will prevent execution on the judgment. 11 U.S.C. § 362(a)(2); *In re Arnold*, 806 F.2d 937, 939 (9th Cir. 1986); *see generally Kalb v. Feuerstein*, 308 U.S. 433, 443 (1940) (holding a state court's confirmation of a property sale to satisfy a debt unauthorized when property owner had pending petition in bankruptcy). In bankruptcy, a judgment creditor is an unsecured creditor, which gives the creditor a relatively low priority. The complex and sometimes strategic consequences of a bankruptcy petition—as it pertains to the imposition of a stay upon a reduced or eliminated supersedeas bond—are explored in Judge Posner's opinion for the Seventh Circuit in *Olympia Equip. Leasing*, 786 F.2d at 797–98, and in Judge Easterbrook's concurring opinion in that case, *id.* at 800–03 (Easterbrook, J., concurring).

What happens if the prevailing party appeals first? Is the judgment debtor thereby entitled to an automatic stay of execution on the judgment? Courts that have addressed the issue have taken divergent views, but the majority view is that "a prevailing party's appeal suspends enforcement of the judgment only when the theory of the appeal is inconsistent with enforcement in the interim." *BASF Corp. v. Old World Trading Co.*, 979 F.2d 615, 617 (7th Cir. 1992); *accord, e.g., Trustmark Ins. Co. v. Gallucci*, 193 F.3d 558, 559 (1st Cir. 1999) (per curiam); *Enserch Corp. v. Shand Morahan & Co.*, 918 F.2d 462, 464 & nn.2 & 3 (5th Cir. 1990); *but see Tenn. Valley Auth. v. Atlas Mach. & Iron Works, Inc.*, 803 F.2d 794, 797 (4th Cir. 1986) ("Where the prevailing party in the lower court appeals from that court's judgment, the appeal suspends the execution of the decree." (citations omitted)).

"[P]remiums paid for a supersedeas bond or other bond to preserve rights pending appeal" are taxable to the appellee in the district court if the appellant prevails and is awarded costs by the appellate court. FRAP 39(e)(3). This can result in a substantial restitutionary award in the event of appellate reversal, given that the costs of supersedeas bonds can, in cases of large judgments, be substantial. *See, e.g., Exxon Valdez v. Exxon Mobil Corp.*, 568 F.3d 1077, 1081–82 (9th Cir. 2009) (denying costs); *id.* at 1082–90 (Kleinfeld, J., concurring in part and dissenting in part) (noting "huge" premiums—$60.6 million—required to secure a $5 billion judgment on appeal, and dissenting from the denial of costs while observing that defendant had successfully reduced the judgment by 90% on appeal).

Proposed amendments to Fed.R.Civ.P. 62 and FRAP 8 and 39 would replace "supersedeas bond" with "bond or other security" in all three rules, thus "mak[ing] explicit the opportunity to post security in a form other than a bond." *See* Preliminary Draft of Proposed Amendments to the Federal Rules of Appellate, Bankruptcy, Civil, and Criminal Procedure, Aug. 2016, at 45–46, 238, *available at* http://www.uscourts.gov/sites/default/files/2016-08-preliminary_draft_of_rules_forms_published_for_public_comment_0.pdf.

§ 7.4 STAY OF INJUNCTION PENDING APPEAL

In contrast to cases involving money judgments, Fed.R.Civ.P. 62(a) does not provide an automatic stay of injunctions. Instead, Fed.R.Civ.P. 62(c) authorizes the district court, while an appeal is pending, to "suspend, modify, restore, or grant an injunction on terms for bond or other terms that secure the opposing party's rights."

In considering applications for a stay of an injunction pending appeal, courts consider four factors: "(1) whether the stay applicant has made a strong showing that he is likely to succeed on the merits; (2) whether the applicant will be irreparably injured absent a stay; (3) whether issuance of the stay will substantially injure the other parties interested in the proceedings; and (4) where the public interest lies." *Hilton v. Braunskill*, 481 U.S. 770, 776 (1987) (citations omitted). As the Court noted in *Nken v. Holder*, 556 U.S. 418 (2009), "[t]here is substantial overlap between these [factors] and the factors governing preliminary injunctions, not because the two are one and the same, but because similar concerns arise whenever a court order may allow or disallow anticipated action before the legality of that action has been conclusively determined." *Id.* at 434 (citations omitted).

The analysis of these four factors is fact-intensive and context-specific; a court will look at the specific factors present in a case, determine how the factors affect each other, and then determine whether a stay should be granted. Since the factors "contemplate individualized judgments in each case, the formula cannot be reduced to a set of rigid rules." *Hilton*, 481 U.S. at 777. For examples, see *Brady v. National Football League*, 640 F.3d 785, 787 (8th Cir. 2011) (per curiam) (granting stay of district court order enjoining NFL from continuing to impose "lockout" of professional football players); *Service Employees Intern. Union Local 1 v. Husted,* 698 F.3d 341, 343–45 (6th Cir. 2012) (per curiam) (granting stay of district court injunction requiring State of Ohio to count provisional ballots cast in the wrong polling place due to poll-worker error; court of appeals noted that, "[a]s a general rule, last-minute injunctions changing election procedures are strongly disfavored").

When analyzing the four factors, courts have often applied a "sliding scale" approach, under which "[t]he probability of success that must be demonstrated is inversely proportional to the amount of irreparable injury plaintiff will suffer absent the stay." *Mohammed v. Reno*, 309 F.3d 95, 101 (2d Cir. 2002) (citation and internal quotation marks omitted). "Simply stated, more of one excuses less of the other." *Id.; see also, e.g., Wildmon v. Berwick Univ. Pictures,* 983 F.2d 21, 23 (5th Cir. 1992) ("[T]he movant need only present a substantial case on the merits when a serious legal question is involved and show that the balance of equities weighs heavily in favor of granting the stay.") (citations and internal quotation marks omitted); *FTC v. Mainstream Mktg. Servs., Inc.,* 345 F.3d 850, 852 (10th Cir. 2003) ("[W]here the moving party has established that the three 'harm' factors tip decidedly in its favor, the 'probability of success' requirement is somewhat relaxed.") (citations omitted). Thus, in cases where the harm is great, and the balance of hardship is overwhelmingly in the movant's favor, "substantial questions," "serious legal questions," or a "substantial case" on the merits—rather than a "likelihood of success" on the merits—may be enough to support a claim to a stay.

Rule 62(c) allows a court to condition a stay "on terms for bond or other terms that secure the opposing party's rights." In appropriate cases, such security might be a bond, *see, e.g.*, *GTE Prods. Corp. v. Kennametal, Inc.*, 772 F.Supp. 907, 920 (W.D.Va. 1991) (granting stay of injunction in patent-infringement case upon posting of surety bond "roughly equal to the amount of profits GTE would lose in one year"), a compulsory license requiring payments for ongoing patent infringement, *see On Demand Mach. Corp. v. Ingram Indus., Inc.*, 442 F.3d 1331, 1337, 1345 (Fed. Cir. 2006), or other similar conditions designed to minimize the temporary loss of the injunctive relief already granted to the plaintiff.

§ 7.5 MOTION FOR STAY IN THE COURT OF APPEALS

FRAP 8 confirms the inherent equitable power of the courts of appeals to grant stays pending appeal. Rule 8(a)(1) makes clear that "ordinarily" a party must move first in the district court to obtain a stay pending appeal, "approval of a supersedeas bond," or "an order suspending, modifying, restoring, or granting an injunction" pending appeal. FRAP 8(a)(2)(A)–(C). If a motion is made to the court of appeals (or to a single judge of the court), FRAP 8(a)(2) requires the motion to either (1) "show that moving first in the district court would be impracticable," or (2) "state that, a motion having been made, the district court denied the motion or failed to afford the relief requested and state any reasons given by the district court for its action." In addition, the motion must state the "reasons for granting the relief requested and the facts relied upon" including "affidavits or other sworn statements supporting facts subject to dispute" and "relevant parts of the record." FRAP 8(a)(2)(B). The movant must also provide reasonable notice to all affected parties. FRAP 8(a)(2)(C).

The standard for obtaining a stay from the court of appeals is "generally the same" as the four-factor test for obtaining a stay from a district court. *Hilton v. Braunskill*, 481 U.S. at 776. That being said, appellate courts are not nearly as well equipped to enforce injunctive relief as are district courts, and while the stay application in the court of appeals is an independent action rather than appellate review, a district court's denial of relief will inevitably be considered as significant (though not dispositive) by the court of appeals.

§ 7.6 ACTION AGAINST A SURETY

FRAP 8(b) provides that: "If a party gives security in the form of a bond or stipulation or other undertaking with one or more sureties, each surety submits to the jurisdiction of the district court and irrevocably appoints the district clerk as the surety's agent on whom any papers affecting the surety's liability on the bond or undertaking may be served. On motion, a surety's liability may be enforced in the district court without the necessity of an independent action. The motion and any notice that the district court prescribes may be served on the district clerk, who must promptly mail a copy to each surety whose address is known."

This rule has a parallel in Rule 65.1 of the Federal Rules of Civil Procedure, on which it is based. Each rule endows the courts (district courts in the case of Fed.R.Civ.P. 65.1 and courts of appeals in the case of FRAP 8(b)) to order security "in the form of a bond or stipulation or other undertaking." *Continuum Co., Inc. v. Incepts, Inc.*, 883 F.2d 333, 335 (5th Cir. 1989). But the appellate version of the rule requires any proceedings to enforce the surety's obligation to take place in the district court, not in the court of appeals, in recognition of the fact that district courts—and their clerks' offices—are better suited to handle such matters, including the resolution of any factual disputes that may arise.

Proposed amendments to FRAP 8(b) and Fed.R.Civ.P. 65.1 would change "surety" to "surety or other security provider" in both Rules. These changes reflect the corresponding proposed amendment to Fed.R.Civ.P. 62, which would "make[ ] explicit the opportunity to post security in a form other than a bond." *See* Preliminary Draft of Proposed Amendments to the Federal Rules of Appellate, Bankruptcy, Civil, and Criminal Procedure, Aug. 2016, at 238–40, *available at* http://www.uscourts.gov/sites/default/files/2016-08-preliminary_draft_of_rules_forms_published_for_public_comment_0.pdf.

§ 7.7 RELEASE OF CRIMINAL DEFENDANTS PENDING APPEAL

The Bail Reform Act of 1966, Pub. L. No. 89–465, § 3146, 80 Stat. 214, established a standard for courts to utilize when making decisions regarding the release of criminal defendants pending trial. That act provided that defendants were entitled to release pending appeals unless "no one or more conditions of release will reasonably assure that the person will not flee or pose a danger to any other person or to the community . . . or if it appears that an appeal is frivolous or taken for delay."

In 1984, however, Congress replaced the 1966 Act with the Bail Reform Act of 1984, 18 U.S.C. § 3141 *et seq.* The 1984 Act provides that a court may allow a convicted defendant to remain free on bond pending appeal only if the court finds: (1) by "clear and convincing evidence" that the defendant "is not likely to flee or pose a danger to the safety of any other person or the community if released"; (2) "that the appeal is not for the purpose of delay"; and (3) the appeal "raises a substantial question of law or fact likely to result in . . . reversal, . . . an order for a new trial, . . . a sentence that does not include a term of imprisonment, or . . . a reduced sentence to a term of imprisonment less than the total of the time already served plus the expected duration of the appeal process." 18 U.S.C. § 3143(b)(1). This change, while not entirely eliminating bail pending appeal, clearly eliminated any presumption in favor of bail, thus making it more difficult for a defendant to obtain a release pending appeal. *See United States v. Ashman*,

964 F.2d 596, 598 (7th Cir. 1992) ("§ 3143(b) 'requires an affirmative finding that the chance for reversal is substantial. . . . [A] conviction is presumed to be correct.' ") (citation omitted); *United States v. Powell*, 761 F.2d 1227, 1233–34 (8th Cir. 1985) (en banc) (requiring "a close question" and not "simply that reasonable judges could differ"). If it is certain that, regardless of how the appellate proceedings are resolved, the defendant would have to return to prison, then there is no basis for release pending appeal. 18 U.S.C. § 3143(b)(1)(B)(iv); *United States v. LaGiglio*, 384 F.3d 925, 926 (7th Cir. 2004).

The procedural aspects of release in a criminal case pending appeal are stated in FRAP 9. Subsection (c) of that Rule confirms that the court's decision on release must be based on the statutory provisions noted above. *See id.* ("The court must make its decision regarding release in accordance with the applicable provisions of 18 U.S.C. §§ 3142, 3143, and 3145(c).").

CHAPTER 8
STANDARDS OF REVIEW

§ 8.1 OVERVIEW

There are few aspects more crucial to a successful appeal than understanding the appropriate standard of appellate review. The standard of review that applies to a given issue dictates how rigorously the appellate court will look at the issue—which is to say, how much deference it will give the district court or administrative agency's ruling.

In turn, that means that ascertaining the correct standard or standards of review is a critical early step in making the determination whether to appeal in the first place (and what issues to press on appeal): If, for example, the appellate standard of review for the issue in question is "abuse of discretion," a lawyer might properly advise his client that the chances of reversal on that particular issue will be slim. Conversely, if the appeal turns on a pure question of law, where review is *de novo*—meaning that the appellate court is required to give no deference to the trial court's ruling—the scope of that review will obviously be more favorable to an appellant.

The standard of review that applies to a given issue will also drive questions of brief writing and argument strategy. If an appeal presents a question of statutory construction (generally a question of law, and thus reviewed *de novo*), a lawyer might present the same arguments to the court of appeals as he or she did in the district court, with a lesser focus on the particular reasoning that the trial judge used in reaching the particular interpretation of the statute. By contrast, if there is any deference inherent in the standard of review (*e.g.*, clear-error review for factual findings or abuse-of-discretion review for evidentiary rulings), the arguments will have to be aimed more at the evidentiary record that was before the court, and at the judge's specific reasoning and ruling. (Of course, stating the proper standard of review for each issue is also a requirement for an appellant's brief under FRAP 28(a)(8)(B).)

Viewed in another way, questions of law that are subject to *de novo* review are those where there can be only one right answer; where deference is appropriate, however, that means there may well be a range of correct answers, any one of which might be upheld as proper in a given case.

The decision of what standard of review applies to a given issue is based on a mixture of practical, institutional, and policy decisions. In cases where the standard of review is unclear or in dispute, lawyers would be well advised to revert to these first principles as support for their preferred standard of review.

§ 8.2 PLAIN ERROR AND HARMLESS ERROR

As discussed earlier in this book (§ 3.6(B), *supra*), the plain-error standard of review comes into play when an issue has not been properly preserved for appeal. *See* Fed.R.Civ.P. 51(d)(2); Fed.R.Crim.P. 52. If an appellate court is presented with an improperly preserved issue, it may only reverse—and it is not obligated to reverse—if the error is "plain" (meaning clear or obvious), and if it affects substantial rights.

As also discussed earlier (§ 3.6(D), *supra*), an appellate court—even if it finds error in the trial court proceedings—will have no basis for reversing or vacating a judgment if the error is harmless, *i.e.*, "justice" does not "require[ ] otherwise," or the error does not "affect any party's substantial rights." *See* Fed.R.Civ.P. 61; Fed.R.Crim.P. 52(a).

§ 8.3 *DE NOVO* REVIEW (LEGAL RULINGS)

"For purposes of standard of review, decisions by judges are traditionally divided into three categories, denominated questions of law (reviewable *de novo*), questions of fact (reviewable for clear error), and matters of discretion (reviewable for 'abuse of discretion')." *Pierce v. Underwood*, 487 U.S. 552, 558 (1988).

In reviewing issues of law, the appellate court gives no explicit deference to the work of the trial court; such legal rulings are reviewed *de novo*. That rule is easy to state, but there are cases at the margins—often denominated as cases presenting "mixed questions of fact and law"—that present lawyers and judges with complicated and difficult questions regarding the proper standard of review.

A helpful discussion of the reasons why *de novo* review is appropriate in such a case presenting mixed questions is contained in the Supreme Court's opinion in *Ornelas v. United States*, 517 U.S. 690 (1996). In *Ornelas*, the Supreme Court held that determinations of probable cause and reasonable suspicion under the Fourth Amendment should be reviewed *de novo* by appellate courts, despite the fact that these questions typically present mixed questions of fact (what happened leading up to the stop or search?) and law (do those facts lead to the conclusion of a constitutional violation?). *Id.* at 696–97.

While not doubting that the underlying factual findings should be reviewed for clear error, the Court nonetheless held that the "ultimate determinations of reasonable suspicion and probable cause," based on the not-clearly-erroneous facts as found, should be reviewed *de novo*. Among the reasons the Court gave for this decision were:

- "A policy of sweeping deference would permit, '[i]n the absence of any significant difference in the facts,' 'the Fourth Amendment's incidence [to] tur[n] on whether different trial judges draw general conclusions that the facts are sufficient or insufficient to constitute probable cause.' Such varied results would be inconsistent with a unitary system of law." *Id.* at 697 (quoting Brinegar v. United States, 338 U.S. 160, 171 (1949)) (alterations in original).

- "In addition, the legal rules for probable cause and reasonable suspicion acquire content only through application. Independent review is therefore necessary if appellate courts are to maintain control of, and to clarify, the legal principles." *Id.* (citing *Miller v. Fenton*, 474 U.S. 104, 114 (1985)).

- "Finally, *de novo* review tends to unify precedent and will come closer to providing law enforcement officers with a defined 'set of rules which, in most instances, makes it possible to reach a correct determination beforehand as to whether an invasion of privacy is justified in the interest of law enforcement.'" *Id.* at 697–98 (quoting *New York v. Belton*, 453 U.S. 454, 458 (1981)).

The Court in *Salve Regina Coll. v. Russell*, 499 U.S. 225 (1991), gave a similar explanation for its decision to apply *de novo* appellate review to federal district court determinations of state-law issues, with an emphasis on the institutional distinctions between trial courts and appellate courts:

> Independent appellate review of legal issues best serves the dual goals of doctrinal coherence and economy of judicial administration. District judges preside alone over fast paced trials: Of necessity they devote much of their energy and resources to hearing witnesses and reviewing evidence. Similarly, the logistical burdens of trial advocacy limit the extent to which trial counsel is able to supplement the district judge's legal research with memoranda and briefs. . . . Courts of appeals, on the other hand, are structurally suited to the collaborative juridical process that promotes decisional accuracy. With the record having been constructed below and settled for purposes of the appeal, appellate

> judges are able to devote their primary attention to legal issues. As questions of law become the focus of appellate review, it can be expected that the parties' briefs will be refined to bring to bear on the legal issues more information and more comprehensive analysis than was provided for the district judge. Perhaps most important, courts of appeals employ multijudge panels that permit reflective dialogue and collective judgment.

Id. at 231–32 (citation omitted).

At the same time, though, the Court in *Salve Regina College* also emphasized that *de novo* review is not a "do over" in the appellate court. "Independent [*i.e.*, *de novo*] appellate review necessarily entails a careful consideration of the district court's legal analysis, and an efficient and sensitive appellate court at least will naturally consider this analysis in undertaking its review." *Id.* at 232. *See also Bose Corp. v. Consumers Union of U.S., Inc.*, 466 U.S. 485, 514 n.31 (1984) (emphasizing that legal determinations are not made *de novo* in the sense of "an original appraisal of all the evidence").

Rulings on motions to dismiss, motions for summary judgment, and motions for judgment as a matter of law are said to present questions of law, and their grant or denial is reviewed *de novo*. *See, e.g., St. Paul Mercury Ins. Co. v. Williamson*, 224 F.3d 425, 440 n.8 (5th Cir. 2000) (motions to dismiss and summary-judgment motions); *Zellner v. Summerlin*, 494 F.3d 344, 371 (2d Cir. 2007) (motions for judgment as a matter of law). Although these motions—particularly summary-judgment and JMOL motions—require an intensive review of the factual records, review is *de novo* because the courts are testing the legal sufficiency of the complaint (under Fed.R.Civ.P. 12(b)(6)), the legal sufficiency of the paper record (under Fed.R.Civ.P. 56), and the legal sufficiency of the trial evidence (under Fed.R.Civ.P. 50).

If the court of appeals corrects the legal standard on appeal, it is not free to find facts under the corrected legal ruling, *Icicle Seafoods, Inc. v. Worthington*, 475 U.S. 709, 713 (1986), but it can—in the context of a properly framed JMOL motion under Fed.R.Civ.P. 50—grant judgment as a matter of law under the corrected standard if the facts were found or undisputed and support such a judgment. *See, e.g., Neely v. Martin K. Eby Constr. Co.*, 386 U.S. 317, 325 (1967).

§ 8.4 CLEAR-ERROR REVIEW (FACTUAL FINDINGS)

Under Fed.R.Civ.P. 52(a)(6), "[f]indings of fact, whether based on oral or other evidence, must not be set aside unless clearly erroneous, and the reviewing court must give due regard to the trial court's opportunity to judge the witnesses' credibility." The Supreme Court has long defined the clear error standard in these terms: "A finding is 'clearly erroneous' when although there is evidence to support it, the reviewing court on the entire evidence is left with the definite and firm conviction that a mistake has been committed." *United States v. U.S. Gypsum Co.*, 333 U.S. 364, 395 (1948).

Although this standard is not entirely toothless, it is deferential to the trial judge's superior vantage point:

> If the district court's account of the evidence is plausible in light of the record viewed in its entirety, the court of appeals may not reverse it even though convinced that had it been sitting as the trier of fact, it would have weighed the evidence differently. Where there are two permissible views of the evidence, the factfinder's choice between them cannot be clearly erroneous.

Anderson v. City of Bessemer City, 470 U.S. 564, 573–74 (1985).

The Supreme Court has on many occasions explained the reasons for this deferential review of district court factfinding:

> The rationale for deference to the original finder of fact is not limited to the superiority of the trial judge's position to make determinations of credibility. The trial judge's major role is the determination of fact, and with experience in fulfilling that role comes expertise. Duplication of the trial judge's efforts in the court of appeals would very likely contribute only negligibly to the accuracy of fact determination at a huge cost in diversion of judicial resources. In addition, the parties to a case on appeal have already been forced to concentrate their energies and

> resources on persuading the trial judge that their account of the facts is the correct one; requiring them to persuade three more judges at the appellate level is requiring too much. As the Court has stated in a different context, the trial on the merits should be "the 'main event' . . . rather than a 'tryout on the road.' " For these reasons, review of factual findings under the clearly erroneous standard—with its deference to the trier of fact—is the rule, not the exception.

Id. at 574–75 (alteration in original) (citation omitted). *See also Salve Regina Coll.*, 499 U.S. at 233 (noting that the clear error standard is "[i]n deference to the unchallenged superiority of the district court's factfinding ability").

As noted above, "mixed questions" of fact and law present difficult questions as to the proper standard of review. "Rule 52(a) does not furnish particular guidance," and there is no "other rule or principle that will unerringly distinguish a factual finding from a legal conclusion." *Pullman Standard v. Swint*, 456 U.S. 273, 288 (1982).

Some cases of mixed questions of law and fact—like *Ornelas v. United States*, discussed in § 8.3, above—result in the ultimate determination being reviewed as a question of law. But others yield the result that the ultimate conclusion is too fact-bound to be reviewed as a matter of law, and is better reviewed as a question of fact.

In *Miller v. Fenton*, 474 U.S. 104 (1985), the Court noted that it had treated the question of juror bias—

a classically "mixed" question of fact and law—as a factual question, reviewable for clear error, despite "the intimate connection between such determinations and the constitutional guarantee of an impartial jury." *Id.* at 115. The Court explained the policy-driven reason why such an issue might be treated as a question of fact rather than one of law. "When, for example, the issue involves the credibility of witnesses and therefore turns largely on an evaluation of demeanor, there are compelling and familiar justifications for leaving the process of applying law to fact to the trial court and according its determinations presumptive weight." *Id.* at 114. (Ultimately, the Court in *Miller v. Fenton* held, consistent with the later reasoning of *Ornelas*, that the proper standard for reviewing trial court determinations of the voluntariness of a confession was to review it as a question of law, not a question of fact. *Id.* at 115–18.)

A line of decisions from earlier in the 20th century, with "an impressive genealogy," asserted that an appellate court may exercise *de novo* review over factual findings that are "not based on credibility determinations." *Anderson v. City of Bessemer City*, 470 U.S. at 574. *See, e.g., Orvis v. Higgins*, 180 F.2d 537 (2d Cir. 1950) ("If [the judge] decides a fact issue on written evidence alone, we are as able as he to determine credibility."). There is a certain logic to this position, based as it is on the institutional differences (or lack thereof) between trial and appellate courts. But it has been repeatedly rejected by the Supreme Court, *Pullman Standard v. Swint*, 456 U.S. 273, 287 (1982); *Anderson v. City of*

Bessemer City, 470 U.S. at 574–75, and properly so based on the text of Fed.R.Civ.P. 52(a), which, without exception, provides for clearly erroneous review of all findings of fact made in a bench trial. *See* Fed.R.Civ.P. 52(a)(6) ("Findings of fact, *whether based on oral or other evidence*, must not be set aside unless clearly erroneous . . .") (emphasis added).

Despite the fact that Fed.R.Civ.P. 52(a) applies, by its terms, only to judicial factfinding made after bench trials, the "clearly erroneous" standard of review applies to most all trial court factual findings, whether or not made in the context of a trial.

§ 8.5 ABUSE-OF-DISCRETION REVIEW

Much scholarly attention has been given to the question of trial-court discretion. *See, e.g.*, Henry J. Friendly, *Indiscretion About Discretion*, 31 Emory L.J. 747 (1982); Maurice Rosenberg, *Appellate Review of Trial Court Discretion*, 79 F.R.D. 173 (1978).

The topic of trial-court discretion seems to be such a fertile source for commentary (and for dispute) because it is difficult to even ascribe a definition to the term "discretion." Judge Friendly's seminal article said that "[m]ost definitions of discretion are not very helpful as applied to the problem of the power of a reviewing court." 31 Emory L.J. at 754. He catalogued some definitions offered by legal scholars—"the power to choose between two or more courses of action each of which is thought as permissible"; or where "no strict rule of law is applicable"—and then offered his own: "I find it more useful to say that the trial judge has discretion in those cases where his ruling will not be reversed simply because an appellate court disagrees. If this be circular, make the most of it!" *Id.*

The essence of the abuse-of-discretion standard, though, is deference to the judgment of the trial court. *See, e.g., Gen. Elec. Co. v. Joiner*, 522 U.S. 136, 143 (1997) ("deference . . . is the hallmark of abuse of discretion review"). The modern cases attempt to define the abuse-of-discretion standard in various ways. A common definition is this description: " 'A district court abuses its discretion when it applies the incorrect legal standard, misapplies the correct legal standard, or relies upon clearly erroneous findings of fact.' " *United States v. Pugh*, 405 F.3d 390, 397 (6th Cir. 2005) (citation omitted).

The late Judge Richard S. Arnold attempted to provide a little more content to the definition in his opinion for the Eighth Circuit in *Kern v. TXO Production Corp.*, 738 F.2d 968 (8th Cir. 1984):

> [W]hen we say a decision is discretionary, or that a district court has discretion to grant or deny a motion, we do not mean that the district court may do whatever pleases it. The phrase means instead that the court has a range of choice, and that its decision will not be disturbed as long as it stays within that range and is not influenced by any mistake of law. An abuse of discretion, on the other hand, can occur in three principal ways: when a relevant factor that should have been given significant weight is not considered; when an irrelevant or improper

> factor is considered and given significant weight; and when all proper factors, and no improper ones, are considered, but the court, in weighing those factors, commits a clear error of judgment. And in every case we as an appellate court must be mindful that the district courts are closer to the facts and the parties, and that not everything that is important about a lawsuit comes through on the printed page.

Id. at 970. But it is probably just as accurate to use Chief Justice Marshall's 200-plus-year-old description: "[A] motion to [a court's] discretion is a motion, not to its inclination, but to its judgment; and its judgment is to be guided by sound legal principles." *United States v. Burr*, 25 F. Cas. 30, 35 (C.C. Va. 1807).

Pierce v. Underwood, 487 U.S. 552 (1988), represents the Supreme Court's first modern attempt to offer an extended explanation of the abuse-of-discretion standard of review—even though the Court there disclaimed any ability to define the standard. *Id.* at 559 ("No more today than in the past shall we attempt to discern or to create a comprehensive test."). The issue there was the proper standard for reviewing a trial court's determination that the litigating position of the United States was not "substantially justified" for purposes of awarding fees under the Equal Access to Justice Act (EAJA), 28 U.S.C. § 2412(d). The lower courts had been divided on the issue—some viewing it as a question of law; others as a discretionary judgment on the part of the trial judge. *Id.* at 558. The Court—again relying on institutional and practical considerations, among others—determined that the proper standard was "abuse of discretion."

In particular, the Court found these factors relevant:

- Contrary to some other statutes, the EAJA did not explicitly prescribe a standard of review. *Id.* at 558.
- There was no historical tradition available from which the Court might have found clues to the proper standard of appellate deference. *Id.*
- The language of the statute—attorneys' fees should be awarded "unless the court finds that the position of the United States was substantially justified"—"suggests some deference to the district court upon appeal." *Id.* at 559.
- Another provision of the EAJA governed fees in agency adjudication, and prescribed a "substantial evidence" standard; "[w]e doubt that it was the intent of this interlocking scheme that a court of appeals would accord more deference to an agency's determination that its own position was substantially justified than to such a determination by a federal district court." *Id.*
- "[S]ome of the elements that bear upon whether the Government's position 'was substantially justified' may be known only to

the district court," such as, *e.g.*, "settlement conferences and other pretrial activities"; and "the district court may have insights not conveyed by the record, into such matters as whether particular evidence was worthy of being relied upon, or whether critical facts could easily have been verified by the Government." *Id.* at 560.

- "[E]ven where the district judge's full knowledge of the factual setting can be acquired by the appellate court, that acquisition will often come at unusual expense, requiring the court to undertake the unaccustomed task of reviewing the entire record." *Id.*

- A *de novo* review of the question whether a litigating position was "substantially justified" would "fail to produce the normal law clarifying benefits" of an appellate decision on a legal question, and might "effectively establish the circuit law in a most peculiar, secondhanded fashion." *Id.* at 560–61.

- " '[T]he sheer impracticability of formulating a rule of decision for the matter in issue [weighs in favor of an abuse of discretion standard]. Many questions that arise in litigation are not amenable to regulation by rule because they involve multifarious, fleeting, special, narrow facts that utterly resist generalization—at least, for the time being.' " *Id.* at 561–62 (quoting Maurice

Rosenberg, *Judicial Discretion of the Trial Court, Viewed From Above*, 22 Syracuse L. Rev. 635, 662–63 (1971)).

The several factors relied upon by the Court in *Pierce v. Underwood* illustrate not only the reasons why an "abuse of discretion" standard might govern appellate review of a particular issue, but also how that review is conducted. Where there are rules, standards, or precedents that govern the exercise of judicial discretion, discretion is thereby limited. Where a particular decision is governed by tests requiring the balancing of diverse, multifarious, or equitable factors, there will be a greater amount of discretion. As the Seventh Circuit has explained, "[t]here is discretion and then there is discretion. The scope of the district court's discretion is greatest when there is no strictly legal rule of decision, when there is no standard against which to compare the district court's decision. When there is no right answer, it becomes difficult to speak of 'error,' and the scope of review shrinks accordingly." *Metlyn Realty Corp. v. Esmark, Inc.*, 763 F.2d 826, 831 (7th Cir. 1985) (citations omitted).

While a comprehensive list of the sorts of rulings subject to abuse-of-discretion appellate review is beyond the scope of this book, several examples will serve to indicate the sorts of issues that are properly subject to abuse of discretion review. Note that many of these fall under the rubric of procedural or case-management rulings:

- Rulings admitting or excluding evidence. *Beech Aircraft Corp. v. Rainey*, 488 U.S. 153, 172 (1988).

- Rulings granting or denying leave to amend a complaint (but note that abuse of discretion is more freely found when amendment is denied). *Zenith Radio Corp. v. Hazeltine Research, Inc.*, 401 U.S. 321, 330–31 (1971).

- Rulings involving discovery. *Moorman v. UnumProvident Corp.*, 464 F.3d 1260, 1264 (11th Cir. 2006).

- Rulings on class-certification motions. *Gulf Oil Co. v. Bernard*, 452 U.S. 89, 103 (1981).

- Certificates under Fed.R.Civ.P. 54(b) that a partial final judgment is appropriate. *Curtiss Wright Corp. v. General Elec. Co.*, 446 U.S. 1, 10–11 (1980).

- Rulings on sanctions. *Cooter & Gell v. Hartmarx Corp.*, 496 U.S. 384 (1990); *Nat'l Hockey League v. Metrop. Hockey Club, Inc.*, 427 U.S. 639, 642 (1976).

- Rulings on attorneys' fees applications. *Hensley v. Eckerhart*, 461 U.S. 424, 437 (1983); *Highmark Inc. v. Allcare Health Mgmt. Sys., Inc.*, 134 S.Ct. 1744, 1747 (2014).

- Dismissals for *forum non conveniens*. *Piper Aircraft Co. v. Reyno*, 454 U.S. 235, 257 (1981).

- Decisions whether to grant a motion for voluntary dismissal without prejudice under Fed.R.Civ.P. 41(a)(1). *Kern v. TXO Production Corp.*, 738 F.2d 968, 970 (8th Cir. 1984).

- Decisions on equitable remedies, such as injunctive relief. *eBay Inc. v. MercExchange, L.L.C.*, 547 U.S. 388, 391, 394 (2006).

- Awards of enhanced damages under Section 284 of the Patent Act, 35 U.S.C. § 284. *Halo Electronics, Inc. v. Pulse Electronics, Inc.*, 136 S.Ct. 1923, 1934 (2016).

- Decisions involving criminal sentencing under the United States Sentencing Guidelines (after they were made non mandatory by the Supreme Court). *United States v. Booker*, 543 U.S. 220, 262 (2005); *Koon v. United States*, 518 U.S. 81, 96–98 (1996) (pre-*Booker*; abuse-of-discretion review for departures from the Guidelines).

- Decisions on intervention. *Georgia v. Ashcroft*, 539 U.S. 461, 476 (2003).

- Rulings on motions for new trial under Fed.R.Civ.P. 59(a). *Allied Chem. Corp. v. Daiflon, Inc.*, 449 U.S. 33, 36 (1980) (per curiam).

- Rulings on motions to vacate judgments under Fed.R.Civ.P. 60(b). *Plaut v. Spendthrift Farm, Inc.*, 514 U.S. 211, 233–34 (1995).

§ 8.6 REVIEW OF JURY VERDICTS

The U.S. Constitution grants the Supreme Court "appellate Jurisdiction, both as to Law and Fact." U.S. Const. art. III, § 2. But at the same time, the Seventh Amendment to the Constitution restricts that power by providing (for civil cases) that "[n]o fact tried by a jury, shall be otherwise reexamined in any Court of the United States, than according to the rules of the common law."

That said, appellate courts do engage in review of jury verdicts—most commonly when a district court is said to have erred by denying a post-judgment Fed.R.Civ.P. 50 motion for judgment as a matter of law. This is permissible, and not a violation of the Seventh Amendment, because it is said that appellate review in these circumstances is a legal question—whether the evidence presented at trial was a "legally sufficient evidentiary basis for a reasonable jury to have found for that party." Because this is a question of law, denials of such motions are reviewed *de novo* on appeal. *See, e.g.*, *Zellner v. Summerlin*, 494 F.3d 344, 371 (2d Cir. 2007).

That *de novo* standard, however, masks what is in practice a deferential standard of review, when the legal standard of Fed.R.Civ.P. 50 is applied: The appellate court " 'consider[s] the evidence in the light most favorable to the party against whom the motion was made and . . . give[s] that party the benefit of all reasonable inferences that the jury might have drawn in his favor from the evidence,' " while " 'disregard[ing] all evidence favorable to the moving party that the jury is not required to believe.' " *Id.* (quoting *Black v. Finantra Capital, Inc.*, 418 F.3d 203, 209 (2d Cir. 2005) (ellipsis in original) and *Reeves v. Sanderson Plumbing Prods., Inc.*, 530 U.S. 133, 151 (2000)). Still, most courts of appeals have rejected the standard that a "mere scintilla" of evidence will suffice to sustain a jury verdict, declaring instead that a verdict must be sustained by "substantial evidence." *See, e.g., PharmaStem Therapeutics, Inc. v. ViaCell, Inc.*, 491 F.3d 1342, 1360 (Fed. Cir. 2007) ("in reviewing the denial of the JMOL motion . . . we examine the evidence in the light most favorable to the verdict and determine whether a reasonable jury could have found all the facts necessary to support the verdict . . . *i.e.,* whether substantial evidence supports the verdict.") (citations omitted); *Peguero Moronta v. Santiago*, 464 F.3d 29, 45 (1st Cir. 2006) ("A non-moving party who bears the burden of proof . . . must have presented 'more than a mere scintilla of evidence in its favor' to withstand a motion for judgment as a matter of law.") (citation omitted); *Am. Home Assurance Co. v. United Space Alliance, LLC*, 378 F.3d 482, 486–87 (5th Cir. 2004) (court of appeals "can reverse a denial of a motion for JMOL only if the jury's factual findings are not supported by substantial evidence or if the legal conclusions implied from the jury's verdict cannot in law be supported by those findings") (citation omitted); *United Int'l Holdings, Inc. v. Wharf (Holdings) Ltd.*, 210 F.3d 1207, 1227 (10th Cir. 2000) ("When a jury verdict is challenged on appeal, our review is limited to determining whether the record—viewed in the light most favorable to the prevailing party—contains substantial evidence to support the jury's decision.") (citation and internal quotation marks omitted).

In the absence of a properly framed Rule 50 or Rule 59 motion, challenges to the sufficiency of the evidence are reviewed, if at all, only under the plain-error standard. *See, e.g.*, *BBA Nonwovens Simpsonville, Inc. v. Superior Nonwovens, LLC*, 303 F.3d 1332, 1338 (Fed. Cir. 2002); *U.S. for use of Wallace v. Flintco, Inc.*, 143 F.3d 955, 969 (5th Cir. 1998); *Image Tech. Servs., Inc. v. Eastman Kodak Co.*, 125 F.3d 1195, 1212 (9th Cir. 1997). It is highly doubtful that even plain-error review is available after the Supreme Court's decision in *Unitherm Food Sys., Inc. v. Swift-Eckrich, Inc.*, 546 U.S. 394 (2006), holding that the courts of appeals are "without power" to grant a new trial based on insufficient evidence in the absence of a proper Rule 50 or Rule 59 motion. *See id.* at 400–02 & n.4.

The denial of a motion for new trial under Fed.R.Civ.P. 59 is reviewed only for abuse of discretion. *Montgomery Ward & Co. v. Duncan*, 311 U.S. 243, 251–52 (1940). This limited standard of review arises from a recognition that a trial judge is in the best position to determine, based on the totality of the record, whether something so prejudicial or inconsistent with the interests of justice occurred at trial that necessitates a new trial. *See, e.g.*, *Caldarera v. Eastern Airlines, Inc.*, 705 F.2d 778, 781 (5th Cir. 1983) ("A trial judge is generally better able than an appellate court to evaluate the prejudice flowing from improper jury arguments. His denial of a motion for new trial based on improper statements is reversible only for abuse of discretion. The district judge . . . was best able to measure the impact of improper argument, the effect of the conduct on the jury, and the results of his efforts to control it.").

Further discussion of the appellate treatment of Rule 50 and 59 motions can be found in § 3.3(E), *supra*.

§ 8.7 REVIEW OF BENCH TRIALS

The standards for appellate review of bench trials in civil cases are guided by Fed.R.Civ.P. 52(a). Findings of fact made by the trial court are subject to clear-error review; the court's conclusions of law are (like most legal rulings) subject to *de novo* review. *See, e.g., Roanoke Cement Co., LLC v. Falk Corp.*, 413 F.3d 431, 433 (4th Cir. 2005) ("We review a judgment following a bench trial under a mixed standard of review—factual findings may be reversed only if clearly erroneous, while conclusions of law, including contract construction, are examined *de novo*.").

In criminal cases tried to the court, the trial evidence is evaluated *de novo*, to determine whether the verdict is supported by substantial evidence, in the same way as in a jury trial: " 'In passing upon the sufficiency of the evidence to sustain an ultimate finding of guilt following a bench trial, we apply the same standard of review that is applied where a defendant has been found guilty by a jury; that is to say, the finding must be sustained if it is supported by substantial evidence.' On review, we will consider the evidence in the light most favorable to the guilty verdict." *United States v. Erhart*, 415 F.3d 965, 969 (8th Cir. 2005) (quoting *United States v. Barletta*, 565 F.2d 985, 991 (8th Cir. 1977)). A defendant does not have to make a motion for judgment of acquittal under Fed.R.Crim.P. 29 to preserve a sufficiency of the evidence challenge for appeal. *See, e.g., United States v. Grace*, 367 F.3d 29, 34 (1st Cir. 2004).

These standards are explained in greater detail in §§ 8.3 and 8.4, *supra*.

§ 8.8 REVIEW OF AGENCY DECISIONS

The Administrative Procedure Act (APA) "empowers federal courts to 'hold unlawful and set aside agency action, findings, and conclusions' if they fail to conform with any of six specified standards." *Marsh v. Or. Nat. Res. Council*, 490 U.S. 360, 375 (1989) (quoting 5 U.S.C. § 706(2)). In full, 5 U.S.C. § 706 provides:

> To the extent necessary to decision and when presented, the reviewing court shall decide all relevant questions of law, interpret constitutional and statutory provisions, and determine the meaning or applicability of the terms of an agency action. The reviewing court shall
>
> (1) compel agency action unlawfully withheld or unreasonably delayed; and
>
> (2) hold unlawful and set aside agency action, findings, and conclusions found to be

> (A) arbitrary, capricious, an abuse of discretion, or otherwise not in accordance with law;
>
> (B) contrary to constitutional right, power, privilege, or immunity;
>
> (C) in excess of statutory jurisdiction, authority, or limitations, or short of statutory right;
>
> (D) without observance of procedure required by law;
>
> (E) unsupported by substantial evidence in a case subject to sections 556 and 557 of this title or otherwise reviewed on the record of an agency hearing provided by statute; or
>
> (F) unwarranted by the facts to the extent that the facts are subject to trial de novo by the reviewing court.
>
> In making the foregoing determinations, the court shall review the whole record or those parts of it cited by a party, and due account shall be taken of the rule of prejudicial error.

Id. There can be no judicial review of agency action, however, if "statutes preclude judicial review," 5 U.S.C. § 701(a)(1), or if "agency action is committed to agency discretion by law." 5 U.S.C. § 701(a)(2).

The two most familiar standards of review that are peculiar to administrative adjudication are the "substantial evidence" standard (for factual findings by administrative bodies) and the "arbitrary and capricious" standard (for some factual findings and most policy judgments made by agencies). In addition, the principle of "*Chevron* deference"—introduced into the law by the Supreme Court in *Chevron U.S.A., Inc. v. Natural Res. Def. Council, Inc.*, 467 U.S. 837 (1984)—has allowed courts reviewing administrative action to defer to agencies' interpretations of law, notwithstanding 5 U.S.C. § 706's command "that the reviewing court shall decide all relevant questions of law." The "substantial evidence" standard—which, as discussed in § 8.7, *supra*, has crept into the realm of judicial review of district court decisions—has long been described by the Supreme Court as requiring "more than a mere scintilla. It means such relevant evidence as a reasonable mind might accept as adequate to support a conclusion." *Consol. Edison Co. of N.Y. v. NLRB*, 305 U.S. 197, 229 (1938). As the Supreme Court has later elaborated, that standard "does not mean a large or considerable amount of evidence," but enough to persuade "a reasonable mind." *Pierce v. Underwood*, 487 U.S. 552, 564–65 (1988).

Under the similar "arbitrary and capricious" standard, "a reviewing court may not set aside an agency rule that is rational, based on consideration of the relevant factors and within the scope of the authority delegated to the agency by the statute." *Motor Vehicle Mfrs. Ass'n v. State Farm Mut. Auto Ins. Co.*, 463 U.S. 29, 42 (1983). "[T]he agency must examine the relevant data and articulate a satisfactory explanation for its action including a 'rational connection between the facts found and the choice made.'" *Id.* at 43 (quoting *Burlington Truck Lines, Inc. v. United States*, 371 U.S. 156, 168 (1962)). An agency rule will be found to be "arbitrary and capricious" where, among other things, "the agency has relied on factors which Congress has not intended it to consider, entirely failed to consider an important aspect of the problem, offered an explanation for its decision that runs counter to the evidence before the agency, or is so implausible that it could not be ascribed to a difference in view or the product of agency expertise." *Id.*

There are facial similarities between "arbitrary and capricious" review of administrative action and "abuse of discretion" review of judicial action. But they are different (as the statute suggests by naming each separately, *see* 5 U.S.C. § 706(2)(A)), and the differences are important. For one, arbitrary and capricious review requires the agency to articulate the reasons for its rule somewhere in the record. *See, e.g., SEC v. Chenery Corp.*, 332 U.S. 194, 196 (1947); 5 U.S.C. § 553(c) ("the agency shall incorporate in the rules adopted a concise general statement of their basis and purpose"). By contrast, discretionary decisions of trial courts are often made without reasoned explanation, especially trial rulings that are made, of necessity, "on the fly." *See, e.g., United States v. Mitchell*, 365 F.3d 215, 233 (3d Cir. 2004) ("The vast majority of evidentiary rulings are made on the fly and without written findings of fact, yet this Court routinely affords deference to such judgments.").

This discussion highlights a fundamental difference between review of agency action and review of judicial action. Agencies are part of the Executive Branch, and are charged with execution of the Nation's laws. As a result, judicial review of administrative agencies must respect separation-of-powers concerns. That is the principal lesson of *SEC v. Chenery Corp.*, 318 U.S. 80 (1943), which holds that a court may not uphold an agency's action on a ground that is different than that supplied by the agency itself. *Id.* at 93–94 (". . . [T]he Commission's order cannot be upheld. Its action must be measured by what the Commission did, not by what it might have done. . . . There must be such a responsible finding.").

Finally, as noted, there is the rule of *Chevron* deference, so named because of its origin in the Supreme Court's 1984 decision in *Chevron U.S.A., Inc. v. Natural Res. Def. Council, Inc.*, 467 U.S. 837. The *Chevron* doctrine was stated by the Court in these terms:

> When a court reviews an agency construction of the statute which it administers, it is confronted with two questions. First, always, is the question whether Congress has directly spoken to the precise question at issue. If the intent of Congress is clear, that is the end of the matter; for the court, as well as the agency, must give effect to the unambiguously expressed intent of Congress. If, however, the court determines Congress has not directly addressed the precise question at issue, the court does not simply

> impose its own construction on the statute, as would be necessary in the absence of an administrative interpretation. Rather, if the statute is silent or ambiguous with respect to the specific issue, the question for the court is whether the agency's answer is based on a permissible construction of the statute.
>
> * * *
>
> If Congress has explicitly left a gap for the agency to fill, there is an express delegation of authority to the agency to elucidate a specific provision of the statute by regulation. Such legislative regulations are given controlling weight unless they are arbitrary, capricious, or manifestly contrary to the statute. Sometimes the legislative delegation to an agency on a particular question is implicit rather than explicit. In such a case, a court may not substitute its own construction of a statutory provision for a reasonable interpretation made by the administrator of an agency.

Id. at 842–44 (footnotes omitted).

Critics of the *Chevron* approach have argued that this rule of deference runs contrary to the congressional command of 5 U.S.C. § 706, that "the reviewing court shall decide all relevant questions of law," and also contrary to the command of *Marbury v. Madison*, 5 U.S. (1 Cranch) 137, 177 (1803), that "[i]t is emphatically the province and duty of the judicial department to say what the law is." The *Chevron* standard has been the subject of proposals for legislative change, as well as judicial criticism, *see, e.g.*, *Gutierrez-Brizuela v. Lynch*, 834 F.3d 1142, 1149–57 (10th Cir. 2016) (Gorsuch, J., concurring), each on the ground that it takes too much of the legislative power and improperly reassigns it to the executive branch's administrative agencies. Nonetheless, absent an amendment to the APA, *Chevron* not only is here to stay, but is being applied to an increasing number of agency determinations.

Whether *Chevron* deference applies to a particular agency action is often the focus of dispute and litigation; many law review articles have attempted to provide coherence to its application, with limited success. *See, e.g.*, Thomas W. Merrill, *Judicial Deference to Executive Precedent*, 101 Yale L.J. 969 (1992). The exceptions to *Chevron* deference—or, perhaps more accurately, the areas where *Chevron* deference will not be given—tend to "reflect a desire to limit *Chevron* in accordance with its original justifications to those situations in which the agency has legitimate expertise, where congressional delegation may be appropriately inferred, and where the agency interpretation is likely to constitute a good faith effort to implement the overall congressional design." Timothy B. Dyk & David Schenck, *Exceptions to* Chevron, Admin. L. News, Winter 1993, at 1, 16.

If *Chevron* deference is inappropriate in a given case, a lesser level of deference—so-called *Skidmore* deference—may be appropriate. *See Skidmore v. Swift & Co.*, 323 U.S. 134 (1944). Statutory "[i]nterpretations such as those in opinion letters—

like interpretations contained in policy statements, agency manuals, and enforcement guidelines, all of which lack the force of law—do not merit *Chevron* style deference." *Christensen v. Harris Cty.*, 529 U.S. 576, 587 (2000). Rather, those informal interpretations are only subject to *Skidmore* deference: Such interpretations, "while not controlling upon the courts by reason of their authority, do constitute a body of experience and informed judgment to which courts and litigants may properly resort for guidance. The weight of such a judgment in a particular case will depend upon the thoroughness evident in its consideration, the validity of its reasoning, its consistency with earlier and later pronouncements, and all those factors which give it power to persuade." *Skidmore*, 323 U.S. at 140. The Supreme Court has held that "*Chevron* did nothing to eliminate *Skidmore*'s holding." *United States v. Mead Corp.*, 533 U.S. 218, 234 (2001).

§ 8.9 REVIEW OF DISTRICT-COURT DETERMINATIONS OF STATE LAW

Under *Erie R. Co. v. Tompkins*, 304 U.S. 64 (1938), federal courts in diversity cases must apply the forum state's substantive law. In this context, the issue has arisen whether the federal appellate court should give deference to the district court's determination of state law. In *Salve Regina Coll. v. Russell*, 499 U.S. 225 (1991), the Supreme Court held that no deference should be given, and that the district court's determination of state law should be reviewed de novo. The Court concluded that "deferential appellate review invites divergent development of state law among the federal trial courts even within a single State." *Id.* at 234.

The Court rejected the argument that district judges possessed more expertise on matters of state law because they frequently presided over diversity cases. "[T]he bases of state law are as equally communicable [by the parties] to the appellate judges as they are to the district judge," and there is "no sense in which a district judge's prior exposure or nonexposure to the state judiciary can be said to facilitate the rule of reason." *Id.* at 239.

At the same time, however, the Supreme Court has in the past deferred to constructions of state law rendered by the relevant regional court of appeals: "In dealing with issues of state law that enter into judgments of federal courts, we are hesitant to overrule decisions by federal courts skilled in the law of particular states unless their conclusions are shown to be unreasonable." *Propper v. Clark*, 337 U.S. 472, 486–87 (1949) (citing cases). *See also Bishop v. Wood*, 426 U.S. 341, 346 n.10 (1976).

§ 8.10 REVIEW OF DISTRICT-COURT DETERMINATIONS OF FOREIGN LAW

In a world where cross-border transactions are increasingly common, foreign law may well supply a rule of decision in a case tried in U.S. courts. Under Fed.R.Civ.P. 44.1, district courts may determine the content of foreign law by "consider[ing] any relevant material or source, including testimony, whether or not submitted by a party or admissible under the Federal Rules of Evidence." Rule 44.1 further provides that "[t]he court's determination [of foreign law] must be treated as a ruling on a question of law." As a result, the federal courts have held that questions of foreign law are reviewed *de novo* on appeal. *See, e.g., Karaha Bodas Co., L.L.C. v. Perusahaan Pertambangan Minyak Dan Gas Bumi Negara ("Pertamina")*, 313 F.3d 70, 80 (2d Cir. 2002); *SEC v. Dunlap*, 253 F.3d 768, 777 (4th Cir. 2001).

Prior to the adoption of Rule 44.1 in 1966, foreign law was understood to present a question of fact, which would "be proved like other facts." *Church v. Hubbart*, 6 U.S. (2 Cranch) 187, 187 (1804) (Marshall, C.J.). The content of foreign law was to be "proved at trial and reviewed on appeal only for clear error." *Rationis Enters. Inc. of Panama v. Hyundai Mipo Dockyard Co.*, 426 F.3d 580, 585 (2d Cir. 2005). However, treating other nations' law like a fact, while treating U.S. (and U.S. states') law as questions of law, was an affront to comity, and the 1966 amendments to the Federal Circuit Rules of Civil Procedure changed that divergent approach.

The unique practice under Rule 44.1 can present curious issues for appellate courts, largely because the content of foreign law is still "proved," at least in part, by the same instruments used to prove facts—declarations and testimony. Justice Holmes long ago observed that contemplating a foreign legal system from the outside may cause it to appear "like a wall of stone." *Diaz v. Gonzalez*, 261 U.S. 102, 106 (1923). In large part, this is because of judges' (and lawyers') familiarity with the Anglo-American legal system and its nuances, and their concomitant unfamiliarity with those foreign legal systems. Yet Rule 44.1's basic command—some might say fiction—is that U.S. judges should be equally competent at ascertaining, and reviewing, foreign law, even though the content of that law may be as alien to them as the unique facts of each case.

Still, there are meaningful procedural and practical differences. Ordinary legal determinations involving U.S. law are made by courts, predominantly based on publicly available information (laws, case decisions) and the arguments of counsel. Moreover, there is no prohibition upon citing new cases and authorities on appeal that were not cited in the trial court, and it is rare that evidence-like materials (such as the "testimony" specifically permitted by Rule 44.1) are allowed in the mine run of cases in order to establish a proposition of U.S. or state law. By contrast, where the content of foreign law is at issue, it is often supplied by affidavit, or live testimony—the typical conduits for the proof of facts, not law.

And, it might be the case that a party seeking to prove that the district court's ruling of foreign law was incorrect (or correct) would wish to supply new legal materials, including affidavits, to the appellate court for consideration. Should this practice of late filed affidavits in the appellate court be allowed? Some courts have forbidden it, on the grounds that Rule 44.1 is also concerned with "notice," and that it is unfair to allow such late-injected materials into a case on appeal. *See, e.g.*, *DP Aviation v. Smiths Aerospace & Def. Sys. Ltd.*, 268 F.3d 829, 847–48 (9th

Cir. 2001). Other courts of appeals hold that they may consider foreign law materials that were not presented to the district court, in the same way that litigants may cite additional judicial decisions or other authorities on appeal, even though those authorities were not cited in the trial court. *See, e.g.*, *Grupo Protexa, S.A. v. All Am. Marine Slip*, 20 F.3d 1224, 1239 & n.23 (3d Cir. 1994); *Mobile Marine Sales, Ltd. v. M/V Prodromos*, 776 F.2d 85, 89 (3d Cir. 1985); *Kalmich v. Bruno*, 553 F.2d 549, 552 (7th Cir. 1977).

A lengthy—and informative—exploration of some of the challenges inherent in applying Rule 44.1 can be found in the Ninth Circuit's opinion in *de Fontbrune v. Wofsy*, 838 F.3d 992, 996–1000 (9th Cir. 2016), which comes down emphatically on the side of treating questions of foreign law like any other question of U.S. or U.S. State law. The court held that "Rule 44.1 authorizes district courts to consider foreign legal materials outside the pleadings in ruling on a motion to dismiss" "where foreign law provides the basis for the claim." *Id.* at 994, 996.

CHAPTER 9

THE RECORD ON APPEAL

§ 9.1 COMPOSITION

FRAP 10(a) sets out three categories of items that comprise the "record on appeal": "(1) the original papers and exhibits filed in the district court; (2) the transcript of proceedings, if any; and (3) a certified copy of the docket entries prepared by the district clerk." *Id.* This Rule is subject to certain limited exceptions, as described in § 9.5, *infra.* It is worth emphasizing at the outset that FRAP 10's purpose is not to allow the parties to provide the appellate court with new evidence. Instead, the Rule is meant to ensure that the record on appeal correctly reflects the record that was before the district court. *See also* § 3.5, *supra.*

§ 9.2 THE TRANSCRIPT

RULE 10(b) describes the parties' obligations with respect to obtaining and providing the appellate court with a transcript of the district court proceedings. Under FRAP 10(b)(1), "[w]ithin 14 days after filing the notice of appeal or entry of an order disposing of the last timely remaining motion of a type specified in [FRAP] 4(a)(4)(A), whichever is later, the appellant must: do either of the following": (A) order (in writing) a transcript from the court reporter "of such parts of the proceedings not already on file as the appellant considers necessary," or (B) "file a certificate stating that no transcript will be ordered." *Id.*

How much of the record is needed in a given case will depend in large part on the arguments the appellant seeks to make on appeal. In general, an appellant who "intends to urge on appeal that a finding or conclusion is unsupported by the evidence or is contrary to the evidence . . . "must include in the record a transcript of all evidence relevant to that finding or conclusion." FRAP 10(b)(2).

By its terms, FRAP 10(b)(3) (entitled "Partial Transcript") only comes into play where the appellant does not order the entire transcript. In that event, the appellant must, within the 14-day period specified in FRAP 10(b)(1), "file a statement of the issues that the appellant intends to present on the appeal," and serve the appellee with a copy of the transcript order (or a certificate that no transcript will be ordered). FRAP 10(b)(3)(A). The appellee then has 14 days to designate additional parts of the record that the appellant considers necessary. FRAP 10(b)(3)(B). If the appellant fails to order the additional portions within a subsequent 14-day period, the appellee may either order those portions itself, or "move in the district court for an order requiring the appellant to do so." FRAP 10(b)(3)(C).

When a party orders a transcript, it must, "[a]t the time of ordering, . . . make satisfactory arrangements with the reporter for paying the cost of the transcript." FRAP 10(b)(4). Failing to do so may result in a forfeiture of the appellant's claims, especially any challenge to the sufficiency of the evidence. *See, e.g.*, *Fogle v. Roadway Express, Inc.*, 10 Fed. Appx. 267, 268 (6th Cir. 2001). For a fuller understanding of when a violation of Rule 10(b) will—and will not—result in a forfeiture of appellant's claims, *compare Roberts v. Ferman*, 826 F.3d 117, 121–22 (3d Cir. 2016) *with Lehman Bros. Holdings, Inc. v. Gateway Funding Diversified Mtge. Servs., L.P.*, 785 F.3d 96, 101 (3d Cir. 2015).

§ 9.3 UNAVAILABILITY OF THE TRANSCRIPT

Subsection (c) of FRAP 10 sets forth the process for providing a record on appeal when the proceedings in the district court were not recorded or the transcript is otherwise "unavailable" (*e.g.*, the court reporter lost the notes of the proceeding). In these circumstances, Rule 10(c) permits the appellant to "prepare a statement of the evidence or proceedings from the best available means, including the appellant's recollection." That statement must then be served on appellee, who has 14 days to respond by "serv[ing] objections or proposed amendments[.]" *Id.* The district court must then resolve any disputes before approving the statement for inclusion in the record. Id.; *see also United States v. Todd*, 287 F.3d 1160, 1162 (D.C. Cir. 2002); *United States v. Krynicki*, 689 F.2d 289, 291 n.3 (1st Cir. 1982).

It should also be noted that a number of courts have held that a party's inability to pay for a transcript does not make the transcript "unavailable" within the meaning of FRAP 10(c). Rather, the applicability of Rule 10(c) has been limited to situations "where the record of the trial court proceedings is physically unobtainable." *Thomas v. Computax* Corp., 631 F.2d 139, 142 (9th Cir. 1980); *accord, e.g., Richardson v. Henry*, 902 F.2d 414, 415–16 (5th Cir. 1990).

Note that a district court's disposition of a Rule 10(c) motion is a final order under 28 U.S.C. § 1291, and is reviewable for abuse of discretion. *United States v. Caramadre*, 807 F.3d 359, 376–77 (1st Cir. 2015). As a practical matter, however, because a district judge may appropriately rely on the judge's own recollection in order to approve, reject, or modify a Rule 10(c) statement, appellate review is likely to be exceedingly deferential.

§ 9.4 AGREED STATEMENT

In lieu of the record on appeal, the parties "may prepare, sign, and submit to the district court a statement of the case showing how the issues presented by the appeal arose and were decided in the district court." FRAP 10(d). Under that rule, "[t]he statement must set forth only those facts averred and proved or sought to be proved that are essential to the court's resolution of the issues." Assuming the statement is truthful, the district court must approve it and certify it to the court of appeals (along with any additions that the district court deems necessary for a "full presentation of the issues on appeal") as the record on appeal. *See McLaurin v. Cole*, 46 Fed. Appx. 802, 805 (6th Cir. 2002) (unpublished).

§ 9.5 CORRECTIONS AND SUPPLEMENTATION

FRAP 10(e) permits correction or modification of the record below in two limited circumstances. First, if the parties disagree "about whether the record truly discloses what occurred in the district court, the difference must be submitted to and settled by that court and the record conformed accordingly." FRAP 10(e)(1). Second, "[i]f anything material to either party is omitted from or misstated in the record by error or accident, the omission or misstatement may be corrected and a supplemental record may be certified and forwarded" by stipulation of the parties, by the district court (even if after the record was forwarded to the appellate court), or by the court of appeals. FRAP 10(e)(2)(A)–(C). Apart from these two circumstances, "[a]ll other questions as to the form and content of the record must be presented to the court of appeals." FRAP 10(e)(3). *See, e.g., Salinger v. Random House,* 818 F.2d 252, 253 (2d Cir. 1987) (adding trial judge's marked copy of trial exhibit to the record).

Of course, if the proposed supplemental material is simply a different format of what was considered below (for example, an indisputably accurate transcript of a tape that was heard by the judge or jury), then supplementation would not be creating new material. But this latter situation is relatively rare. For instance, one court has held—in a case with "facts . . . so unique that they could originate only in the District of Puerto Rico"—that an English transcript of a tape played to the jury in the original

Spanish could not be added to the record under FRAP 10(e) because the opposing party disputed the accuracy of the translation. *United States v. Rivera-Rosario,* 300 F.3d 1, 4, 9 (1st Cir. 2002).

In addition, as one court noted, an appeals court may "take judicial notice" and "exercise inherent authority to supplement the record in extraordinary cases." *Lowry v. Barnhart*, 329 F.3d 1019, 1024 (9th Cir. 2003). *See also, e.g., Dakota Industries, Inc. v. Dakota Sportswear, Inc.*, 988 F.2d 61, 63 (8th Cir. 1993) (court's "authority to enlarge a record is rarely exercised and is a narrow exception to the general rule that an appellate court may consider only the record made before the district court"). The latter ground is rarely utilized; courts do so only when the interests of justice compel the court to include something that was not before the district court.

In all circumstances, however, "[o]nly the court may supplement the record"; the parties may not do it unilaterally or even by agreement. *Lowry, supra,* at 1024. As the *Lowry* court explained, a party seeking supplementation "should proceed by motion or formal request so that the court and opposing counsel are properly apprised of the status of the documents in question." *Id.* at 1025.

A party attempting to add materials to the record without seeking permission or obtaining a stipulation under FRAP 10(e)(2) may be subject to sanctions. In *Lowry*, for example, the Ninth Circuit found a "particularly serious violation" and awarded the opposing party reasonable attorneys' fees incurred in making the motion to strike the improper extra-record materials. *Id.* at 1025–26 & n.8.

§ 9.6 FORWARDING THE RECORD

Under FRAP 11(a), the appellant must, in addition to complying with FRAP 10(b), "do whatever else is necessary to enable the clerk to assemble and forward the record." As noted in § 9.2, *supra*, because the burden is on the appellant to compile the record on appeal, if the record fails to support appellant's claim, appellant cannot prevail.

The duties of the reporter and district court are set forth at length in FRAP 11(b). First, the reporter must prepare and file a transcript when one is ordered. Upon receiving an order, the reporter is required to "enter at the foot of the order the date of its receipt and the expected completion date and send a copy, so endorsed, to the circuit clerk." FRAP 11(b)(1)(A). If the reporter cannot complete the transcript within 30 days, the reporter may ask the circuit court clerk to grant additional time. (The clerk must then note on the docket the response to the request and so inform the parties.) FRAP 11(b)(1)(B). The court reporter must file "the completed transcript" with the district court clerk and notify the circuit court clerk of that filing. FRAP 11(b)(1)(C). If the reporter cannot complete the transcript in a timely manner, "the circuit clerk must notify the district judge and do whatever else the court of appeals directs." FRAP 11(b)(1)(D). A reporter who fails to comply with FRAP 11 may be subject to sanctions. *Matter of Holloway*, 884 F.2d 476, 477–78 (9th Cir. 1989).

Upon completion of the record, "the district clerk must number the documents constituting the record and send them promptly to the circuit clerk together with a list of the documents correspondingly numbered and reasonably identified." FRAP 11(b)(2). The clerk shall not send to the appellate court unusually bulky physical exhibits (other than documents) unless directed by a party or by the circuit court clerk. *Id.*

By stipulation or order of the district court on motion, the parties may retain the record temporarily in the district court for use in preparing their appellate filings. FRAP 11(c). Also, the appellate court may determine (by order or local rule) that only a certified copy of the docket entries be sent to the appellate court, as opposed to the entire record. In that event, a party may request that designated portions of the record be sent to the appellate court. FRAP 11(e)(1). The district court may also order that it shall retain some or all of the record during the pendency of the appeal, subject to the right of the appellate court to instruct that the record be transferred. FRAP 11(e)(2). The parties may also stipulate that portions of the record remain in the district court (subject to request by the appellate court). FRAP 11(f).

Under FRAP 11(g), if prior to the forwarding of the record a party moves in the appellate court for dismissal, release, stay pending appeal, additional security on the appeal or supersedeas bond, or "any other immediate order," the district court clerk must send to the appellate court "any parts of the record designated by any party."

A proposed amendment to FRAP 11(g) would replace "supersedeas bond" with "bond or other security provided to obtain a stay of judgment" to conform to a parallel amendment in Fed.R.Civ.P. 62(b)(2). Preliminary Draft of Proposed Amendments to the Federal Rules of Appellate, Bankruptcy, Civil, and Criminal Procedure, Aug. 2016, at 25–26, *available at* http://www.uscourts.gov/sites/default/files/2016-08-preliminary_draft_of_rules_forms_published_for_public_comment_0.pdf.

§ 9.7 DOCKETING THE APPEAL

For the most part, FRAP 12 deals with the duties of the circuit clerk. FRAP 12(a) provides that it is the duty of the clerk of the court of appeals to docket the appeal "under the title of the district-court action" and to "identify the appellant, adding the appellant's name if necessary." This is when the court of appeals provides its own docket number for the case. The "under the title of the district-court action" provision means that, in most cases, the title of the action will be the same on appeal as in the district court. According to the Advisory Committee Notes to the original Rule 12(a), this was intended to ease "future reference and citation and location of cases in indexes." (Note that at the U.S. Supreme Court level, however, the title of the action often changes, with the petitioner or appellant always listed first.)

FRAP 12(b) is the only part of Rule 12 imposing an obligation on attorneys. It provides that, "unless the court of appeals designates another time," the attorney who filed the notice of appeal in the district court has 14 days to file a representation statement—"a statement . . . naming the parties that the attorney represents on appeal." FRAP 12(b). In many circuits, the representation statement is, by local rule, combined with the notice of appearance or the corporate disclosure statement. Some circuits also impose the additional requirement of a "docketing statement," which may require a carefully detailed statement of the bases for district-court and federal appellate jurisdiction. *See, e.g.*, 7th Cir. R. 3(c).

Finally, FRAP 12(c) makes it the duty of the circuit clerk, upon receipt, to file the record (or partial record, or district clerk's certificate) as provided in FRAP 11, and to "immediately" notify the parties of the fact. Of course, it is the appellant's duty to facilitate the district court's transmission of the record to the circuit court under FRAP 11, and, as noted in §§ 9.2 and 9.6, *supra*, the failure of the appellant to do so can result in a forfeiture of the right to appeal.

CHAPTER 10

SPECIAL RULES FOR REVIEW OF BANKRUPTCY, TAX COURT, AND ADMINISTRATIVE AGENCY ORDERS

§ 10.1 INTRODUCTION

The Federal Rules of Appellate Procedure contain special provisions addressing the practice of the courts of appeals in appeals in bankruptcy cases (FRAP 6), appeals from the U.S. Tax Court (FRAP 13–14), and petitions for review or enforcement of administrative agency orders (FRAP 15–20). Each of these rules, or sets of rules, takes the same general approach—each provides that the Federal Rules of Appellate Procedure generally apply, sets forth the FRAP provisions that do not apply, and provides for special rules applicable to those classes of cases. This chapter is limited to addressing the particular provisions of the rules that apply to each of these classes of cases.

§ 10.2 BANKRUPTCY APPEALS

The major reason that FRAP 6 is even necessary lies in the unique nature of the U.S. Bankruptcy Courts. Bankruptcy judges are not "Article III judges," in that they serve for a term of 14 years (28 U.S.C. § 152(a)(1)), and may be removed by the judicial council of each circuit for "incompetence, misconduct, neglect of duty, or physical or mental disability" (28 U.S.C. § 152(e)); they do not receive the lifetime appointments (technically, appointments that last "during good Behaviour," U.S. Const., Art. III, § 1) that are guaranteed to the Article III federal judiciary. Bankruptcy judges nonetheless are considered to be "a unit of the district court" (28 U.S.C. § 151), and as "judicial officers of the United States district court established under Article III of the Constitution." 28 U.S.C. § 152(a)(1).

One of the special features of bankruptcy litigation is that appeals in bankruptcy cases can go directly from the district court to the court of appeals, or they can take one of two other appellate routes before reaching the court of appeals. Under 28 U.S.C. § 158(a), the federal district courts have limited appellate jurisdiction to hear appeals from bankruptcy courts. Alternatively, a bankruptcy case may be appealed to a bankruptcy appellate panel established in the circuit under 28 U.S.C. § 158(b) (and composed of bankruptcy judges from within the circuit). FRAP 6(b) provides that a final decision from either type of tribunal may be appealed to the appropriate court of appeals.

If the appeal is from a district court ruling, where the district court was exercising original jurisdiction under 28 U.S.C. § 1334, the appeal proceeds as though it were any other appeal in a civil case. FRAP 6(a). If the appeal is from a district court or bankruptcy appellate panel exercising appellate jurisdiction, then FRAP 6(b) applies. FRAP 6(b)(2)(A) sets forth specific provisions regarding the timing of notices of appeal when rehearing is sought in an appellate bankruptcy case under the bankruptcy rules, and FRAP 6(b)(2)(B) has special provisions regarding redesignation of the record on appeal from an appellate decision; these latter provisions recognize that "[a]fter an intermediate appeal [in the district court], a party may well narrow the focus of its efforts on the second appeal and a redesignation of the record may eliminate unnecessary material." Advisory Committee Notes to 1989 addition of FRAP 6.

FRAP 6(b)(1) sets forth the specific exceptions to the general applicability of the Federal Rules of Appellate Procedure for appeals from bankruptcy appellate decisions.

§ 10.3 TAX COURT APPEALS

Under FRAP 13 and 14, appeals from decisions of the U.S. Tax Court proceed in much the same fashion as appeals from a U.S. district court, with the following significant exceptions:

- The notice of appeal must be filed within 90 days of entry of the Tax Court's decision (FRAP 13(a)(1)).
- If a timely appeal is filed, any other party may file a notice of appeal within 120 days of entry of the Tax Court's decision (*id.*).
- Unlike an ordinary notice of appeal under FRAP 4(a), the postmark date of a mailed notice of appeal is deemed to be the date of filing (FRAP 13(a)(2); 26 U.S.C. § 7502).

A section of the Internal Revenue Code, 26 U.S.C. § 7482(b), specifies the appropriate circuit for an appeal from a Tax Court decision to be taken. Although that subsection contains a number of provisions separately applicable to different kinds of taxpayers, it generally provides that the proper venue for an appeal from a Tax Court decision is the circuit within which the taxpayer resides or has his principal office or principal place of business. Alternatively, the parties can stipulate to a different venue. 26 U.S.C. § 7482(b)(2); *Maloof v. Comm'r*, 456 F.3d 645, 652 (6th Cir. 2006).

FRAP 14 sets forth the rules that do not apply to appeals from Tax Court decisions (FRAP 4, 6–9, 15–20, and 22–23), while providing that "[a]ll other provisions of these rules . . . apply to appeals from the Tax Court." *Id.*

§ 10.4 ADMINISTRATIVE AGENCY ORDERS—REVIEW AND ENFORCEMENT

FRAP 15 sets forth the procedure for petitioning a court of appeals for review of an administrative agency's order, as well as the procedure for an agency to petition a court of appeals for enforcement of the agency's order. Although the governing jurisdictional statute relevant to the particular agency may refer to the document initiating court of appeals review as a "petition for review" or as a "notice of appeal," the Federal Rules of Appellate Procedure refer to such documents collectively as a "petition for review." FRAP 15(a)(1).

Petition for Review. The content requirements for a petition for review are similar to those for a notice of appeal under FRAP 3(c). A petition for review must name each party seeking review, either in the caption or in the body of the petition. Here, however, unlike the 1993 amendments to FRAP 3(c), use of terms like "petitioners," "respondents," or "*et al.*" are ineffective. FRAP 15(a)(2)(A); *cf.* § 5.2, *supra.* The petition must also "name the agency as a respondent," and "specify the order or part thereof to be reviewed." FRAP 15(a)(2)(B), (C).

Application for Enforcement. Alternatively, the agency itself might seek to have the court of appeals enforce its order, via an application or cross-application for enforcement. FRAP 15(b). Such an application is available only if the court of appeals is "authorized to enforce the order" by statute. FRAP 15(b)(1). The content requirements for such an application are quite different and more involved than for a petition for review: It "must contain a concise statement of the proceedings in which the order was entered, the facts upon which venue was based, and the relief requested." FRAP 15(b)(3). The respondent has 21 days to file an answer to the application, and if the respondent defaults by failing to answer in time, "the court will enter judgment for the relief requested." FRAP 15(b)(2).

Timing. The statute authorizing court of appeals review or enforcement is the source of any timing requirements for a petition for review or application for enforcement. Because such statutory timing requirements would be jurisdictional, FRAP 26(b)(2) forbids the court of appeals from extending the time for the filing of such a document.

Where to File. Unlike a notice of appeal, a petition or application under Rule 15 is filed in the court of appeals specified by statute. FRAP 15(a)(1); FRAP 15(b)(1). The fees, likewise, are paid to the court of appeals clerk. FRAP 15(e). FRAP 15(c) provides that the clerk takes care of service of a petition or application under this rule, as under FRAP 3(d).

Intervention. If the applicable statute or statutes permit intervention, a potential intervenor must file a motion (or notice, if intervention is allowed as of right rather than by the discretion of the court of appeals) within 30 days of the filing of the petition for review; it "must contain a concise statement of the interest of the moving party and the grounds for intervention." FRAP 15(d); *cf.* § 6.4, *supra.* A motion to intervene is not jurisdictional, and so an untimely motion to intervene may be granted upon an appropriate showing of good cause and excusable neglect. *Canadian Tarpoly Co. v. U.S. Int'l Trade Comm'n*, 649 F.2d 855, 857 (C.C.P.A. 1981); *Krupp Int'l, Inc. v. U.S. Int'l Trade Comm'n*, 644 F.2d 869, 872 (C.C.P.A. 1981).

The Record. The record in an administrative review action consists of "the order involved"; "any findings or report on which it is based"; and "the pleadings, evidence, and other parts of the proceedings before the agency." FRAP 16(a)(1)–(3). Under FRAP 16(b), an omission or misstatement in the record can be corrected by stipulation of the parties, or by the direction of the court, which may also order the preparation and filing of a supplemental record. The court's power in this respect is somewhat constrained, however, by principles of separation of powers and appropriate respect for the proper institutional roles of executive agencies and federal courts, respectively. *Cf. E.I. du Pont de Nemours & Co. v. Collins*, 432 U.S. 46, 56–57 (1977) (reversing where court of appeals had employed a university professor to help it interpret the record materials and noting that such an approach "clearly departed from [the court's] statutory appellate function"). FRAP 17 contains directions to the agency regarding the preparation and filing of the record.

Stays. FRAP 18 provides that a court may grant a stay pending review of the agency's order. The language and standards of FRAP 18 are substantially similar to the language and standards of FRAP 8, respecting stays of district court orders pending appeal. *See* § 7.5, *supra.*

Settling Judgments Enforcing Agency Orders in Part. FRAP 19 provides that where a court of appeals determines to enforce an agency order only in part, the agency must file and serve on the opposing party a proposed judgment conforming to the opinion within 14 days. The opposing party, if it disagrees, may file its own version within 10 days, and the court will thereafter settle the issue without further briefing or argument. The apparent purpose of this rule—which is unique to appellate review of agency action—is to allow the agency to shape the revised ruling in the first instance, consistent with separation-of-powers concerns and respect for the proper roles of the agency and the courts. The court's ultimate entry of judgment after this FRAP 19 procedure is followed is the judgment under FRAP 36 that will trigger further deadlines, *e.g.*, for filing a petition for rehearing, or for filing a petition for certiorari. *See* FRAP 36; § 17.1, *infra*.

FRAP 20 lists the provisions of the Federal Rules of Appellate Procedure that *do not* apply to the review and enforcement of an agency order (FRAP 3–14 and 22–23).

CHAPTER 11

RULES GOVERNING FILING, SERVICE, TIME LIMITS, AND CORPORATE DISCLOSURE

§ 11.1 FILING OF DOCUMENTS

FRAP 25(a) is a relatively simple rule, but it requires close attention, lest a lawyer's assumptions result in an inadvertent forfeiture of substantial rights. FRAP 25(a)(2)(A) sets forth the default rule, that a paper is not timely unless received by the clerk before the deadline set for filing. FRAP 25(a) then excepts briefs and appendices from this rule, which are timely filed when mailed via first class U.S. mail ("or other class of mail that is at least as expeditious"), or when "dispatched to a third party commercial carrier," *e.g.*, UPS or FedEx, "for delivery to the clerk within 3 days." FRAP 25(a)(2)(B)(i), (ii). And because of the special disabilities of incarcerated persons, their filings are deemed timely if accompanied by either (i) a declaration or notarized statement stating the date the paper was deposited in the institution's mail system and that first-class postage is prepaid, or (ii) evidence (such as a postmark or date stamp) showing that the paper was deposited and the postage prepaid. FRAP 25(a)(2)(C)(i)–(ii). Alternatively, the court of appeals has discretion to permit the later filing of a declaration or notarized statement that otherwise meets the Rule's requirements. FRAP 25(a)(2)(C)(iii).

Litigants have effectively forfeited cases by erroneously assuming that a notice of appeal or petition for review was deemed filed upon mailing. *See, e.g., Ludgood v. Apex Marine Corp. Ship Mgmt.*, 311 F.3d 364, 367–68 (5th Cir. 2002) (per curiam) (dismissing appeal where notice of appeal was mailed the day before the deadline expired, but received by clerk after expiration); *Felt v. Dir., Office of Workers' Comp. Programs*, 11 F.3d 951, 952 (9th Cir. 1993) (dismissing, for lack of jurisdiction, petition for review mailed on last day of period for filing and received by the clerk after the deadline). Similarly, even though FRAP 25(a) excepts briefs and appendices from the "received by the clerk" rule for filing, that exception does not apply to petitions for rehearing and rehearing *en banc*; those documents must be actually received by the clerk prior to the deadline. *See, e.g., Ludgood*, 311 F.3d at 367 n.2; FRAP 40(a)(1).

Every court of appeals provides for electronic filing of documents 24 hours a day, seven days a week (except for routine or emergency maintenance), through the Case Management/Electronic Case Files system (CM/ECF), as permitted by FRAP 25(a)(2)(D). Attorneys must be registered with the circuit to use the system. Information on individual circuits' e-filing requirements, procedures, manuals, and other pertinent information is available on the individual court home pages (links to each court's website may be found through the United States Courts home page, at www.uscourts.gov). An electronic filing constitutes a "written paper" where required by the rules, such that where electronic filing is allowed, the date and time of electronic uploading of the document constitutes the date and time of filing for purposes of deadlines. FRAP 25(a)(2)(D).

Proposed amendments to FRAP 25 would "establish . . . a new national rule that generally makes electronic filing mandatory" while recognizing "exceptions for persons proceeding without an attorney, exceptions for good cause, and variations established by local rule." Preliminary Draft of Proposed Amendments to the Federal Rules of Appellate, Bankruptcy, Civil, and Criminal Procedure, Aug. 2016, at 37, *available at* http://www.uscourts.gov/sites/default/files/2016-08-preliminary_draft_of_rules_forms_published_for_public_comment_0.pdf. The proposed amendments would further "establish national rules regarding the methods of signing and serving electronic documents" and would "dispense with the requirement of proof of service for electronic filings." *Id.*

§ 11.2 SERVICE OF DOCUMENTS

FRAP 25 sets forth the requirement, applicable in all litigation, that any filed paper must also be served on all parties, unless a rule requires service by the clerk (such as with a notice of appeal or petition for review). FRAP 25(b). Unrepresented parties must be served themselves; represented parties must be served via counsel. *Id.*

FRAP 25(c) sets forth the manner of service allowed by the rule. A paper may be served personally, which includes delivery to a responsible person at the office of counsel. Alternatively, a paper may be served by mail, by commercial carrier (so long as delivery is for within three calendar days), or by electronic means (so long as the party being served consents to such service, in writing). FRAP 25(c)(1)(A)–(D). The ECF systems generate a "notice of docket activity"—an email message containing a hyperlink to the document filed—whenever a document is filed with the court. Under local court rules, this notice provides immediate electronic service to parties registered with the court's filing system. *See, e.g.*, 11th Cir. Guide to Electronic Filing 7.2.

"When reasonable considering such factors as the immediacy of the relief sought, distance, and cost," counsel "must" serve other counsel in the case at least as expeditiously as it makes filings with the court. FRAP 25(c)(3). As much as this is a mandate of the federal appellate rules, it is also driven by considerations of professionalism and civility. For example, it would be highly inappropriate for a Cincinnati-based counsel to file by hand a motion with the Sixth Circuit (which is located in Cincinnati) seeking an immediate stay of a district court's injunction, while serving opposing counsel in Los Angeles by first class mail. In that circumstance, it would be appropriate for the Cincinnati counsel to serve his opposing Los Angeles counsel with a faxed or emailed copy of his motion, with a hard copy to follow by overnight courier.

FRAP 25(c)(4) provides that service (not filing) by mail or commercial carrier is complete upon mailing or delivery to the carrier. Service by electronic means is completed by transmission, unless the party making the service is notified that the paper was not received by the party served. *Id.* This provision is important for, among other things, calculating the due date for filing of responsive briefs, whose due dates are calculated based on "service" of the opposing party's brief. *See, e.g.*, FRAP 31(a) (providing, *inter alia*, that "[t]he appellee must serve and file a brief within 30 days after the appellant's brief is served").

Finally, pursuant to FRAP 25(d), each document filed with the court must contain a proof of service. That proof can be an acknowledgement by the party being served, but more commonly, it is a certification by the person who made service certifying (i) the date and manner of service; (ii) the name(s) of the persons served; and (iii) their addresses, fax numbers, email addresses, etc., as appropriate to the manner of delivery. With respect to briefs or appendices, the certification must also state the date and manner by which the document was mailed or dispatched to the clerk.

§ 11.3 COMPUTING AND EXTENDING TIME

FRAP 26 sets forth general provisions regarding computation and extension of time limits. As for computing time limits, FRAP 26(a) was amended in 2009 to provide that all deadlines stated in days, regardless of the length, are computed in the same way. Previously, time periods of less than 11 days did not include weekends or holidays, leading to unnecessary complications and counterintuitive results: *e.g.*, a 14-day period might well expire before a 10-day period. Advisory Comm. Note to 2009 Amendments to FRAP 26(a)(1).

Under amended FRAP 26(a), the day of the event that triggers the deadline is not counted. All other days, including weekends and legal holidays, are counted. If the due date lands on a weekend or legal holiday, "the period continues to run until the end of the next day that is not a Saturday, Sunday, or legal holiday." FRAP 26(a)(1)(C). Likewise, if the clerk's office is inaccessible on the last day for filing, the time is extended to the first accessible day that is not a weekend or legal holiday. FRAP 26(a)(3)(A). A clerk's office might be inaccessible due to causes such as weather, or an outage of the electronic filing system. Advisory Committee Note to 2009 Amendments to FRAP 26(a)(3). Only an official closure of a clerk's office is generally considered as rendering it "inaccessible," thereby extending deadlines, and even then, the untimely filer may have to justify why electronic filing was not an option. *See, e.g., Chao Lin v. U.S. Atty. Gen.*, 677 F.3d 1043, 1045–46 (11th Cir. 2012) (dismissing petition for review because, while inclement weather delayed commercial carrier's delivery, clerk's office was open and appellants also could have filed electronically).

The FRAP sets both forward-looking time periods, requiring something to be done within a certain time *after* an event (*e.g.*, notice of appeal after judgment is entered), and backward-looking time periods, requiring an act at least a period of time *before* an event (*e.g.*, filing a reply brief before scheduled oral argument). If the last day for filing falls on a weekend or holiday, the "next day" is determined by continuing to count in the same direction, *i.e.*, counting forward and delaying the deadline when the period is measured after an event, and counting backward and making the deadline earlier when measured before an event. *See* Advisory Comm. Note to 2009 Amendments to FRAP 26(a)(5).

Under the 2009 amendments, a "legal holiday" is defined as one of the 10 statutory federal holidays; "any day declared a holiday by the President or Congress;" and "any other day declared a holiday by the state where either of the following is located: the district court that rendered the challenged judgment or order, or the circuit clerk's principal office." FRAP 26(a)(6)(A)–(C). For purposes of FRAP 26(a)(6)(C), however, state holidays are legal holidays only "for periods that are measured after an event"—not for periods measured back from an event. The Advisory Committee Notes to the 2009 amendments explain:

> For forward-counted deadlines, treating state holidays the same as federal holidays extends the deadline. Thus, someone who thought that the federal courts might be closed on a state holiday would be safeguarded against an inadvertent late filing. In contrast, for backward-counted deadlines, not giving state holidays the treatment of federal holidays allows filing on the state holiday itself rather than the day before.

Advisory Comm. Note to 2009 Amendments to FRAP 26(a)(6). This distinction aims to "protect those who may be unsure of the effect of state holidays" on filing deadlines against inadvertent late filing. *Id.*

Under the 2009 amendments to FRAP 26(a)(4), the time of day by which papers must be filed depends on the manner of filing. Thus, with respect to electronically filed papers, unless local rules, a statute, or court order sets a different deadline, papers may be filed electronically before midnight of the last day (in the time zone of the district court or of the circuit clerk's principal office); documents filed by mail may be filed on the due date at the latest time the post office, commercial carrier, or prison mailing system accepts papers for delivery; and documents filed in person may be filed on the due date in the court clerk's office before scheduled closing. FRAP 26(a)(4)(A)–(D). Local rules will sometimes address issues that arise if a single district has clerk's offices in different time zones, or offers a drop box that date-stamps documents filed after normal office hours. Furthermore, if a filer uses a drop box maintained by a commercial carrier, the "last day" ends at the time of that drop box's last scheduled pickup. Advisory Comm. Note to 2009 Amendments to FRAP 26(a)(4).

FRAP 26(b) provides that the courts of appeals, upon a showing of "good cause," have the power to "extend the time prescribed by these rules or by its order to perform any act, or may permit an act to be done after that time expires." Courts of appeals may not, however, extend the time for filing a notice of appeal (except under the terms provided in FRAP 4, *see* § 5.3(A), *supra*), a petition for permission to appeal, or a petition for review (however denominated by the governing statute), unless the law otherwise allows such an extension to be granted by the court of appeals. *See* § 10.4, *supra*.

Finally, FRAP 26(c) sets forth a rule that adds three extra days for an action when the time for acting runs from service, and the service was made by any means other than personal delivery. Under a 2016 amendment to the Federal Rules of Appellate Procedure, papers served electronically are now—contrary to prior practice—treated as delivered in person on the stated date of service, so they do not receive the added three days. FRAP 26(c). The Committee Notes to the amendment explain that "advances in technology and widespread skill in using electronic transmission" have "substantially alleviated" the concerns about delayed transmissions and "incompatible systems" that gave rise to the previous version of the Rule.

Note that this rule applies only to time periods that run from the date of service, such as the due date for a brief under FRAP 31(a); it does not, for example, extend the time for filing a notice of cross appeal, which is "14 days after the date when the first notice was filed." FRAP 4(a)(3) (emphasis added).

Thus, to give an example of the application of all of these rules: If the certificate of service on an appellant's brief indicates that it was served by mail on Tuesday, January 14, 2014, FRAP 31(a)(1) would provide that the appellee's brief would be due "within 30 days after the appellant's brief is served." Thirty days from January 14 would be Thursday, February 13, 2014. Service of appellant's brief by mail, however, entitles the appellee to an additional three days under FRAP 26(c). That would move the due date to Sunday, February 16, 2014, but FRAP 26(a)(3) provides that the last day cannot be a weekend or holiday. The next day, Monday, February 17, 2014, is Presidents' Day (known officially as "Washington's Birthday," which is one of the specified holidays in FRAP 26(a)(4)), so the due date for the appellee's brief is the next non-weekend, non-holiday day, or Tuesday, February 18, 2014.

§ 11.4 CORPORATE DISCLOSURE STATEMENTS

Under FRAP 26.1(a), any "nongovernmental corporate party" must file with the court of appeals a statement that "identifies any parent corporation and any publicly held corporation that owns 10% or more of its stock"; if there is no such corporation, the statement must make that clear. The reason for this disclosure is to provide a statement that allows judges to make an informed decision regarding recusal. *See* Advisory Committee Notes to 1989 Addition of FRAP 26.1. *Cf.* § 14.2, *infra*. Unless a court's local rules provide otherwise, the statement must be filed with the first filed brief, motion, response, petition, or answer in the court of appeals. FRAP 26.1(b). The statement must be supplemented whenever the information changes. *Id.* There is great variety among the circuits as to the form and requirements of this statement, so it is imperative to consult and follow the local rules.

CHAPTER 12
MOTIONS

§ 12.1 MOTIONS

FRAP 27 guides motion practice before the federal appellate courts. The Rule provides that "[a]n application for an order or other relief is made by motion, unless these rules prescribe another form," and that a "motion must be in writing unless the court permits otherwise." FRAP 27(a)(1). Additionally, subsection (e) provides that a "motion will be decided without oral argument unless the court orders otherwise." FRAP 27(e).

§ 12.2 GENERAL REQUIREMENTS FOR MOTIONS

Under FRAP 27(a)(2)(A), "[a] motion must state with particularity the grounds for the motion, the relief sought, and the supporting legal argument necessary to support it." If an affidavit or other paper is necessary to support the motion, it must be served and filed with the motion. FRAP 27(a)(2)(B)(i). If a motion seeks "substantive relief"—*e.g.*, a motion to dismiss or otherwise determine an appeal—the motion "must include a copy of the trial court's opinion or agency's decision as a separate exhibit." FRAP 27(a)(2)(B)(iii).

All motion papers—motions, responses, and replies—must be printed in black on "light paper" 8½ by 11 inches in size; their text must have margins of at least one inch on all sides (the page numbers—but nothing else—may be in the margins); must be double spaced (although quotations more than two lines long may be indented and single spaced, and headings and footnotes may be single spaced); must bear the caption of the case (a cover is permitted but not required) and contain "a brief descriptive title indicating the purpose of the motion and identifying the party or parties for whom it is filed"; must be bound in a secure manner, in a way that does not obscure the text, and the binding must allow the document to "lie reasonably flat when open"; and must be set in a type that is in a "plain, roman style" with serifs (if proportionally spaced). FRAP 27(d)(1); FRAP 32(a)(5) and 32(a)(6).

Under the 2016 amendments to FRAP 27(d)(2), the Rule's former page limits have now been supplemented by with type-volume limits (*i.e.*, limits stated in terms of number of words or lines of text) for all papers produced using a computer: motions and responses are limited to 5,200 words, and replies limited to 2,600 words. FRAP 27(d)(2)(A), (C). Page limits (20 pages; 10 pages) remain for handwritten or typewritten documents. FRAP 27(d)(2)(B), (D). The corporate disclosure statement and other documents required by FRAP 27(a)(2)(B) do not count toward these limits. FRAP (d)(2).

An original and three copies of all motion papers must be filed with the court of appeals unless the court directs otherwise. FRAP 27(d)(3). Motion papers must be accompanied by proof of service. FRAP 25(d). In addition, some circuits by local rule require the parties to meet and confer prior to the filing of a motion, and further require the movant to include a statement to this effect (as well as a statement whether the other party will oppose the motion and file a response). *See, e.g.*, Fed. Cir. R. 27(a)(5).

§ 12.3 RESPONSES TO MOTIONS

"Any party may file a response to a motion." FRAP 27(a)(3)(A). A response "must be filed within 10 days after service of the motion, unless the court shortens or extends the time." *Id.* However, a motion for a procedural order (including a motion to extend time under FRAP 26(b)) may be granted at any time, without even awaiting a response. Motions under FRAP 8 (stay or injunction pending appeal), 9 (release pending appeal in criminal cases), 18 (stay pending review of administrative cases), or 41 (issuance or stay of mandate) may be granted before the 10-day period runs, but only if the court gives "reasonable notice to the parties" that it intends to act sooner. FRAP 27(a)(3)(A).

The requirements of FRAP 27(a)(2) also apply to responses to motions (grounds and relief sought, accompanying documents, etc.). In addition, a response to a motion may contain a request for affirmative relief on behalf of the respondent, but the title of the response must alert the court that the response is also requesting relief. FRAP 27(a)(3)(B).

§ 12.4 REPLIES IN SUPPORT OF MOTIONS

"Any reply to a response must be filed within 7 days after service of the response." FRAP 27(a)(4).

The Rule strictly limits the scope of any such reply, stating that a "reply must not present matters that do not relate to the response." *Id.*

§ 12.5 PROCEDURAL ORDERS

As noted above, the court may act on a motion for a procedural order at any time—even before a response has been filed. FRAP 27(b). The rule provides that a party aggrieved by such court action may file a motion to reconsider, vacate, or modify that action; the rule further provides that a late filed opposition (*i.e.*, one filed after the court has acted) does not constitute a motion to reconsider, etc.; "a motion requesting that relief must be filed." *Id.*

§ 12.6 POWER OF A SINGLE JUDGE

A single judge has the power to entertain and act upon a motion, except that a single judge may not dismiss or otherwise determine a case. FRAP 27(c). Any ruling made by a single judge may be reviewed by a panel of the court, or the court *en banc*. *See id.* ("The court may review the action of a single judge."); *see also, e.g., Fieldturf, Inc. v. Sw. Recreational Indus., Inc.*, 357 F.3d 1266, 1268 (Fed. Cir. 2004) ("A motion to dismiss denied by the order of a single judge, however, does not become the law of the case.").

CHAPTER 13

BRIEFS

§ 13.1 FORMAL REQUIREMENTS

FRAP 32 contains the requirements for the form of briefs, including length limits, layout specifications, and physical production details such as the color of the cover and binding requirements. Even in an age of universally available electronic filing, courts still require paper filings, and these formal requirements remain important. A court that accepts electronic filings of briefs may also, by local rule, require paper copies to be mailed, dispatched to a third-party commercial carrier, or delivered to the clerk's office the next business day. *See, e.g.*, 4th Cir. R. 25(a). Other courts delay submission of the required paper copies until ordered by the clerk. *See, e.g.*, 9th Cir. R. 31–1; Fed. Cir. R. 31(b).

There are significant local variations on the federal rules' requirements. *Compare, e.g.*, 10th Cir. R. 32(a) (Court "prefers 14-point type, . . . but 13-point type is acceptable") *with* 7th Cir. R. 32(b) ("A brief is acceptable if proportionally spaced type is 12 points or larger in the body of the brief, and 11 points or larger in footnotes."). FRAP 32(e) provides that "[e]very court of appeals must accept documents that comply with the form requirements of [Rule 32]," but also that, "[b]y local rule or order in a particular case a court of appeals may accept documents that do not meet all of the form requirements of [FRAP 32]." *Id.*

A. FORMATTING THE BRIEF

The brief must be printed with clear black images on light-colored opaque and unglazed paper, on one side only (thereby enabling judges and clerks to use the blank side for notes). Photographs, illustrations, and tables may be reproduced by any method yielding a good copy. FRAP 32(a)(1).

The brief must be printed on 8½ by 11 inch paper, double-spaced (except for quotes longer than two lines, which may be indented and single-spaced), with single-spaced headings and footnotes. FRAP 32(a)(4). Margins must be at least an inch on all four sides; only page numbers may appear in the margins. *Id.*

The typeface of a brief may be either "proportionally spaced" or "a monospaced face." FRAP 32(a)(5). The Advisory Committee Notes to the 1998 Amendments to Rule 32 explain the distinction between the two kinds of typefaces:

> A proportionally-spaced typeface gives a different amount of horizontal space to characters depending upon the width of the character. [For example, a] capital "M" is given more horizontal space than a lower case "i". [FRAP 32(a)(5)(A)] requires that a proportionally-spaced typeface have serifs. Serifs are small horizontal or vertical strokes at the ends of the lines that make up the letters and numbers. Studies have shown that long passages of serif type are easier to read and

> comprehend than long passages of sans-serif type. * * *
>
> A monospaced typeface is one in which all characters have the same advance width. That means that each character is given the same horizontal space on the line. A wide letter such as a capital "M" and a narrow letter such as a lower case "i" are given the same space. * * *

Adv. Comm. Notes to 1998 Amendments to FRAP 32(a)(5). A proportionally spaced typeface "must be 14-point or larger." FRAP 32(a)(5)(A). A monospaced typeface, by contrast, "may not contain more than 10 ½ characters per inch." FRAP 32(a)(5)(B). Note, however, that as contemplated by FRAP 32(e), individual circuits can deviate from Rule 32's stated requirements. For example, as noted above, the Seventh Circuit's Local Rule 32 allows a smaller type size than the Federal Rules would otherwise permit. *See* 7th Cir. R. 32(b) ("A brief is acceptable if proportionally spaced type is 12 points or larger in the body of the brief, and 11 points or larger in footnotes."). A font is proportionally spaced when, as in this book, some letters are narrower than others; "I" takes less space than "M." In typewriter-style monospaced fonts, such as Courier, each letter takes the same amount of space. Some circuits allow smaller font sizes, including the Seventh (12 points in the body, 11 points in footnotes, if proportionally spaced, *see* 7th Cir. R. 32(b)), and the Tenth (14-point type is preferred, but 13-point type is acceptable, *see* 10th Cir. R. 32(a)).

The typeface must be a "plain, roman style." Italics and boldface "may be used for emphasis," and "[c]ase names must be italicized or underlined." FRAP 32(a)(6). These may sound like just technical requirements, but producing a readable brief is crucial to getting the points in a case across to the judges. The Seventh Circuit's Practitioner's Handbook for Appeals (*available at* http://www.ca7.uscourts.gov/Rules/handbook.pdf) contains an extensive discussion of this topic, including some specific tips for practitioners. *See id.* at 128–34 (section entitled Requirements and Suggestions for Typography in Briefs and Other Papers). For a helpful, and thoughtful, guide to making briefs' form support their function, *see* Matthew Butterick, *Typography for Lawyers* (2d ed. 2015).

B. COVERS AND BINDING

The color of the cover is specified by the Federal Rules: blue for appellant, red for appellee, green for intervenor or *amicus*, gray for reply, and tan for any supplemental brief. FRAP 32(a)(2). (The appellant's combined response and reply brief in a cross-appeal must have a yellow cover. FRAP 28.1(d).) The cover must contain certain specified information, including the case number (top, center), name of court, title of case, nature of proceeding, title of brief (with identity of party filing), and name, office location, and phone number for the filing party's counsel. FRAP 32(a)(2). Binding must be "secure," must "not obscure the text," and must "permit[ ] the brief to lie reasonably flat when open." FRAP 32(a)(3).

The "lie reasonably flat when open" requirement typically means spiral binding (rather than VeloBinding), although some courts' local rules express preferences that should be honored. *See, e.g.*, Fed. Cir. R. 32 Practice Note ("The court prefers . . . that a ring-type binding, plastic or metal, or a binding that protrudes from the front and back covers (*e.g.*, VeloBind) not be used; and that any externally positioned staple be covered with tape."); 7th Cir. R. 32(a) ("A brief need not comply with the portion of [FRAP] 32(a)(3) requiring it to 'lie reasonably flat when open.' A brief's binding is acceptable if it is secure and does not obscure the text.").

C. LENGTH OF BRIEFS

The rules contain specific requirements for page length. FRAP 32(a)(7) recognizes three ways to measure a brief's length: by number of pages, *see* FRAP 32(a)(7)(A); by number of words, *see* FRAP 32(a)(7)(B)(i); or by the number of lines of text, *see id.* Word processing programs provide quick and accurate word counts (for example, in Microsoft Word, one can simply highlight the text, and then click on "Tools" and "Word Count").

Under FRAP 32(a)(7), a "principal brief" (appellant's opening brief or appellee's response brief) is limited to 30 pages, unless it "uses a monospaced face and contains no more than 1,300 lines of text" or "contains no more than 13,000 words." FRAP 32(a)(7)(A), (B). A reply brief is limited to half the length of the principal brief: 15 pages, 650 lines of text or 6,500 words, depending on the measure used. *Id.* Headings, footnotes, and quotations count towards these limits but the corporate disclosure statement, tables of citation and authority, statement regarding oral argument, statutory, regulatory or rule addendum, and certificates of counsel do not count. FRAP 32(a)(7)(B)(iii). An attorney who selects a type-volume limit instead of the page limit must file a certificate, based on a word or line count of the word processing program, specifying the length of the brief. FRAP 32(g)(1).

When a case involves a cross-appeal, somewhat different page or type/volume restrictions apply. Each of the appellant's two briefs (the principal brief and the response-and-reply brief) is allowed 30 pages, 1,300 lines, or 13,000 words. The appellee's principal and response brief is allowed 35 pages, 1,500 lines or 15,300 words, and his reply brief (limited to the issues raised on his cross-appeal) 15 pages, 650 lines, or 6,500 words. FRAP 28.1(e).

These word limits, which were adopted in the 2016 amendments to the FRAP, are more stringent than the pre-2016 word limits (14,000 words for an appellant's opening brief or an appellee's response brief, 7,000 words for reply brief, and 16,500 words for an appellee's principal and response brief in a cross-appeal). This reduction in 2016 was not without controversy, however. *See* Elizabeth Olson, *Judges Push Brevity in Briefs, and Get a Torrent of Arguments*, N.Y. Times (Oct. 3, 2016). The 2016 amendments, however, also allow appellate courts to vary these limits by local rule. FRAP 32(e). And, as of the publication of this edition, the Second, Seventh, Ninth, and Federal Circuits have retained the previous word limits. *See* 2d Cir. R. 32.1(a)(4); 7th Cir. R. 32(c); 9th Cir. R. 32–1(a)–(b); Fed. Cir. R. 32(a).

Failure to comply with length requirements can subject the lawyer to possible sanctions, as *DeSilva v. DiLeonardi*, 181 F.3d 865 (7th Cir. 1999), illustrates. The appellants filed a brief with a certificate representing that it contained 13,824 words, but the Seventh Circuit said that "[o]ur check reveals that the certificate is false," and that the brief actually included 15,056 words, well over the 14,000-word maximum. *Id.* at 867 n.†. Counsel were ordered to show cause why they should not be sanctioned for disobeying the type-volume rules, and for filing a false statement with the court. *Id. See also, e.g.*, *Kano v. Nat'l Consumer Co-op. Bank*, 22 F.3d 899, 899 (9th Cir. 1994) (fining attorney $1,500 for filing a brief that met FRAP 32(a)'s 50-page limit only by using one-and-a-half- instead of the required double spacing; the court estimated that the brief "was the equivalent of at least sixty-five pages in length").

Parties may move for permission to file briefs in excess of FRAP 32's length limits. Convincing a court to grant such a motion, however, is no easy task: courts make clear that such motions are discouraged, absent "extraordinary and compelling reasons." 11th Cir. Rule 32–4. That means convincing the court that the issues are unusually complex or novel, such that they require longer treatment. Excessively long briefs are generally not well received. *See* § 13.8(1), *supra.* By way of illustration, motions to exceed the limits—usually by at least 20 percent—were filed in one-quarter of appeals before the Third Circuit. The court noted that the standard length should almost always suffice to address all issues on appeal, and it issued a standing order to discourage parties from seeking to exceed the limits:

> Notice is hereby given that motions to exceed the page or word limitations for briefs are strongly disfavored and will be granted only upon demonstration of extraordinary circumstances. Such circumstances may include multi-appellant consolidated appeals in which the appellee seeks to file a single responsive brief or complex/consolidated proceedings in which the parties are seeking to file jointly or the subject matter clearly requires expansion of the page or word limitations.

3rd Cir. Page Limit Order. Other circuits take a similar approach. *See, e.g.*, 9th Cir. R. 32–2 ("Such motions will be granted only upon a showing of diligence and substantial need."), 11th Cir. R. 32–4 ("The court looks with disfavor upon such motions and will only grant such a motion for extraordinary and compelling reasons.") Wholly apart from the limitations imposed by the Rule, filing a brief that is *shorter* than the page or word limits is often effective as a matter of advocacy. *See also* § 13.8, *infra*, on writing persuasive briefs.

D. ELECTRONIC FILINGS

All of the formatting requirements above—*e.g.*, font size, margins, line spacing—apply equally to briefs filed electronically. Counsel should consult the local rules of the applicable circuit for the precise requirements, including the number of physical copies needed. *See*, *e.g.*, 11th Cir. Rule 31–3 ("One originally signed brief and six copies (total of seven) shall be filed in all appeals" other than pro se parties); 3d Cir. Rule 31.1(a) (requiring "an original and nine copies of each brief," plus an extra copy in cases from the Virgin Islands).

In particular, electronic briefs should be filed as PDF (Portable Document Format) files, a non-modifiable format with the ".pdf" file extension. PDF files generated within the original word-processing program (rather than scanned from a hard copy) are text-searchable. Every brief should be in text-searchable PDFs to make the court's review more convenient. See, *e.g.*, 5th Cir. ECF Filing Standards at 3 ("All documents must be submitted in native PDF text format (not scanned to PDF)" unless local rules or the court allow otherwise).

§ 13.2 CONTENTS OF PRINCIPAL BRIEFS

FRAP 28 governs briefs in an appeal. The rule explains what the briefs must contain and how they are to be organized. Unless there is a cross-appeal, three main briefs will be filed: the appellant's brief, the appellee's brief, and the appellant's reply brief. Each type of brief is governed by a separate subsection of Rule 28. *See* FRAP 28(a) (appellee's brief); 28(b) (appellant's brief); 28(c) (reply brief).

Appellant's Brief. According to FRAP 28(a), the appellant's brief must contain the following ten items (in the following order):

- ***A corporate disclosure statement.*** FRAP 28(a)(1). Rule 26.1 will determine whether a corporate disclosure statement is required.
- ***A table of contents, with page references.*** FRAP 28(a)(2).
- ***A table of authorities.*** FRAP 28(a)(3). This table must list all authorities cited or referred to in the brief. These include cases, statutes, regulations, and secondary sources. The cases and secondary sources should be in alphabetical order. For every authority, the table must list the page or pages of the brief where the authority is cited. Local rules may add some requirements (*see, e.g.*, D.C. Cir. R. 28, requiring an asterisk next to principal authorities relied upon).
- ***A jurisdictional statement.*** FRAP 28(a)(4). This statement must include the district court's or agency's basis for subject-matter jurisdiction. The statement must also include the basis for the appellate court's subject-matter jurisdiction—why the court has the power to hear the case at hand. The basis for subject-matter jurisdiction must be supported by statutes, cases, and relevant facts. The jurisdictional statement should also list any

filing dates in order to demonstrate that the appeal is timely. The jurisdictional statement must assert that the appeal is from a final order or judgment, or provide relevant information showing that the court of appeals otherwise has jurisdiction to hear the case.

- ***A statement of the issues presented for review.*** FRAP 28(a)(5). This statement identifies the issues the party wants the court to consider. Although courts have been somewhat liberal in finding issues raised if presented anywhere in the brief, the failure to list an issue in the statement of issues can result in a finding of waiver. *See, e.g., Suarez-Valenzuela v. Holder*, 714 F.3d 241, 249 (4th Cir. 2013) (appellant waived issue raised in reply, but not opening brief).

The lawyer should consider, in drafting the statement of issues, whether the statement provides sufficient context to be understandable, and to preview the arguments that will follow. For example, an issue stated as "Did the district court err in excluding plaintiff's expert's testimony" is less helpful than one that briefly describes the excluded testimony and, perhaps, additional details that preview the argument, *e.g.*, "Did the district court err by excluding plaintiff's expert's testimony with respect to causation of plaintiff's disease, where that testimony was based on research that was tested, repeatable, and peer-reviewed?"

- ***A concise statement of the case, setting out relevant facts, procedural history and rulings presented for review.*** FRAP 28(a)(6). Rule changes in 2013 removed the requirement of separate statements of the case and of the facts, which caused "confusion and redundancy." Advisory Committee Notes, FRAP 28(a). The statement should describe the "nature of the case," including facts relevant to the issues raised on review, relevant aspects of the procedural history, and the rulings presented for review. The attorney may present the information chronologically, but the attorney has flexibility in that choice, and subheadings may be used. *See* Advisory Committee Notes, FRAP 28(a). Rule 28(e) dictates how to refer to the record: to pages of the appendix (if prepared by the time the brief is filed), or by reference to pages of an original document, such as a filed motion or trial transcript. And, of course, local rules may prescribe different forms of citation to the record.

- ***A summary of the argument.*** FRAP 28(a)(7). The summary must contain "succinct, clear, and accurate" statements of the arguments that are made later in the briefs. This is an important section, and should not be treated as an afterthought, or minimized merely to conserve words for other parts of the brief. The goal of this section is not only to lay out the arguments at the beginning, but also to make the brief easier to understand, by serving as a guide to the reader. The argument summary should provide a synopsis of the brief's major points, and, ideally, begin to strike the themes that will be repeated in the argument section. Of course, the summary of argument must not merely repeat the argument headings. On the other hand, courts have been equally critical of unduly long argument "summaries." *See, e.g.*, *Chen v. Gonzales*, 162 Fed. Appx. 39, 40 (2d Cir. 2006) (unpublished) ("The summary of the argument is longer than the argument itself, which constitutes only one page.")

- ***The argument.*** FRAP 28(a)(8). The argument section is critical. It lays out the heart of the case: what the party claims and why. This section must be well-written and articulate; the arguments will not be convincing or successful if they cannot be understood. Strong, clear, and concise writing is important throughout the brief (*see* § 13.8, *infra*) but especially in the argument section. Powerful and tightly-edited prose will make the argument more persuasive. Verbose arguments should be avoided. At the same time, it is critical to spell out the arguments: Failure to do so can waive the entire argument on appeal. *See, e.g.*, *Flanigan's Enterprises, Inc. of Ga. v. Fulton Cty., Ga.*, 242 F.3d 976, 987 n.16 (11th Cir. 2001) (declining to address plaintiffs' substantive due process argument where briefs "fail[ed] to elaborate or provide any citation of authority in support"). An argument articulated, but not supported by citations to authority and the record, likewise can be waived. *See, e.g., Becker v. Kroll*, 494 F.3d 904, 913 n.6 (10th Cir. 2007) ("An issue or argument insufficiently raised in the opening brief is deemed waived."). Finally, the argument section must contain the applicable standard of review for each issue raised. *See N/S Corp. v. Liberty Mut. Ins. Co.*, 127 F.3d 1145, 1146 (9th Cir. 1997) (striking brief for, *inter alia*, failure to include the standards of review). The standard of review may appear within the discussion of an issue, or under its own sub-heading before the discussion.

- ***A short conclusion.*** FRAP 28(a)(9). The conclusion must state the "precise relief sought" (*e.g.*, "The judgment should be reversed"). The conclusion should not be a lengthy summation of the argument that has just concluded. Rather, it is the place to tell the court exactly what relief is sought. In addition, failing to ask specifically for the desired relief may lead the appellate court to conclude that an argument has been forfeited for failure to adequately brief the issue. *See, e.g., Cross Med. Prods., Inc. v. Medtronic Sofamor Danek, Inc.*, 424 F.3d 1293, 1320 n.3 (Fed. Cir. 2005) (holding that argument was waived where, *inter alia*, appellant "never request[ed] relief" on the subject); § 3.3, *supra*.

- ***The certificate of compliance.*** FRAP 28(a)(10). As previously mentioned, briefs have page or type-volume limits. Rule 32(a)(7) provides that a certificate of compliance is required where the type-volume measurement is elected, and requires a certification of compliance with those requirements, as well as a representation of the number of words (or the number of lines of type) in the text. The rule further provides that the certifier may rely on the count of words or lines provided by the word-processing program used.

These requirements are mandatory, and failure to comply with them can result in serious consequences, including waiver or abandonment of issues as well as sanctions. For instance, as previously noted, "the failure to elaborate or provide any citation of authority in support of an argument on appeal acts as a waiver of the argument for appellate purposes." *Guevara v. U.S. Attorney General*, 132 Fed. Appx. 314, 318 (11th Cir. 2005) (citation omitted). Similarly, "failure to offer an argument on an issue abandons it." *Id.* And, "passing references to issues are insufficient to raise the claim on appeal." *Id. See also* § 3.4, *supra.*

At a minimum, failure to comply with the rules may result in the briefs being returned to counsel with an order requiring the re-filing of a corrected brief. In the Eighth Circuit, for example, the clerk notifies counsel that the brief is defective and allows five days to submit a brief that complies with the rules; failure to do so can lead to dismissal for failure to prosecute. 8th Cir. R. 28A(b).

At the extreme, the court can dismiss the appeal with prejudice, as the First Circuit did in an opinion faulting an appellant's briefs—which contained no specific citations to the record to support appellant's version of the facts allegedly in dispute—as "textbook examples of how *not* to litigate a case on appeal:"

> Plaintiff's lackluster way offends some major appellate procedural rules and controlling caselaw. Being human, lawyers of course will not always dot every "i" and cross every "t" in trying to live up to their obligations under the rules. And occasional mistakes—minor infringements of the rules that neither create unfairness to one's adversary nor impair the court's ability to comprehend and scrutinize a party's papers—typically will not warrant Draconian consequences. But major breaches call for severe decrees, and the violations here are certainly major, given that they cripple any attempt to review the issues intelligently.

Rodriguez-Machado v. Shinseki, 700 F.3d 48, 50 (1st Cir. 2012) (per curiam) (citations and internal quotation marks omitted).

Appellee's Brief. Under FRAP 28(b), the appellee's brief must generally comply with the requirements of FRAP 28(a). Indeed, the appellee's brief must include many of the same items as the appellant's, and in the same order. If, however, the appellee agrees with the appellant's versions, the following items need not be included:

- the jurisdictional statement;
- the statement of the issues;
- the statement of the case; and
- the statement of the standard of review.

FRAP 28(b). The appellee may still include those statements in his brief if he or she is "dissatisfied with the appellant's statement[.]" *Id.* Moreover, some circuits' local rules may require an appellee to "state explicitly whether the jurisdictional summary in the appellant's brief is complete and correct." 7th Cir. R. 28(b). In addition, an appellee's brief need not contain a conclusion. *Compare* FRAP 28(b) (providing that an appellee's brief "must conform to the requirements of Rule 28(a)(1)–(8) and (10)") *with* FRAP 28(a)(9) (requiring an appellant's brief to contain "a short conclusion stating the precise relief sought"). As a practical matter, however, it is usually good practice for an appellee to end his brief with a short conclusion, *e.g.*, "the judgment of the district court should be affirmed."

§ 13.3 CONTENTS OF REPLY BRIEFS

FRAP 28(c) sets forth minimal guidelines for the reply brief. Only the appellant may file a reply brief without the court's permission (unless the appellee is also cross-appealing). The reply brief must have its own table of contents and table of authorities. FRAP 28(c). A reply brief is not required, but "may" be filed.

Id. An appellant's usual reason for filing a reply brief is to rebut an argument in the appellee's brief or to clarify an argument from the appellant's opening brief; the reply brief is not an opportunity to raise new issues. After the appellant submits a reply brief, no other briefs may be submitted without the court's permission. *Id.*

§ 13.4 BRIEFS IN CASES WITH CROSS-APPEALS

Rule 28.1, added to the Federal Rules of Appellate Procedure in 2005 and amended in 2013, brings together all the rules specifically dealing with cross-appeals under one heading. The major points are:

- ***Designation of "Appellant".*** Under Rule 28.1(b), the first party to file a notice of appeal is designated the appellant. If both parties file a notice of appeal on the same day, the plaintiff in the district court is designated as the appellant. *Id.* This is important for the order of briefs (the appellant files the first and third briefs; the designated appellee, or cross-appellant, files the second and fourth); and even more important as to the total size of briefs allotted (in type-volume terms, the appellant gets 26,000 words total; the cross-appellant gets 21,800). Those designations (*i.e.*, which party is the "appellant" and which one is the "appellee") may be modified by the parties' agreement or by court order. FRAP 28.1(b).

- ***Appellant's Principal Brief.*** The designated appellant files a principal brief that complies with Rule 28(a). FRAP 28.1(c)(1). It may contain no more than 13,000 words, 30 pages, or 1,300 lines of text. FRAP 28.1(e)(1)–(2). It must have a blue cover. FRAP 28.1(d). The appellant's principal brief must be served and filed within 40 days after the record is filed. FRAP 28.1(f)(1).

- ***Appellee's Principal and Response Brief.*** The appellee must file a principal brief in the cross-appeal that also, in the same brief, responds to the appellant's brief. FRAP 28.1(c)(2). This principal and response brief must include the same required sections as the appellant's brief, except that the statement of the case is not required if the appellee agrees with the appellant's version. *Id.* The dual-purpose brief is allowed to be larger than any other brief in the case: 15,300 words, 35 pages, or 1,500 lines of text, depending on the measure used. FRAP 28.1(e)(1)–(2). As the appellee's principal and response brief, it must have a red cover. FRAP 28.1(d). This brief must be filed and served within 30 days after the appellant's principal brief. FRAP 28.1(f)(2).

- ***Appellant's Response and Reply Brief.*** This is the appellant's dual-purpose brief. The appellant must respond to the principal brief in the cross-appeal, and in the same brief may reply to the appellee's response to the appeal.

FRAP 28.1(c)(3). This brief need not include the jurisdictional statement, statement of issues, statement of case, statement of the standard of review, or a conclusion. It bears a yellow cover. FRAP 28.1(d). The response and reply brief may be up to 13,000 words, 30 pages, or 1,300 lines of text. FRAP 28.1(e)(1)–(2). Appellant's response and reply brief is to be filed and served within 30 days after the appellee's principal and response brief is served. FRAP 28.1(f)(3).

- ***Appellee's Reply Brief.*** The appellee may file a brief to reply to appellant's response in the cross-appeal. If filed, the brief must include a table of contents, a table of authorities, and a certificate of compliance. FRAP 28.1(c)(4). It must be limited to the issues presented by the cross-appeal. *Id.* The reply brief may contain no more than 6,500 words, 15 pages, or 650 lines of text. *See* FRAP 28.1(e)(2)(C) ("The appellee's reply brief is acceptable if it contains no more than half of the type volume specified in Rule 28.1(e)(2)(A)"). As a reply brief, it bears a gray cover. FRAP 28.1(d). The appellee's reply brief is to be filed within 14 days after the appellant's response and reply brief, but at least seven days before argument, unless the court allows a later filing for good cause. FRAP 28.1(f)(4).

§ 13.5 ADDITIONAL REQUIREMENTS FOR BRIEFS

Referring to Parties in the Briefs. FRAP 28(d) describes how the parties should be referred to in the briefs (and at oral argument). The rule indicates that "counsel should minimize use of the terms 'appellant' and 'appellee.'" *Id.* "To make briefs clear, counsel should use the parties' actual names or the designations used in the lower court or agency proceeding, or such descriptive terms as 'the employee,' 'the injured person,' 'the taxpayer,' 'the ship,' [or] 'the stevedore.'" *Id.*

Referring to the Record in the Briefs. FRAP 28(e) contains guidelines for referring to the record in a brief. The record should be cited using only "clear abbreviations." *Id.* If the cited material appears in the appendix, such references "must be to the pages of the appendix." *Id.* This makes it more efficient for the court to locate the portion of the record being cited, since the record can often encompass many volumes. In some cases, a party may wish to refer to evidence whose admissibility is disputed; in that case, the brief "must cite the pages of the appendix or of the transcript at which the evidence was identified, offered, and received or rejected." *Id.*

Reproduction of Statutes, Rules, and Regulations. Under FRAP 28(f), if the argument will require the court to analyze or study a particular statute, rule, or regulation, the relevant parts of the statute, rule, or regulation must be set forth in the brief itself, in an addendum at the end of the brief, or in a separate pamphlet.

Joining Another Party's Brief and Adopting by Reference. FRAP 28(i) provides that, in a case involving multiple appellants or appellees, "any number of appellants or appellees may join in a brief" or reply brief (that is, multiple parties may join together to file a single brief), and "any party may adopt by reference a part of another's brief." The latter provision allows one party to refer to a particular argument in another party's brief without repeating it, so that the writer may use the limited length of his or her own brief more effectively (and also save the court from having to read duplicative arguments).

Appellate courts, however, have rejected attempts by litigants to circumvent the word and page limitations of FRAP 32(a) by incorporating by reference documents filed in the district court. As one court explained, " 'Petitioners direct us to a document filed in the district court, but we have not read it because adoption by reference amounts to a self-help increase in the length of the appellate brief.' " *Northland Ins. Co. v. Stewart Title Guar. Co.*, 327 F.3d 448, 452 (6th Cir. 2003) (citation omitted).

The Addendum. The Federal Rules mention an addendum to a brief only as the proper place to provide the relevant statutes, rules, and regulations. FRAP 28(f). Local rules, however, may allow, or even require, inclusion of other materials in an addendum for the convenience of the court:

- The judgment, decision, rulings, or orders appealed from, including explanation such as a written or transcript opinion. *See also* FRAP

32.1 (governing citation to unpublished opinions.)

- Short excerpts of the records at issue, such as disputed jury instructions, the issued patent, or contractual provisions. The court may require a motion for leave to file these optional supplemental materials under separate cover.

The addendum is intended to be an easy reference for the court, not a comprehensive appendix: Only documents essential to the case should be included. Materials included in an addendum should be limited in page length, and generally should not also appear in the appendix. The local rules should be consulted before filing any addendum, as the circuits differ in their requirements. *See, e.g.*, 4th Cir. R. 28(b) (an appellant who wishes to supplement a brief beyond the requirements of FRAP 28(f) and FRAP 32.1(b) must present "the additional material . . . to the Court under separate cover, accompanied by a motion for leave to file such supplemental material as an attachment to the brief."); 6th Cir. R. 28(b)(1)(A)(i) (principal briefs must include, in addition to FRAP 28's requirements, a "designation of relevant documents from the lower court record" in an addendum); 8th Cir. R. 28A(g)(2) (addendum not to exceed 15 pages, excluding copies of the court or agency decision(s) below).

Letter Briefs Regarding Supplemental Authority. Under FRAP 28(j), "[i]f pertinent and significant authorities come to a party's attention" after briefing or after oral argument (but before decision), a party may notify the clerk by letter (with copies to all other parties), providing the citation of such authority. Under the rule, "[t]he letter must state the reasons for the supplemental citations, referring either to the page of the brief or to a point argued orally." FRAP 28(j). The rule further provides that "[t]he body of the letter must not exceed 350 words," and "[a]ny response [to the letter] must be made promptly and must be similarly limited." *Id.* Prior to 2002, FRAP 28(j) prohibited argument in such supplemental submissions. The amended rule, however, "no longer forbids 'argument,' " and now "permits parties to decide for themselves what they wish to say about supplemental authorities." Advisory Committee Notes to 2002 Amendments to FRAP 28. "The only restriction upon parties is that the body of a Rule 28(j) letter—that is, the part of the letter that begins with the first word after the salutation and ends with the last word before the complimentary close—cannot exceed 350 words." *Id.*

§ 13.6 *AMICUS CURIAE* BRIEFS

FRAP 29 governs *amicus curiae* (translated, "friend of the court") briefs. The Rule was amended in 2016 to distinguish between amicus filings during the court's initial consideration of the merits, *see* FRAP 29(a), and amicus filings during the court's consideration of requests for panel rehearing or rehearing *en banc*, *see* FRAP 29(b). Many of the same requirements apply under both subdivisions, with the differences noted below. As the Notes to the 2016 amendments explain, "[s]ubdivision (b) sets default rules that apply when a court does not provide otherwise by local rule or by order in a case." *Id.*

However, "[a] court remains free to adopt different rules governing whether amicus filings are permitted in connection with petitions for rehearing, and governing the procedures when such filings are permitted." *Id.*

When Permitted. Under FRAP 29(a)(2) and (b)(2), whether an *amicus* brief is permitted without leave of court or consent of the parties depends upon the particular party seeking to file such a brief. "The United States or its officer or agency, or a state" may file an *amicus* brief "without the consent of the parties or leave of court." *Id.* (A "state" includes the District of Columbia and any U.S. commonwealth or territory. FRAP 1(b).) For all other proposed *amici*, at the merits stage, a brief may be filed "only by leave of court or if the brief states that all parties have consented to its filing." FRAP 29(a)(2). In connection with a petition for panel rehearing or rehearing *en banc*, "[a]ny other amicus curiae may file a brief only by leave of the court," unless the court provides otherwise by local rule or case order. FRAP 29(b)(1)–(2).

Motion Required. A motion for leave to file an *amicus* brief "must be accompanied by the proposed brief" and must "state . . . the movant's interest," "the reason why an amicus brief is desirable and why the matters asserted are relevant to the disposition of the case." FRAP 29(a)(3). The requirements for a motion for leave to file apply both at the merits stage and during consideration of rehearing. FRAP 29(b)(3).

Courts have broad discretion whether to permit the filing of an *amicus* brief (when leave of the court is required). Most courts are fairly liberal in permitting the filing of *amicus* briefs, especially when the brief does not simply duplicate the briefs of the parties but instead provides a new perspective, argument or information that is useful to the court.

Some appellate judges, however, have expressed concern regarding the potential burden on the court that *amicus* briefs can represent. Illustrative of this restrictive approach is *NOW, Inc. v. Scheidler*, 223 F.3d 615 (7th Cir. 2000). There, Judge Posner, writing for the court, noted that "amicus curiae briefs can be a real burden on the court system," given the already-heavy reading load of federal judges. *Id.* at 616. Such briefs may also impose a burden on the parties, who must study—and possibly reply to—such briefs. The *NOW, Inc.* opinion further noted that *amicus* briefs "are more often than not sponsored or encouraged by one or more of the parties" and may be a device to "circumvent the page limitations on the parties' briefs, to the prejudice of any party who does not have an amicus ally." *Id.* at 617. And the court noted that *amicus* briefs "are often attempts to inject interest-group politics into the federal appellate process by flaunting the interest of a trade association or other interest group in the outcome of the appeal." *Id.*

Thus, in the Seventh Circuit, leave to file an *amicus* brief will be granted "only when (1) a party is not adequately represented (usually, is not represented at all); or (2) when the would-be *amicus* has a direct interest in another case, and the case in which he or she seeks permission to file an *amicus curiae* brief may, by operation of stare decisis or res judicata, materially affect that interest; or (3) when the *amicus* has a unique perspective, or information, that can assist the court of appeals beyond what the parties are able to do." *Id. See also Voices for Choices v. Ill. Bell Tel. Co.*, 339 F.3d 542, 544–46 (7th Cir. 2003) (Posner, J., in chambers); *Ryan v. CFTC*, 125 F.3d 1062, 1063 (7th Cir. 1997) (Posner, J., in chambers).

Other judges, however, have been more receptive to *amicus* briefs. For instance, in *Neonatology Assoc. v. Comm'r*, 293 F.3d 128 (3d Cir. 2002), then-Circuit Judge Alito granted a motion for leave to file an *amicus* brief over appellant's opposition. In doing so, Judge Alito first determined, contrary to appellant's contention, that an *amicus* need not be "impartial"—indeed, FRAP 29's requirement that *amicus* have an "interest" conflicts with any rule of impartiality. *Id.* at 131. The fact that an *amicus* has a pecuniary interest also is not disqualifying. *Id.* Finally, according to Judge Alito, an *amicus* need not show that the party whose side the *amicus* wishes to support "is either unrepresented or inadequately represented." *Id.* at 132. Even when a party has capable representation, "an amicus may provide important assistance to the court." *Id.* Judge Alito was not concerned that a liberal approach to *amicus* briefs would materially increase the workload of judges. In Judge Alito's view, a court should grant leave to an *amicus* to file a brief "unless it is obvious that the proposed briefs do not meet Rule 29's criteria as broadly interpreted." *Id.* at 133.

Contents and Form of Brief. Pursuant to FRAP 29(a)(4), an *amicus* brief must comply with FRAP 32, dealing with the form of briefs. *See* § 13.2, *supra*. The cover of the *amicus* brief must be green, and "must identify the party or parties supported and indicate whether the brief supports affirmance or reversal." FRAP 29(a)(4), 32(a)(2). If the proposed *amicus* is a corporation, a corporate disclosure statement (like that required of parties under FRAP 26.1, *see* § 11.4, *supra*) must be included. FRAP 29(a)(4)(A). An *amicus* brief does not need to conform to *all* of the rules governing briefs submitted by parties (*see* § 13.2, *supra*, discussing FRAP 28). Like a principal brief, however, an *amicus* brief must contain a table of contents, table of authorities, an argument, and a certificate of compliance with the length limits under FRAP 32(a)(4) (*see* § 13.2, *supra,* discussing FRAP 32). A summary of the argument and statement of the governing standard of review are not required, FRAP 29(a)(4)(F), although the former may be helpful in giving the court a preview of the longer argument that follows.

The requirements for form and content are the same at the merits stage and the petition for reconsideration stage, as stated by FRAP 29(b)(4) ("Rule 29(a)(4) applies to the amicus brief" filed during consideration of whether to grant rehearing). However, different length limits may apply depending on when the proposed amicus brief is submitted: Under FRAP 29(a)(5), at the merits stage, "an amicus brief may be no more than one-half the maximum length authorized by these rules for a party's principal brief" (typically 6,500 words), except by the court's permission. By contrast, FRAP 29(b)(4) simply provides that "[t]he [amicus] brief must not exceed 2,600 words." When the court gives a party permission to file a longer brief, that permission "does not affect the length of an amicus brief." FRAP 29(a)(5). *See also* § 13.2, *supra* (discussing length of parties' principal briefs).

FRAP 29(c), however, does add two special requirements for the *amicus* brief. First, the brief must include a "concise statement of the identity of the *amicus curiae*, its interest in the case, and the source of its authority to file." FRAP 29(a)(4)(D). Second, if the *amicus* is not one of the government parties listed in Rule 29(a)(2), the brief must also include a statement that indicates whether a party's counsel authored the brief (in whole or in part); whether a party or party's counsel provided funding to prepare or submit the brief (general membership dues do not count); and whether any person besides the *amicus*, its members, or its counsel helped fund the brief, and if so, who. FRAP 29(a)(4)(E)(i)–(iii). These disclosures help deter parties from using an *amicus* brief to circumvent the word limits on their briefs; they also provide one measure for the court of whether the *amicus* truly considers the issue important enough to put its own effort and money into the filing. Advisory Committee Notes to the 2010 Amendments to FRAP 29.

Time of Filing of Brief. At the merits stage, an *amicus* brief is due "no later than 7 days after the principal brief of the party being supported is filed." FRAP 29(a)(6). If the brief does not support either side, it must be filed "no later than 7 days after the appellant's or petitioner's principal brief is filed." *Id.* The court "may grant leave for later filing" of an *amicus* brief, "specifying the time within which an opposing party may answer." *Id.* Similarly, during consideration of whether to grant rehearing, "[a]n amicus curiae supporting the petition for rehearing or supporting neither party must file its brief, accompanied by a motion for filing when necessary, no later than 7 days after the petition is filed." FRAP 29(b)(5). "An amicus curiae opposing the petition must file its brief, accompanied by a motion for filing when necessary, no later than the date set by the court for the response." *Id.*

***Reply Briefs and Oral Argument by* Amici.** An *amicus* is not permitted to file a reply brief or to participate in oral argument absent leave of court. FRAP 29(a)(7), (8).

Expanding the Scope of Arguments. Absent extraordinary circumstances, an *amicus* brief may not inject issues into a case that have not been raised by the parties. This is frowned upon as an effort to expand the pages, lines, or words allowed to a party, as well as an attempt to "expand the scope of an appeal to implicate issues that have not been presented by the parties to the appeal." *Resident Council of Allen Pkwy. Vill. v. U.S. Dep't of HUD*, 980 F.2d 1043, 1049 (5th Cir. 1993). *See also Riverkeeper, Inc. v. Collins*, 359 F.3d 156, 163 n.8 (2d Cir. 2004); § 6.7, *supra.*

Strategy for Obtaining* Amicus *Support. Sometimes *amici curiae* appear in cases without being solicited by a party. In many instances, however, *amicus* briefs are solicited by the parties. Indeed, many industry associations or advocacy groups will not file briefs unless parties actively seek their participation, and convince the organization's counsel or advisory board that participation as *amicus* would be helpful to the party and in the best interest of the organization. Some organizations will even require the party to be (or become) a member of the organization before the organization will consider filing an *amicus* brief in support of that party. As noted, such general membership dues do not need to be disclosed under Rule 29(c)(5). *See* Advisory Committee Notes to 2010 Amendments to FRAP 29.

There is nothing inherently wrong with an *amicus curiae* brief that was obtained by a party's request of the *amicus*. So long as the organization has a true interest in the case, and has relevant views to offer the court, there should be no objection to a party obtaining such *amicus* support by reaching out to potential *amici*. Indeed, the Advisory Committee Notes to the 2010 Amendments point out that "coordination between the amicus and the party whose position the amicus supports is desirable, to the extent that it helps to avoid duplicative arguments." *Id.* Since the *amicus* brief is due seven days after that of the party being supported, this staggered schedule helps to reduce the likelihood of duplication. *Id.*

§ 13.7 SERVING AND FILING OF BRIEFS

FRAP 31(c) provides that "[i]f an appellant fails to file a brief within the time provided by this rule, or within an extended time, an appellee may move to dismiss the appeal." Courts have not hesitated to dismiss appeals or order other serious sanctions for flagrant violations of the time limits for filing briefs. To avoid sanctions, the offending party must show " 'extraordinary and compelling circumstances' [giving] the court cause to excuse the violation." *Matute v. Procoast Navigation Ltd.*, 928 F.2d 627, 631 (3d Cir. 1991) (citation omitted) (finding "extraordinary and compelling personal circumstances excusing [counsel's] neglect in failing to file on time" where counsel's wife and son were hospitalized during the 40-day period for preparing the brief and appendix).

Some courts have warned that extension requests will not be routinely granted, especially requests that are made only *after* the due date of the brief. As one judge stated:

> The movant, and all those who practice before this Court, should consider themselves on notice that motions to extend time to file briefs will be carefully scrutinized, and denied unless good cause is shown. Moreover, good cause shall not be deemed to exist unless the movant avers something more than the normal (or even the reasonably anticipated but abnormal) vicissitudes inherent in the practice of law. When such a motion is not made in a timely fashion, it will be scrutinized all the more

carefully, as will the reasons for its untimely filing. If an untimely motion is denied, no brief will be accepted for filing by the Clerk.

United States v. Raimondi, 760 F.2d 460, 462 (2d Cir. 1985) (Kaufman, J., in chambers). In addition, many courts provide by local rule that extension requests (*e.g.*, those made in the last days of a briefing period) must satisfy a higher standard than the usual "good cause" for an extension. *See, e.g.*, Fed. Cir. R. 26(b)(1) (providing that motion to extend time for filing a brief must be made "at least 7 days" before due, and that a motion brought later than that must be supported by affidavit or declaration under 28 U.S.C. § 1746 describing not merely "good cause," but "extraordinary circumstances" for the late filing of the motion).

Sanctions for untimely filings (or filing no briefs) apply not only to appellants but to appellees as well. FRAP 31(c), for example, provides that "[a]n appellee who fails to file a brief will not be heard at oral argument unless the court grants permission."

§ 13.8 WRITING PERSUASIVE BRIEFS

Extensive commentary exists on persuasive brief writing, much of it written by very experienced appellate judges and practicing lawyers. *See, e.g.*, Douglas E. Abrams, *One Judge's "Top Ten Tips for Effective Brief Writing" (Part I)*, Precedent (Spring 2014), *available at* http://www.mobar.org/uploaded Files/Home/Publications/Precedent/2014/Spring/abr ams.pdf; and *Part II*, *available at* http://www. mobar.org/uploadedFiles/Home/Publications/Preced ent/2014/Summer/abrams.pdf. No Nutshell could possibly hope to cover the entirety of this subject. Still, the authors' experience in the field leads to the following key points.

1. Keep the brief as short as possible, focused on the key issues and authorities. Do not feel compelled to reach the page or word limits, and think long and hard about asking for additional words or pages (requests which are rarely granted in any event). *See* § 13.1(C), *supra*. Out of respect for the overburdened courts, advocates should file a brief just long enough to present issues both "clearly and comprehensively." *Smith v. Town of Eaton, Ind.*, 910 F.2d 1469, 1470 (7th Cir. 1990). The message sent by an overly wordy brief is that the arguments are too complicated to be stated succinctly, and the court may view a complicated argument with skepticism. *See* § 13.1(C), *supra* (discussing length limits).

Keep in mind "the four percent rule." A typical appellate judge, sitting to hear a week of arguments, may hear and decide 25 or more cases. Although not every case will be equally complex or deserving of the same amount of attention, this means that, on average, the typical appellate judge has only four percent of his or her time to devote to your case. Not each brief—your *entire* case, including hearing argument and authoring (or reviewing) the draft opinion. (The authors are indebted to Judge William Bryson of the Federal Circuit for putting a name to this very sensible rule.)

2. Do not violate page, word, and type restrictions. Ninth Circuit Judge Alex Kozinski

writes colorfully about the dangers of such dishonesty:

> Chiseling on the type size and such has two wonderful advantages: First, it lets you cram in more words, and when judges see a lot of words they immediately think: LOSER, LOSER. You might as well write it in big bold letters on the cover of your brief. But there is also a second advantage: It tells the judges that the lawyer is the type of sleazeball who is willing to cheat on a small procedural rule and therefore probably will lie about the record or forget to cite controlling authority.

Alex Kozinski, *The Wrong Stuff*, 1992 B.Y.U. L. Rev. 325, 327.

3. Limit the number of issues to the strongest ones. A lawyer who raises a large number of issues does his client a disservice: The strong arguments may be hidden in a maze of weak ones, and the lawyer's need to raise weak arguments will betray a lack of confidence in the stronger ones. *Cf.* Robert H. Klonoff & Paul L. Colby, *Winning Jury Trials: Trial Tactics and Sponsorship Strategies* 32–35 (NITA 3d ed. 2007).

4. Limit the number of citations. Long string cites rarely have value. Pick the cases that are the most persuasive—cases that are legally controlling, and others that are especially well-reasoned. For example, there is no reason, in an ordinary case, to supply three case citations to establish the proper

standard of review, or the Fed.R.Civ.P. 56 standard for granting summary judgment. One will do.

5. Where citations (even a string of citations) are necessary, use parentheticals to help the reader. The following example, borrowed from a presentation given by Seventh Circuit Judge David Hamilton, makes the point. The example—which applies with full force to briefs—is from Judge Hamilton's opinion for the court in *Bausch v. Stryker Corp.*, 630 F.3d 546, 553 (7th Cir. 2010), where the issue was whether a hip replacement was manufactured in violation of applicable federal safety standards, and the point of the citations was to demonstrate that there is nothing unusual about such reliance on government standards to prove product defect or common-law negligence. The first is from the opinion:

> Illinois treats a violation of a statute or ordinance designed to protect human life or property as prima facie evidence of negligence, though the violation may not always be conclusive on the issue of negligence. *See, e.g., Kalata v. Anheuser-Busch Companies, Inc.*, 581 N.E.2d 656, 661 (Ill. 1991) (violation of public safety ordinance regulating handrails is prima facie evidence of negligence); *Batteast v. Wyeth Laboratories, Inc.*, 560 N.E.2d 315, 323 (Ill. 1990) (violation of safety statute is prima facie evidence of negligence if law designed to (1) protect class to which plaintiff belongs and (2) injury has direct, proximate connection with regulation); *Barthel v. Illinois Central Gulf Railroad Co.*, 384 N.E.2d 323, 326 (Ill. 1978),

> citing *Davis v. Marathon Oil Co.*, 356 N.E.2d 93 (Ill. 1976) (a defendant's violation of a statute designed to protect human life or property is ordinarily prima facie evidence of negligence); *First National Bank in DeKalb v. City of Aurora*, 373 N.E.2d 1326, 1329–30 (Ill. 1978) (citing violation of ordinances regulating street and sidewalk safety was sufficient to state a cause of action); *Hartje v. Moxley*, 85 N.E. 216, 217 (Ill. 1908) (driving at prohibited rate of speed is prima facie evidence of negligence).

The second example removes the descriptive parentheticals, and, while shorter, is basically a "to-do list" for the judge or law clerk:

> Illinois treats a violation of a statute or ordinance designed to protect human life or property as prima facie evidence of negligence, though the violation may not always be conclusive on the issue of negligence. *See, e.g.*, *Kalata v. Anheuser-Busch Companies, Inc.*, 581 N.E.2d 656, 661 (Ill. 1991); *Batteast v. Wyeth Laboratories, Inc.*, 560 N.E.2d 315, 323 (Ill. 1990); *Barthel v. Illinois Central Gulf Railroad Co.*, 384 N.E.2d 323, 326 (Ill. 1978), citing *Davis v. Marathon Oil Co.*, 356 N.E.2d 93 (Ill. 1976); *First National Bank in DeKalb v. City of Aurora*, 373 N.E.2d 1326, 1329–30 (Ill. 1978); *Hartje v. Moxley*, 85 N.E. 216, 217 (Ill. 1908).

6. In the same spirit of not giving the judge or law clerk a to-do list, try to use direct quotes from cases where possible, rather than merely paraphrasing their holdings. This demonstrates to

the court that your briefs are credible, and lessens the chance of misstating or overstating a case's holding.

7. Display absolute candor in everything written in the brief—including representations about the record and discussions of cases. The obligation of candor requires an advocate to bring to the court's attention controlling adverse authority. *See, e.g.*, *Amoco Oil Co. v. United States*, 234 F.3d 1374, 1378 (Fed. Cir. 2000) ("By failing to cite controlling adverse authority, the conduct of appellant's counsel was inappropriate and potentially a violation of counsel's duty of candor toward the court.") (citing Model Rules of Prof'l Conduct R. 3.3(a)(3) ("A lawyer shall not knowingly . . . fail to disclose to the tribunal legal authority in the controlling jurisdiction known to the lawyer to be directly adverse to the position of the client and not disclosed by opposing counsel.")).

8. Avoid name calling—whether the target is the lower court judge or opposing counsel. *See, e.g.*, 11th Cir. R. 25–6(a)–(b) (when any paper filed with the court contains "ad hominem or defamatory language," the court may take "appropriate action," including ordering that the document be struck from the record); *cf. In re Wilkins*, 782 N.E.2d 985 (Ind. 2003) (sanctioning counsel for writing a footnote in an appellate brief suggesting that the state court of appeals' opinion was "so factually and legally inaccurate that one is left to wonder whether the Court of Appeals was determined to find for Appellee . . . and then said whatever was necessary to reach that conclusion"). Most judges react very unfavorably

to such tactics. Stick to the facts and the law. Any unsavory or inappropriate conduct will be apparent to the reader without the need for *ad hominem* attacks. *See, e.g., Garrett v. Selby Connor Maddux & Janer*, 425 F.3d 836, 840 (10th Cir. 2005) ("We affirm the judgment below because Plaintiff has forfeited his right to a review of that decision. His briefs in this court contain no argument of substance, and the scurrilous tone convinces us to refrain from exercising any discretion we may have to delve for substance in a pro se pleading.").

9. Avoid block quotes unless the language is absolutely critical and compelling. Even then, snippets of the key language, interspersed with paraphrasing, may be more apt to focus the court's attention on the important language. Many judges have openly acknowledged their tendency simply to skip over long block quotes. *See, e.g., United States v. Ulloa-Porras*, 1 Fed. Appx. 842, 845 n.1 (10th Cir. 2001) ("Counsel are advised that the inclusion of lengthy block quotes—here, two sets of nearly identical quotes spanning twelve consecutive pages each—is not the most effective use of the limited pages permitted for appellate briefing."). On the other hand, if a case turns on the precise wording of a law or regulation, or is governed by the specific holding of a prior case, quoting the relevant law or case—even in a block quote—may be necessary. Even there, however, the advocate may want to consider including the relevant language in an appendix rather than in the text of the brief. *See* FRAP 28(f) ("If the court's determination of the issues presented requires the study of statutes, rules, regulations, etc.,

the relevant parts must be set out in the brief or in an addendum at the end, or may be supplied to the court in pamphlet form.").

10. Limit the number of footnotes. Judges find them distracting and often ignore them. If a footnote is essential, the best place is at the end of a paragraph; the worst place is the middle of a sentence in the middle of a paragraph. As with block quotes, many judges have claimed, in open court or elsewhere, that they do not read footnotes. And, on top of that, many courts have held that an argument made only in a footnote is insufficiently developed and thus forfeited on appeal. *See* § 3.3, *supra*.

11. Address the grounds for jurisdiction and standard of review in a coherent way. These are two areas that judges virtually always will study, for they go directly to the appellate courts' power to hear the appeal in the first place, and the scope of that power if it exists. The brief must have clear, persuasive arguments for dealing with them.

12. Address the opponent's key issues, arguments, and authorities. The problems in one's case will not go away simply by ignoring them.

13. Write in plain English using short, declarative sentences. Avoid using legalese or arcane words that no one will understand without having a dictionary at hand. Whenever possible, use the active voice. And avoid excessive use of acronyms. Judge Kozinski gives a real example of excessive use of acronyms: " 'LBE's complaint more specifically alleges that NRB failed to make an appropriate determination of RPT

and TIP conformity to SIP.' " 1992 B.Y.U. L. Rev. at 328. As Judge Kozinski notes, "[e]ven if there was a winning argument buried in the midst of that gobbledygook, it was DOA." *Id.* Judge Laurence Silberman of the D.C. Circuit has also written, passionately, about "[t]he use of obscure acronyms, sometimes those made up for a particular case, [which] is an aggravating development of the last twenty years." *Delaware Riverkeeper Network v. F.E.R.C.*, 753 F.3d 1304, 1320–21 (D.C. Cir. 2014) (Silberman, J., concurring) ("Petitioner's brief, unfortunately, was laden with obscure acronyms notwithstanding the admonitions in our handbook (and on our website) to avoid uncommon acronyms. Since the brief was signed by a faculty member at Columbia Law School, that was dismaying both because of ignorance of our standards and because the practice constitutes lousy brief writing.").

14. Lengthy paragraphs are difficult to follow, so keep paragraphs short.

15. Make liberal use of headings and subheadings. Headings and subheadings break up the monotony and provide a roadmap for the reader. They enable the reader to zero in quickly on a specific point or argument.

16. Organize the brief in a logical and coherent manner. Depending on the circumstances, options include (among others): strongest arguments first; jurisdictional arguments first; or statutory arguments before constitutional arguments.

17. Avoid fundamentally inconsistent arguments (*e.g.*, the evidence demonstrated that defendant acted in self-defense or, in the alternative, the evidence demonstrated that defendant was nowhere near the scene of the crime or incident). Inconsistent arguments cast serious doubt on the brief writer's credibility. Of course, alternative arguments may be pursued as long as they are not inconsistent. *Cf.* Klonoff & Colby, *Winning Jury Trials* 39–40.

18. Exercise care in finalizing the brief, making sure to cite-check the cited authorities and to catch any misspelled words, grammatical errors, or poorly copied (or missing) pages. If time allows, ask a colleague unfamiliar with the case to proof your brief; fresh eyes will catch errors you may have missed. You should also consider closing your office door and reading your brief out loud to yourself. That technique will often identify a surprising number of errors.

19. Consider choices of typography to make the typeface clear and easy to read, keeping in mind the "four percent rule" and the need to make your brief inviting to a busy judge or law clerk. *See* "Requirements and Suggestions for Typography in Briefs and Other Papers," a publication issued by the Seventh Circuit, *available at* http://www.ca7.uscourts.gov/Rules/type.pdf.

20. Use extreme caution in making arguments that depend on the court's willingness to reassess findings of fact by the court or jury. Appellate courts are very reluctant to re-examine factual findings, *see*

Fed.R.Civ.P. 52(a), and an argument premised on factual error is unlikely to be well received.

21. Update any research shortly before oral argument and provide, as supplemental authority under FRAP 28(j), any significant new case law or legislative developments.

22. Be sure to cite the record when making record-based arguments. The failure to do so can be devastating to an appeal. At the same time, do not provide a long list of record cites with the expectation that the court will figure out which ones are relevant. *See, e.g., Racicky v. Farmland Indus., Inc.*, 328 F.3d 389, 398 & nn.8 & 9 (8th Cir. 2003) (expressing "frustrat[ion]" at "the failure of the Racickys to cite specifically to the record," describing their litigation approach as similar to "the pasta sauce commercial where the actor claims 'It's in there!' ", and noting that "[w]ith a record spanning thousands of pages, citing scores of scattered pages at a time [*i.e.*, long string citations of record materials] is not helpful").

CHAPTER 14
THE APPENDIX

§ 14.1 FORM

FRAP 32(b) covers the requirements for the form of an appendix. In general, an appendix must satisfy the procedures for reproducing a brief, including the text, cover, binding, and paper requirements of FRAP 32(a)(1)–(4). Additionally, the following special requirements exist for an appendix:

- The appendix must be "separately bound" with a white cover (FRAP 32(b)(1));
- The appendix "may include a legible photocopy of any document found in the record or of a printed judicial or agency decision" (FRAP 32(b)(2)); and
- If "necessary to facilitate inclusion of odd-sized documents such as technical drawings," the appendix need not be 8½ by 11 inches and "need not lie reasonably flat when opened" (FRAP 32(b)(3)).

With appendices—as with briefs, motions, and other court documents—it is essential that counsel review the local circuit rules before filing. Every federal circuit now allows electronic filing, while also requiring (in at least some instances) that appendices be filed in paper form. Every circuit has implemented electronic filing (*see* § 13.1(D), *supra*), but the transition is not complete. Local rules related to electronic filing are still evolving; each circuit's website provides not only the latest local rules, but usually also offers manuals to help attorneys comply with the latest requirements.

Appendices generally must be submitted in one PDF document. That file may be created by compiling the preferred searchable text (or "native") PDF documents, as well as scanned PDFs of documents unavailable in their original electronic format. Further, technological limitations may mean that larger files (over a certain number of megabytes) may not be uploaded electronically. *See, e.g.,* 7th Cir. ECF User Manual ("Any attachment exceeding 50 megabytes may not be submitted electronically. Counsel seeking to submit attachments so large they cannot be filed via ECF must submit a motion prior to submission seeking exemption from the electronic filing requirements and justifying the need to submit attachments of this size." (emphasis deleted)).

§ 14.2 CONTENTS

FRAP 30 covers the contents of the appendix. Under FRAP 30(a)(1), the appellant is responsible for preparing the appendix, which must include "the relevant docket entries in the proceeding below"; "the relevant portions of the pleadings, charge, findings, or opinion"; "the judgment, order, or decision in question"; and "other parts of the record to which the parties wish to direct the court's attention." FRAP 30(a)(1)–(d). (Although it is often referred to as a "joint" appendix, the rule simply calls this document an "appendix," and makes it the responsibility of the appellant to prepare it, albeit with the input of all parties.) Rule 30 instructs counsel *not* to include memoranda of law "unless they have independent relevance" (*e.g.*, demonstrating that an issue was in fact raised in the lower tribunal), and also makes clear that the parties and court may rely on items in the record "even though not included in the appendix." FRAP 30(a)(2).

This last provision points out a crucial distinction between "the record," FRAP 10, and "the appendix," FRAP 30. While the appendix includes portions of "the record," it is not meant to contain the entire record on appeal. *Cf.* Chapter 9, *supra.*

FRAP 30(a)(3) provides that, "[u]nless filing is deferred under Rule 30(c), the appellant must file 10 copies of the appendix with the brief and must serve one copy on counsel for each party separately represented." (An unrepresented party proceeding *in forma pauperis* need only provide four copies along with service of a copy on each separately represented party.) *Id.* Importantly, however, the court of appeals "may by local rule or order in a particular case require the filing or service of a different number." *Id.* As a result, it is essential to consult the local rules before filing an appendix. *Compare, e.g.*, 2d Cir. R. 30.1(b) ("A counseled party must submit 6 paper copies of an appendix in cases in which an appendix is required. A pro se party must submit 3 paper copies of its appendix in cases in which an appendix is required."); *with, e.g.*, 3d Cir. R. 30.1(b) ("In addition to the electronic appendix, four paper copies of the appendix must be filed for the convenience of the court, unless otherwise ordered.").

The parties should attempt to agree on the contents of the appendix. If they cannot, the appellant must (within 14 days after the record is filed) serve on appellee a designation of what appellant intends to include in the appendix, and appellee then has 14 days to designate additional items, which appellant must include. FRAP 30(b)(1). "[U]nnecessary designation" of record items should be avoided, because "the entire record is available to the court." FRAP 30(b)(1). Appellant must pay for the appendix, including portions designated by appellee, unless appellant deems appellee's designations "unnecessary," in which case appellee must advance the costs of its designation. FRAP 30(b)(2). Costs of the appendix are "taxable" costs, although a party making "unnecessary" designations may be required to bear those costs. FRAP 30(b)(2). Each circuit must provide for sanctions against attorneys who "unreasonably and vexatiously increase litigation costs by including unnecessary material in the appendix." *Id.* These requirements—which vary from circuit to circuit because of local rules—apply both to regular appendices and deferred appendices.

The appendix must start with a table of contents, followed by the relevant docket entries. FRAP 30(d). Subsequent items should be organized chronologically. *Id.* When transcript pages are included, "the transcript page numbers must be shown in brackets immediately before the included pages." *Id.* In addition, the Rule provides that "[i]mmaterial formal matters (captions, subscriptions, acknowledgments, etc.) should be omitted." *Id.* Exhibits that are included "may be reproduced in a separate volume, or volumes, suitably indexed." FRAP 30(e). The court has authority to dispense with an appendix "either by rule for all cases or classes of cases or by order in a particular case." FRAP 30(f).

Courts have at times expressed frustration with deficient appendices, including omitted items, poor binding, and inclusion of unnecessary items. *See, e.g.*, *Vitello v. J.C. Penney Co.*, 107 F.3d 869, 1997 WL 87248, at *3 n.1 (4th Cir. 1997) (table) (per curiam) (describing index as "useless," complaining about poor binding and omitted items, and calling the product a "disaster"). Courts have not hesitated to sanction counsel for submitting appendices that do not comport with the rules, including awarding costs of preparing supplemental appendices and attorneys' fees incurred by challenging violations of the rules, and—in extreme cases—dismissal of the appeal. *See, e.g.*, *Kushner v. Winterthur Swiss Ins. Co.*, 620 F.2d 404, 407 (3d Cir. 1980) (dismissing appeal "for failure to file an appendix that conforms to [the court's] rules").

Despite the detail contained in FRAP 30, counsel should be cautious about the applicability of local rules, which result in wide variations in the specific requirements for an appendix.

CHAPTER 15
ORAL ARGUMENT

§ 15.1 INTRODUCTION

In 1967, Rule 34(b) of the Federal Rules of Appellate Procedure provided that, "[u]nless otherwise provided by rule for all cases or classes of cases," oral argument was set at 30 minutes per side. Indeed, the Advisory Committee Notes to the 1967 adoption of FRAP 34 contains the now-quaint statement that "[a] majority of circuits now *limit* oral argument to thirty minutes for each side, with the provision that additional time may be made available upon request." (emphasis added.) Now, some fifty years later a 30-minutes-per-side argument in a federal court of appeals seems like an extraordinary event—a luxury reserved only for the most complex and compelling cases. The continuing shrinkage of oral argument brings with it extra challenges for the advocate, who must—within these strictures—ensure that his client's case is presented in the best fashion possible.

A survey of the rules and practices of the federal appellate courts shows that the norm for oral argument today is 15 minutes per side—when oral argument is granted at all—and the trend line is pointing downward, particularly in the circuits with the busiest caseloads:

- First Circuit: "Normally the court will permit no more than 15 minutes per side for oral argument." 1st Cir. R. 34.0(c)(1).

- Second Circuit: "The clerk notifies the parties of the argument time the court has allotted to each side." 2d Cir. R. 34.1(d). Cases on recent dockets have been allotted 5, 7, 8, 10, 12, or 15 minutes per side.

- Third Circuit: The maximum request (absent a majority ruling of the panel) is "20 minutes per side." "Usually, 15 minutes per side is allotted." 3d Cir. I.O.P. 2.1.

- Fourth Circuit: "Each side is normally allowed 20 minutes." 4th Cir. R. 34(d).

- Fifth Circuit: "Most cases are allowed 20 minutes to the side." 5th Cir. R. 34.11.

- Sixth Circuit: "Each side has 15 minutes for oral argument unless the notice of oral argument provides otherwise." 6th Cir. R. 34(f).

- Seventh Circuit: "The amount of time allotted for oral argument will be set based on the nature of the case." 7th Cir. R. 34(b)(1). "[T]he court . . . limits the time in many [appeals] to 10 to 20 minutes per side. . . . On some occasions more than 30 minutes per side is allowed, usually in a complex case." Practitioner's Handbook for Appeals to the United States Court of Appeals for the Seventh Circuit at 147–48 (2014), *available at* www.ca7.uscourts.gov.

- Eighth Circuit: "Cases screened for full oral argument usually will be allotted 10, 15 or 20 minutes per side. Extended argument of 30 minutes or more per side occasionally will be allotted." 8th Cir. R. 34A(b).

- Ninth Circuit: If oral argument is allowed, the amount of time, which is within the Court's discretion, generally ranges between 10 and 20 minutes per side." Local Rules of the U.S. Court of Appeals for the Ninth Circuit, "Court Structures and Procedures," at xix (July 1, 2016), *available at* www.ca9.uscourts.gov.

- Tenth Circuit: "Fifteen minutes is allotted to each side for argument." Practitioners' Guide to the United States Court of Appeals for the Tenth Circuit at 51 (Jan. 2016), *available at* www.ca10.uscourts.gov.

- Eleventh Circuit: "The time for oral argument will be indicated on the calendar." 11th Cir. I.O.P. 10 to Rule 34. The court's general practice is to allow 15 minutes per side, except in extraordinary cases.

- D.C. Circuit: "Counsel will be afforded such time for oral argument as the court may provide." D.C. Cir. R. 34(b). "There is no standard length of argument time, although the allotment of 15 minutes per side is perhaps the most common." Handbook of Practice and Internal Procedures, United States Court of Appeals for the District of Columbia Circuit at 49 (Jan. 26, 2017), *available at* www.cadc.uscourts.gov.

- Federal Circuit: "Time allotted for oral argument is ordinarily 15 minutes per side (not per party or attorney), although the court may vary this depending on the nature of the case." Fed. Cir. R. 34 Practice Notes.

Those rules and practices, however, do not fully capture the shrinking nature of the federal courts of appeals' oral argument dockets. All of the circuits maintain a substantial non-argument docket; most of the federal courts of appeals hear oral argument in no more than 30% of the cases they decide.

Moreover, according to statistics collected by the federal judiciary, over 80% of the cases resolved by the federal courts of appeals are now decided without oral argument: over the last 20 years, the percentage of orally argued appeals has dropped from 40.1% (in 1996–97) to 17.5% (in 2015–16). Even the Second Circuit, which had long prided itself on hearing oral argument in all cases (except those involving an incarcerated person acting pro se), adopted a non-argument calendar in 2007 as a response to the court's increasing caseload—including the flood of immigration related cases now coming before that court. *See* 2d Cir. R. 34(d).

Despite the shrinking time available for oral argument, and the fact that many courts of appeals hear oral argument in fewer than half of the cases submitted for decision, most judges still say that they value the opportunity for oral argument, because it gives them the opportunity to test the validity of the parties' arguments, as well as probe the consequences of a decision in one party's or the other's favor. Even though oral arguments now may be 10 minutes (or less) instead of 30 minutes a side, arguments are no less important to the administration of justice in the courts of appeals than they were in 1967. The challenge for the lawyer today is how to obtain argument in the first instance (or to oppose it), and, if argument is allowed, to present an oral argument to the court, within the limited time available, that best serves the interests of the client and the court.

§ 15.2 PROCEDURE FOR REQUESTING ORAL ARGUMENT

Under FRAP 34(a)(1), "[a]ny party may file, or a court may require by local rule, a statement explaining why oral argument should, or need not, be permitted." Here, lawyers should be sensitive to the local court of appeals' rules, because many of them prescribe specific procedures for making such statements. The Eleventh Circuit, for example, requires the parties to set forth such a statement in their briefs. 11th Cir. R. 28–1(c).

FRAP 34(a)(2) provides that "[o]ral argument must be allowed in every case unless a panel of three judges who have examined the briefs and record unanimously agrees that oral argument is unnecessary"—either because the appeal is frivolous; because there is already an authoritative decision on the issues in the case; or because the briefs and record are sufficiently "adequat[e]" that "the decisional process would not be significantly aided by oral argument." These exceptions are vast; in some circuits the unargued appeals represent as much as 75% of the court's docket.

Alternatively, the attorneys for all parties to a case may agree that the case can be submitted for decision on the briefs, without oral argument. FRAP 34(f). Notwithstanding the parties' agreement, however, the court may still order oral argument if it desires. *Id.*

§ 15.3 NOTIFICATION OF ORAL ARGUMENT

The clerk will inform the parties whether oral argument has been granted, and, if so, how much time has been allotted for argument, as well as where and when it will take place. FRAP 34(b).

Rule 34(b) also provides that motions to postpone arguments, or requests for additional time for oral argument, must be made "reasonably in advance" of the scheduled argument date. However, in most circuits a motion to postpone argument will be granted only in exceptional circumstances, as the notification of scheduling of argument comes after the judges have been assigned to the panel, and after the judges and their clerks have begun their review of the briefs and record in the case. *See*, *e.g.*, 1st Cir. R. 34.1(d) ("Once a case is scheduled for argument, continuances may be allowed only for grave cause."). The committee comments to Third Circuit Rule 34 reflect this practice and explain the reasons for it: "Because the panels are constituted in advance for a specific sitting, rescheduling of an argument may result in a second panel being assigned an appeal when one panel has already performed the necessary study of the briefs and appendix. Alternatively, it may result in members of the panel having to travel to Philadelphia at additional government expense, disrupting previously established schedules. Such needless waste of judicial resources underlies this court's precedent of declining to reschedule except upon a showing of extraordinary circumstances."

To avoid these problems, the clerk's offices in some circuits send out preliminary notices of tentative or proposed argument dates (or collections of dates) before confirming the calendar. In other circuits, the court invites counsel to notify the court, by letter, once briefing is completed, about intractable conflicts with upcoming argument sessions. This allows the attorneys in the case to respond to the notice with any schedule conflicts they may have. The clerk's offices in circuits that do not follow these practices may nonetheless be receptive to letters from counsel, preceding the notice of oral argument, indicating dates when counsel will be unavailable for oral argument.

§ 15.4 NOTIFICATION OF IDENTITY OF JUDGES

FRAP 34 contains no provision requiring the courts of appeals to notify counsel of the identity of the judges who will hear argument in an appeal. As a result, the circuits have developed individual practices regarding this notification:

- First Circuit: "The names of the judges on each panel may be disclosed for a particular session seven (7) days in advance of the session." 1st Cir. I.O.P. VIII(B).

- Second Circuit: "The names of the judges are made public at noon on Thursday of the week before the panel sits." How to Appeal a Civil Case to the United States Court of Appeals for the Second Circuit at 12–13, *available at* www.ca2.uscourts.gov.

- Third Circuit: "No later than 10 calendar days prior to the first day of the panel sitting, the clerk communicates to counsel in each case listed the names of the members of the panel and whether the case is to be orally argued." 3d Cir. I.O.P. 2.5.

- Fourth Circuit: "The identity of the panel assigned to hear argument pursuant to I.O.P. 34.1 is not disclosed until the morning of the argument." Oral Argument Calendar page, *available at* www.ca4.uscourts.gov/oral-argument.

- Fifth Circuit: "The clerk may not disclose the names of the panel members for a particular session until 1 week in advance of the session." 5th Cir. I.O.P. to FRAP 34.

- Sixth Circuit: "The names of the judges who will hear the case are posted on the court's website and are available from the clerk's office on the first business day of the week two weeks before oral argument." 6th Cir. I.O.P. 34(b)(5).

- Seventh Circuit: "When the court is sitting, oral arguments are generally scheduled for 9:30 A.M. The panel of judges and the order of cases to be argued that day is posted at 9:00 A.M. each morning that the court is in session." Practitioner's Handbook for Appeals to the United States Court of Appeals for the Seventh Circuit at 149 (2014), *available at* www.ca7.uscourts.gov.

- Eighth Circuit: "The printed argument calendar lists the judges on each panel." 8th Cir. I.O.P. III(K)(2). "The clerk's office prepares and publishes an oral argument calendar approximately one month before the court session." *Id.* I(D)(1).

- Ninth Circuit: "The names of the judges on each panel are released to the general public on the Monday of the week preceding argument." Local Rules of the U.S. Court of Appeals for the Ninth Circuit, Court Structure and Procedures § E(3), at xvii (Dec. 1, 2016), *available at* www.ca9.uscourts.gov.

- Tenth Circuit: "The panel members for each case are made public 7 days before the first day of the calendar (that is, on the Monday prior to the start of the court's week long calendar). Counsel and parties may access that information on the court's website." Practitioners' Guide to the United States Court of Appeals for the Tenth Circuit at 52 (Dec. 2016), *available at* www.ca10.uscourts.gov.

- Eleventh Circuit: "The clerk's office may disclose the names of the panel members for a particular session two weeks in advance of the session, or earlier as determined by the court. At the time the clerk issues a calendar assigning an appeal to a specific day of oral argument, the clerk will advise counsel of when the clerk's office may be contacted to learn the identity of panel members." 11th Cir. I.O.P. 7 to Rule 34.
- D.C. Circuit: "The composition of the merits panel will be posted on the Court's internet site, usually 30 days before the date of oral argument, and will not be disclosed before that time." Handbook of Practice and Internal Procedures, United States Court of Appeals for the District of Columbia Circuit at 48 (Jan. 26, 2017), *available at* www.cadc.uscourts.gov.
- Federal Circuit: Identity of panel members is not disclosed until 9:00 a.m. on the day of morning arguments (which begin at 10:00 a.m.), and 11:00 a.m. for afternoon arguments (which begin at 2:00 p.m.).

Some courts are wary of allowing lawyers to know the identity of the panel before the argument, for fear that the advocates will tailor their arguments to a specific judge or judges on the panel. Indeed, the Federal Circuit in late 2004 started experimenting with posting the names of panel members on its website on the Thursday before the week of oral arguments. It abruptly truncated the experiment after six months, amid reports that the circuit's judges perceived that " 'the arguments were distorted as opposed to arguing the strongest points.' " Pamela A. MacLean, *Federal Circuit Stops Early Notice of Panels*, Nat'l L. J. (May 9, 2005) at 4 (quoting the Circuit Executive of the Federal Circuit, Jan Horbaly). But experienced advocates generally prefer to know the identities of the judges who will decide their case, on the basic principle that it is better to know one's audience, their prior views and preferences, and how active they are as questioners.

§ 15.5 PROCEDURES FOR THE ORAL ARGUMENT

FRAP 34(c)—which, in the case of a cross-appeal, must be read in conjunction with FRAP 34(d) and FRAP 28.1—sets forth a limited amount of guidance regarding the procedures and protocol of the oral argument session.

The appellant argues first and last. FRAP 34(c). In the event of a cross-appeal, FRAP 28.1(b) denotes which party is deemed to be the appellant. Although the rule does not explicitly allow it, some courts allow the cross-appellant (*i.e.*, the party deemed to be the appellee under FRAP 28.1(b)) to conclude the argument, but in doing so limit that final argument to rebuttal of points relevant to the cross-appeal.

FRAP 34(c) also sets forth a flat prohibition on "read[ing] at length from briefs, records, or authorities," which is never good advocacy practice in any event.

Finally, FRAP 34(e) provides that if one party does not appear for oral argument, the opposing party may still give its argument: If it is the appellee who is a no-show, "the court must hear appellant's argument"; if the appellant is a no-show, "the court may hear the appellee's argument." Attorneys (and, occasionally, judges) may appear by audio or video from a remote location, with advance coordination with the clerk's office and the permission of the court.

Beyond these points, however, the Federal Rules of Appellate Procedure are silent as to oral argument procedure. Advocates should consult the specific court's local rules and internal operating procedures—typically available on the court's website—for further guidance on local argument practices. (By way of example, the Third Circuit's Instructions for Oral Argument in the Third Circuit (available at www.ca3.uscourts.gov) provides that "[a]t the outset of argument, counsel shall state for the record . . . [h]is or her name; . . . [t]he party represented; and . . . [t]he amount of rebuttal time reserved (for appellant).") In addition, several circuits offer a "practitioner's handbook" on their websites. These handbooks, each of which is sponsored by the court in question, provide useful guidance on the practices, preferences, and expectations of that court's judges with respect to oral argument.

If possible, an advocate arguing in an unfamiliar court would do well to attend arguments the day before, to watch the court, even if not the same judges, in action.

§ 15.6 USE OF EXHIBITS

An attorney is allowed to use exhibits in oral argument. FRAP 34(g) provides that exhibits must be set up or displayed before court convenes and must be promptly removed at the conclusion of the arguments, "unless the court directs otherwise." Unclaimed exhibits are subject to destruction or other disposition within a reasonable time after the clerk has notified the party or parties to claim them.

Counsel contemplating the use of exhibits at oral argument should also consult local rules, practices, and practitioners' handbooks, where available. Local rules may well require notice and disclosure of exhibits to the opposing side by a date well in advance of the oral argument.

Some appellate courts disfavor the use of exhibits during the oral argument. Additionally, the use of exhibits in oral argument can pose a challenge to effective advocacy—if not carefully considered, a skilled opponent can use an exhibit to hoist the proponent of the exhibit on his own petard, so to speak, leaving an indelible impression on the judges as they retire to deliberate on the outcome of the case.

More prosaically, some exhibits—particularly large "blow ups" requiring easels—can require the advocate to leave the podium (and the microphone), thus making it difficult for the judges to hear the advocate, and difficult for the court's recording devices to pick up counsel's voice. For this reason, some courts are equipped with wireless microphone packs that counsel can wear during argument.

Counsel should check on the availability of such microphones as part of the process of deciding whether to use an exhibit at argument.

Finally, in considering the use of an exhibit, the advocate should keep in mind the arrangement of the courtroom, and in particular the distance that the exhibit will be from the judges. It may be difficult for the judges see the exhibit if it is far from the bench. The authors have had better luck using handouts for the judges as exhibits, or simply pointing the panel to a page of the briefs or appendix to guide their discussions.

As a tactical matter, we are hesitant to suggest that an advocate should "never" use an exhibit during oral argument, for we have seen (on occasion) such exhibits used to great effect. But in making the decision whether to use an exhibit, an advocate might profitably engage in a strong presumption against using any exhibits, and then consider whether there is a compelling reason involving that particular case—and that particular exhibit (or exhibits)—sufficient to overcome that strong presumption against its use.

§ 15.7 DIVIDED ARGUMENT

At times, it may be appropriate for more than one counsel to present argument for a "side" in a case. Often, that will be because multiple parties with different issues or divergent interests are aligned as appellants or appellees; alternatively, on rare occasions, divided argument will be sought when two or more lawyers representing the same client wish to present argument.

The Federal Rules of Appellate Procedure do not speak to the question of divided argument. Some local rules do, however, and the topic is covered in several of the circuit handbooks mentioned above. Above all, consider these issues in respect to divided argument: Is it really necessary to the case? (The authors believe that counsel should try to avoid divided argument if it is possible to do so.) If it is deemed necessary, is a motion to the court and to opposing counsel required? If no motion is required, is notice to the court required? If so, when is the notice required? How will the arguing counsel divide responsibility for the case? How will counsel communicate the division of responsibility to the court? Will it be by notice, by statement made to the clerk when signing in for the argument, or by a statement at the outset of argument? Will each lawyer be prepared only for his part of the case, or will the lawyers be prepared to answer questions relevant to each other's portion of the case? (The latter is definitely advisable.)

§ 15.8 PERSUASIVE ORAL ARGUMENT

As with brief writing, extensive commentary exists on how to deliver an effective oral argument. Much of this commentary has been written by judges, and since they are the ones who have to be convinced by an oral argument, we are particularly fond of those tips. *See, e.g.*, Ruggero J. Aldisert, *Winning on Appeal: Better Briefs and Oral Argument* 305–79 (2d ed. 2003) (containing the late Third Circuit Judge Aldisert's views on effective arguments, as well as tips from many other judges and appellate advocates). In addition, although it is focused primarily on Supreme Court advocacy, David Frederick's book *Supreme Court and Appellate Advocacy* (2003), is a useful guide to the keys to success—and perhaps even more importantly, the common errors—in appellate advocacy.

As well, the various practitioners' handbooks endorsed by the courts of appeals—particularly the Seventh Circuit's version—provide very helpful, and sometimes court specific, guidance. And, although it is tailored to U.S. Supreme Court practice, which is in some respects unique, that Court offers a Guide for Counsel in Cases to be Argued Before the Supreme Court of the United States, which is available from the Court and is on the Court's website, www.supremecourtus.gov. Most of the guidance for advocates contained there can be translated into advocacy in most appellate courts.

The authors' experience, as well as much of this helpful commentary, leads to the advice that follows.

A. PREPARATION

1. Even though the argument may be only 10 or 15 minutes long, you have to be prepared for anything. Don't expect that you'll be delivering a 15-minute-long speech. You have to be familiar with the entire record, and you have to know the critical parts of the record cold. That can be a daunting task, but consider this: The appendix may be thousands of

pages long, and the full record many thousands more, but the truly relevant portions of an appeal typically boil down to only a few of those pages. Also, if you are the appellant, know where in the record the particular error was preserved, whether by objection, by motion, or otherwise. *See* § 3.3, *supra*.

2. You also have to know the briefs and the cases that are cited in the briefs—both yours and your opponent's. (Ideally, you were the author of the briefs in some substantial way.) A common approach is to prepare an "oral argument notebook" containing all of the cases cited in all of the parties' briefs, and to read the entirety of those cases—not just the pages or portions cited or quoted in the briefs.

3. Prepare a brief oral introduction that begins with "May it please the Court," and then provides a "roadmap" articulating the two or three crucial points that you need to make. Writing this (and rewriting this) will help you boil down your case to the two or three points you need the judges to take away from your argument. Again, remember the "four percent rule" when you are preparing for argument—the judges hearing your case have only been able to devote, on average, 4% of their preparation time to your case, so this is your opportunity to focus the court on the most critical part of your case for reversal or affirmance. This may be the only uninterrupted period in your entire presentation.

4. In outlining the rest of the argument you hope to give, focus on those two or three points from your roadmap and highlight those. Do not expect to have

time to cover all of the arguments contained in the brief. (Indeed, an oral argument that simply attempts to summarize the brief will be of no value to the judges—they already have your brief.) In preparing this argument, don't forget the equities of your case—advocacy means not just showing the judges how (doctrinally) to decide the case in your favor; it also means showing the judges why they should decide it that way.

5. Recite your introductory roadmap out loud, and time it with a stopwatch (or a watch with a second hand). If it is any longer than 45 seconds, go back and rewrite it until it is short enough that you'll have a fighting chance of getting it out before the first judicial interruption. Additionally, the process of saying your roadmap out loud will give you ideas for areas where you can sharpen the focus, and choose different words. Eventually, you want this portion of your argument (at the very least) internalized so that you could give it without notes.

6. Then, go on and try to give your "entire" argument (the one you would give if you were entirely uninterrupted, which you hope is not the case) out loud. If that takes more than half the time allotted by the court for argument, go back and shorten, focus, and simplify that argument.

7. Using those notes, prepare whatever document you intend to take to the podium when your case is called for argument. One useful way of doing this is to use a simple file folder with the notes affixed to the two inside faces of the folder. Other advocates prefer to have a small notebook with tabs

with them at the podium; yet others take only a single piece of paper or two. A handful of outstanding advocates have so internalized the record, the authorities, and their argument that they can go to the podium with no materials or notes. (Even though we agree that the goal is to have your argument so internalized that you won't lean on your notes during the argument, we do not recommend that latter practice: Human memory is fallible, and the inevitable nervousness of presenting oral argument can cause even the finest advocate's mind to go temporarily blank on a subject.)

8. You may wish to prepare a separate document containing anticipated questions and your answers to those questions. Add to and refine that list as you continue your preparations, especially after you practice your argument in "moot courts."

9. Do at least one "moot court"—preferably at least two, and definitely at least two if it is your first argument—with colleagues who have read the briefs and are willing to "play judge." Make the moot court as realistic as possible—conduct it in a private, quiet room, and have a lectern available to replicate the courtroom experience (if you don't have a lectern, you can follow the practice of one of our former colleagues—a leading advocate turned court of appeals judge—and use an inverted office wastebasket on top of a conference table). If you have some doubts about an argument strategy, or the way you intend to answer a question, try it out in the moot court; here, there's no penalty if it turns out you say something ill-advised. The more questions you get,

and the more ruthless the "judges" are on you, the better.

10. After your first moot court, you may think you need to substantially revise—maybe even scrap—the argument you prepared. Do not be surprised, or depressed, if that is the case. That is why you do moot courts.

11. Nor should you be surprised if, after all of this practice, preparation, and internalization, you are still nervous. Many of the finest and most experienced advocates freely admit that they still get nervous before presenting an argument.

12. Prior to argument, research the particular judges on the panel (if they have been disclosed). Research should focus on the judges' background, work experience, temperament, and political orientation. Also, the advocate should identify any relevant precedent (both helpful and harmful) authored or joined by the particular judges on the panel. Although the occasions should be carefully chosen, it can sometimes be effective to reference a judge on the panel by name when discussing a particular precedent. For instance:

> Smith versus Jones is especially instructive. Judge Miller, in that case, you wrote for the court, in language directly applicable here, that [give very brief quote from the decision].

At the same time, though, this strategy has its risks. Counsel should remember that appellate courts' holdings are those of the court, not of individual authoring judges. So it is inappropriate to refer to "Judge Miller's holding" or "Judge Miller's opinion"; rather, it is "the court's opinion, written by Judge Miller," or "Judge Miller's opinion for the court." Moreover, it may be the case that other members of the court have criticized Judge Miller's opinion for the court in later opinions, so pursuing this strategy without full knowledge of the opinion's treatment by later panels borders on the foolhardy.

B. THE DAY OF ARGUMENT

1. Make sure to consult the local rules and practices to see what is required on the morning (or afternoon) of argument. Most courts require advocates to sign in at the clerk's office; some require the appellant's (or cross appellant's) rebuttal time to be reserved at that point.

2. Entering the courtroom, identify the proper table (often, they have nameplates identifying the tables as for "Appellant" and "Appellee"). If yours is the first argument, you should be able to take a seat at the table. If not, you should pick a seat in the courtroom that allows you to approach the table quickly and quietly and to arrange your materials appropriately in a matter of seconds. You might also walk to the podium, just to get a feel for the imminent experience, and to determine whether its height can be adjusted, whether it will need to be adjusted for your height, and if so, how to accomplish that. (Some courts have electronically adjustable podiums that are controlled by the deputy clerk on duty in the courtroom; others are adjustable either electronically or manually by the advocate; still others do not

permit any adjustment.) Ascertain what the court's timing system is (Are there lights that will warn the advocate that time is running out? Or is it counsel's obligation to keep track of time?).

3. If you have a colleague who will sit with you at counsel table, agree—in advance—about what your expectations are of that colleague. Preferably, you'll be accompanied by someone who also knows the case, and who can find on the fly, in the materials you've brought with you, record excerpts, cases, or statutes that you may need to refer to. Courts dislike it when arguing counsel is constantly getting notes from co-counsel, but in extreme situations the occasional note may be necessary in order for counsel to be of maximum aid to the court. Ideally, if the courtroom is oriented with the tables next to the podium, co-counsel can write such a note in big, bold lettering on a notepad, so that arguing counsel can unobtrusively glance at it during argument.

4. When you are called to the podium, stand up, button your suit coat (where applicable), approach the podium, arrange your materials (and a glass of water, which the court personnel should provide), and then look up to the presiding judge, who should give you some indication (even if just a nod) that the court is ready for your argument. Unless the court has a different prescribed introduction, begin with "May it please the Court," add any identifying material required for the record by court rule or practice (such as your name and the identity of your client), and proceed into your roadmap.

5. Speak clearly, and be attuned to the speed of your delivery. (Nerves tend to make advocates speed up.) Speak in an appropriately modulated tone.

6. The best oral advocates approach the task of oral argument as one of having a conversation with the court; one advocate has called this attitude one of "respectful equality." Gary L. Sasso, *Appellate Oral Argument*, 20 Litig. 27, 30 (Summer 1994). This means a low-key question-and-answer session—not a trial lawyer's summation. Make eye contact with the judges, just as though you are having a conversation with them. Oral arguments that come across as jury arguments are usually unpersuasive—even counterproductive.

7. Do not oversell the case. As Ninth Circuit Judge Kozinski has humorously explained:

> A good way to improve your chances of losing is to overclaim the strength of your case. When it's your turn to speak, start off by explaining how miffed you are that this farce—this travesty of justice—has gone this far when it should have been clear to any dolt that your client's case is ironclad. Now the reason this is a good tactic is that it challenges the judges to get you to admit that there is just some little teensy weensy weakness in your case. So if you overstate your case enough, pretty soon one of the judges will take the bait and ask you a question about the very weakest part of your case. And, of course, that's precisely what you want the judges to be focusing on—the flaws in your case.

Kozinski, *The Wrong Stuff*, 1992 B.Y.U. L. Rev. at 330–31.

C. ANSWERING QUESTIONS

1. Remember that you want questions from the judges. This is the only opportunity you will have to engage directly with the judges who will decide the case, so listening to those judges' concerns and doing one's best to meet those concerns is crucial.

2. Answer the judges' questions—clearly, promptly, and directly. This means stopping an argument mid-sentence if the judge interrupts. If the question calls for a "yes" or "no" answer, give the precise answer—"yes" or "no"—before attempting to explain: "The answer to your question, Your Honor, is 'yes.' The reason is that. . . ." Then try to transition your answer back to one of your main points. This is difficult and is learned only with practice, but it is a good exercise for moot courts.

3. It is risky (to say the least) to answer a question by saying, "I plan to cover that point later." Judges want their questions answered when those questions are asked, and will be frustrated when lawyers are evasive. Lawyers should view questions as an opportunity to address the judges' concerns, not as an irritation or disruption of the flow of a prepared text. Indeed, in addition to telegraphing the judges' concerns, questions can be used to reinforce counsel's themes. The goal is not to give a perfect, oratorical speech, but to be an effective communicator and advocate for the client. As the late First Circuit Judge Frank M. Coffin wrote, "I've seen attorneys bumble,

stammer, and read their argument, but be effective because they had this ability to say to the court, 'Look, I believe in this case; this is important, and you fellows better do the right thing.' " Frank M. Coffin, *The Judge as Advocate's Consumer: On Reading Briefs and Hearing Argument*, (Feb. 27, 1979), *available at* files.mainelaw.maine.edu/Coffin/Public_Speeches/pdf/IV-TheJudgeasAdvocatesConsumer.pdf.

4. In addressing an individual judge, refer to the judges correctly: In the federal courts of appeals, the jurists are called "Judge," not "Justice." In federal courts, the title "Justice" is reserved for the nine members of the Supreme Court of the United States. (Years ago, some wag explained the difference between "Judge" and "Justice" by saying, "There are no judges on the Supreme Court, and there is no justice in the Court of Appeals.") And, unless you are confident that you know the name of the judge (some courtrooms identify the judges on the bench with nameplates; others do not), call the judge "Your Honor"—but not "Sir" or "Ma'am." In one of the highest profile cases ever, *Bush v. Gore*, the lawyer for the Florida Secretary of State referred to Justice Stevens as "Justice Brennan" (who had retired from the Court ten years earlier and passed away three years before the argument). Undeterred by his error, he then referred to Justice Breyer as "Justice Souter," prompting Justice Souter to interject, "I'm Justice Souter—you'd better cut that out." Justice Scalia then followed with a question that he sarcastically began, "Mr. Klock—I'm Scalia." Tr. of Oral Arg., *Bush v. Gore*, No. 00–949, at 34–35 (U.S. S. Ct. Dec. 11, 2000). The gaffe was not only ill-

received by the Justices; it was reported all over the newswires.

5. You are likely to get hypothetical questions from the judges. Answer them. Don't try to dismiss hypotheticals by saying, "That's not this case." By asking hypothetical questions, the judges are testing the rule of law that you are advocating, to see whether it will have negative consequences if applied in another case.

6. Not all questions are hostile to your position. Indeed, a judge who favors your case may ask a friendly question in the hopes that your answer will help the judge convince one of his colleagues to vote with him or her. That makes it critical that you listen closely to the question that is being asked.

7. Flexibility is very important. Thus, if counsel finds that a particular argument is not resonating, based on the judges' comments or demeanor, he or she must be prepared to move immediately to another point.

D. APPELLEE'S ARGUMENT

1. The appellee must be even more flexible. Even the initial two minutes of prepared text may have to be scrapped based on what occurred during the appellant's argument. Instead, it may be appropriate to begin with something like "I'd like to start by addressing the question about jurisdiction that Judge Hutchinson asked my opponent."

2. When appropriate, appellee's counsel should harken back to questions and answers during the

appellant's argument, using those points to reinforce the appellee's themes. As an example:

> Judge Jones, your question to my opponent about the wording of subsection 3 of the statute underscores the fundamental flaw in plaintiff's case.

3. Address the hard arguments made by your opponent. Meet them head-on. Too many appellees' arguments are like ships passing the appellants' arguments in the night. Our late colleague Dean Erwin Griswold, the former Solicitor General of the United States (1967–73), was admired by many Justices of the Supreme Court of the United States for tackling the hardest question in his case in the first few words of his argument.

E. CONCLUDING THE ARGUMENT

1. Have a prepared and clear request for relief, such as: "The judgment of the district court should be reversed," "affirmed," etc. "The injunction should be vacated," "modified," etc. "The judgment should be reversed and the case remanded with instructions to. . . ." You may not get the opportunity to use this request because of the expiration of time, or you may choose not to conclude your argument this way (preferring instead to end with something like "Unless the Court has additional questions, I have nothing further."). Nonetheless, preparing such a statement will ensure that you are able to respond to judges who are unclear as to what relief you are requesting for a particular alleged error.

2. Do not feel compelled to use the entire allotted time. As with arguments in briefs, the more lengthy and complicated an argument is, the less likely the judges will view it as correct. Both authors have had the experience of arguing cases in the U.S. Supreme Court (where 30 minutes of argument per side is the norm) and using much less than the allotted time—and winning, 9–0.

CHAPTER 16

OPINION AND DECISIONMAKING PROCESS

§ 16.1 OPINIONS

In cases set for oral argument, at some point shortly after argument, the judges on the panel will meet in conference to discuss the case. Typically, that conference takes place at the end of the argument day, although in courts where the same three judges sit together for more than one day during the argument week, the conference might take place at the end of the week. These conferences take place with only the three judges (or, if the court is sitting *en banc*, the entire *en banc* court) present. There are no law clerks, secretaries, or other personnel at this conference; only the three judges are there.

At the conclusion of that discussion, the judges will have voted on how the case should be decided, and, in some fashion, decided which of them should be responsible for writing the court's opinion. The assignment power resides in the presiding judge, who is either the seniormost active judge or the Chief Judge, if on the panel (assuming that judge is in the majority and not dissenting). But if a particular judge has a specific interest in the subject matter of a case and expresses a desire to be the author of the opinion, that judge's wishes are often accommodated. Generally, the judges attempt to spread the opinion writing work evenly, so that no judge is overloaded or underutilized. The judges typically reach a tentative understanding at that point whether the opinion will be a signed one or a *per curiam* (by the court) opinion, whether the opinion will be published or unpublished, and whether there will be a dissent from the court's judgment.

The authoring judge and the judge's law clerks will return to their chambers and write a draft opinion. Once the authoring judge is satisfied with the draft opinion, the judge will send it along to his two colleagues. They may, upon reviewing the draft, indicate their concurrence in the opinion. Alternatively, they may make suggestions and offer proposed changes. Minimal stylistic suggestions may be left to discussions between law clerks.

All of the votes and judgments made at the conference are necessarily tentative; a judge who votes to dissent at conference may find himself ultimately swayed by his colleague's draft opinion, or the judge may be able to suggest and secure sufficient changes to the draft opinion, once it is circulated, that his objections to the judgment are minimized or eliminated, thereby allowing the dissenting judge to join the court's opinion. (In rare cases, the authoring judge may ultimately determine that "the opinion will not write," *cf. Arlinghaus v. Ritenour*, 543 F.2d 461, 464 (2d Cir. 1976) (per curiam), and circulate a draft that goes a different direction than the judges tentatively agreed upon at conference.)

A judge may, however, simply be unable to go along with the draft opinion, and will write a separate opinion, concurring on a different ground, or dissenting in whole or in part. (On occasion, a judge will indicate that he or she dissents, but not offer reasons for that decision.) When the dissenting (or concurring) judge completes the separate opinion, that opinion will also be circulated to the rest of the panel. The authoring judge may wish to make some changes to the majority opinion in order to respond to some points made by the dissenting opinion, and if so, the authoring judge will recirculate the opinion, so revised. (On rare occasions, the force of the draft dissenting opinion will be such that one or both of the other judges switch their vote, which would likely result in the dissenting opinion being revised to become the majority opinion, and the former dissenter becoming the author of the court's opinion.)

Recently, some controversy has arisen regarding whether appellate judges should be allowed to engage in factual research, using the Internet or otherwise, in the course of writing the court's opinion. Seventh Circuit Judge Richard Posner has been at the center of this debate. A recent panel decision of the Seventh Circuit, authored by Judge Posner but occasioning separate opinions from each of his colleagues, explores this unsettled issue in some detail. *See Rowe v. Gibson,* 798 F.3d 622, 629–32 (7th Cir. 2015) ; *id.* at 635 (Rovner, J., concurring); *id.* at 635–44 (Hamilton, J., concurring in part and dissenting in part).

In some courts—for example, the Third Circuit and the Federal Circuit—some or all of the court's draft opinions are sent to all of the active judges, not just the judges on the panel, for their review and comment. *See, e.g.*, 3d Cir. I.O.P. 5.5.4; Fed. Cir.

I.O.P. 10.5. In rare cases, that process may cause the court to order an *en banc* rehearing before a panel opinion ever sees the light of day.

After the internal back-and-forth of the judges results in a final opinion for the court, the authoring judge (or judges) forward the opinion (or opinions) to the clerk's office, which issues the court's ruling. With the adoption of e-filing in all 13 judicial circuits, counsel are notified of an opinion's issuance by an emailed notice from the CM/ECF system; opinions are typically posted to the Court's website shortly thereafter. The opinion is either accompanied by, or by itself represents, the "judgment" of the court under FRAP 36.

A more extensive recounting of the inner workings of an appellate court, with respect to the judges' conference and the opinion writing process, and based on the author's longtime experience as a judge on the U.S. Court of Appeals for the First Circuit, can be found in Chapters 8–11 of Frank M. Coffin, *On Appeal: Courts, Lawyering, and Judging* (1994).

§ 16.2 RECUSAL AND REASSIGNMENT

Section 455 of Title 28 of the United States Code is the general judicial recusal statute applicable to appellate judges. (Section 144 of Title 28 is another recusal statute, but it only applies, by its terms, to district judges.)

Recusal is required when a judge's "impartiality might reasonably be questioned." *Id.* § 455(a). The scope of this subsection is limited by the "extrajudicial source" doctrine, which generally forbids a judge's rulings and on the record expressions of opinion from being a ground for recusal. *Liteky v. United States*, 510 U.S. 540, 555 (1994). Recusal under this subsection (a) of Section 455 may be waived by the consent of the parties, but only if "preceded by a full disclosure on the record of the basis for the disqualification." 28 U.S.C. § 455(e).

Recusal is also required under § 455(b) where the judge—

- "has a personal bias or prejudice concerning a party, or personal knowledge of disputed evidentiary facts concerning the proceeding" (§ 455(b)(1));
- "in private practice . . . served as lawyer in the matter in controversy" or "a lawyer with whom [the judge] previously practiced law served during such association as a lawyer concerning the matter, or the judge or such lawyer has been a material witness concerning it" (§ 455(b)(2));
- "has served in governmental employment and in such capacity participated as counsel, adviser or material witness concerning the proceeding or expressed an opinion concerning the merits of the particular case in controversy" (§ 455(b)(3));
- "knows that he, individually or as a fiduciary, or his spouse or minor child residing in his household, has a financial interest in the subject matter in controversy or in a party to

the proceeding, or any other interest that could be substantially affected by the outcome of the proceeding" (§ 455(b)(4));

- is, or the judge's spouse is, or a person "within the third degree of relationship to either of them" is a party, lawyer, material witness, or "is known by the judge to have an interest that could be substantially affected by the outcome of the proceeding." § 455(b)(5).

Recusal under the provisions of subdivision (b) of the recusal statute may not be waived, even with the agreement of all parties. 28 U.S.C. § 455(e).

The case law on appellate judge recusals under Section 455 is sparse, for several reasons. For one, the corporate disclosure form required by FRAP 26.1 allows judges and clerks' offices to avoid assigning judges having a financial interest in one of the parties to the panel in the first place. For another, an appellate judge's decision to recuse, whether on motion or *sua sponte*, is a personal decision; it cannot be reviewed by a panel of an appellate court, or the court *en banc*.

One issue that does arise with some frequency in a narrow class of cases is the "rule of necessity." That rule dates back to the common law; under that rule, a judge is qualified to hear a case even if the judge has an interest in it, if "the case cannot be heard otherwise." *United States v. Will*, 449 U.S. 200, 213–14 (1980). This has most frequently arisen where the plaintiffs in an action are federal judges, and the outcome of the case would affect the compensation of all federal judges, *e.g.*, *id.* at 213–17 (challenge under Compensation Clause of U.S. Constitution, Art. III, § 1, to judicial salaries set by Congress), or where the plaintiff has sued all of the judges in a circuit, *e.g.*, *Tapia-Ortiz v. Winter*, 185 F.3d 8, 10–11 (2d Cir. 1999). In the latter circumstance, the case may—but is not required to—be heard by judges from another circuit sitting by designation. *See, e.g.*, *In re Nettles,* 394 F.3d 1001, 1003 (7th Cir. 2005) (where mandamus petitioner was charged with conspiring to attempt to blow up the Dirksen Courthouse in Chicago—where the Seventh Circuit and the Northern District of Illinois both sit—the judges of the Seventh Circuit recused themselves); *United States v. Nettles*, 476 F.3d 508, 510 (7th Cir. 2007) (in a later appeal in the same case, a panel of the Seventh Circuit comprising Judges Martin, Gibbons, and Sutton of the Sixth Circuit, each sitting by designation, affirmed Nettles' conviction before Judge Keenan of the district court for the Southern District of New York, who sat by designation as a judge of the district court for the Northern District of Illinois).

There is another recusal statute that applies uniquely to appellate judges. Section 47 of Title 28 provides that "no judge shall hear or determine an appeal from the decision of a case or issue tried by him." In the main, this statute prevents a district judge (or former district judge) from sitting on an appellate panel that is reviewing a decision in a case tried by him. But in at least one case (involving school desegregation), it has resulted in the recusal of an appellate judge who was not involved in the case below that was under review, but who had filed an opinion five years earlier in the same dispute under the same docket number. *Swann v. Charlotte-Mecklenburg Bd. of Ed.*, 431 F.2d 135, 135–37 (4th Cir. 1970).

These recusal provisions are treated at much greater length in a comprehensive publication issued by the Federal Judicial Center, Charles Gardner Geyh, *Recusal: Analysis of Case Law Under 28 U.S.C. §§ 455 and 144* (Fed. Judicial Ctr. 2d ed. 2010).

An issue related to recusal—that of reassignment of a case to a different district judge on remand—crops up on occasion. The power of a court of appeals to reassign cases is confirmed by 28 U.S.C. § 2106, which authorizes a court of appeals (or the Supreme Court) to "direct the entry of such appropriate judgment, decree, or order, or require such further proceedings to be had as may be just under the circumstances." Reassignment upon remand does not require a showing of bias or prejudice, but it is nonetheless rarely granted. Most circuits, in evaluating reassignment requests, adhere to a three-factor evaluation: "(1) whether the original judge would reasonably be expected to have substantial difficulty putting out of his or her mind previously expressed views or findings; (2) whether reassignment is advisable to preserve the appearance of justice; and (3) whether reassignment would entail waste and duplication out of proportion to any gain in preserving the appearance of fairness." *Solomon v. United States*, 467 F.3d 928, 935 (6th Cir.

2006). *See also United States v. Robin*, 553 F.2d 8, 10 (2d Cir. 1977) (originating the three-factor inquiry).

§ 16.3 CITATION OF UNPUBLISHED CASES

For many years, courts and commentators debated the soundness of local rules prohibiting citation of unpublished opinions. The Eighth Circuit, in a controversial opinion authored by a very respected appellate judge (the late Richard S. Arnold), held that such a rule was "unconstitutional under Article III, because it purports to confer on the federal courts a power that goes beyond the 'judicial.'" *Anastasoff v. United States*, 223 F.3d 898, 899–905 (8th Cir. 2000). That decision was later vacated as moot by the *en banc* Eighth Circuit. 235 F.3d 1054 (8th Cir. 2000) (en banc). Nonetheless, in *Anastasoff*'s wake, some courts and judges continued to express support for the ability of advocates to cite unpublished opinions. By contrast, the Ninth Circuit, in an opinion authored by another respected judge, Judge Alex Kozinski, held that such rules were constitutional, *Hart v. Massanari*, 266 F.3d 1155 (9th Cir. 2001), and various other courts have agreed with that view.

The debate is now largely academic. FRAP 32.1, which became effective December 1, 2006, forbids courts of appeals from "prohibit[ing] or restrict[ing] the citation of" unpublished opinions handed down on or after January 1, 2007. Despite that rule, however, the courts of appeals are not prohibited from giving "unpublished" dispositions less weight than "binding" authority by local rule or practice. *See, e.g.*, Fed. Cir. R. 32.1(d) ("The court . . . will not give one of its own nonprecedential dispositions the effect of binding precedent.").

§ 16.4 BINDING NATURE OF PRIOR PANEL OPINIONS

Later panels of an appellate court are bound by earlier decisions of that court, whether rendered by another three-judge panel or by the court *en banc*. *United States v. Prince-Oyibo*, 320 F.3d 494, 498 (4th Cir. 2003) ("Absent an en banc overruling or a superseding contrary decision of the Supreme Court," an appellate court is bound by earlier panel precedents.). An exception to this rule appears where a prior panel decision is "clearly inconsistent" with a subsequent Supreme Court decision. *Sheehan v. United States*, 896 F.2d 1168, 1172 n.7 (9th Cir. 1990). The same rule applies with respect to *prior* Supreme Court precedent, "if the Court determines that the prior panel would have reached a different conclusion if it had considered controlling precedent." *Atlantic Thermoplastics Co. v. Faytex Corp.*, 970 F.2d 834, 838 n.2 (Fed. Cir. 1992); *see also Tucker v. Phyfer*, 819 F.2d 1030, 1035 n.7 (11th Cir. 1987).

What happens if a second panel of the same court reaches a decision inconsistent with an earlier panel decision, but neither the parties nor the court are aware of the earlier decisions? Which one of the two decisions is binding precedent? Generally, the earlier decision is the binding precedent if the conflict is irreconcilable, since—even though it failed to do so—the second panel was obligated to follow the first panel's decision. *See, e.g., McMellon v. United States*,

387 F.3d 329, 333 (4th Cir. 2004) (en banc) (collecting cases; agreeing with "[m]ost of the other circuits" and "follow[ing] the earlier of conflicting opinions"). The Eighth Circuit appears to stand alone in giving a panel the choice to follow either line of conflicting circuit precedent, *Graham v. Contract Transp., Inc.*, 220 F.3d 910, 914 (8th Cir. 2000) (a panel "faced with conflicting precedents [is] free to choose which line of cases to follow"); even then, however, a later Eighth Circuit opinion has suggested that "the better practice normally is to follow the earliest opinion, as it should have controlled the subsequent panels that created the conflict." *T.L. ex rel. Ingram v. United States*, 443 F.3d 956, 960 (8th Cir. 2006).

Resolving intra-circuit conflicts becomes even more complicated when there have been intervening Supreme Court decisions that arguably undercut the earlier decision, *see, e.g., id.* at 960–61, because a court of appeals is bound by directly applicable Supreme Court precedent, even if its logical moorings appear to have been cut out from underneath it by subsequent decisions. *Rodriguez de Quijas v. Shearson/Am. Express, Inc.*, 490 U.S. 477, 484 (1989) ("If a precedent of this Court has direct application in a case, yet appears to rest on reasons rejected in some other line of decisions, the Court of Appeals should follow the case which directly controls, leaving to [the Supreme] Court the prerogative of overruling its own decisions.").

Of course, such an intra-circuit conflict in decisions is a significant ground for *en banc* review. FRAP 35(b)(1)(A) (it is a ground for *en banc* rehearing if "the panel decision conflicts with a decision . . . of the court to which the petition was addressed . . . and consideration by the full court is therefore necessary to secure and maintain uniformity of the court's decisions").

CHAPTER 17

ENTRY OF JUDGMENT, REHEARING, REHEARING EN BANC, AND ISSUANCE OF MANDATE

§ 17.1 ENTRY OF JUDGMENT

Under FRAP 36, "[a] judgment is entered when it is noted on the docket." That usually occurs contemporaneously with the issuance of the court's opinion. Rule 36 also instructs clerks on preparing, signing, and entering the judgment (FRAP 36(a)), as well as notifying the parties of the judgment (FRAP 36(b)). But the more important role of Rule 36 is that it clears up confusion as to when a judgment becomes effective. Prior to the Rule's adoption in 1967, it was uncertain as to whether a judgment took effect on the date it was decided, or on the date the mandate was issued. *See, e.g.*, *Comm'r v. Bedford's Estate*, 325 U.S. 283, 286–87 (1945). Now, it is clear from the text of Rule 36 that a judgment is considered entered, and thus takes effect, "when it is noted on the docket." FRAP 36(a).

There are important differences between a court's "judgment" and its "mandate." The judgment is the document that is entered on the docket and contains the court's disposition of the case (*e.g.*, "affirmed," "reversed," etc.). FRAP 36. The mandate, by contrast, is the court of appeals' direction to the district court, and it includes the judgment, the court's opinion (if there was one), and any direction as to the recovery of costs. FRAP 41(a); *see* § 22.4(D), *infra*. The mandate typically issues to the district court several weeks after the opinion and judgment are issued—seven days after the period for filing a petition for rehearing expires, or seven days after such a petition is denied, unless the court of appeals shortens the time or orders that the mandate issue forthwith, *i.e.*, at the same time as the opinion and judgment. FRAP 41(b).

It is important to know the difference between the judgment and the mandate. The date on which the judgment issues is important for computing the time for taking post-decision action in the court of appeals, seeking further relief in the U.S. Supreme Court, and sometimes even for post-judgment relief on remand in the district court. Confusion between judgments and mandates can have profound (and often fatal) effects on issues of timeliness. The confusion is exacerbated by the fact that the courts reach different results in similar or analogous cases with respect to which one (judgment or mandate) starts a particular clock.

For example, in *United States v. Reyes*, 49 F.3d 63 (2d Cir. 1995), a criminal defendant's conviction had been affirmed by the Second Circuit in a judgment entered on April 26, 1991. The mandate, however, did not issue until May 31, 1991. *Id.* at 65. On April 28, 1993, the defendant moved for a new trial in the district court based on newly discovered evidence; at the time, Fed.R.Crim.P. 33 required such motions to be made "before or within two years after final judgment." Had the two years started running from the date of the court of appeals' "judgment," the motion would have been untimely by two days. The Second Circuit nonetheless held (despite the "judgment" language in the rule) that the two-year period begins when the appellate mandate issues, not when the judgment is entered. *Id.* at 67. (The rule now makes the period "3 years after the verdict or finding of guilty," thereby seemingly obviating this problem for future cases.) By contrast, the district court in *Davis v. U.S. Steel Corp.*, 528 F.Supp. 220 (E.D. Pa. 1981), ruled that the tolling of the jurisdictional time limitations for individual Title VII claims ceased when the court of appeals' judgment affirming the denial of class action status was entered, not when the court of appeals' mandate issued. *Id.* at 221–22.

Under the U.S. Supreme Court's Rule 13.3, "[t]he time to file a petition for a writ of certiorari runs from the date of entry of the judgment or order sought to be reviewed, and not from the issuance date of the mandate," unless a timely petition for rehearing is filed in the court of appeals—in which case the 90-day period "runs from the date of the denial of rehearing or, if rehearing is granted, the subsequent entry of judgment." Understanding the operation of this rule is crucial to getting a case before the Supreme Court: Without any apparent exception, the Court routinely denies motions to accept late-filed petitions for certiorari. *See* § 22.4(D), *infra*.

§ 17.2 PANEL REHEARING

FRAP 40 addresses the timing and requirements for a petition for rehearing before the panel initially deciding a case. A petition for panel rehearing must be filed within 14 days after the entry of judgment, except that if the United States or its officer or agency is a party, any party to the suit has 45 days to file a petition for panel rehearing. In either event, the court can shorten or extend the time allowed for filing. FRAP 40(a)(1). This time limit is not "jurisdictional," as a court of appeals has the power to allow a petition and treat it as timely even though it is filed late. *Young v. Harper*, 520 U.S. 143, 147 n.1 (1997).

A petition for rehearing is limited to 3,900 words (or 15 typewritten pages), FRAP 40(b), and must "state with particularity each point of law or fact" that the party seeking rehearing believes was erroneous or overlooked. FRAP 40(a)(2). An opposing party may not respond unless asked to do so by the court; nonetheless, the court "ordinarily" will not grant rehearing without requesting such a response. FRAP 40(a)(3). If the petition is granted, the court can render a new decision without oral argument, or schedule new arguments. FRAP 40(a)(4). The rule forbids oral argument on the petition itself, however. FRAP 40(a)(2).

Securing panel rehearing is somewhat easier than securing rehearing *en banc* (*see* § 17.3, *infra*), but that reflects the different purposes of each kind of petition. A mistake of fact is enough to get panel rehearing, but it would not normally be enough to get rehearing *en banc*. Moreover, a mistake of law might also warrant panel rehearing, even if the issue is not sufficiently important to justify rehearing *en banc*.

The court might grant rehearing in a case simply to clarify its opinion or issue a revised opinion, without any effect on the ultimate judgment of the court. Alternatively, a panel may grant rehearing in order to make a change to the court's opinion that would eliminate the need for an *en banc* proceeding; this might occur in response to the circulation of internal memoranda among the court's judges suggesting that *en banc* treatment of a case would be appropriate unless corrections are made to the panel's opinion.

§ 17.3 REHEARING *EN BANC*

The federal courts of appeals conduct over 99% of their business in panels of three judges. For the various circuits to maintain coherent bodies of precedent, it is vital that later panels, even though comprising different judges who might want to reach a different result, respect the earlier panel decisions as binding precedent. *See* § 16.4, *supra*. Thus, in general, only an *en banc* decision of the same court, or a decision by the U.S. Supreme Court, can overrule a three-judge panel's precedent.

There are exceptions, however. A panel might determine that an intervening Supreme Court decision has removed the logic of a prior panel opinion, and therefore find that the prior opinion was implicitly overruled. Or, a panel might purport to provide "clarification" of earlier decisions. *In re Initial Pub. Offering Sec. Litig.*, 471 F.3d 24, 35–37, 39–40 & n.6 (2d Cir. 2006) (effectively rejecting two prior panel decisions, each one authored by a member of the panel in the *IPO* case). And, of course, a panel may unwittingly create a conflict with an earlier decision in the circuit by not locating that decision prior to ruling. *See* § 16.4, *supra*. *En banc* decision making allows each court of appeals a more straightforward process for unifying its precedent and considering questions of overwhelming importance.

Obtaining rehearing *en banc* is much more difficult than obtaining panel rehearing; indeed, FRAP 35(a) states explicitly that *en banc* hearings are "not favored and ordinarily will not be ordered." FRAP 35 sets out the procedure for requesting rehearing *en banc*. The party must petition for rehearing *en banc* based upon the same deadlines that apply to petitions for panel rehearing under FRAP 40. FRAP 40(a); *see* § 15.2, *supra*. The petition may not exceed 3,900 words or 15 typewritten pages. FRAP 35(b)(2). A response may not be filed unless the court requests one. FRAP 35(e). And as a matter of substance, the petition must demonstrate (1) that "en banc consideration is necessary to secure or maintain uniformity of the court's decisions," including harmony with the Supreme Court's decisions, or (2) that "the proceeding involves a question of exceptional importance." FRAP 35(a)(1), (2). The petition must begin with a statement affirming that one or the other condition exists. FRAP 35(b)(1)(A), (B). If a party seeks both panel rehearing under FRAP 40 and rehearing *en banc* under FRAP 35, the requests are subject to a combined 3,900-word (or 15-typewritten-page) limit, "even if they are filed separately, unless separate filing is required by local rule." FRAP 35(b)(3).

An *en banc* hearing or rehearing can be initiated by the court *sua sponte*, even without the filing of a petition for rehearing *en banc*. The courts of appeals may issue a notice of *en banc* rehearing without notice to the parties, although the Ninth Circuit has an internal rule requiring the court to seek the views of the parties when the *en banc* process is initiated from within the court. 9th Cir. General Order 5.4(c)(3).

A petition for rehearing *en banc* is determined by "the circuit judges who are in regular active service and who are not disqualified." FRAP 35(a); 28 U.S.C. § 46(c). That means that only "active" circuit judges (*i.e.*, not senior judges, and not district judges or judges from other courts "sitting by designation") may vote on the petition. A majority of those active judges must vote to rehear a case *en banc*; otherwise, the petition will be denied. If the number of "active" judges on a court is an even number, and only half vote to accept a case for *en banc* review, the petition is denied. *See* 28 U.S.C. § 44(a); Chapter 2, *supra*.

Prior to the 2005 amendments to Rule 35, which added the "and who are not disqualified" language, there was a national split over whether recused judges counted as "judges . . . in regular active service." Seven circuits followed an "absolute majority" rule (if a judge or judges are recused from consideration of an *en banc* petition, that does not reduce the number of judges needed to vote in favor of *en banc* proceedings). The remaining six circuits provided that recused judges were excluded from consideration of what was a "majority." *See Allapattah Servs., Inc. v. Exxon Corp.*, 362 F.3d 739, 744–45 n.6 (11th Cir. 2004) (Tjoflat, J., dissenting from denial of rehearing en banc). The 2005 amendments adopted the latter approach. Advisory Committee Notes to 2005 Amendments to FRAP 35.

If rehearing *en banc* is ordered, however, the *en banc* court may include more—or fewer—judges than just the non-recused "judges who are in regular active service." A senior judge who was a member of the original panel may participate, at his election and pursuant to 28 U.S.C. § 294(c) and 28 U.S.C. § 46(c), as a member of the *en banc* court (that judge may not vote in the poll regarding whether to accept the case for *en banc* treatment, however). And the Omnibus Judgeship Act of 1978, Pub. L. 95–486, § 6, 92 Stat. 1633, provides that circuits with more than 15 active judges may perform its *en banc* functions with fewer judges, as prescribed by court rule. Only the Fifth and Ninth Circuits qualify for these special procedures; presently, only the Ninth Circuit has implemented them, via a rule providing for a "limited en banc court." *See* 9th Cir. R. 35–3 (providing that "[t]he en banc court . . . shall consist of the Chief Judge of this circuit and 10 additional judges to be drawn by lot from the active judges of the Court" and that, "[i]n appropriate cases, the Court may order a rehearing by the full court following a hearing or rehearing en banc").

FRAP 35's provisions allow for either an initial hearing *en banc* or a rehearing *en banc*. As rare as rehearing *en banc* is, initial hearings *en banc* (that is, where the full court hears the appeal in the first instance without an argument and decision having first occurred before the panel) are even rarer. *See Belk v. Charlotte-Mecklenburg Bd. of Educ.*, 211 F.3d 853, 854–55 (4th Cir. 2000) (Wilkinson, C.J., concurring in the denial of an initial hearing *en banc*) (noting the rarity of initial *en banc* hearings and stating that "[h]earing the case for the first time *en banc* would be like the Supreme Court bypassing the winnowing function of the court of appeals, which it routinely refuses to do").

§ 17.4 ISSUANCE OF MANDATE

A. BASIC PRINCIPLES

As noted above (§ 17.1, *supra*), FRAP 41(a) provides that the mandate of the court of appeals consists of a "certified copy of the judgment, a copy of the court's opinion, if any, and any direction about costs." Although the mandate includes the judgment of the court of appeals (*see* FRAP 36), it serves different purposes: It provides direction to the district court upon remand, ends the proceedings in the court of appeals, and re-vests the district court with jurisdiction over the entire case. *See, e.g., Fort Gratiot Sanitary Landfill, Inc. v. Mich. Dept. of Nat. Resources*, 71 F.3d 1197, 1200 (6th Cir. 1995) (noting that the issuance of the court's mandate "returned jurisdiction to the district court"); *United States v. Rivera*, 844 F.2d 916, 921 (2d Cir. 1988) ("Simply put, jurisdiction follows the mandate."). The judgment, by contrast, notifies the parties and the public of the disposition of a case, and triggers timing requirements for further review by the court of appeals or by the Supreme Court. § 17.1, *supra*.

The mandate of the court of appeals is to be issued by the clerk's office either "7 days after the time to file a petition for rehearing expires" (*i.e.*, 21 days after the entry of judgment, in the ordinary course) or "7 days after entry of an order denying a timely petition for panel rehearing, petition for rehearing en banc, or motion for stay of mandate, whichever is later." FRAP 41(b). The court may, however, "shorten or extend the time" for issuance of the mandate, *id.*, and may exercise its discretion to shorten the time—including to direct in its opinion that "the mandate shall issue forthwith"—where prompt action in the district court may need to be taken.

The "mandate rule" is, at its most basic level, the rule that a lower court must follow the directions of a superior court. It is sometimes said to be a corollary to the "law of the case" doctrine, *see, e.g.*, *Ute Indian Tribe v. Utah*, 114 F.3d 1513, 1520 (10th Cir. 1997), but that may not be the most accurate analogy. The "law of the case" doctrine is generally considered to be the "amorphous," flexible, and ultimately discretionary practice that a ruling made at one stage of a case "*should* continue to govern the same issues in subsequent stages in the same case." *Arizona v. California*, 460 U.S. 605, 618 (1983) (emphasis added). But the mandate rule—as the name suggests—is *mandatory*. It holds that "a district court *must* comply strictly with the mandate rendered by the reviewing court," and "may not deviate" from that mandate. *Huffman v. Saul Holdings Ltd. P'ship*, 262 F.3d 1128, 1132 (10th Cir. 2001) (internal quotation marks and citations omitted; emphasis added). Nonetheless, the interpretation of an appellate court's mandate may require close examination of not only the judgment, but the opinion as well. *See, e.g., Exxon Chem. Patents, Inc. v. Lubrizol Corp.*, 137 F.3d 1475, 1483 (Fed. Cir. 1998) ("the nature of the district court's remaining tasks is discerned not simply from the language of the judgment, but from the judgment in combination with the accompanying opinion").

B. STAYING THE MANDATE BY MOTION OR REHEARING PETITION

The issuance of the mandate is automatically stayed by the timely filing of a petition for rehearing or rehearing *en banc*, or by the timely filing of a motion for stay of mandate. FRAP 41(d)(1). As noted (§ 17.4(A), *supra*), those acts cause the mandate to be held in the court of appeals until 7 days following the disposition of the last of such petitions or motions, unless the court orders otherwise. FRAP 41(b).

Sometimes, a clerk's office will issue a mandate prematurely (*i.e.*, before the disposition of a timely petition for rehearing), or other circumstances are present after the mandate has issued in which the court of appeals desires to reassert its authority over the case. In such cases, the court of appeals has the inherent authority to recall its mandate. However, that power is subject to review for abuse of discretion, and is to be exercised (save in the case of a clerical error by the court) "only in extraordinary circumstances," as a power "of last resort, to be held in reserve against grave, unforeseen contingencies." *Calderon v. Thompson*, 523 U.S. 538, 549–50 (1998). The reason for this exceptional treatment can be found in "the profound interests in repose" that attend the judgments of federal courts of appeals. *Id.* at 550. The recall power may be used to correct "clerical errors," but it cannot be used by a court of appeals to "revisit the merits of its earlier decision" absent extraordinary circumstances. *Id.* at 557.

For example, in *United States v. Crawford,* 422 F.3d 1145 (9th Cir. 2005), the court of appeals found just such "extraordinary circumstances" and ordered the mandate recalled in a case where the sentencing judge had expressed reservations about the sentence he was imposing against the defendant, and where the U.S. Supreme Court had foreshadowed its later holding that certain aspects of the United States Sentencing Guidelines were inconsistent with the Sixth Amendment's jury trial right before the original mandate had issued. *Id.* at 1145–46.

C. STAY OF MANDATE PENDING CERTIORARI

The losing party in the court of appeals will sometimes seek a stay of the mandate pending a petition for certiorari. Under FRAP 41(d)(2)(A), such party must identify a substantial issue for presentation to the Supreme Court and good cause for a stay. The court of appeals must decide "whether the applicant has a reasonable probability of succeeding on the merits and whether the applicant will suffer irreparable injury." *Nanda v. Bd. of Tr. of Univ. of Ill.*, 312 F.3d 852, 853 (7th Cir. 2002) (Ripple, J., in chambers). In the context of certiorari, which requires four votes to grant certiorari and five votes to reverse a court of appeals' judgment (*see* § 22.12(D), *infra*), this means that "the applicant must show a reasonable probability that at least four Justices will vote to grant certiorari and a reasonable possibility that at least five Justices will vote to reverse the judgment of this court." *Id.* at 853–54. Showing a conflict among the circuits is one way to show a reasonable probability that certiorari will be granted. *See, e.g., United States v. Holland*, 1 F.3d 454, 456 (7th Cir. 1993) (Ripple, J., in chambers); *see generally California v. American Stores, Co.*, 492 U.S. 1301, 1304–07 (1989) (O'Connor, J., in chambers).

A stay cannot exceed 90 days (the time allowed for the filing of a petition for certiorari, *see* S. Ct. R. 13.1), except for good cause. The filing of a petition, however, extends the stay until the Supreme Court's "final disposition," so long as counsel notifies the clerk of the court of appeals, in writing, before the stay expires, that a petition has been timely filed. FRAP 41(d)(2)(B). If the final disposition is the denial of certiorari, the court of appeals' mandate must issue immediately upon the filing of a Supreme Court order denying certiorari. FRAP 41(d)(2)(D).

A stay of mandate is not a prerequisite to the filing of a petition for certiorari, however, as the issuance of the court of appeals' mandate does not in itself eliminate the power of the Supreme Court to review the court's judgment. *See, e.g.*, *Aetna Cas. & Sur. Co. v. Flowers*, 330 U.S. 464, 467 (1947); *Carr v. Zaja*, 283 U.S. 52, 53 (1931). Indeed, even compliance with the terms of a district court judgment (such as payment of the amount of a money judgment) will not impede Supreme Court review; money can always be repaid. A stay of mandate might be appropriate, however, where actions taken in the district court upon remand might cause the dispute to become moot, *e.g.*, where the mandate directs the district court to order the disclosure of allegedly privileged or confidential materials. *See, e.g.*, *John Doe Agency v. John Doe Corp.*, 488 U.S. 1306, 1307–08 (1989) (Marshall, J., in chambers).

CHAPTER 18

APPELLATE COSTS, SANCTIONS, ATTORNEY DISCIPLINE, AND VOLUNTARY DISMISSALS

§ 18.1 COSTS

FRAP 39 contains provisions addressing the substance and procedure of the payment of costs associated with an appeal. It both supplements and complements Fed.R.Civ.P. 54(d), which deals with the allowance of costs in district-court proceedings.

A. WHO PAYS THE COSTS?

One side or the other (or both of them) must pay the costs of an appeal. FRAP 39(a)(1)–(3) creates a default rule that the prevailing party is entitled to recover its costs, "unless the law provides or the court orders otherwise." FRAP 39(a); *see generally, e.g., American Auto. Mfrs. Ass'n v. Comm'r, Mass. Dept. of Envtl. Prot.*, 31 F.3d 18, 28 (1st Cir. 1994). If the case is dismissed or the judgment is affirmed, the appellant bears the costs—even if the dismissal was at the request of the appellant. *Id.*; FRAP 39(a)(1) & (2). If the judgment is reversed, the costs are assessed against the appellee. FRAP 39(a)(3). The court of appeals has virtually unfettered discretion (constrained only by the remote possibility of Supreme Court review) to award or deny costs under this rule. *See, e.g., Tung Mung Dev. Co. v. United States*, 354 F.3d 1371, 1381–82 (Fed. Cir. 2004).

The court can grant—or deny—costs for numerous reasons, including the good or bad faith of the parties, the history of the case, and the actual amount of money involved. Indeed, a court can even deny costs to a winning party. For example, the Second Circuit in *Varda, Inc. v. Insurance Co. of North America*, 45 F.3d 634 (2d Cir. 1995), denied costs to a successful appellee who "brazenly" used single-spaced footnotes to evade the page limits under the then-existing FRAP 28(g). *Id.* at 640. (The court then humorously waxed "nostalgi[c] for the rigors of the common law," recalling an ancient English chancery decision ordering an offending lawyer to be led through the courts with his head sticking through a hole in his brief. *Id.* at 641.) The Federal Circuit views its discretion in this regard as so unlimited that it has held that costs need not be routinely awarded to the prevailing party—and in fact has suggested that it "routinely . . . den[ies] costs to the prevailing party." *Tung Mung Dev. Co. v. United States*, 354 F.3d at 1382. *But see id.* at 1382–83 (Friedman, J., dissenting) ("It has long been my understanding that costs are awarded routinely to the prevailing party. . . . [T]he routine denial of costs seems inconsistent with [FRAP] 39.").

If, however, a judgment is reversed in part and affirmed in part, then there is no default rule, and "costs are taxed only as the court orders." FRAP 39(a)(4). The court of appeals might indicate "no costs" or "each party is to bear its own costs" in its opinion (meaning that the costs initially incurred by the parties are not shifted in any way). Alternatively, the court has the virtually unfettered discretion to award costs to one or the other party (*e.g.*, if one of the parties substantially prevailed in the appeal), or it might allocate costs among the parties (*e.g.*, by providing that each side should " 'pay fifty percent of the costs on appeal to be taxed by the Clerk of this Court' "). *Conway Groves, Inc. v. Coopers & Lybrand*, 158 F.R.D. 505, 506 (M.D.Fla. 1994) (quoting Eleventh Circuit mandate).

These rules apply even if the United States is a party, unless another law specifies otherwise. FRAP 39(b). Indeed, the Equal Access to Justice Act, 28 U.S.C. § 2412(a), expressly provides that the United States may be liable for costs.

As noted, the standards of FRAP 39(a) apply "unless the law provides or the court orders otherwise." In some cases, other laws provide for or deny the awarding of costs, and will override FRAP 39(a). For example, the cost-shifting provision of the Endangered Species Act has been read to entitle a prevailing defendant to an award of costs only when the losing plaintiff's litigation was "frivolous." *See, e.g., Marbled Murrelet v. Babbitt*, 182 F.3d 1091, 1096 (9th Cir. 1999); 16 U.S.C. § 1540(g)(4). That provision, the Ninth Circuit held, "overrides" FRAP 39. *See, e.g., Ocean Conservancy, Inc. v. Nat'l Marine Fisheries Serv.*, 382 F.3d 1159, 1161–62 (9th Cir. 2004) (per curiam). Similarly, the *in forma pauperis* statute provides that "[j]udgment may be rendered for costs at the conclusion of the suit or action as in other proceedings, but the United States shall not be liable for any of the costs thus incurred." 28 U.S.C.

§ 1915(f)(1). *See, e.g.*, *Maida v. Callahan*, 148 F.3d 190, 192–93 (2d Cir. 1998).

In forma pauperis litigants can present other special issues with respect to costs as well. Such litigants are not immune from having to pay costs, although the court may take their indigency into account in determining whether to award costs and how much to award. *See, e.g.*, *Singleton v. Smith*, 241 F.3d 534, 539–40 (6th Cir. 2001). Two courts have divided on the issue of whether costs may be assessed against a prisoner proceeding *in forma pauperis* under 28 U.S.C. § 1915, which provides, in relevant part, that costs may only be assessed against an *in forma pauperis* prisoner "[i]f the judgment against [the] prisoner includes the payment of costs." *Id.* § 1915(f)(2)(A). The Second Circuit has held that the judgment itself must include an award of costs and cannot be entered later in connection with the issuance of the mandate; the Sixth Circuit has expressly disagreed with that analysis, and held that § 1915(f) simply means that prisoners, like other litigants, can be required to pay costs. *Compare Feliciano v. Selsky*, 205 F.3d 568, 572 (2d Cir. 2000) *with Skinner v. Govorchin*, 463 F.3d 518, 521–23 (6th Cir. 2006).

B. WHAT COSTS ARE RECOVERABLE?

The costs that can be taxed in the court of appeals include:

- the fee for filing the notice of appeal, if the appellant (who initially incurred the cost) is the prevailing party in the court of appeals, FRAP 39(e)(4);

- the "cost[s] of producing necessary copies of a brief or appendix," or necessary copies of records authorized by FRAP 30(f) (dealing with appeals on the record without an appendix), FRAP 39(c); and
- the costs of "the preparation and transmission of the record," "the reporter's transcript, if needed to determine the appeal," and "premiums paid for a supersedeas bond or other bond to preserve rights pending appeal," FRAP 39(e)(1)–(3).

These types of costs are typical, but not exhaustive; FRAP 39(a) does not provide a list of recoverable costs. *See Adsani v. Miller*, 139 F.3d 67, 74 (2d Cir. 1998).

The majority rule is that attorneys' fees are not within the meaning of "costs" as defined by Rule 39, even where a federal statute provides for the award of "a reasonable attorney's fee as part of the costs." In *Family PAC v. Ferguson*, 745 F.3d 1261 (9th Cir. 2014), the Ninth Circuit surveyed the law of other circuits and concluded that "the term 'costs' under Federal Rule of Appellate Procedure 39 does not include attorney's fees recoverable as part of costs under 42 U.S.C. § 1988 and similar statutes." 745 F.3d. at 1269. *See also id.* at 1266–67 (surveying circuits and describing the D.C. Circuit as an outlier). The Ninth Circuit in *Family PAC* rejected the argument that its prior mandate, providing that "[e]ach party shall bear its own costs of appeal," *Family PAC v. McKenna*, 685 F.3d 800, 814 (9th Cir. 2012), precluded the statutory fee award, noting, *inter alia*, that the "costs" enumerated in Rule 39 and in 28 U.S.C. § 1920 (the statute on which Rule 39 is based) were in the nature of "a set of uniformly administrative costs, not including attorney's fees." 745 F.3d at 1266.

In the D.C. Circuit case identified by the Ninth Circuit as conflicting with this majority rule, however, the court held that the prevailing appellee had not timely filed a request for statutory *attorneys' fees* because it had not made its fee request within the period prescribed by Rule 39 for the recovery of *costs*. *Montgomery & Assocs., Inc. v. Commodity Futures Trading Comm'n*, 816 F.2d 783, 784–85 (D.C. Cir. 1987) ("Since [7 U.S.C. § 18(e)] specifically and expressly requires every attorney's fee 'to be taxed and collected as a part of [appellee's] costs,' the conclusion seems unavoidable that all fee requests must be filed in accord with the established deadline for costs" in FRAP 39). The D.C. Circuit's "timeliness" holding is nonetheless in accord with the decisions of other circuits—even those that have interpreted "costs" in Rule 39 as excluding attorneys' fees—holding that such statutory fee requests are untimely if not made within the period of time provided by Rule 39 for claiming costs. *See, e.g.*, *Mills by Mills v. Freeman*, 118 F.3d 727, 734–35 & n.5 (11th Cir. 1997) (holding that, even though "[t]he award of costs pursuant to rule 39 is 'separate and distinct from and totally unrelated to an award of attorney's fees pursuant to the directions of [section] 1988,' " a party wishing to obtain fees on appeal nonetheless "must file a petition with the clerk of this circuit within fourteen days of the issuance of the opinion of this court"). Accordingly, there is a potential trap for the unwary here: While an appellate court's award or refusal of Rule 39 costs will not preclude a fee award based on a federal statute, Rule 39's timeliness provision may nonetheless control.

Note the difference in language between FRAP 39(a) and 39(e): Under Rule 39(a), "costs *are taxed*" by the court of appeals; by contrast, Rule 39(e) provides that certain "costs on appeal *are taxable* in the district court for the benefit of the party entitled to costs under this rule." (Emphases added). The logic of this separation of categories of costs is that the costs available under FRAP 39(a) were incurred in the court of appeals, whereas the FRAP 39(e) costs were incurred while the case was still in the district court, making it more appropriate that the district court exercise its discretion as to those categories of appeal-related costs. That means that if the court of appeals has awarded costs, then the district court has discretion to award such further costs to that prevailing party under Rule 39(e); it is not required to make such an award, however. *See Campbell v. Rainbow City, Ala.*, 209 Fed. Appx. 873, 875 (11th Cir. 2006) (collecting cases).

Still, courts have held that under Fed.R.Civ.P. 54(d), there is a "strong presumption that the prevailing party will recover costs," and the discretion of a district court to deny costs to a prevailing party is "narrowly confined." *Weeks v.*

Samsung Heavy Indus. Co., 126 F.3d 926, 945 (7th Cir. 1997). "Generally, only misconduct by the prevailing party worthy of a penalty or the losing party's inability to pay will suffice to justify denying costs." *Id. See also, e.g.*, *Chapman v. AI Transp.*, 229 F.3d 1012, 1039 (11th Cir. 2000) (stating that Fed.R.Civ.P. 54(d) "establishes a presumption that costs are to be awarded to a prevailing party," and "[t]o defeat the presumption and deny full costs, a district court must have and state a sound basis for doing so").

One significant cost that can be taxed in the district court under FRAP 39(e) is "premiums paid for a supersedeas bond or other bond to preserve rights pending appeal." When the appeal has resulted in the reversal of a large money judgment, these costs can be substantial, and the district court has discretion to award them in whole or in part post-appeal in the event that appellate costs are awarded. *See, e.g.*, *Emmenegger v. Bull Moose Tube Co.*, 324 F.3d 616, 627 (8th Cir. 2003). However, if the court of appeals' judgment is an affirmed-in-part, reversed-in-part judgment, these costs cannot be awarded unless the court of appeals first makes a specific order for the award of costs under FRAP 39(a)(4). *See, e.g.*, *Reeder-Simco GMC, Inc. v. Volvo GM Heavy Truck Corp.*, 497 F.3d 805, 808–09 (8th Cir. 2007); *Golden Door Jewelry Creations, Inc. v. Lloyds Underwriters Non-Marine Assn.*, 117 F.3d 1328, 1340–41 (11th Cir. 1997).

FRAP 39(c) mandates that "[e]ach court of appeals must, by local rule, fix the maximum rate for taxing the cost of producing necessary copies of a brief or appendix, or copies of records authorized by Rule 30(f)." That rule further provides that the rate set by each court of appeals "must not exceed that generally charged for such work in the area where the clerk's office is located and should encourage economical methods of copying." *Id.* The rule was amended in 1979 to allow for variations based on differing prevailing prices in different localities. Advisory Committee Notes to 1979 Amendments to FRAP 39. When originally adopted in 1967, Rule 39(c) did not allow for such variability in costs; indeed, the Advisory Committee Notes to its adoption stated that it was designed to create a uniform rule for cost recovery "in keeping with the principle of this rule that all cost items expended in the prosecution of a proceeding should be borne by the unsuccessful party." Advisory Committee Notes to 1967 Adoption of FRAP 39.

C. PROCEDURES REGARDING COSTS

FRAP 39(d) sets forth the procedures for filing and objecting to a bill of costs in the court of appeals. "[W]ithin 14 days after entry of judgment," a party seeking to have costs taxed must file an itemized and verified bill of costs. FRAP 39(d)(1). (Note that under FRAP 36(a), an appellate court's judgment is entered when it is noted on the docket. Typically, this is the date the appellate court's opinion—not its mandate—is issued.) Objections to the statement "must be filed within 14 days after service of the bill of costs, unless the court extends the time." FRAP 39(d)(2). The court (often, a single judge) will then rule on the objections.

If there is no objection, the clerk will include an itemized list of costs as part of its mandate under FRAP 41(a).

If the U.S. Supreme Court reverses or substantially modifies an appellate court's judgment, or the *en banc* court of appeals does the same to a panel's decision, "any costs awarded to the previously prevailing party are automatically vacated." *Furman v. Cirrito*, 782 F.2d 353, 355 (2d Cir. 1986) (citations omitted).

§ 18.2 SANCTIONS

FRAP 38 provides that "[i]f a court of appeals determines that an appeal is frivolous, it may, after a separately filed motion or notice from the court and reasonable opportunity to respond, award just damages and single or double costs to the appellee." That rule enforces 28 U.S.C. § 1912, which provides that when an appellate court (including the U.S. Supreme Court) affirms a judgment, "the court in its discretion may adjudge to the prevailing party just damages for his delay, and single or double costs." It is also authorized by 28 U.S.C. § 1927, which allows courts to penalize *attorneys*—"personally"—for "unreasonably and vexatiously" "multipl[ying] the proceedings in any case." Section 1927 penalties can include "the excess costs, expenses, and attorneys' fees reasonably incurred because of such conduct." Rule 11 of the Federal Rules of Civil Procedure, however, applies only to actions in district courts. *See* Fed.R.Civ.P. 1 (rules "govern the procedure . . . in

United States district courts"); *Cooter & Gell v. Hartmarx Corp.*, 496 U.S. 384, 405–07 (1990) (same).

A. WHAT IS A "FRIVOLOUS" APPEAL?

An appeal can be frivolous as filed, or frivolous as argued. An appeal is frivolous as filed if "the judgment by the tribunal below was so plainly correct and the legal authority contrary to appellant's position so clear that there really is no appealable issue." *Finch v. Hughes Aircraft Co.*, 926 F.2d 1574, 1579 (Fed. Cir. 1991). In other words, an appeal is frivolous as filed if the appeal is a "complete loser." *In re Perry*, 918 F.2d 931, 935 (Fed. Cir. 1990) (internal quotation marks and citations omitted).

Alternatively—and more commonly—an appeal may be frivolous as argued if there is an appealable issue in the case, but "the appellant's contentions in prosecuting the appeal are frivolous." *Finch*, 926 F.2d at 1579. *See also Mars Steel Corp. v. Cont. Bank N.A.*, 880 F.2d 928, 938 (7th Cir. 1989) (en banc) (appeal is frivolous if the "result is foreordained by the lack of substance to the appellant's arguments"). The Federal Circuit's *Finch* decision catalogued numerous ways that an appeal might be frivolous as argued, including: submitting rambling briefs, filing numerous documents with irrelevant arguments and authority, seeking to relitigate issues already decided, failing to explain the lower court's error, failing to exclude impermissible opponents from the appeal, rearguing frivolous and already-sanctioned arguments, citing irrelevant authorities, and misrepresenting facts or law to the court. 926 F.2d at 1579–80.

In addition, parties making unjustified motions and requests for sanctions have frequently been sanctioned for those acts. *See, e.g.*, *Foy v. First Nat'l Bank of Elkhart*, 868 F.2d 251, 258 (7th Cir. 1989) ("A frivolous request for sanctions is itself sanctionable."). Even the United States can be sanctioned for a frivolous appeal. *See In re Good Hope Indus.*, 886 F.2d 480, 481–82 (1st Cir. 1989) (per curiam) (holding that 28 U.S.C. § 2412(b), which allows an award of attorneys' fees against the United States under "any statute which specifically provides for such an award," applies to FRAP 38). Moreover, there is no categorical exclusion of criminal cases from the rule, even though "[t]he rule must be applied with caution in such cases to avoid discouraging convicted defendants from exercising their right to appeal." *United States v. Cooper*, 170 F.3d 691, 692 (7th Cir. 1999) (issuing order to show cause), *sanctions imposed* (7th Cir. June 14, 1999) (unpublished). And, despite the special solicitude that is typically given to *pro se* litigants, they, too, can be sanctioned for a frivolous appeal. *See, e.g.*, *Haworth v. Royal*, 347 F.3d 1189, 1192 (10th Cir. 2003) ("'The fact that [an appellant] is a pro se litigant does not prohibit the court from imposing sanctions.'").

However, sanctions should not be used to penalize and deter good-faith but ultimately unsuccessful appeals. Thus, "[t]he fact that an appeal is without merit does not mean that the appeal is necessarily a frivolous one." *Abbs v. Principi*, 237 F.3d 1342, 1345 (Fed. Cir. 2001). Nor does the fact that an appeal is blocked by circuit precedent automatically make an appeal frivolous, especially if the legal question is open in the U.S. Supreme Court and an appeal is the only way to preserve the issue for further review. *See McKnight v. Gen. Motors Corp.*, 511 U.S. 659, 660 (1994) (per curiam) (reversing sanctions imposed by Seventh Circuit).

B. PROCEDURES REGARDING SANCTIONS

Under FRAP 38, a party seeking sanctions must present the request in "a separately filed motion." The request cannot come in the merits brief; absent a separate request, the courts will not consider the request. *See, e.g., In re I Don't Trust*, 143 F.3d 1, 4 (1st Cir. 1998). In the absence of a motion, a court must provide "notice . . . and reasonable opportunity to respond" to the notice, consistent with the basic requirements of due process. FRAP 38.

Sanctions may be directed at parties or at their attorneys—or at both, jointly and severally. *See, e.g., Hilmon Co. (V.I.) Inc. v. Hyatt Int'l*, 899 F.2d 250, 253–54 (3d Cir. 1990) (cataloging cases where attorneys have been held personally liable for FRAP 38 sanctions). That decision is left to the court of appeals' discretion, and will likely be based on the particular facts and circumstances of the case, especially any indicia of who (the party or the attorney) is most responsible for the frivolous appeal.

The fact that a court lacks subject-matter jurisdiction over the underlying dispute does not deprive a court of jurisdiction to impose and enforce sanctions, including Rule 38 sanctions. *Chemiakin v. Yefimov*, 932 F.2d 124, 126–29, 130 (2d Cir. 1991); *see also Willy v. Coastal Corp.*, 503 U.S. 131, 137–38 (1992) (lack of subject-matter jurisdiction does not deprive district court of power to award and enforce Fed.R.Civ.P. 11 sanctions); *Cooter & Gell*, 496 U.S. at 395–96 (dismissal of underlying action does not terminate court's authority to award Fed.R.Civ.P. 11 sanctions).

C. "JUST DAMAGES AND SINGLE OR DOUBLE COSTS"

FRAP 38 provides that courts may award "just damages and single or double costs" as a penalty for a frivolous appeal. "Just damages" may take the form of a lump sum of money, *see, e.g., Marino v. Brown*, 357 F.3d 143, 147 (1st Cir. 2004), or the reasonable attorneys' fees incurred in opposing the appeal. *See, e.g., Mustafa v. City of Chicago*, 442 F.3d 544, 549 (7th Cir. 2006) (FRAP 38 "permit[s] the discretionary award of attorneys' fees to the victorious party").

§ 18.3 ATTORNEY ADMISSIONS AND DISBARMENT

FRAP 46(a) provides instructions regarding eligibility, application, and admission to the bar of the courts of appeals; the rule is supplemented by local rules. Rules 46(b) and (c) authorize the courts of appeals to suspend or disbar lawyers or otherwise discipline them.

Once an attorney is admitted to the bar, he or she is expected to follow the rules of professional conduct and act in an ethical manner. If an attorney acts in an unprofessional manner, the court must determine whether the attorney's actions warrant discipline. The court may look to the professional rules of conduct as well as Fed.R.Civ.P. 11 for guidance in making this determination. *See, e.g.*, *In re Hendrix*, 986 F.2d 195, 201 (7th Cir. 1993). Possible disciplinary actions, if warranted, include fines, suspension, or disbarment. *United States v. Song*, 902 F.2d 609, 610 (7th Cir. 1990). Some misconduct will result in fines only. *Williams v. Leach*, 938 F.2d 769, 775–76 (7th Cir. 1991). As with suspension or disbarment, a disciplinary order imposing a fine can only be made after giving the attorney in question notice and an opportunity to respond. *Id.*; FRAP 46(b)(2) & 46(c).

Not all unprofessional actions warrant discipline, however. For example, an attorney who stipulated to subject-matter jurisdiction while planning to challenge jurisdiction as a strategy was not disciplined, even though his conduct was deemed "perilously close to 'conduct unbecoming a member of the bar.' " *Aves v. Shah*, 997 F.2d 762, 767 (10th Cir. 1993).

As an alternative to disbarment, suspension, or fines, the court may make a "public reprimand" of a lawyer who engages in inappropriate conduct. *See, e.g.*, *United States v. Williams*, 952 F.2d 418, 422 (D.C. Cir. 1991) (per curiam) (reprimanding "inexperienced" government lawyer).

A suspended member of the bar of a court of appeals remains a member of the bar, and can be subjected to additional discipline while suspended. *In re Mitchell*, 901 F.2d 1179, 1183 (3d Cir. 1990). Such a suspended attorney may not act or appear as counsel before the court, but may act in effect as a "law clerk," provided that he or she has "the close supervision of a member in good standing of the bar of this court, and then only so long as the suspended attorney has no contact with clients, [the] Court, or its staff." *Id.* at 1190–91. After being suspended or disbarred, an attorney may apply for reinstatement to the bar; FRAP 46 is silent as to such procedures, but reinstatement procedures are often governed by local rule. A court may impose reasonable conditions on reinstatement motions. *Cf. In re Kandekore*, 460 F.3d 276, 280 (2d Cir. 2006) (per curiam) (affirming denial of petitioner's application to be reinstated to federal district court bar on ground that petitioner had not been reinstated to state bar).

§ 18.4 VOLUNTARY DISMISSALS

FRAP 42 governs voluntary dismissals of appeals. Such dismissals may occur when both parties agree to end the litigation and seek to have the case dismissed. This relief can be granted at the district-court level (FRAP 42(a)) or the appellate-court level (FRAP 42(b)), depending on the circumstances.

The district court can grant a voluntary dismissal after a notice of appeal has been filed, but before the appeal has been docketed by the circuit clerk. A stipulation must be filed by both parties agreeing to the dismissal. In the alternative, the case may be dismissed if the appellant moves for dismissal and properly notifies all parties. FRAP 42(a).

After docketing has occurred in the court of appeals, the rule requires the parties to sign and file a dismissal agreement. Such an agreement must state how and by whom costs will be paid, and all fees due to the court of appeals must also be paid by that time. Absent agreement, the appellant can also move for dismissal at the appellate court level. The parties can either agree on the terms for dismissal or the court can set the terms. FRAP 42(b). However, those court-imposed terms cannot include an award of attorneys' fees. *See, e.g.*, *Overseas Cosmos, Inc. v. NR Vessel Corp.*, 148 F.3d 51, 52 (2d Cir. 1998).

The court has discretion as to whether to grant voluntary dismissals. Although these motions are generally granted, they "may be denied in the interest of justice or fairness." *American Auto. Mfrs. Ass'n v. Comm'r, Mass. Dept. of Envtl. Prot.*, 31 F.3d 18, 22 (1st Cir. 1994) (discussing case law). If the parties cannot agree on the terms of the dismissal, then the court must exercise its discretion in determining whether the case should be dismissed. The presumption favors dismissal. However, the court can deny a dismissal "to curtail strategic behavior." *Albers v. Eli Lilly & Co.*, 354 F.3d 644, 646 (7th Cir. 2004) (per curiam). For example, in *Albers*, the appellant moved to dismiss the case after "oral arguments had not gone well" in order to avoid creating precedent that could adversely affect other cases the attorney was handling. In those circumstances, the court denied the voluntary dismissal. *Id.*

And, although a voluntary dismissal does not allow an appellant to escape sanctions for a frivolous appeal under FRAP 38, courts have held that sanctions in that sort of circumstance will be imposed only in "an exceptional case," since "a readiness to grant sanctions" upon the voluntary dismissal of a case would "discourage voluntary dismissals." *Ormsby Motors Inc. v. Gen. Motors Corp.*, 32 F.3d 240, 241–42 (7th Cir. 1994) (concluding that, by requesting sanctions after its opponent's voluntary dismissal, "GM is behaving like a sore winner").

CHAPTER 19
CERTIFICATION OF STATE-LAW ISSUES TO STATE COURT

§ 19.1 INTRODUCTION

Federal judges often become uneasy when they are asked to decide an unsettled issue of state law. Considerations of federalism, comity, and deference all support allowing state courts to decide unsettled issues of state law, rather than have a federal court guess what that law might be. In some cases, these considerations might lead a court to abstain from deciding a case, *see, e.g., Railroad Comm'n v. Pullman Co.*, 312 U.S. 496 (1941). In others, the federal courts may be asked to make an "*Erie* prediction" (*see Erie R. Co. v. Tompkins*, 304 U.S. 64 (1938)) about what the content of state law may be. In neither situation, however, do the courts and the litigants get an authoritative answer about the content of state law. By allowing a federal appellate court to certify a question of state law for the state's highest court to answer, however, a state's certification procedure "allows a federal court faced with a novel state-law question to put the question directly to the state's highest court, reducing the delay, cutting the cost, and increasing the assurance of gaining an authoritative response." *Arizonans for Official English v. Arizona*, 520 U.S. 43, 76 (1997).

§ 19.2 HISTORY OF CERTIFICATION PROCESSES

The practice of certifying legal questions to an authoritative court appears to have first arisen in English practice with the passage of the British Law Ascertainment Act of 1859. 22 & 23 Vict., ch. 63 (Eng.), *reprinted in* 17 Halsbury's Laws of England 104 (Lord Hailsham of St. Marlyebone, ed., 4th ed. 1976)). It would not arrive in American practice for almost 100 years. In 1945, in response to the rise in the use of abstention doctrines to avoid deciding unsettled questions of state law, Florida enacted the first certification law. The statute, however, remained unused until 1960, when the U.S. Supreme Court, in *Clay v. Sun Insurance Office, Ltd.*, 363 U.S. 207 (1960), invoked the Florida certification law in a diversity of citizenship case presenting an undecided question of Florida law. The Court remanded and instructed the Fifth Circuit to certify the action to the Florida Supreme Court, with praise for the Florida law and its enactors: "The Florida Legislature, with rare foresight, has dealt with the problem of authoritatively determining unresolved state law involved in federal litigation by a statute which permits a federal court to certify such a doubtful question of state law to the Supreme Court of Florida for its decision." *Id.* at 212.

By 1974, when the Supreme Court again voiced its emphatic approval of the state-law certification process by noting that it "save[s] time, energy, and resources and helps build a cooperative judicial federalism," *Lehman Bros. v. Schein*, 416 U.S. 386,

391 (1974), at least ten states had adopted laws or rules allowing federal courts to "certify" unsettled questions of state law to the state's highest court, so that the federal courts may utilize an authoritative answer to an unsettled question of state law, rather than guessing under *Erie*, or "punting" under one of the abstention doctrines. *Id.* at 390 n.7. As the court in *Lehman Brothers* explained, it is never mandatory for a federal appellate court to use these certification procedures; rather, their use is left to the courts' discretion. *Id.* at 390–91. Nonetheless, these procedures are "particularly appropriate" when the state whose law is in question is not located within the geographic confines of the federal court in question. *Id.* at 391 ("When federal judges in New York attempt to predict uncertain Florida law, they act, as we have referred to ourselves on this Court in matters of state law, as 'outsiders' lacking the common exposure to local law which comes from sitting in the jurisdiction."). Certification is also especially appropriate if resolution of a question of state law may obviate the need for the federal court to pass on an issue of federal constitutional law. *See, e.g., Bellotti v. Baird*, 428 U.S. 132, 151 (1976); *Ass'n of Surrogates & Supreme Ct. Reporters Within the City of N.Y. v. State of N.Y.*, 940 F.2d 766, 770–71 (2d Cir. 1991).

§ 19.3 CURRENT USE OF CERTIFICATION

Presently, 49 of the 50 states, the District of Columbia, Puerto Rico, the Northern Mariana Islands, and Guam, have laws or rules that allow a federal court to certify an issue of state (or territorial) law to the state's (or territory's) highest court for resolution. North Carolina is the only state that has never enacted such a law or rule. A special note on Missouri's situation is warranted, however: The Missouri legislature enacted a certification statute in 1989, but that state's supreme court held in *Grantham v. Mo. Dep't of Corr.*, No. 72576, 1990 WL 602159, at *1 (Mo. July 13, 1990) (en banc), that answering a certified question would exceed the Missouri Constitution's limited grant of powers to the state supreme court. In 2000, the Missouri legislature reenacted the certification statute notwithstanding the *Grantham* holding; the state's General Assembly acknowledged the decision but interpreted the ruling to mean that only questions certified by the district court in *Grantham* itself were barred. *See* V.A.M.S. § 477.004 (West 2002) (update). The Missouri statute remains on the books, but has not been invoked in the years since it was reenacted.

§ 19.4 REQUIREMENTS FOR CERTIFICATION

Certification is only available if, *inter alia*, the particular state in question has a statute, law, or rule allowing it; a resolution of the question is consistent with state law (including state constitutional prohibitions on advisory opinions, *see, e.g.*, *In re Richards*, 223 A.2d 827, 833 (Me. 1966)); and the state court accepts the certification—which it is not obliged to do. *Cf. Chrysler Capital Realty, Inc. v. Grella*, 942 F.2d 160, 161 (2d Cir. 1991) ("[B]ecause the issue appeared to be one of particular importance to the state of Michigan, we certified the state law issue to the Michigan Supreme Court at plaintiff's request. That court, however, declined (by a 4–3 vote) to answer our query, so we are left to determine on our own plaintiff's attempt to extend Michigan law so as to provide relief from defendant's alleged fraud.").

§ 19.5 CERTIFICATION PROCEDURES

Certification procedures differ from state to state. It is generally the case that the court of appeals will suggest certification *sua sponte*, although there is nothing to prohibit a party from suggesting certification. *See id.* In some courts of appeals, the court will ask the parties to agree upon a certified question and statement of facts; in others, the court will draft the question itself. The state court is generally given the power to reformulate the question, however, to avoid the problem encountered by the Fifth Circuit in *Green v. Am. Tobacco Co.*, 304 F.2d 70 (5th Cir. 1962) & 409 F.2d 1166 (5th Cir. 1969), where the federal court, after certifying a Florida-law question in 1962 and receiving an answer to that question, realized in 1969 that it had asked the wrong question—and decided the case *en banc* under Florida law rather than returning to the Florida Supreme Court for an answer to the proper question. *See id.* at 1168–70 (Brown, C.J., dissenting).

A standard threshold requirement is that the question of state law be both unsettled and potentially determinative of an issue in the pending litigation. A certification order from a federal court of appeals generally contains (to comply with state law):

- the question of law to be answered;
- the facts relevant to the question;
- a statement acknowledging that the state supreme court may reformulate the question; and
- the names and addresses of counsel of record, and of parties appearing without counsel.

See Uniform Certification of Questions of Law Act, § 6(a)(1)–(4) (Nat'l Conf. of Comm'rs on Uniform State Laws 1995). The record in the federal case is typically transmitted to the state court, and the federal court of appeals holds the case on its docket without conducting any further proceedings until the certified question is either answered or declined by the state court. *See, e.g.*, *Reilly v. Alcan Aluminum Corp.*, 181 F.3d 1206, 1210 (11th Cir. 1999).

Once the state court decides the question of state law, the federal appellate court is bound by that decision. *See, e.g.*, *Engel v. CBS, Inc.*, 182 F.3d 124, 125–26 (2d Cir. 1999). It may then conduct further proceedings in the case as appropriate.

The U.S. Supreme Court, too, may certify questions directly to a state's highest court, provided that the state certification statute in question allows for that practice. In this regard, note that New Jersey's certification rule only allows that state's supreme court to "answer a question of law certified to it by the United States Court of Appeals for the Third Circuit. . . ." N.J. R. 2:12A–1. All other states' and territories' certification rules allow the U.S.

Supreme Court to certify state-law questions. The U.S. Supreme Court has utilized this procedure infrequently, but consistently, over the years. *See, e.g., Cline v. Okla. Coalition for Reproductive Justice*, 133 S.Ct. 2887 (2013); *Stewart v. Smith*, 534 U.S. 157, 159 (2001); *Arizonans for Official English v. Arizona*, 520 U.S. 43, 77–78 (1997); *Virginia v. American Booksellers Ass'n*, 484 U.S. 383, 393–94 (1988); *Zant v. Stephens*, 456 U.S. 410, 416–17 (1982); *Elkins v. Moreno*, 435 U.S. 647, 663 (1978); *Massachusetts v. Feeney*, 429 U.S. 66 (1976). That being said, the Supreme Court is no more obliged than any other federal appellate court to certify such an unsettled question; the vigorous disagreement between the majority (per Justice Scalia) and dissent (per Justice Stevens) in *Town of Castle Rock v. Gonzales*, 545 U.S. 748 (2005), illustrates that well.

CHAPTER 20

SPECIAL ISSUES INVOLVING PRO SE APPEALS, APPOINTED COUNSEL, AND HABEAS CORPUS

§ 20.1 PARTIES APPEARING *PRO SE*

Parties who prosecute (or defend) appeals in the federal courts in their own name present special concerns for courts and opposing parties. In the district courts, *pro se* complaints are "h[e]ld to less stringent standards than formal proceedings drafted by lawyers," *Haines v. Kerner*, 404 U.S. 519, 520 (1972), and the same lenient standards are generally applied to the construction of their appellate submissions. *See, e.g.*, *Triestman v. Fed. Bureau of Prisons*, 470 F.3d 471, 475 (2d Cir. 2006) (per curiam).

But the "special solicitude" that federal courts show to *pro se* litigants, *id.*, does not insulate such litigants from meeting jurisdictional deadlines, from generally obeying the court's rules or procedures, or even from being subjected to sanctions. *See, e.g.*, *Stearman v. Comm'r*, 436 F.3d 533, 538 (5th Cir. 2006) (per curiam) ("Sanctions on *pro se* litigants are appropriate if they were warned . . . that their claims are frivolous and if they were aware of 'ample legal authority holding squarely against them.' ") (citation omitted);; *Haworth v. Royal*, 347 F.3d 1189, 1192 (10th Cir. 2003).

Some circuits offer guidebooks for *pro se* litigants (*e.g.*, the Federal Circuit's *Guide for Pro Se*

Petitioners and Appellants, available on that court's website). Others, such as the Second Circuit, also maintain a staff of "*pro se* clerks," a specialized kind of staff attorney position that assists the judges with the review and processing of *pro se* appeals.

§ 20.2 PARTIES PROCEEDING *IN FORMA PAUPERIS*

FRAP 24 sets forth procedures, consistent with 28 U.S.C. § 1915(a), for allowing a party to pursue an appeal *in forma pauperis*—literally, "in the manner of a pauper," meaning that the basic court costs associated with bringing or maintaining a lawsuit are ameliorated. If a party was allowed to proceed *in forma pauperis* in the district court, that status continues on appeal, unless the district court certifies, in writing, that the appeal is not taken in good faith or that the party is not otherwise entitled to continue to proceed *in forma pauperis*. FRAP 24(a)(3), (4). If a party wishes to appeal *in forma pauperis* and was not already granted that status, he or she must make the application in the district court, and make the required showing (via affidavit) of impoverishment, along with a statement of the issues that the party intends to present on appeal. FRAP 24(a). The court then must make the twin determinations of (1) economic eligibility and (2) non-frivolousness of the appeal before a party will be allowed to proceed *in forma pauperis*. *Id.* The granting of such status generally allows a party to proceed without prepayment of fees and costs, FRAP 24(a)(2), and allows such a party to request that the appeal be heard on the original record without the necessity of incurring the expense of reproducing any parts of it for an appendix or otherwise. FRAP 24(c).

By contrast, if the appeal is from a decision of an administrative agency or United States Tax Court, then the application for permission to appeal *in forma pauperis* is to be made in the court of appeals. FRAP 24(b).

§ 20.3 APPOINTED COUNSEL AND *ANDERS* BRIEFS

The Constitution has been interpreted to provide a right to counsel for a first appeal that is available as of right in a criminal case. *Douglas v. California*, 372 U.S. 353, 355 (1963). To carry out this right, in appropriate cases a court of appeals may appoint appellate counsel for a criminal defendant or habeas corpus petitioner pursuant to the Criminal Justice Act (CJA), 18 U.S.C. § 3006A, and Rule 44 of the Federal Rules of Criminal Procedure. The CJA provides for appointment and limited compensation of lawyers accepting such appointments.

The question of when an appointed counsel may withdraw from representation has been the subject of several Supreme Court decisions. Under *Anders v. California*, 386 U.S. 738 (1967), if appointed criminal defense counsel finds his or her client's case to be

> wholly frivolous, after a conscientious examination of it, he should so advise the court and request permission to withdraw. That request must, however, be accompanied by a brief referring to anything in the record that

> might arguably support the appeal. A copy of counsel's brief should be furnished [to the client] and time allowed him to raise any points that he chooses; the court—not counsel—then proceeds, after a full examination of all the proceedings, to decide whether the case is wholly frivolous. If it so finds it may grant counsel's request to withdraw and dismiss the appeal insofar as federal requirements are concerned, or proceed to a decision on the merits, if state law so requires. On the other hand, if it finds any of the legal points arguable on their merits (and therefore not frivolous), it must, prior to decision, afford the indigent the assistance of counsel to argue the appeal.

Id. at 744. *See also Penson v. Ohio*, 488 U.S. 75 (1988) (reaffirming *Anders*); *Smith v. Robbins*, 528 U.S. 259 (2000) (allowing states to use alternate procedures to guarantee the right of representation). Although *Anders* does not strictly apply to retained counsel, *see McCoy v. Court of Appeals of Wisconsin, District 1*, 486 U.S. 429, 437 (1988), several courts of appeals have allowed the same *Anders* procedures for retained counsel as well, in light of *McCoy*'s recognition that "retained and appointed counsel share the responsibility not to 'consume the time and the energies of the court or the opposing party by advancing frivolous arguments.'" *United States v. Urena*, 23 F.3d 707, 708 (2d Cir. 1994) (per curiam) (quoting *McCoy*, 486 U.S. at 436).

§ 20.4 HABEAS CORPUS CASES

The Federal Rules of Appellate Procedure contain two rules (FRAP 22 and 23) dealing with the special circumstance of habeas corpus cases.

FRAP 22(a), which addresses procedures when a habeas application is directed to a court of appeals judge, is necessary because the governing statute, 28 U.S.C. § 2241(a), provides that "[w]rits of habeas corpus may be granted by the Supreme Court, any justice thereof, the district courts *and any circuit judge* within their respective jurisdictions." (Emphasis added.) Rule 22(a), however, provides that a habeas application "*must* be made to the appropriate district court," and, "[i]f made to a circuit judge, the application must be transferred to the appropriate district court," and it may not be "renew[ed]" before a single court of appeals judge. This transfer procedure is specifically permitted by 28 U.S.C. § 2241(b), and, as a practical matter, it means that the power granted to circuit judges under subsection (a) of Section 2241 will never be exercised in the first instance by a court of appeals judge.

FRAP 22(b) sets forth procedures for implementing the certificate-of-appealability requirement of 28 U.S.C. § 2253(c)(1), which provides that a district court's habeas decision may not be appealed unless "a circuit justice or judge issues a certificate of appealability." Under the statute, no certificate may issue unless "the applicant has made a substantial showing of the denial of a constitutional right." *Id.* § 2253(c)(2). Rule 11 of the Rules Governing § 2254 Cases provides that "[t]he district court must issue or deny a certificate of appealability when it enters a final order adverse to the applicant." Further, Rule 11 states: "[i]f the court denies a certificate, the parties may not appeal the denial but may seek a certificate from the court of appeals under" FRAP 22. If the applicant addresses his or her request to the court of appeals, it may be considered either by a single circuit judge or by multiple judges, "as the court prescribes" by local rule or procedure. FRAP 22(b)(2). And, if the applicant fails to make a specific request, the notice of appeal will be construed as a request for such a certificate. *Id.* Any granted certificate must set forth the issue or issues satisfying the showing, 28 U.S.C. § 2253(c)(3), and the scope of the appeal is thereby limited.

FRAP 22(b)(3) also resolves an ambiguity in the habeas statute. Section 2253(c), which was drafted in the passive voice, provides that "an appeal may not be taken" in a habeas case without a certificate of appealability, which arguably required such a certificate when the state defendant was the loser in the district court and sought to appeal. Rule 22(b)(3) confirms, consistent with the purpose of the certificate-of-appealability requirement, that such a certificate is not required when the state, the United States, or its respective representative, is the appellant.

FRAP 23 deals with the custody of the prisoner during the pendency of a habeas appeal. It is based on a similar rule contained in the U.S. Supreme Court rules (S. Ct. R. 36), and it contains essentially four provisions:

- Subsection (a) forbids a prisoner who is the subject of a habeas proceeding from being transferred to another facility (with a different custodian) without the court's authorization. This rule prevents habeas petitions, which are directed to a prisoner's custodian, from being mooted by the unilateral action of the defendant (typically, the warden of the correctional facility where the plaintiff is incarcerated), and it further provides that when the court authorizes transfer, the new custodian will be substituted for the former one.

- Subsection (b) gives the court flexibility for dealing with the custody of the prisoner pending review of a *denied* habeas petition—it may leave the prisoner in the custody of the custodian defendant; order the prisoner detained in "other appropriate custody"; or order the prisoner released on personal recognizance, with or without bond.

- Subsection (c), which deals with the prisoner's custodial arrangements pending review of a *granted* habeas petition, is similar; however, it establishes a default rule that "the prisoner must . . . be released on personal recognizance, with or without surety," unless a court or judge "orders otherwise."

- Finally, subsection (d) gives the court some flexibility to modify the initial order governing custody pending review where there are "special reasons" for doing so.

§ 20.5 VEXATIOUS LITIGANTS

The American legal system is renowned for its openness to litigants of all types, and its availability to adjudicate a wide variety of legal claims. There is a price to be paid for the ready availability of the American adjudicatory system, however, and that can sometimes be exhibited by a category of litigants commonly called "vexatious litigants." In the extreme, a vexatious litigant may exhibit a pathology, causing the late judge and professor Jerome Frank to label such a litigant a "litigious paranoiac," which he defined as one who "uses trumped-up claims—in the validity of which he comes to believe—to assuage a 'persecution complex.' And, this side the extreme pathologue, there are many others eager to seek in litigation a solace for their inner disturbances." Jerome Frank, *Courts on Trial: Myth and Reality in American Justice* 374–75 (1949).

Often—but not necessarily—the vexatious litigant poses special problems for appellate courts, and courts have adopted mechanisms for dealing with such litigants while preserving access to the courts for the resolution of valid disputes. *See, e.g.*, *De Long v. Hennessey*, 912 F.2d 1144, 1146–47 (9th Cir. 1990). In most cases, the ordinary rules and tools of litigation—summary judgments, preclusion doctrines, sanctions, and the like—sufficiently equip the courts to deal with repeat litigants who mount *seriatim*, frivolous claims. However, in extreme cases, courts may have to resort to injunctions in order to effectively stop such abuses of the judicial system, and ensure that the system has sufficient bandwidth to fairly adjudicate reasonable claims.

Anthony R. Martin-Trigona is one of the more infamous vexatious litigants known to the American judicial system:

> He is the source of literally hundreds of lawsuits, motions and miscellaneous pleadings, all but a small fraction of which lack any merit whatsoever. Viewing Martin-Trigona's litigious conduct in its entirety yields the inescapable conclusion that he persistently resorts to legal processes without regard to the merits of the claims asserted and that he invokes those processes largely to harass persons who have unluckily crossed his path. His abuse of legal processes is exemplified not only by the number and variety of meritless actions but also by his recent use of pleadings and other legal papers, the contents of which are set out in their appalling detail in the district court's opinion, as a vehicle to launch vicious attacks upon persons of Jewish heritage.

In re Martin-Trigona, 737 F.2d 1254, 1256 (2d Cir. 1984). After entertaining—and rejecting—a number of his claims over the years, a federal district court finally enjoined Martin-Trigona from making all but the most essential court filings—except for appellate filings—without first obtaining leave of court. That injunction was upheld in the main (although remanded for minor modifications) by the Second Circuit, and that court of appeals further imposed its own injunction upon Martin-Trigona, forbidding him from making future filings in the Second Circuit without seeking leave of that court. *Id.* at 1264.

However, such injunctions are extreme, and should not be imposed without rigorous attention to providing the litigant due process—including notice, the opportunity to be heard, a record with "substantive findings as to the frivolous or harassing nature of the litigant's actions," and "findings as to any pattern constituting harassment." *In re Powell*, 851 F.2d 427, 431 (D.C. Cir. 1988).

CHAPTER 21

LOCAL RULES, INTERNAL OPERATING PROCEDURES, AND SPECIAL MASTERS

§ 21.1 LOCAL RULES

As many of the prior chapters have illustrated, the practices in the thirteen federal courts of appeals are far from uniform in a number of areas. FRAP 47(a) both allows and limits this variation.

The 1995 amendments to FRAP 47 made several significant changes in the rule: (1) The rule provides that a "generally applicable direction to parties or lawyers" must be in a local rule, and not in an internal operating procedure (I.O.P.) or standing order; (2) it requires that local rules must be consistent with—but not duplicative of—laws and rules adopted under the Rules Enabling Act (*e.g.*, the Federal Rules of Appellate Procedure); (3) it requires that local rules conform with uniform numbering systems prescribed by the Judicial Conference of the United States; and (4) it provides that any local rule "imposing a requirement of form" may not be enforced in a way that "causes a party to lose rights because of a nonwillful failure to comply." FRAP 47(a)(1), (2). With respect to the uniform numbering requirement of FRAP 47(a)(1), the Advisory Committee Notes acknowledge that the requirement was necessary to "make it easier for an increasingly national bar and for litigants to locate a local rule that applies to a particular procedural issue."

FRAP 47(b) goes on to provide that, when there is no controlling law, a court of appeals is permitted to "regulate practice in a particular case in any manner consistent with federal law, these rules [*i.e.*, the Federal Rules of Appellate Procedure], and local rules of the circuit," but prohibits sanctions or other penalties for noncompliance with any such requirement "unless the alleged violator has been furnished in the particular case with actual notice of the requirement."

Because of these local variations among the circuits, it is imperative that the lawyer be familiar with the local court of appeals rules before pursuing an appeal in a particular circuit.

§ 21.2 INTERNAL OPERATING PROCEDURES

Also important, on a circuit-by-circuit basis, are the internal operating procedures, or I.O.P.s, of each court of appeals. Each circuit has such I.O.P.s (the Ninth Circuit calls theirs "General Orders"), but their detail, like that of local rules, varies from circuit to circuit. Here, too, it is very useful for the advocate to know the local I.O.P.s—even though they may not have the force of law—because they can demystify some of the seemingly arcane processes of court operation. For example, the I.O.P.s might explain the process of case assignment, both with respect to motions panels and with respect to decisions on the merits. Some I.O.P.s set forth the expectations with regard to when draft opinions will be circulated. Yet others may describe the roles of the staff attorneys within the court.

Similarly, several federal courts of appeals offer "handbooks" for counsel on their websites. These publications are extremely useful, too, in that they are typically written—or at least approved—by court personnel who truly understand the inner workings of a particular court of appeals. If a court of appeals offers such a handbook, counsel pursuing a case in that circuit would be well advised to become familiar with its contents.

§ 21.3 APPOINTMENT OF SPECIAL MASTERS

FRAP 48, which was added to the Federal Rules of Appellate Procedure in 1994, authorizes the use of special masters to hold hearings and make recommendations "in matters ancillary to proceedings in the court." According to the Advisory Committee Notes to the newly framed rule, this is not a new practice, as "[t]he courts of appeals have long used masters in contempt proceedings where the issue is compliance with an enforcement order."

The operative phrase in FRAP 48(a) is "ancillary to proceedings in the court." The phrase is not otherwise defined, except that the Advisory Committee Notes offer some examples of what sorts of matters ought to be viewed as "ancillary," *e.g.*, "an application for fees or eligibility for Criminal Justice Act status on appeal." For example, in *Gallop v. Cheney*, 667 F.3d 226 (2d Cir. 2012) (per curiam), the Second Circuit appointed a judge of the Eastern District of New York "to serve as Special Master to ensure full and prompt compliance with the Court's mandate," which imposed monetary and other sanctions upon plaintiff-appellant's lawyers. *Id.* at 231 & n.5. (A special master is not required where attorneys' fees on appeal are at issue, however. *In re Maurice*, 73 F.3d 124, 127 (7th Cir. 1995).) There are few reported cases even mentioning the modern FRAP 48, but the challenge for courts applying the rule in the future appears to lie in limiting the scope of the rule to matters that are truly "ancillary to proceedings in the court," and not allowing the rule to expand into areas of factfinding that have been traditionally reserved for the district courts. Despite the lack of clarity in the text, the Advisory Committee Notes, which refer to the rule's proper use with respect to "factual issues [that] *arise in the first instance in the court of appeals*" (emphasis added), may provide courts with a useful limiting principle in future cases so that the application of FRAP 48 does not intrude upon district court factfinding.

PART 3

U.S. SUPREME COURT

CHAPTER 22

U.S. SUPREME COURT PRACTICE

§ 22.1 INTRODUCTION

In many ways, practice before the Supreme Court of the United States is just practice before another appellate court. But at the same time, it is anything but ordinary. For one, practice before the Supreme Court is not governed by the Federal Rules of Appellate Procedure; rather, an entirely different set of rules—the Rules of the Supreme Court of the United States—addresses practice before that Court. And, for another, there are significant differences between intermediate appellate courts and the Supreme Court, largely attributable to the latter's role as the ultimate appellate court, both for the federal court system and for state-court cases that present issues of federal law. Thus, Supreme Court practice has certain features and facets that make practice before that tribunal different than practice before any other appellate court anywhere.

Consider how these differences are driven by the institutional role of the Supreme Court. The Supreme Court is the body tasked with making sure that important issues of federal law—including interpretation of the U.S. Constitution—are settled in a uniform way for the entire country. (The Court *only* hears and decides appellate cases presenting federal-law issues.) But as a practical matter, the Court could not possibly hear every case involving any issue of federal law, so it must be selective in hearing only the cases presenting the most important of those issues. That institutional role is the overarching reason why the Court has almost total discretionary power over the cases it decides to hear. In turn, that aspect of its institutional role drives the certiorari process, as well as the process the Court uses to determine whether to give plenary treatment to the handful of cases on its otherwise "mandatory" docket. Almost every case that is heard on the merits by the Supreme Court involves two separate stages of advocacy—the stage where the advocates convince the Court to entertain the case (or not), followed by the stage where the advocates brief and argue the merits of affirmance or reversal in those cases passing the first stage.

That institutional role, particularly when compared to the work of the federal courts of appeals, in turn explains some of the differences in advocacy between those two types of fora. When issues come to the Supreme Court, their proper answer is not likely to have been settled by a prior Supreme Court decision—after all, if a prior Supreme Court decision had already settled an issue, there would not likely be a compelling reason for the Court to take up the issue again and, in effect, re-decide it (unless the Court were determined to revisit and perhaps modify or overrule its prior disposition of that legal issue). In the courts of appeals, by contrast, many of the legal issues that those courts face have already been decided—either by the Supreme Court or by the courts of appeals themselves. As a result, persuasive advocacy in the Supreme Court (on the merits of a case) will have to focus much more on argument by analogy, on lower courts' experiences with the issue, and on the consequences of a decision one way or the other.

There is, also, the fact that the Supreme Court sits *en banc* in all of its cases. The Constitution does not define the number of Justices on the Court, but Congress has, for some time now, fixed the number at nine—eight Associate Justices and the Chief Justice of the United States. 28 U.S.C. § 1. If some Justices are recused from a case, it still takes six Justices to constitute a quorum. *Id.*; S. Ct. R. 4.2. If an insufficient number of Justices to make up a quorum are qualified to hear a case, and a majority of the qualified Justices do not believe that the case can be heard and decided in the next term of the Court, then the judgment is affirmed as though affirmed by an equally divided court. 28 U.S.C. § 2109; *see Sibley v. Breyer*, 128 S.Ct. 514 (2007) (suit naming seven of the Supreme Court's Justices as defendants).

The fact that the Supreme Court always sits *en banc* contributes to a number of other differences between Supreme Court practice and court of appeals practice. For one, nine sitting Justices almost always means a "hot" bench at oral argument. For another, owing to the institutional considerations outlined above, questions from the bench are even more likely to test the ruling that the advocate seeks, with policy concerns, hypothetical questions about the next case having similar but not identical facts, etc. Finally, because a nine-member bench can divide in any number of ways, advocacy in the Supreme Court includes trying to shape a theory that—based on prior opinions and other known facts about each of the Justices—is going to be palatable to five (or more) Justices.

Unlike the courts of appeals, virtually all cases in which review is granted by the Supreme Court are orally argued, except for rare cases in which the Court rules (usually to reverse) based on the petition for certiorari and the opposition thereto. Compared to the ten or 15 minutes allowed for argument—when argument is granted at all—in the courts of appeals, the Supreme Court allows 30 minutes per side in almost every case, and occasionally allows more in extraordinary cases. The oral argument transcripts are placed on the Court's website, www.supreme courtus.gov, later the same day for the public and press to read, and, since 2010, the audio of argued cases has been placed on the Court's website on the Friday at the end of each argument week.

Moreover, unlike the courts of appeals, which typically carry over undecided cases from year to year, the Supreme Court has a single annual term (designated "October Term 2017," "October Term 2018," etc.). The term is designated as the "October Term" because the term traditionally starts on the first Monday in October and ends on the day before the first Monday in October in the following year. 28 U.S.C. § 2; S. Ct. R. 3. Although the Court's rules provide that all cases pending on the docket at the end of a term are continued to the next term, the Court's practice is to decide (by the end of June) all cases that were orally argued during the particular term—often contributing to a flurry of decisions, typically involving some of the Court's higher-profile cases, at the end of each June. On occasion, the Court will hear argument but not decide a case during the term, preferring instead to order reargument in the following term. For example, in *Kungys v. United States*, a case argued by one of the authors, the Court had heard argument on April 27, 1987. On June 26, 1987, however, the Court issued an order not merely restoring the case to the calendar for reargument, but directing the parties to file supplemental briefs addressing three specified questions. 483 U.S. 1017 (1987). The Court then heard reargument in October 1987 and decided the case in May 1988. *Kungys v. United States*, 485 U.S. 759 (1988). Reargument is rare—in the last ten years, the Court has ordered argument in only two cases, *Kiobel v. Royal Dutch Petroleum Co.*, 133 S.Ct. 1659 (2013) (argued February 28, 2012; reargument and supplemental briefs ordered March 5, 2012; reargued October 1, 2012); and *Citizens United v. Federal Election Comm'n*, 130 S.Ct. 876 (2010) (argued March 24, 2009; reargument and supplemental briefs ordered June 29, 2009; reargued September 9, 2009).

Layered on top of that are all of the other factors that make practice before the Supreme Court unique: the national stage that it creates for advocates; the grand courthouse and courtroom; the traditions of the institution; and the Court's own special rules and practices. The trick—if it is indeed a "trick" at all—of transitioning from a skilled appellate advocate to a skilled Supreme Court practitioner is starting from a baseline of excellent appellate advocacy, and then adding on the knowledge of what makes practice before the Supreme Court different and special.

§ 22.2 THE WORK OF THE SUPREME COURT

In the 2015 Term, the Supreme Court issued 80 opinions on the merits (because of consolidated cases resulting in a single opinion, these 80 opinions represented the disposition of 87 distinct cases). Of those 80 opinions, 63 were issued after oral argument; 13 opinions were summary reversals (that is, the Court reversed the judgment based entirely on the papers requesting certiorari, without briefs on the merits or oral argument); and four cases were affirmed by an equally divided Court (this was attributable to the in-Term death of Justice Scalia). One additional case was dismissed as improvidently granted (*i.e.*, the Court ultimately determined that it should not have granted certiorari in the case). The Court affirmed in 27 cases (31%), affirmed by an equally divided Court in four (5%), and reversed in 55 (64%). One opinion arose from a case decided under the Supreme Court's original jurisdiction, meaning that there was no lower-court decision to affirm or reverse.

Compare the Supreme Court's affirmance rate of 31% to the affirmance rate in the federal courts of appeals, which is around 90%. *See* Chapter 2, *supra*.

One important phenomenon of the Supreme Court's opinions is the even distribution of the writing assignments. In the 2015 Term, six of the Justices authored either seven or eight opinions for the Court. (The Chief Justice authored only six; Justice Scalia, who passed away mid-Term, authored only two; and Justice Kennedy authored nine.) The differences in opinion-writing workloads lie in separate opinions: In the 2015 Term, the Justices collectively issued 86 concurring or dissenting opinions to go along with the 76 majority opinions; Justice Thomas alone authored 32 of those (14 concurring; 18 dissenting), while Justice Kennedy wrote only three separate opinions (two concurring; one dissenting).

Nonetheless, a study only of the Court's decided cases does not even begin to paint a complete picture of the Supreme Court's workload. The 70 or so cases that result in a decision on the merits are the result of an extensive winnowing process that begins in most cases with the filing of a petition for certiorari. Over 8,000 such petitions are presented to the Court each year; the approximately 70 cases that now make it to oral argument and decision—less than 1%—are the survivors of that rigorous process. Roughly one-fourth of those 8,000 or so petitions are what are known as "paid petitions," *i.e.*, they were not filed by a petitioner proceeding *in forma pauperis* (this is colloquially known as "the I.F.P. docket"). The reason this distinction is significant is that I.F.P. petitions—most of which are filed by *pro se* petitioners—stand an uncommonly low chance of being granted. (The statistics demonstrate that typically only two or three tenths of one percent of I.F.P. petitions are granted.) In turn, that means that paid petitions stand a 3–4% chance of being granted—still a small number, but slightly more heartening odds than the 1% overall figure.

Moreover, there has been a historical downturn in the number of cases that the Court has accepted for review. From 1927 until the mid-1980s, the Court (with certain significant downward fluctuations in the late 1940s and early 1950s) was issuing 150 to 175 opinions per Term. But the number has been well under 100 cases per Term for well over 20 years now. In fact, statistics compiled by *The Supreme Court Compendium* suggest that the 62 signed opinions issued by the Court in its 2015 Term represented its lowest level of productivity in over 150 years—since October Term 1864, when the Court issued only 55 signed opinions.

Numerous commentators have evaluated the several hypotheses regarding this downturn—the elimination of most of the Court's "mandatory" appellate jurisdiction in 1988; the Court's 1995 "tightening" of the considerations favoring certiorari (*see* S. Ct. R. 10); the increase in the political homogeneity of court of appeals judges and the Supreme Court's Justices; the lack of as many "big social issue" cases as populated the docket in the 1960s and 1970s; and many others. For the most part, the various hypotheses have been found individually lacking, and no one theory completely explains the trend.

§ 22.3 THE JURISDICTION OF THE SUPREME COURT

The Supreme Court is the only court created by the Constitution. Article III, section 1 of the Constitution provides that "[t]he judicial Power of the United States shall be vested in one supreme Court, and in such inferior Courts as the Congress may from time to time ordain and establish." The Constitution then goes on to outline the Supreme Court's two types of jurisdiction—"original Jurisdiction" and "appellate Jurisdiction." In the very narrow class of original jurisdiction (which means that the Supreme Court sits as a trial court of first—and, necessarily, last-instance), fall "all Cases affecting Ambassadors, other public Ministers and Consuls, and those in which a State shall be a Party." U.S. Const., art. III, § 2; *see* § 22.6, *infra*. The other category—"appellate Jurisdiction, both as to Law and Fact"—is subject to "such Exceptions, and under such Regulations as the Congress shall make." U.S. Const., art. III, § 2.

The congressional enactments that have regulated the Court's appellate jurisdiction have, since the time of the first Judiciary Act, divided federal cases from state cases, and treated the two classes of cases somewhat differently. Generally speaking, as explained in greater detail below, cases coming to the Supreme Court from the highest court of a state must exhibit a greater degree of finality than cases coming to the Court out of the federal system; this important statutory distinction is grounded in congressionally enacted values of federalism and judicial restraint—to avoid "precipitat[ing] interference with state litigation." *Cox Broadcasting Corp. v. Cohn*, 420 U.S. 469, 478 (1975).

A. CASES COMING FROM THE FEDERAL COURTS

Under 28 U.S.C. § 1254(1), the Supreme Court is granted jurisdiction to review "[c]ases in the courts of appeals . . . [b]y writ of certiorari . . . before or after rendition of judgment or decree." The Supreme Court no longer has mandatory appellate jurisdiction over any class of federal court of appeals decisions; this means that the Supreme Court has total control over its docket with respect to cases coming from the federal courts, subject, of course, to any mandatory jurisdiction that Congress might prescribe in a given type of case, as it did, for example, in connection with the federal flag-burning statute (discussed in § 4.1, *supra*).

The reference to "cases in" the federal courts of appeals has been interpreted extremely broadly, so that virtually any federal-law dispute that ever reaches the court of appeals can be reviewed by the Supreme Court. It can include, for example, review of a denied certificate of appealability in a habeas corpus case, *see Hohn v. United States*, 524 U.S. 236, 241–50 (1998), even though the effect of the denial of the certificate is to deprive the petitioner of access to court of appeals review. *See* § 21.4, *supra*.

The statutory language "before or after rendition of judgment or decree" similarly indicates that the Court can review nonfinal rulings of a federal court of appeals, including interlocutory orders as well as orders remanding the matter to the district court for further proceedings. The Court may prefer to await finality as a matter of discretion, but there is no jurisdictional bar to Supreme Court review of such matters. Indeed, the statute even authorizes the Court to determine to grant review *before* the court of appeals renders judgment, but that procedure is reserved for truly exceptional cases, *see Coleman v. PACCAR, Inc.*, 424 U.S. 1301, 1304 n.* (1976) (Rehnquist, J., in chambers) ("the exercise of such power by the Court is an extremely rare occurrence"); the only jurisdictional requirement is that the case be "in"—meaning docketed in—the court of appeals. *Gay v. Ruff*, 292 U.S. 25, 30 (1934); *see also* 28 U.S.C. § 2101(e) ("An application to the Supreme Court for a writ of certiorari to review a case before judgment has been rendered in the court of appeals may be made at any time before judgment."). The exceptional nature of this procedure is confirmed by the few cases that have merited such treatment, and the need for immediate resolution of the issues decided in those cases. *See, e.g.*, *United States v. Nixon*, 418 U.S. 683 (1974) (Watergate tapes); *Bolling v. Sharpe*, 347 U.S. 497, 498 (1954) (school desegregation; companion case to *Brown v. Bd. of Educ.*); *United States v. United Mine Workers*, 330 U.S. 258 (1947) (enjoined national strike of mine workers). In recent years, the Court has also used this procedure to grant certiorari before judgment in companion cases to cases coming to the court on certiorari after judgment. *See, e.g.*, *Gratz v. Bollinger*, 539 U.S. 244, 259–60 (2003) (companion case to *Grutter v. Bollinger*, 539 U.S. 306 (2003)); *United States v. Booker*, 543 U.S. 220, 229

(2005) (noting that companion case, *United States v. Fanfan*, was granted certiorari before judgment).

Section 1254(1) of Title 28 allows for "any party" to file a writ of certiorari. That includes an appellant or appellee, as well as any party that has been granted intervenor status. *See Dir., Office of Workers' Comp. Progs. v. Perini N. River Assocs.*, 459 U.S. 297, 304 n.13 (1983). The Court has even, on rare occasions, permitted a party to intervene in the Supreme Court in order to file a petition for certiorari, where the intervenor was effectively the real party in interest. *See, e.g., Banks v. Chicago Grain Trimmers Ass'n*, 390 U.S. 459 (1968). Of course, the petitioner must be a losing party in the court below, *see, e.g., Public Service Comm'n v. Brashear Freight Lines, Inc.*, 306 U.S. 204, 206 (1939) ("the successful party below has no standing to appeal"), although it is arguable that this requirement does not apply to petitions for certiorari before judgment, where parties that had prevailed in the district court have nonetheless succeeded in seeking certiorari before judgment in the court of appeals—in effect, petitioning to have the case transferred to the Supreme Court for appellate resolution. *See, e.g., United States v. Nixon*, 418 U.S. at 686–87.

In *Camreta v. Greene*, 563 U.S. 692 (2011), the Ninth Circuit had ruled that two government officials had violated the Fourth Amendment by failing to obtain a warrant to conduct an interview of a minor child, but that the officials were shielded from monetary liability because of qualified immunity; despite having prevailed, the officials petitioned for certiorari. The Court agreed that it had jurisdiction under section 1254(1), and that Article III of the Constitution did not stand in the way of adjudicating the officers' claims, because the officials might wish to engage in the same conduct again; without Supreme Court review, the official "must either change the way he performs his duties or risk a meritorious damages action" in the future. *Id.* at 703. The Court also noted that, "[a]s a matter of practice and prudence, we have generally declined to consider cases at the request of a prevailing party," *id.* at 703–04, but that qualified-immunity cases were in a "special category when it comes to this Court's review of appeals brought by winners." *Id.* at 704 (The dispute was nonetheless held to be moot, because the minor child had moved outside the Ninth Circuit and was about to reach the age of majority, and therefore could not possibly be affected by the Ninth Circuit's ruling. *See id.* at 709–14.)

Under 28 U.S.C. § 1254(2), a court of appeals may certify a question to the Supreme Court of the United States in a manner similar to the way courts of appeals may certify unsettled state-law questions to state supreme courts (*see* Chapter 19, *supra*). The Court has been generally unwilling to accept such certifications in the rare instances when that provision has been invoked, on the ground that it is generally the job of the court of appeals to decide the issues *before* the Supreme Court is asked to hear the case. *See, e.g., Wisniewski v. United States*, 353 U.S. 901, 902 (1957) (per curiam). The last time this provision was successfully invoked by a court of appeals was in 1981, when the Second Circuit certified three questions to the U.S. Supreme Court arising out of executive orders entered by President Carter during the Iran hostage crisis. *See Iran Nat'l Airlines Corp. v. Marschalk Co.*, 453 U.S. 919 (1981). In 1974, the Fourth Circuit certified to the Supreme Court a question regarding the proper composition of an *en banc* court in the Fourth Circuit. *See Moody v. Albemarle Paper Co.*, 417 U.S. 622, 624 (1974). The certified-question procedure has not otherwise been successfully invoked in the past 50 years. Today, it appears to be a provision in a state of total disuse, and there have been calls for its repeal.

There are two other general jurisdictional statutes governing Supreme Court review of federal-court decisions. Under 28 U.S.C. § 1253, the Supreme Court hears direct "appeal[s]" from injunctive orders (whether granting or denying) entered by three-judge district courts, "[e]xcept as otherwise provided by law." This provision is typically invoked in cases "challenging the constitutionality of the apportionment of congressional districts or the apportionment of any statewide legislative body." 28 U.S.C. § 2284(a). Additionally, as noted above, a handful of federal statutes allow direct appeals to the Supreme Court from district-court decisions, *e.g.*, 15 U.S.C. § 29(b) (allowing district judges in antitrust cases to enter an order, upon application of a party to the case, that "immediate consideration of the appeal by the Supreme Court is of general public importance in the administration of justice"), but their invocation—particularly in recent years—has been rare.

Finally, 28 U.S.C. § 1259 gives the Supreme Court the power to review decisions of the U.S. Court of Appeals for the Armed Forces in a manner similar to its certiorari review of other court of appeals' decisions. The Court may not, however, review that court's decisions denying a petition for review; its certiorari jurisdiction is limited to cases decided on the merits by the Court of Appeals for the Armed Forces. *Cf. Matias v. United States*, 923 F.2d 821, 824 (Fed. Cir. 1990) (discussing legislative history of jurisdictional statute); § 1.5(C), *supra*.

B. CASES COMING FROM THE STATE COURTS

Finality Requirement. Under 28 U.S.C. § 1257(a), the Supreme Court's appellate jurisdiction over state-court cases is restricted to review of "[f]inal judgments or decrees rendered by the highest court of a State in which a decision could be had." The important requirement here, which distinguishes the Court's review of state-court decisions from that of federal-court decisions, is the prerequisite of a "final judgment or decree."

For many years, the Court took an exceedingly narrow view of Section 1257, interpreting that provision to hold that review of a state-court decision was barred "where anything further remain[ed] to be determined by a State Court, no matter how dissociated from the only federal issue that ha[d] finally been adjudicated by the highest court of the state." *Radio Station WOW, Inc. v. Johnson*, 326 U.S. 120, 124 (1945).

Nonetheless, the Court frequently faced cases where, despite the pendency of further proceedings in state court, the federal question had been conclusively resolved by the highest court of the state. Thus, eventually, the Court arrived at a more practical construction of Section 1257's "finality" requirement. In *Cox Broadcasting Corp. v. Cohn*, 420 U.S. 469 (1975), the Court identified "four categories of . . . cases in which the Court has treated the decision on the federal issue as a final judgment for the purposes of 28 U.S.C. § 1257 and has taken jurisdiction without awaiting the completion of the additional proceedings anticipated in the lower state courts." *Id.* at 477. These four categories can be confusing and difficult to understand, and at times they seem to overlap.

First, there are "cases in which there are further proceedings—even entire trials—yet to occur in the state courts but where for one reason or another the federal issue is conclusive or the outcome of further proceedings preordained." *Id.* at 479. To illustrate the point, the Court cited *Mills v. Alabama*, 384 U.S. 214 (1966). In *Mills*, the state trial court granted a demurrer in a criminal case based on the U.S. Constitution, but the state supreme court reversed and sent the case back for trial. The Supreme Court granted review because the defendant's only defense was his federal challenge, and thus postponing review would be "a completely unnecessary waste of [the state court's] time and energy." *Id.* at 217–18.

Second, there are cases "in which the federal issue, finally decided by the highest court in the State, will survive and require decision regardless of the outcome of future state-court proceedings." *Cox Broadcasting*, 420 U.S. at 480. The Court in *Cox Broadcasting* cited several examples, including *Radio Station WOW*, 326 U.S. at 124, in which the Nebraska Supreme Court had mandated the transfer of a federally licensed radio station's assets and ordered an accounting. As the Court in *Cox Broadcasting* explained the case, the question whether the transfer order interfered with the radio station's federal license would remain for U.S. Supreme Court review, and there was no likelihood that the accounting would generate additional federal questions. 420 U.S. at 480.

The third category involves "situations where the federal claim has been finally decided, with further proceedings on the merits in the state courts to come, but in which later review of the federal issue cannot be had, whatever the ultimate outcome of the case." *Id.* at 481. As the Court in *Cox Broadcasting* explained, "if the party seeking interim review ultimately prevail[ed] on the merits, the federal issue [would] be mooted; if he were to lose on the merits, however, the governing state law would not permit him again to present his federal claims for review." *Id.* Among the examples cited was *California v. Stewart*, a case decided in conjunction with *Miranda v. Arizona*, 384 U.S. 436 (1966). In that case, the state court overturned a criminal conviction based on violations of the U.S. Constitution and remanded the case for a new trial. As the *Cox Broadcasting* Court explained the *Stewart* case: "Although the State might have prevailed at trial, . . . the state judgment was 'final' since an acquittal of the defendant at trial would preclude, under state law, an appeal by the State." 420 U.S. at 481. As this language suggests, the third category is probably limited to criminal cases; after *Jefferson v. City of Tarrant*, 522 U.S. 75 (1997), it is difficult to conceive of a civil case that would satisfy the third *Cox Broadcasting* category. In *Jefferson*, the Court ruled that the likelihood that a state supreme court would adhere to its earlier ruling as "law of the case" on a second appeal did not merit application of the third category. *Id.* at 82–83.

Fourth are cases "where the federal issue has been finally decided in the state courts with further proceedings pending in which the party seeking review [in the U.S. Supreme Court] might prevail on the merits on nonfederal grounds, thus rendering unnecessary review of the federal issue by [the U.S. Supreme Court], and where reversal of the state court on the federal issue would be preclusive of any further litigation on the relevant cause of action rather than merely controlling the nature and character of, or determining the admissibility of evidence in, the state proceedings still to come." *Id.* at 482–83. As the Court in *Cox Broadcasting* explained, "if a refusal immediately to review the state-court decision might seriously erode federal policy, the Court has entertained and decided the federal issue, which itself has been finally determined by the state courts for purposes of the state litigation." *Id.* at 483. The Court cited several examples, including *Miami Herald Publ'g Co. v. Tornillo,* 418 U.S. 241 (1974) , where an electoral candidate sued the Miami Herald, arguing that the paper violated a state statute by refusing to allow him to respond to a critical editorial published by the paper. The trial court held that the statute violated the First and Fourteenth Amendments, but the state supreme court reversed and remanded for trial, finding the statute constitutional. In upholding its jurisdiction, the Court in *Tornillo* opined that, were it to conclude there was no final judgment, the result would be an "intolerable" situation in which "an important question of freedom of the press" would be left "unanswered." *Id.* at 247 n.6.

The Court has struggled since *Cox Broadcasting* to apply the four categories. For example, in *Johnson v. California*, 541 U.S. 428 (2004) (per curiam), the Court granted certiorari, but after briefing and oral argument concluded *sua sponte* that there was not a sufficiently "final" state-court judgment under 28 U.S.C. § 1257. There, the California state intermediate court reversed petitioner's criminal conviction under *Batson v. Kentucky*, 476 U.S. 79 (1986), because of the prosecution's use of racially based peremptory challenges to prospective jurors. The California Supreme Court reversed without reaching various state-law evidentiary and prosecutorial misconduct challenges, which were left open for the state's court of appeal on remand. The U.S. Supreme Court held that *Cox Broadcasting's* third category did not apply: "In the event that the California Court of Appeal on remand affirms the judgment of conviction, petitioner could once more seek review of his *Batson* claim in the Supreme Court of California—albeit unsuccessfully—and then seek certiorari on that claim from this Court." 541 U.S. at

430–31. Likewise, *Cox Broadcasting*'s fourth category was inapplicable because "petitioner can make no convincing claim of erosion of federal policy that is not common to all decisions rejecting a defendant's *Batson* claim." *Id.* at 430.

In *Kansas v. Marsh*, 548 U.S. 163 (2006), the Court again faced *Cox Broadcasting* finality issues. The issue was whether Kansas' death penalty statute, which mandated a death sentence when the sentencing jury found aggravating and mitigating circumstances in equipoise, violated the U.S. Constitution. The Kansas Supreme Court had found that the statute violated the Eighth and Fourteenth Amendments to the U.S. Constitution. Under that order, Marsh was to be retried on murder and aggravated arson counts without a death-penalty claim, but the U.S. Supreme Court held that the third *Cox Broadcasting* category was applicable because, absent immediate U.S. Supreme Court review, "the State [would] be unable to obtain further review of its death penalty law later in [the] case," regardless of whether Marsh was convicted. If, without immediate review, he were acquitted, the State would be barred by double jeopardy from appealing. On the other hand, if he were convicted, the State could not seek the death penalty. 548 U.S. at 167–68.

Adequate and Independent State-Law Grounds. Aside from the finality requirement of 28 U.S.C. § 1257, as elaborated in *Cox Broadcasting* and subsequent cases, where a state court decides both federal-law and state-law issues, but the state-law ground is an "independent and adequate" ground for the state court's judgment, the Supreme Court is "utterly without jurisdiction to review" such cases. William J. Brennan, *State Constitutions and the Protection of Individual Rights*, 90 Harv. L. Rev. 489, 501 (1977). The state-law ground of decision must be both "independent" and "adequate" to support the state court's decision in order to preclude Supreme Court jurisdiction; the two requirements are separate. The Court will consult the state court's opinion to make these determinations, and, if necessary, other materials as well, such as the record in the case and the course of state law leading to that decision. *See, e.g., Staub v. City of Baxley*, 355 U.S. 313, 318 (1958); *Ake v. Oklahoma*, 470 U.S. 68, 74–75 (1985).

The rationale behind the "independent and adequate state-law ground" doctrine is that for the Court to decide a question of federal law in that circumstance would be, in effect, to render an advisory opinion, since it would make no difference to the outcome. *Herb v. Pitcairn*, 324 U.S. 117, 125–26 (1945). In some cases, however, the state-law ground will be so interrelated with questions of federal law that the Court can hear and decide the federal-law question and then remand to the state court for further consideration of its state-law holding in light of the Court's federal-law ruling. *See, e.g., Three Affiliated Tribes v. Wold Eng'g, P.C.*, 467 U.S. 138, 152 (1984).

A lack of clarity in the grounds for the state-court's decision will yield the presumption that it was grounded in federal law. However, "[i]f the state court decision indicates clearly and expressly that it is alternatively based on bona fide separate, adequate, and independent grounds, [the Court] will not undertake to review the decision." *Michigan v. Long*, 463 U.S. 1032, 1040–41 (1983). In *Long*, the Michigan Supreme Court had purported to ground its decision declaring a vehicle search illegal in both the United States and Michigan constitutions; the state court, however, cited no state decisions in support of its judgment, and relied exclusively on federal decisions interpreting and applying the Fourth Amendment to the U.S. Constitution. In view of that lack of clarity, the Supreme Court applied the newly crafted presumption and asserted jurisdiction. *Id.* Although this "*Long* presumption" has not been without controversy, it has continued in effect. *See, e.g.*, *Arizona v. Evans*, 514 U.S. 1, 8 (1995) *with id.* at 23–34 (Ginsburg, J., dissenting) (advocating abandonment of the *Long* presumption and its replacement with the opposite presumption); *Washington v. Recuenco*, 126 S.Ct. 2546, 2554 (2006) (Stevens, J., dissenting) (criticizing the Court's "expansionist post-*Michigan v. Long* jurisprudence").

§ 22.4 HOW THE SUPREME COURT TAKES JURISDICTION—CERTIORARI

The discussion in § 22.3, *supra*, addresses when the Supreme Court has the *power* to hear a case. But, as noted above, the Court's docket is almost entirely discretionary—that is, the Court is almost never *required* to hear a case. All but a fraction of the cases that the Court decides on the merits come to the Court by way of the granting of a writ of certiorari, and it is critical for an advocate to understand how that rule works, in practice, if there is to be any hope of making a case fall within that small number of cases that are granted review each year.

A. SUPREME COURT RULE 10

Rule 10 of the Supreme Court Rules outlines the considerations that will motivate the Court to grant certiorari. Generally, Rule 10 provides that review on certiorari is a matter of "judicial discretion," and that "[a] petition for a writ of certiorari will be granted only for compelling reasons." Without being controlling or exhaustive, Rule 10 lists reasons that reflect "the character of the reasons the Court considers":

> (a) a United States court of appeals has entered a decision in conflict with the decision of another United States court of appeals on the same important matter; has decided an important federal question in a way that conflicts with a decision by a state court of last resort; or has so far departed from the accepted and usual course of judicial proceedings, or sanctioned such a departure by a lower court, as to call for an exercise of this Court's supervisory power;
>
> (b) a state court of last resort has decided an important federal question in a way that conflicts with the decision of another state court of last resort or of a United States court of appeals;

(c) a state court or a United States court of appeals has decided an important question of federal law that has not been, but should be, settled by this Court, or has decided an important federal question in a way that conflicts with relevant decisions of this Court.

Rule 10 further provides that a petition "is rarely granted when the asserted error consists of erroneous factual findings or the misapplication of a properly stated rule of law."

As the rule suggests, the most critical factors for obtaining certiorari are (i) an important federal question; and (ii) the existence of a "conflict" of one of the specified kinds on that question. Most frequently, the conflict is between decisions of the various circuits, or between circuits and the highest courts of the states. But even a conflict where the courts of appeals are hopelessly divided will not be enough to secure review if the question is not sufficiently important, or if a particular feature of the case makes it a less attractive vehicle for resolving the question presented. Again, a petition for certiorari is an appeal to the unreviewable discretion of the Justices of the Supreme Court; the Court follows the longstanding but unwritten "rule of four," which means that four Justices must vote to hear a case for certiorari to be granted.

There is a special category of cases where certiorari is sometimes appropriate on a lesser showing—where the Court determines to grant certiorari, summarily vacate the lower court's judgment, and remand the case to the lower court for reconsideration. These so-called "GVR" (grant-vacate-remand) orders are typically available "[w]here intervening developments, or recent developments that we have reason to believe the court below did not fully consider, reveal a reasonable probability that the decision below rests on a premise that the lower court would reject if given the opportunity for further consideration, and where it appears that such a redetermination may determine the ultimate outcome of the litigation." *Lawrence v. Chater*, 516 U.S. 163, 167 (1996) (per curiam). GVR orders have most commonly been utilized to give the lower courts the opportunity to apply intervening Supreme Court decisions that were not available when the lower court issued its decision; indeed, when a Supreme Court decision is issued, it is not uncommon for the Court's "Orders List" in the following weeks to feature a number of GVR orders sending cases back to the lower courts for reconsideration in light of the Court's new decision. GVR practice is available in other areas, too, including in cases of statutory, regulatory, or agency interpretive change, or where the opposing side has "confessed error" in the lower court's decision. The Court has indicated that the standard for certiorari under Rule 10 where a GVR order is contemplated is not as rigorous as the standard for certiorari to be followed by plenary review. *Id.* at 167.

It is also possible that, even absent a conflict or issue of exceptional importance, a decision may be so profoundly wrong as to warrant summary reversal—where the Court simultaneously grants certiorari and issues an opinion summarily reversing the lower court without receiving briefs on the merits or hearing oral argument. One of the authors personally handled such a case during his tenure in the Solicitor General's Office, *INS v. Hector*, 479 U.S. 85 (1986), and, more recently, the Court has aggressively reversed (using summary procedures) a number of decisions of the Ninth Circuit that have probably not satisfied the typical requirements of conflict in decisions and overwhelming importance.

Additionally, even if the Court grants certiorari in a case, it may later determine, based on the course of the briefing and oral argument, that the petition for certiorari should be dismissed as improvidently granted. A "DIG" (as it is known colloquially) may arise, for example, when the Court determines that an antecedent question has to be answered but is not properly before the Court, *see, e.g., Izumi Seimitsu Kogyo Kabushiki Kaisha v. U.S. Philips Corp.*, 510 U.S. 27 (1993) (discussed in § 22.4(C), *infra*), or where further study indicates to the Court that the question presented was not properly raised in the lower courts, *cf. Laboratory Corp. of Am. Holdings v. Metabolite Labs., Inc.*, 126 S.Ct. 2921, 2925 (2006) (Breyer, J., dissenting); *but see United States v. Williams*, 504 U.S. 36, 40–41 (1992) (suggesting that the grant of certiorari disposes of such a contention). The Court may also DIG only part of a case. *See, e.g., Board of Trustees of Univ. of Ala. v. Garrett*, 531 U.S. 356, 360 n.1 (2001).

The criteria of Rule 10, and how they are best presented to the Supreme Court, are discussed at greater length in § 22.4(E), *infra*.

B. THE "CERT. POOL" AND THE "DISCUSS LIST"

As noted, a grant of certiorari requires the vote of at least four Justices. The question of how the Justices can select the 70 or so cases to hear in a term out of the roughly 8,000 certiorari petitions presented to the Court annually is a mystery to many. Obviously, if each Justice read and studied each petition (along with the lower court opinion, opposition to certiorari, *amicus curiae* briefs, and other materials), he or she would have far less time to devote to the cases selected for review, argument, and opinion writing.

Not surprisingly, the Court has developed a process to streamline the review of petitions for certiorari—the so-called "cert. pool." The cert. pool was created in 1973 by then-Chief Justice Burger in order to distribute the workload of reviewing petitions for certiorari. As currently applied, all of the Justices (with the exception of Justice Alito) pool their law clerks to review and analyze petitions for certiorari on behalf of all of the participating Justices. One of the 32 or so law clerks to the participating Justices is assigned a specific petition and writes a (typically) short memorandum recommending either granting or denying the petition. The clerk's work product, the "cert. pool memo," is distributed to the eight participating Justices and their law clerks. Based on the pool memos, the individual chambers may engage in further review of some of the cases. An example pool memo can be seen in Zachary Wallander & Sara C.

Benesh, *Law Clerks as Advisors: A Look at the Blackmun Papers*, 98 Marq. L. Rev. 43, 68–72 (2014).

The cert. pool process has been the subject of intense criticism by some commentators, as well as by certain Justices, principally on the ground that it delegates too much of the judicial function to the Justices' law clerks, who are typically highly credentialed young lawyers with a year's experience clerking for a federal court of appeals judge. It appears, however, that the cert. pool memo process is here to stay, at least for the foreseeable future. Prior to joining the Court, Chief Justice Roberts (when he was a Supreme Court advocate) had openly expressed concerns about the process. Since his 2005 confirmation as Chief Justice, however, he has chosen to participate in the pool. Justice Alito participated in the cert. pool upon his 2006 confirmation, but withdrew in 2008. Adam Liptak, *A Second Justice Opts Out of a Longtime Custom: The 'Cert. Pool'*, N.Y. Times (Sept. 25, 2008) at A21. The newest member of the Court, Justice Gorsuch, has also opted out of the cert. pool. Adam Liptak, *Gorsuch, in Sign of Independence, Is Out of Supreme Court's Clerical Pool*, N.Y. Times (May 2, 2017) at A22.

Based on the filing date of the brief in opposition to certiorari (or the waiver thereof), the Clerk of Court assigns each petition a conference date. That is the date on which the petition will be considered by the nine Justices for grant or denial, and the Court publicly notes the fact and date of distribution on its docket. As that date approaches, and based on the pool memo and whatever other work is done by the individual chambers, the hundreds of petitions set for consideration at a conference get winnowed to a much smaller number for actual discussion among the Justices. Appearance on that list—called the "discuss list"—is essential for a petition to be granted, for the ones that do not make it to that list are, in effect, dead on arrival, and their denial will be announced on the Court's next full orders list. The discuss list is a confidential, internal Court document; it is not available to the public.

The Justices' conference is attended by no one except the nine Justices; not even a secretary attends. Typically, the conference is held on Fridays during the Court's regular sessions. Here, the Justices discuss and vote on whether to grant certiorari in those cases that made the discuss list. When the conference is complete, the Court forwards the list of granted cases to the Clerk of Court, along with the cases from the discuss list for which the Court has ultimately determined to deny certiorari.

In previous years, a few cases from the discuss list might be held, or "re-listed," for a later conference, for one or more of several reasons: to provide the Justices with additional time to consider the question of certiorari; because the decision to grant certiorari is better considered along with another case coming up later on the Court's docket; or because a pending case, once decided by the Court, may better inform the need for certiorari in a given case. In more recent years, starting toward the end of October Term 2012, the Court appears to have begun to relist cert-worthy cases as a matter of course—almost 80% of the cases granted certiorari in the October Term 2015 were relisted at least once.

Thus, maximizing the chances for a grant of certiorari requires an understanding of how the pool process works in practice. The advocate must recognize that, in many cases, a law clerk will devote only an hour or two to a petition and related papers. Drafting a petition to separate a legitimate case from one that is patently unworthy of a grant is a true skill. *See* § 22.4(E), *infra*.

C. CONTENTS OF A PETITION FOR CERTIORARI—RULE 14

A petition for a writ of certiorari must contain, in the order specified by S. Ct. R. 14, the following nine items:

1. "The questions presented for review, expressed concisely in relation to the circumstances of the case, without unnecessary detail." Such questions should be "short," and not "argumentative or repetitive." Such questions shall be set forth "on the first page following the cover," and nothing else may be included on that page. "Only the questions set out in the petition, or fairly included therein, will be considered by the Court." S. Ct. R. 14.1(a).

2. A list of all parties to the proceeding. S. Ct. R. 14.1(b).

3. For petitions longer than 1,500 words or five pages, a table of contents and a table of authorities. S. Ct. R. 14.1(c).

4. Citations to court and agency opinions and orders. S. Ct. R. 14.1(d).

5. "A concise statement of the basis for jurisdiction in this Court," providing the following information: the date of the judgment or order being appealed; the date of any order with respect to rehearing; the date and terms of any order extending the time for filing a petition for a writ of certiorari; express reliance on S. Ct. R. 12.5 (involving cross-petitions for certiorari); the statute conferring jurisdiction in the Supreme Court; and (if applicable) a statement that the special notification requirements of S. Ct. R. 29.4(b) or (c) have been met (*see* § 22.12(E), *infra*). S. Ct. R. 14.1(e).

6. The laws and regulations at issue (if lengthy, the laws and regulations should be set out in the appendix). S. Ct. R. 14.1(f).

7. A "concise statement of the case" setting forth the material facts and showing the bases for federal jurisdiction. S. Ct. R. 14.1(g).

8. "A direct and concise argument amplifying the reasons relied on for allowance of the writ." S. Ct. R. 14.1(h).

9. An appendix, containing (in order) the opinion sought to be reviewed, other relevant orders, any order on rehearing, the judgment sought to be reviewed (if the date of the judgment differs from the date of the opinion at issue), and any lengthy laws or regulations that are at issue. S. Ct. R. 14.1(i).

The rules further provide that all contentions supporting a petition must be set forth in the body of the petition and not in a separate brief (S. Ct. R. 14.2); that a petition should be written in "plain terms" and subject to S. Ct. R. 33's page limits (S. Ct. R. 14.3); that a petition may be denied simply because it is not clear, accurate, and brief (S. Ct. R. 14.4); and that the clerk may return a petition that does not comply with the rules (with a corrected version due within 60 days) (S. Ct. R. 14.5).

The importance of properly phrasing the question presented cannot be overstated. The purpose of the question presented is twofold: (i) it "provides the respondent with notice the grounds upon which the petitioner is seeking certiorari, and enables the respondent to sharpen the arguments as to why certiorari should not be granted"; and (ii) it "assists the Court in selecting the cases in which certiorari will be granted," by identifying the specific "particularly important questions" and thus "enabling [the Court] to make efficient use of [its] resources." *Yee v. City of Escondido*, 503 U.S. 519, 535–36 (1992).

On a number of occasions, the Court has granted certiorari, only to later discover that an antecedent issue, not fairly presented by the petition or the question, would have to be resolved before the Court could get to the question presented. That is what happened in *Izumi Seimitsu Kogyo Kabushiki Kaisha v. U.S. Philips Corp.*, 510 U.S. 27 (1993). There, the petition raised the following question: "Should the United States Court of Appeals routinely vacate district court final judgments at the parties' request when cases are settled on appeal?" *Id.* at 30. In the court of appeals, however, petitioner was not permitted to intervene in the case. Since the petitioner did not present a question addressed to the propriety of the court of appeals' denial of its motion to intervene, the Supreme Court found that omission fatal, and dismissed the petition. Although the Court's rules allow consideration of additional questions that are "fairly included" within the question presented, the Court noted that the intervention issue could not be deemed "fairly included" within the question presented. *Id.* at 31–33. Eventually, the Court granted certiorari in another case presenting the same issue, but which was unaffected by the antecedent issue of whether the petitioner was a party to the case. *U.S. Bancorp Mortgage Co. v. Bonner Mall P'ship*, 513 U.S. 18 (1994) (discussed at § 6.10, *supra*).

D. TIMING OF A PETITION FOR A WRIT OF CERTIORARI

The Court's Rule 13.1 states that, "[u]nless other provided by law," and subject to extension granted under S. Ct. R. 13.5, a petition for a writ of certiorari to review a judgment of a state court of last resort or a federal court of appeals must be filed within 90 days after entry of judgment (or, in the case of a lower-state-court decision that is subject to discretionary review by a state court of last resort, within 90 days after the order denying discretionary review). A Justice, "[f]or good cause," may extend the filing time for up to 60 days, provided that ("except in extraordinary circumstances") the application is filed at least 10 days before the original due date. S. Ct. R. 13.5. The application must identify the judgment being challenged, include the opinion and any order on rehearing, and specify why an extension is necessary. *Id.* Note that the time runs from *judgment* in the court of appeals, not from the issuance of the *mandate*. *See* § 17.4, *supra*.

The application for extension is referred to a Justice based on the circuit (or state) out of which the case arises. Every Justice has a "Circuit Justice" assignment for at least one of the thirteen judicial circuits; the current list of such assignments may be found on the Supreme Court's website, www.supremecourtus.gov, or in the prefatory pages of the most recent bound edition of the *Federal Reporter*.

Missing the deadline for filing a petition for certiorari is inevitably fatal. It does not matter whether the deadline was missed by neglect, miscalculation, or otherwise, nor does it matter whether the petition presents a compelling issue or has been filed by one of the Court's regular advocates or preeminent law firms—the Court's regular orders lists are filled with notations denying motions to file out of time. *See* S. Ct. R. 13.2 ("The clerk will not file any petition for a writ of certiorari that is jurisdictionally out of time. See, *e.g.*, 28 U.S.C. § 2101(c)."); *Riley v. Dow Corning Corp.*, 510 U.S. 803, 803 (1993) (Stevens, J., dissenting) ("the Court consistently denies motions to direct the Clerk to file a petition for a writ of certiorari out-of-time").

E. SEEKING CERTIORARI: STRATEGY

Several strategies can assist the drafter in maximizing the chances of having a petition for a writ of certiorari granted. The following strategies are adapted in part from an earlier publication co-authored by one of the authors, Timothy B. Dyk & Gregory A. Castanias, *Certiorari in Business Cases: Improving Your Chances*, The Practical Litigator, Vol. 7, No. 6 (Nov. 1996) at 27–37.

The drafter should carefully limit the number of issues presented for review. If, out of more than 8,000 petitions a year, the Court grants fewer than 80, the likelihood that a single case raises more than one "cert-worthy" issue is exceedingly low. This is especially true if the issues are truly independent (*e.g.*, a statutory question and a constitutional question). Sometimes a broad issue breaks down naturally into two or three sub-issues that, for clarity, may best be set out separately. Even here, however, it is a rare case that warrants more than two issues. The very strong presumption in drafting a petition is to limit the petition to a single question presented.

In the past 10 to 20 years, regular U.S. Supreme Court advocates—including members of the Office of the Solicitor General—have, in appropriate cases, used the practice of prefacing the question presented with a short statement in order to frame the context of the question. Used correctly, this can aid in providing clarity to the question presented. In a case argued by one of the authors, the question presented was drafted in a way that not only stated the question presented, but foreshadowed the conflict among the circuits and the importance of the case:

> A divided panel of the Court of Appeals for the Third Circuit held that a district court must first conclusively determine if it has personal jurisdiction over the defendant before it may dismiss the suit on the ground of *forum non conveniens*. The court acknowledged that its holding was inconsistent with the interests of judicial economy, recognized that its decision in the case deepened an already-existing 2–4 split among the circuits, and invited this Court's review.
>
> The question presented is:
>
> Whether a district court must first conclusively establish jurisdiction before dismissing a suit on the ground of *forum non conveniens*?

Pet. for Certiorari, *Sinochem Int'l Co., Ltd. v. Malay. Int'l Shipping Corp.* (No. 06–102), at i (July 21, 2006).

Although the merits of a case may have some impact on whether the Court grants a petition (the Court reverses the vast majority of cases it accepts, *see* § 22.2, *supra*), the certiorari process is separate from the merits. The real question at the certiorari stage is whether the case warrants review, not whether the decision below was correctly decided. Thus, it is normally ineffective to make the principal focus of a petition for certiorari an analysis of the merits.

Instead, the principal focus of the petition should be to explain why the case is "cert-worthy" under traditional criteria. If there is a conflict among the federal courts of appeals (or among the highest state courts, or between federal circuits and highest state courts), that conflict should be the major focus of the petition. If the courts themselves have recognized the conflict, that fact should be prominently noted (indeed, such recognition should usually be quoted). The courts' recognition of a conflict is far more credible than the advocate's bare claim of a conflict. (Of course, where an appellate court possesses exclusive federal jurisdiction over particular categories of cases, such as the Federal Circuit's exclusive jurisdiction over cases arising under the U.S. patent laws, a petition for certiorari directed to a decision of such a court will have to demonstrate importance through means other than conflicts of authority.)

Equally important, if the Court itself has previously identified a conflict, that point should be featured prominently. For instance, in *Free v. Abbott Labs., Inc.*, 529 U.S. 333 (2000) (mem.), the Court decided a federal jurisdictional question by an equally divided Court, leaving no binding precedent (the Court divided 4–4 because of Justice O'Connor's recusal). The fact that the Court had already granted review on the issue in *Free* made the certiorari petition in a later case raising the issue especially strong, and the Court granted review. *Exxon Mobil Corp. v. Allapattah Servs., Inc.*, 545 U.S. 546 (2005). Similarly, when the Court has already granted certiorari on an issue in a case but never reached the merits, either because of settlement or dismissal, a later case presenting the same issue is a prime candidate for certiorari. *See, e.g.*, § 22.4(C), *supra* (discussing *Izumi Seimitsu Kogyo Kabushiki Kaisha v. U.S. Philips Corp.*, 510 U.S. 27 (1993), and *U.S. Bancorp Mortgage Co. v. Bonner Mall P'ship*, 513 U.S. 18 (1994)).

Credibility is crucial. The advocate should not overstate the purported conflict. The law clerk from the cert. pool will study the purported conflict and review the supposedly conflicting authority. An exaggerated claim of conflict will ensure a rapid denial of certiorari. In some instances, even if a conflict is not direct, a conflict in approach, or "conflict in principle" can be asserted. The important point is that, whatever the nature of the conflict, the advocate must not overstate or misrepresent it.

It is also possible that a decision may conflict with a prior Supreme Court decision. This is unlikely, however, since lower courts are bound by Supreme Court authority and will rarely decide a case in a manner that overtly conflicts with a Supreme Court case. Such conflicts do occur, however, and an egregious case may warrant summary reversal (granting the petition and reversing based on the certiorari papers, without further briefing and without oral argument). As the Court is fond of saying, "the prerogative of overruling its own decisions" belongs to the Supreme Court itself, and so lower courts are obligated to follow Supreme Court precedent, even if that Supreme Court precedent "appears to rest on reasons rejected in some other line of decisions." *Rodriguez de Quijas v. Shearson/Am. Express, Inc.,* 490 U.S. 477, 484 (1989).

After demonstrating a conflict (if possible), the next part of the petition should demonstrate that the issue is important and likely to recur. If the issue impacts few people and rarely arises, even a true conflict may be of little interest to the Court.

Finally, at the end of the petition, counsel should briefly explain why the decision below is incorrect. The claim of error should not, of course, be the focus of the petition, but it is nonetheless helpful to briefly illustrate why the approach taken in the court below was faulty.

There will, of course, be cases where these models will not apply. Overall, the Court's unreviewable discretion to accept cases for review is exercised where a case is sufficiently important to merit the Court's limited time and resources; the existence of a conflict in lower-court decisions is part of the typical showing of importance or "cert-worthiness." But some cases may be cert-worthy even if there is no conflict—the 2000 presidential-election dispute resolved by the Court in *Bush v. Gore*, 531 U.S. 98 (2000) (per curiam), is an example of that phenomenon. Similarly, the Court granted review in *McNally v. United States*, 483 U.S. 350 (1987), and ultimately reached a decision on the proper construction of the wire-fraud statute that left it "stand[ing] alone, or virtually so, against a tide of well-considered opinions issued by state or federal courts." *Id.* at 376 (Stevens, J., dissenting). And, as discussed earlier (§ 22.4(A), *supra*), certiorari will sometimes be granted simultaneously with GVR orders and summary reversals on showings that are quite different from the typical showings of cert-worthiness.

F. OPPOSING CERTIORARI: REQUIREMENTS

The Court's Rule 15 addresses the requirements for and timing of a brief in opposition to a petition for certiorari. Significantly, such a brief is not "mandatory," except in capital cases and where requested by the Supreme Court. S. Ct. R. 15.1. Where a petition for certiorari is so plainly frivolous, or the case is otherwise not substantial enough to be deserving of certiorari, a respondent may wish to file a waiver of opposition to the petition. This can be accomplished either via the waiver form that is provided to petitioner for service of the notice of docketing on the respondent's counsel, or by letter addressed to the Clerk of Court, indicating that the respondent waives the right to file a brief in opposition. The Court may, however, request a waiving respondent to file a response to a petition in a "CFR" (call for response) order. The Court rarely, if ever, will grant a petition for certiorari without calling for a response from such a respondent.

If a brief in opposition is filed, it must be filed within 30 days of the docketing of the petition, a date that can be learned from the Court's docket, and is available via the Court's website or by telephone call to the Court. S. Ct. R. 15.3. The brief in opposition should contain all of the requirements of the Court's

Rule 24 (governing respondents' briefs on the merits), "except that no summary of the argument is required." *Id.* In addition, respondent is not required to include questions presented, a list of parties, a statement of the opinions below, a statement of jurisdiction, the statutes involved, or the statement of the case—all of which have already been presented in the petition—unless the respondent disagrees or is otherwise dissatisfied with petitioner's statements. S. Ct. R. 24.2.

If the petition contains any misstatement of law or fact bearing on "what issues properly would be before the Court if certiorari was granted," the brief in opposition should point that out. Indeed, the Court's rules "admonish[ ]" counsel that they "have an obligation to the Court to point out in the brief in opposition, and not later, any perceived misstatement made in the petition." S. Ct. R. 15.2. Additionally, there can be severe consequences for failing to raise, in the brief in opposition, an argument that petitioner waived a point by failing to properly raise it in the courts below; the Court's rules provide that any such objection (so long as not jurisdictional) "may be deemed waived" if it is not contained in the brief in opposition. *Id.* This latter rule grew out of the Court's experience in receiving waiver arguments in respondents' briefs *after* the Court had made the determination to hear the case: "Our decision to grant certiorari represents a commitment of scarce judicial resources with a view to deciding the merits of one or more of the questions presented in the petition. Nonjurisdictional defects of this sort should be brought to our attention *no later* than in respondent's brief in opposition to the petition for certiorari; if not, we consider it within our discretion to deem the defect waived." *Okla. City v. Tuttle*, 471 U.S. 808, 816 (1985).

G. OPPOSING CERTIORARI: STRATEGY

The strategy for opposing certiorari is almost the mirror image of the strategy for seeking certiorari. In most circumstances, that will mean first arguing (if possible) that there is no conflict, then arguing (if possible) that the case is not sufficiently important to merit certiorari, then arguing that the decision below is correct.

Depending on the case, some very strong additional arguments for denying certiorari may exist. For example, one of the most common reasons for the denial of certiorari is that the issue presented is a "factbound" one. If the proper resolution of the case turns on factors that are unique to that case, or to a narrow class of cases, then the Supreme Court's review of the question may not make national law for a large number of similar cases in the future. Such factbound cases cannot be said to have the "important" and recurring qualities that mark most cert-worthy issues.

Another common situation meriting the denial of certiorari is where the question presented by the petition has not been presented to, or passed upon by, the lower courts. In that circumstance, the brief in opposition should highlight the failure to allow the lower courts to decide the issue; the Supreme Court generally prefers the opportunity to decide cases where the issue presented has been considered not only by other courts of appeals, but by the lower courts in the particular case as well. Additionally, as noted in § 22.4(F), *supra*, the respondent is obligated to raise such preservation issues in the brief in opposition, lest the objection be considered waived if the case proceeds to the merits.

Obviously, jurisdictional problems in the case—lack of standing, lack of Article III jurisdiction, insufficient finality of a state-court decision under *Cox Broadcasting*, or the presence of an adequate and independent state-law ground for decision—are potentially lethal to the possibility of certiorari, and if they are present, an effective brief in opposition will highlight those factors as well.

If the certiorari petition asserts a conflict among the lower courts and the assertion is incorrect (or, at least exaggerated), the opposition should make that clear. Even if the existence of the conflict cannot be disputed, the opposition may have several points, depending on the circumstances:

- If there are only a couple of conflicting cases, the Court should let the issue "percolate," so that, if and when the Court ultimately *does* take the issue up, it will do so in a future case with the benefit of the considered views of several court of appeals judges and panels.

- There may be a trend in favor of the approach taken in the recent case, and it may make sense to give the court rendering the decision in the earlier case an opportunity in a future case to reconsider the issue (*e.g.*, through its *en banc* process).

- It may be possible to argue that the issue is unimportant or arises only infrequently.
- There may be some reason why the conflict will go away on its own (*e.g.*, through a legislative change that does away with the issue in future cases, or by *en banc* review in one of the assertedly conflicting circuits).

Of course, the opposition should also explain briefly at the end why the decision below is correct. As with the petition, however, the discussion of the merits should be kept relatively brief.

H. REPLY BRIEFS IN SUPPORT OF CERTIORARI

If a brief in opposition is filed by the respondent, the petitioner may file a reply brief in support of the petition. S. Ct. R. 15.6. There are few formal requirements for such a brief contained in the Court's rules, and there is no court-imposed deadline for the filing of such a reply brief, except for a practical one: When a brief in opposition has been filed, the clerk's office will distribute the petition and other briefs in the case to the Justices' chambers "no less than 14 days after the brief in opposition is filed." S. Ct. R. 15.5. The clerk will not delay distribution if a reply brief has not been filed. S. Ct. R. 15.6. Thus, to allow a reply brief to be considered by the law clerk writing the cert. pool memo, *see* § 22.4(B), *supra*, the reply brief should be filed within 14 days of the filing of the brief in opposition.

§ 22.5 HOW THE SUPREME COURT TAKES JURISDICTION—APPEALS

In 1988, Congress "eliminate[d] substantially all of [the Supreme Court's] appellate jurisdiction" in Public Law No. 100–352, 102 Stat. 662. *Duquesne Light Co. v. Barasch*, 488 U.S. 299, 307 n.4 (1989). Despite the fact that almost all of the Supreme Court's docket is now filled with cases coming to the Court on petition for certiorari, there are still, as noted above, *see* § 22.3, *supra*, narrow classes of cases that come to the Supreme Court as "appeals" from district courts rather than on certiorari review. Even in those cases, however, the Court follows a process parallel to the certiorari process, first receiving preliminary filings ("jurisdictional statements" and "motions to dismiss" rather than petitions for certiorari and briefs in opposition) in order to make the determination of whether plenary consideration (briefs on the merits and oral arguments) should be allowed before reaching a decision.

One substantive difference between appeals and petitions for certiorari is the nature of the Court's decision. Because a denied petition for certiorari reflects the Court's decision not to consider a case, the Court has said, "again and again," that the denial of a petition for certiorari has no precedential effect and "does not remotely imply approval or disapproval of what was said by" the lower courts. *Maryland v. Baltimore Radio Show*, 338 U.S. 912, 919 (1950)

(Frankfurter, J., respecting denial of petition for writ of certiorari). But where the Court disposes of an appeal—even by summary affirmance or by "dismiss[al] for want of a substantial federal question"—that decision *is* precedential and binding on lower courts. "Votes to affirm summarily, and to dismiss for want of a substantial federal question, it hardly needs comment, are votes on the merits of a case." *Ohio v. Price*, 360 U.S. 246, 247 (1959) (separate opinion of Brennan, J.). *See generally Hopfmann v. Connolly*, 471 U.S. 459, 459–61 (1985) (per curiam) (providing a short but useful explanation of the differences). As the Supreme Court has explained, "the lower courts are bound by summary decisions by [the Supreme] Court 'until such time as the Court informs [them] that [they] are not.'" *Hicks v. Miranda*, 422 U.S. 332, 344–45 (1975) (quoting *Doe v. Hodgson*, 478 F.2d 537, 539 (2d Cir. 1973)).

One procedural difference between certiorari practice and appeal practice in the Supreme Court involves the requirement of a notice of appeal. When a losing party in the district court takes a direct appeal to the U.S. Supreme Court, that party must file a notice of appeal in the district court. The time for filing a notice of appeal is governed by 28 U.S.C. § 2101(a)–(c), or by the specific statute conferring appellate jurisdiction on the Supreme Court. Unless a specific statute applies, in cases where a federal statute has been held unconstitutional, this is a 30-day period, *id.* § 2101(a); in other appeals from district courts it is a 30-day period for interlocutory decisions and a 60-day period for final decisions, *id.*

§ 2101(b), and in all other cases (including those where only certiorari review is available) it is 90 days. *Id.* § 2101(c). Note, however, that in certain cases the overriding federal statute can shorten the time for filing a notice of appeal to as little as 10 days. *See, e.g.*, 2 U.S.C. § 692(b) (line-item-veto act). No extensions of time for filing a notice of appeal can be obtained. S. Ct. R. 18.1.

Like the contents of a notice of appeal to the federal courts of appeal (*see* § 5.2, *supra*), a notice of appeal to the U.S. Supreme Court is relatively simple: "The notice of appeal shall specify the parties taking the appeal, designate the judgment, or part thereof, appealed from and the date of its entry, and specify the statute or statutes under which the appeal is taken." S. Ct. R. 18.1.

After the notice of appeal is filed, the appellant has the responsibility for docketing the case in the Supreme Court. This is accomplished by the appellant's filing of a "jurisdictional statement" and payment of the docketing fee. S. Ct. R. 18.3. The time for docketing is 40 days from the filing of the notice of appeal in the district court, but that time period may be extended by a Justice for as many as 60 days. The appellee then has 30 days (also extendable) to file a response to the jurisdictional statement—typically a "motion to dismiss," a "motion to affirm," or a "motion to dismiss or affirm." S. Ct. R. 18.6. The same 30-day period applies to the filing of a conditional cross-appeal. S. Ct. R. 18.4.

The contents of a jurisdictional statement parallel those of a petition for certiorari, although the argument section, which in a petition for certiorari is entitled "reasons for granting the writ," is instead entitled "the questions are substantial" in a jurisdictional statement. *See* S. Ct. R. 18.3 (providing that "[t]he jurisdictional statement shall follow, insofar as applicable, the form for a petition for a writ of certiorari prescribed by Rule 14"). The argument serves a similar purpose to the argument section of a petition for certiorari—it is designed to convince the Court to at least receive briefs and hear oral argument instead of simply affirming the judgment of the lower court (or, in extreme cases, to convince the Court to summarily reverse the decision below). The motion to dismiss or affirm, similarly, should resemble the brief in opposition to certiorari, explaining to the Court the reasons why there is no jurisdiction, or why the questions presented by the appeal are too insubstantial to merit plenary treatment and can be affirmed summarily. As with certiorari practice, a reply brief opposing the motion to dismiss (or affirm) may be filed, and counsel are advised to file such a reply brief within 14 days of the filing of the motion to dismiss (or affirm) in order to have it considered by the Justices and their law clerks. S. Ct. R. 18.7, 18.8

§ 22.6 HOW THE SUPREME COURT TAKES JURISDICTION—ORIGINAL ACTIONS

As noted above, *see* § 22.3, *supra*, the Supreme Court's "appellate" jurisdiction is accompanied by a class of cases where the Court has "original" jurisdiction. Article III, § 2 of the Constitution provides that "[i]n all cases affecting Ambassadors, other public Ministers and Consuls and those in which a State shall be a party, the supreme Court shall have original Jurisdiction." This means that in a narrow class of cases, the Supreme Court of the United States serves as a trial court. In effect, that makes the Court—in a very limited set of cases—a court of first *and last* resort.

The constitutional command is supplemented by 28 U.S.C. § 1251, which provides:

> (a) The Supreme Court shall have original and exclusive jurisdiction of all controversies between two or more States.
>
> (b) The Supreme Court shall have original but not exclusive jurisdiction of:
>
> > (1) All actions or proceedings to which ambassadors, other public ministers, consuls, or vice consuls of foreign states are parties;
> >
> > (2) All controversies between the United States and a State;
> >
> > (3) All actions or proceedings by a State against the citizens of another State or against aliens.

Note the difference between subsections (a) and (b). In subsection (a), involving state-to-state disputes, the Court's original jurisdiction is also *exclusive* jurisdiction. But in the categories of cases covered by subsection (b), the Court's jurisdiction is "original but not exclusive," meaning that those kinds of disputes can also be litigated in the lower courts and make their way to the Supreme Court through the ordinary appellate channels.

Typically, the Court's original jurisdiction is invoked in cases involving boundary disputes between states, *e.g.*, whether New Jersey or New York owns Ellis Island, and which parts. *See New Jersey v. New York*, 523 U.S. 767 (1998). But the Court's original jurisdiction has also included the state "su[ing] as a proprietor to redress wrongs suffered by it as the owner of [property]." *Georgia v. Pa. R.R. Co.*, 324 U.S. 439, 446–47 (1945); *see also South Dakota v. North Carolina*, 192 U.S. 286 (1904). An "official state instrumentality" is considered to be the "state" for purposes of § 1251. *See Arkansas v. Texas*, 346 U.S. 368, 370 (1953). However, a political subdivision of a state, such as municipal corporation or county, is *not* considered a "state" for original—jurisdiction purposes; rather, it is considered a "citizen of [the] State." *Illinois v. City of Milwaukee*, 406 U.S. 91, 97–98 (1972).

Procedure in original actions is governed by the Court's Rule 17. The Federal Rules of Civil Procedure govern "[t]he form of pleadings and motions," S. Ct. R. 17.2, and in other respects, those Rules and the Federal Rules of Evidence "may be taken as guides." *Id.* The complaint in an original action "shall be preceded by a motion for leave to file," and those documents may also be accompanied by a brief in support of the motion for leave. Such a brief resembles a petition for certiorari or jurisdictional statement, in that it seeks to convince the Court to agree to accept the complaint. In original but nonexclusive jurisdiction cases, this is particularly crucial, as the Court could decide that the case is not sufficiently meritorious or important to warrant the exercise of original jurisdiction. Even in cases falling within the Court's original *and exclusive* jurisdiction, this can be important, as the Supreme Court still has the discretion "not to accept original actions" even in "actions between two States, where [its] jurisdiction is exclusive." *Mississippi v. Louisiana*, 506 U.S. 73, 77 (1992).

Within 60 days of the filing of the motion for leave to file, an adverse party may file a brief in opposition to the motion. S. Ct. R. 17.5. A plaintiff may then file a reply brief, but—as with reply briefs in support of certiorari and in opposition to motions to dismiss (*see* S. Ct. R. 15.6, 18.8)—the papers will be distributed to the Justices after 10 days have elapsed from the filing of the responsive paper, and that distribution will not be delayed in order to receive a reply brief.

Rule 17.5 also provides that upon consideration of the submitted papers, "[t]he Court thereafter may grant or deny the motion, set it for oral argument, direct that additional documents be filed, or require that other proceedings be conducted." If the Court accepts the case, and no facts are contested, the Court will set the case for oral argument. However, if factual issues are in dispute, the Court will typically appoint a Special Master to hear evidence and make findings and recommendations to the Court. The parties are generally allowed to present arguments to the Master, to file objections and exceptions to the Master's recommendations, and, ultimately, to present briefs and arguments to the Court itself before final decision.

§ 22.7 MERITS BRIEFING IN THE SUPREME COURT

A merits brief is generally limited to the issues presented to the Court in the petition for a writ of certiorari. Of course, issues going to the jurisdiction of the Court to hear the dispute, although not raised in the petition, may be raised at any time.

Much of the advice that applies to the crafting of superior appellate briefs in the federal courts of appeals applies with full force to Supreme Court merits briefs. *See* § 13.2(H), *supra*. Nonetheless, a merits brief in the Supreme Court differs in important ways from a typical appellate brief in a federal appellate court.

One important difference stems from the fact that federal court of appeals panels are bound by Supreme Court decisions, *en banc* decisions of the circuit, and prior panel opinions of the circuit. It is not uncommon to find controlling case law on a particular issue before a court of appeals. In that circumstance, there is little, if any reason, to focus on what the rule of law "should" be, and long discussions of policies underlying prior precedent are frequently unnecessary and even counterproductive. By contrast, it is exceedingly rare that the Supreme Court will grant plenary review in a case that is already squarely controlled by a prior Supreme Court case.

In those rare instances in which a court of appeals disregards a Supreme Court case squarely on point, the usual Supreme Court approach is summary reversal based on the certiorari papers. But even if a plenary appeal is arguably controlled by a prior Supreme Court decision, the Court is free to overrule that case. For that reason, it is even more essential to a Supreme Court merits brief for the advocate to explain, in detail, *why* a particular approach is correct. Any attempt to suggest that the Court should reflexively rule a certain way simply because of prior case law—and without a discussion of the wisdom of the approach—is likely to be unpersuasive standing on its own.

By the same token, there is little to be gained by simply citing lower-court cases to show the number of courts that have taken a particular position. The Supreme Court does not conduct a headcount in resolving issues. For example, in *McNally v. United States*, 483 U.S. 350 (1987) (discussed at § 22.4(E), *supra*), the Court reached a decision that was at odds with every lower court to have addressed the issue up to that point.

What *is* important, however, is if a particular decision articulates a well-reasoned and persuasive rationale for the approach being urged by the advocate. This is especially true if the decision is written by a well-respected court of appeals judge. (If so, the author should be identified by name.) Secondary sources—particularly by highly respected academics—may also be persuasive to the Court, though probably less so in constitutional cases if the

Court's opinions are any indication. If a recognized expert in the field supports the position urged by the advocate, a citation (or quotation if the source contains persuasive reasoning) may well be appropriate.

As with court of appeals briefs, multiple alternative arguments in support of a particular result usually are not warranted. The advocate should select and advance only the strongest arguments. Also, as with court of appeals briefs, footnotes and block quotes should be kept to a minimum. And, as with all written and oral representations to any court, absolute candor is critical: Exaggeration or misstatement of authority is unethical and will severely damage the advocate's credibility before the court.

Finally, as in all briefs, the arguments should be as concise as possible. There is no reason why a brief must reach (or even come close to) the page or word limits. In many cases, the most effective briefs are relatively short—demonstrating through sheer simplicity that the advocate's argument is simple, logical, and persuasive.

§ 22.8 *AMICUS CURIAE* BRIEFS IN THE SUPREME COURT

Even more than in the federal courts of appeals, *amicus curiae* briefs play a major role in U.S. Supreme Court advocacy. The rules and the practice of *amicus* filings, however, differ in meaningful ways from the rules and practice that govern in the federal appellate courts. *Cf.* § 12.2(F), *supra*.

A. RULE 37: LEGAL REQUIREMENTS

The overarching principle applicable to *amicus* briefs in the Supreme Court is set forth in the Court's Rule 37.1: "An *amicus curiae* brief that brings to the attention of the Court relevant matter not already brought to its attention by the parties may be of considerable help to the Court. An *amicus curiae* brief that does not serve this purpose burdens the Court, and its filing is not favored."

In certiorari cases, *amicus* briefs may be filed at either the petition stage of the case, or the merits stage, or both. Rule 37.2 governs petition-stage briefs, and provides that such briefs are due within 30 days of the docketing of a case or 30 days of the Court's request for a response from respondent (for *amicus* briefs supporting a petitioner), or within the time for filing respondent's brief (for *amicus* briefs supporting respondent). (The same time periods govern *amicus* briefs supporting the analogous filings in appeals and original-jurisdiction cases.) Rule 37.3 governs *amicus* briefs in cases to be orally argued, and makes the due date seven days after the brief for the party supported is filed, or seven days after the petitioner's brief is filed if the *amicus* brief purports to be in support of neither party.

Regardless of whether the *amicus* brief is to be filed at the petition stage or at the merits stage, the brief must be accompanied for filing by the written consents of all parties to the filing of such a brief. S. Ct. R. 37.2(b) (petition-stage); 37.3(b) (merits-stage). Absent written consents, the proposed *amicus* brief must be accompanied by a motion for leave to file that sets forth the nature of the movant's interest as well as the identities of the party or parties withholding consent. Rule 37.2(b), dealing with petition-stage briefs, but not Rule 37.3(b), dealing with merits-stage briefs, indicates that such a motion for leave "is not favored." A party may file an objection to such a motion, "stating concisely the reasons for withholding consent." S. Ct. R. 37.5. Motions are not required for *amicus* briefs coming from the United States, authorized federal agencies, states, or municipalities. S. Ct. R. 37.4.

Except for the governmental *amici* subject to Rule 37.4, every *amicus* brief filed in the Supreme Court must contain a disclosure of "whether counsel for a party authored a brief in whole or in part and whether such counsel or a party made a monetary contribution intended to fund the preparation or submission of the brief, and shall identify every person other than the *amicus curiae*, its members, or its counsel, who made such a monetary contribution." S. Ct. R. 37.6. That disclosure must be made "in the first footnote on the first page of text" in the *amicus* brief. *Id.* The clerk's comments on this rule indicate that "general membership dues in an organization need not be disclosed"; only monetary contributions "intended to fund the preparation or submission of the brief" need be disclosed. Thus, for example, if a petitioner was a member of the U.S. Chamber of Commerce, that fact would not have to be disclosed in the Chamber of Commerce's *amicus* brief pursuant to Rule 37.6; if the petitioner paid the Chamber of Commerce $5,000 specifically to cover the printing costs of the *amicus* brief, that fact *would* have to be disclosed.

B. STRATEGY

Petition Stage. Recent—and not-so-recent—statistics suggest that having the support of an *amicus* brief at the certiorari stage of a case in the U.S. Supreme Court correlates with a higher likelihood that a petition for certiorari will be granted. *See* "Cert.-Stage amicus all-stars: Where are they now?", *available at* www.scotusblog.com/2013/04/cert-stage-amicus-all-stars-where-are-they-now/ (showing that the top 16 filers of certiorari-stage *amicus* briefs from May 19, 2009 and August 15, 2012 filed 349 briefs supporting certiorari, and 75—or 21%—were granted); "Top Sixteen Cert.-Stage Amicus Brief Filers From May 19, 2004 to August 15, 2007," *available at* http://www.scotusblog.com/movabletype/archives/Top%2016%20Amici.pdf (showing that the top 16 filers of certiorari-stage *amicus* briefs during this time frame filed 269 briefs supporting certiorari, and 67—or 27%—were granted); H.W. Perry, Jr., *Deciding to Decide* 137–38 (1991) (indicating that *amicus* support at the certiorari stage increased the chances of a grant of certiorari to 26.7%, and 37.1% when including the United States as *amicus*); Gregory A. Caldeira & John R. Wright, *Amici Curiae Before the Supreme Court: Who Participates, When, and How Much?*, 52 J. of Politics 782 (1990); Gregory A. Caldeira & John R. Wright, *Organized Interests and Agenda Setting in the U.S. Supreme Court*, 82 Am. Pol. Sci. Rev. 1109 (1988).

It is rare—but not unheard of—for an *amicus curiae* to file a brief at the certiorari stage urging the Court to *deny* a petition. Perversely, the authors' limited experience with such cases shows a 100% correlation between the filing of such *amicus* briefs and the *granting* of a petition for certiorari—review was granted in both cases where *amicus* briefs were filed in opposition to the petition. *See West Lynn Creamery, Inc. v. Watson*, 510 U.S. 811 (1993) (order granting certiorari); *General Motors Corp. v. Tracy*, 517 U.S. 1118 (1996) (order granting certiorari). Perhaps this is attributable to the fact that the *amici* filings opposing certiorari served only to underscore the importance of the case, thereby (paradoxically) proving that the case satisfied the requirements of the Court's Rule 10.

Either way, an *amicus* brief filed at the petition stage can help a petition for certiorari stand out of the pack. In particular, an *amicus* brief from a noted organization with an interest in the case, explaining why a ruling from the Supreme Court would be generally important and affect a number of persons, companies, or entities beyond the parties to the case, is likely to be particularly helpful.

Should counsel consent across-the-board to the filing of *amicus* briefs on the other side? In general, the Court grants leave to file *amicus* briefs at the certiorari stage, even if the motion for leave to file is opposed, and despite the language in the Rule indicating that motions for leave to file certiorari-stage *amicus* briefs are "not favored." At the same time, however, counsel—or, frequently, their clients—may have good and sufficient reasons to oppose the filing of an *amicus* brief. For example, counsel might oppose a proposed brief because he or she knows that the *amicus* will seek to make arguments that go far beyond the issues in the case, or because the proposed *amicus* is seeking to file a brief simply to provide his or her opposing party with additional words or pages to make the party's arguments. Although it is rare that a timely motion for leave to file an *amicus* brief is denied, whether at the certiorari stage or at the merits stage, it does happen on occasion. *See, e.g., Gonzales v. Carhart*, 127 S.Ct. 30 (2006) (merits stage; proposed brief argued that *Roe v. Wade* "is unconstitutional and invalid, and must be overruled," even though that issue was not presented in the case); *Ashcroft v. Raich*, 543 U.S. 977 (2004) (merits stage); *Butler v. FAA*, 544 U.S. 1027 (2005) (certiorari stage); *Allen v. Pacheco*, 540 U.S. 1212 (2004) (same).

Merits Stage. At least one *amicus curiae* brief is typically filed in over 95% of the cases in which the Court hears oral argument. *See* Richard Lazarus, *Advocacy Matters Before and Within the Supreme Court: Transforming the Court by Transforming the Bar*, 96 Geo. L.J. 1487, 1514 (2008) (noting that in the Court's 2005 Term, 96% of the cases on the oral-argument docket had one or more *amicus* briefs filed in the merits stage of the case). Thus, in contrast to *amicus* briefs filed at the certiorari stage, which may help a case stand out from the pack, *amicus* briefs at the merits stage of a case are common, and in the highest-profile cases can be overwhelming in number. As a couple of extreme examples, one of the recent University of Michigan affirmative-action cases, *Grutter v. Bollinger*, 539 U.S. 306 (2003), engendered 89 *amicus curiae* briefs—69 for the University, 15 for the petitioner, and five in support of neither party. More recently, a patent case argued by one of the authors, *Association for Molecular Pathology v. Myriad Genetics, Inc.*, 133 S. Ct. 2107 (2013), occasioned 51 *amicus curiae* briefs—16 supporting the petitioner, 26 supporting the respondent, and nine supporting neither party.

The challenge for lawyers writing *amicus* briefs for the merits stage, therefore, is to provide the Court with, at minimum, a document that is likely to be read. That counsels in favor of a short, succinct brief. Heeding Rule 37.1, and providing "relevant matter" not already in the parties' briefs, is most likely to be useful to the Justices. That "matter" might include factual data (often presented in the form of a "Brandeis Brief"), or narrower arguments than those offered by the parties, or—in extraordinary cases, especially those involving constitutional adjudication—broader arguments or theories that differ from those advanced by the parties. *See, e.g., Freytag v. Comm'r*, 501 U.S. 868 (1991) (adopting constitutional argument advanced only by an *amicus*). But simply filing a "me, too" brief or a brief indicating that a corporation or industry group agrees with the position advanced by one of the parties is not likely to be helpful to the Court.

§ 22.9 CERTIFICATION OF STATE-LAW QUESTIONS

As discussed in Chapter 20, *supra*, federal courts may certify unsettled questions of state law for disposition by 45 of the 50 states' highest courts. The U.S. Supreme Court, too, may utilize this procedure, and it has done so in rare occasions over the years. *See, e.g., Stewart v. Smith*, 534 U.S. 157 (2001); *Va. v. Am. Booksellers Ass'n*, 484 U.S. 383 (1988); *see also* cases cited in Chapter 20, *supra*.

§ 22.10 ROLE OF THE UNITED STATES SOLICITOR GENERAL

No Supreme Court advocate can be fully effective without a clear understanding of the role and importance of the U.S. Solicitor General. The Solicitor General represents the United States in the Supreme Court. And the United States is involved as a party in a high percentage of the Court's cases—over the past 10 years, the United States filed merits briefs and presented argument as a party in 30 to 40% of the Court's orally argued cases. Additionally, the Solicitor General is also involved as *amicus* in many other cases, both filing briefs and presenting argument on behalf of the United States as *amicus*. All told, the Solicitor General commonly participates in 80% or more of the cases on the merits in a given Term.

Indeed, it is not uncommon for the Supreme Court to request the views of the Solicitor General before deciding whether to grant certiorari in a case. Particularly where the proper interpretation of a federal statute or regulation is at issue, the Court will frequently issue an order indicating that "The Solicitor General is invited to file a brief in this case expressing the views of the United States." (Colloquially, this is called a "CVSG" order, short for "call for the views of the Solicitor General.") The Solicitor General's office does not view these "invitations" as discretionary on its part; it responds to the invitations in all cases.

Having the support of the Solicitor General—at the certiorari stage and on the merits—can often make or break a case. Unlike the advocate for a private party, who is inevitably viewed as somewhat of a "hired gun," the Solicitor General (sometimes called "The Tenth Justice," *see* Lincoln Caplan, *The Tenth Justice: The Solicitor General and the Rule of Law* (1987)) has an institutional and historic role that affords great credibility to that office. The Court knows that the Solicitor General is concerned about long-term credibility and will even confess error in a case if that outcome is warranted. Thus, it is not surprising that, while the likelihood of a petition for certiorari being granted is overall very low—in the 1–3% range (depending on which petitions are included in the denominator, *see* § 22.2, *supra*)—a very high percentage (over 50%) of the Solicitor General's certiorari petitions are granted.

Advocates with matters before the Supreme Court should understand that, upon request, members of the Solicitor General's Office may be willing to meet to discuss pending or prospective cases. This is an opportunity to educate the office on the policy implications or other important features of a case that favor the advocate's position. The advocate should, of course, recognize that the Solicitor General will make its decision on a case based on what is best for the United States, and thus the ability to "persuade" the Solicitor General to take a particular side is limited. Nonetheless, the advocate can sometimes highlight features of a case that might not be immediately apparent, especially upon only limited review.

When the Solicitor General has weighed in on the advocate's side in a written brief, the advocate is likely to face a motion by the Solicitor General for "divided argument"—usually a request by the Solicitor General to receive ten minutes of the advocate's 30 minutes of oral argument time. It is a rare case (if any) in which the advocate whose side is being supported should oppose such a request. Although the Court generally disfavors divided argument, it strongly favors divided argument when the request comes from the Solicitor General. The participation of the Solicitor General lends great credibility to the advocate's argument. Indeed, in many cases, only the Solicitor General can argue credibly about the long-term public policy consequences of a case. (The Court assumes that, in most circumstances, a private client's objective is simply to win the case.) The Solicitor General is much more credible in addressing adverse consequences beyond the particular case and the particular clients.

§ 22.11 ORAL ARGUMENT IN THE SUPREME COURT

The points discussed in connection with oral argument in the federal circuits (*see* § 13.8, *supra*) are also generally true at the Supreme Court level. There are, however, some additional considerations in the Supreme Court.

First, with nine Justices, the Supreme Court is virtually always a "hot" bench. (In some federal court of appeals arguments, by contrast, the judges will ask relatively few questions.) And as soon as the advocate has started to answer one Justice's question, another Justice may fire off a question. Brevity in responses is absolutely critical.

Second, with nine Justices and multiple law clerks, the likelihood that difficult problems with the advocate's case will not be picked up on by the Court is exceedingly low. For that reason, while moot courts are important before any appellate argument, they are critical before a Supreme Court argument. Indeed, even the most experienced Supreme Court advocates will often have several moot courts before the actual Supreme Court argument.

An extremely helpful resource for oral argument assistance is the Georgetown University Law Center Supreme Court Institute. The Georgetown Institute offers moot courts, free of charge, on a non-partisan first-come, first-serve basis. In the October 2015 Term, 95% of the cases argued at the Court were mooted through the Georgetown Institute. The mock Justices include many of the country's most experienced Supreme Court advocates; the authors have participated in this program both as advocates preparing for their arguments, and as "Justices." Supreme Court Justices have publicly remarked that the Georgetown program has significantly improved the quality of oral advocacy before the Court.

Finally, there are other unique aspects to Supreme Court oral advocacy that are outlined in the Court's *Guide for Counsel in Cases to be Argued Before the Supreme Court of the United States*, which is prepared by the Clerk of the U.S. Supreme Court, and is available on the Court's website. For instance, one always begins argument with "Mr. Chief Justice and may it please the Court" (unless the Chief Justice is recused or otherwise not sitting, in which case the advocate addresses the senior, and therefore presiding, Associate Justice, *e.g.*, "Justice Kennedy and may it please the Court"). Only the Chief Justice is referred to as "Mr."; the custom of referring to the Justices as "Mr. Justice Douglas," "Mr. Justice Brennan," etc., went out shortly before the 1981 confirmation of Justice Sandra Day O'Connor as the first female Justice of the Supreme Court. Unlike the courts of appeals, moreover, the Supreme Court has traditionally frowned on parties who seek to submit their case on the briefs without presenting oral argument. *See, e.g., Franchise Tax Bd. v. Alcan Aluminium Ltd.*, 493 U.S. 930 (1989) (denying respondent's motion to submit the case on the briefs).

§ 22.12 OTHER ISSUES IN SUPREME COURT PRACTICE

A. ADMISSION AND DISBARMENT OF ATTORNEYS

Admission to the Supreme Court bar is open to any lawyer who has been qualified to practice before the highest court of a state or territory for three years immediately preceding the date of application, and who has not been the subject of any adverse disciplinary action during that three-year period. S. Ct. R. 5.1.

The Court's rules also provide that an applicant "must appear to the Court to be of good moral and professional character." *Id.* In one notable case, *In re Rose*, 71 L.Ed.2d 862 (1982), the Court granted admission to a lawyer over the dissent of Chief Justice Burger, joined by Justice O'Connor, who complained that the Court should not " 'rubber stamp' the actions of a State" bar by granting admission to questionable candidates. *Id.* at 863 (Burger, C.J., dissenting). (The applicant had aroused controversy by representing some Air Force cadets who had been the subject of charges at the Air Force Academy, and his admission to the Bar of Colorado had also been accompanied by some controversy.) Although Rose had been admitted to the bar, his admission would have been accompanied by the "blot" of the dissenting opinion doubting his good moral and professional character, so he resigned from the bar of the Court, and re-applied, this time accompanying his application with affidavits from lawyers who knew of the facts surrounding the prior controversy. Rose was readmitted, with Chief Justice Burger and Justice O'Connor concurring on the ground that "the record presented at this time demonstrates that the applicant is 'of good moral and professional character.'" *In re Rose*, 92 L.Ed.2d 764 (1986). A fuller account of this episode appears in our late colleague Erwin Griswold's biography, *Ould Fields, New Corne: The Personal Memoirs of a Twentieth Century Lawyer* 381–83 (West 1992); Dean Griswold represented Mr. Rose in connection with his second application and moved his second admission to the court.

Admission can take place by mail or in open court. The latter provides the applicant and his or her sponsor a ceremonial opportunity to appear before the Justices and have the application for admission publicly granted.

B. MOTIONS AND APPLICATIONS

A number of the Court's rules refer to motions, and the Court's Rule 21 generally governs most of those sorts of motions. In addition, Rule 22 addresses "applications" made to an individual Justice.

The Court's Rule 21.1 requires every motion to "clearly state its purpose," as well as the facts in support of the motion; a motion also "may" include argument in support. The only page or word-count requirement is that motions "should be concise and shall comply with any applicable page limits." *Id.* Certain case-dispositive and other types of motions must be prepared in booklet format, *see* S. Ct. R.

21.2(b) & 33.1; all others may be prepared on 8½-by-11-inch-paper. *See* S. Ct. R. 21.2(c) & 33.2. Responses to motions should be filed "as promptly as possible considering the nature of the relief sought," and in all events within 10 days of receipt, unless otherwise ordered by the Court or a Justice thereof. S. Ct. R. 21.4. Oral argument is not allowed on motions unless the Court directs otherwise; the only type of motion that is routinely orally presented is the ceremonial motion for admission to the bar of the Court. S. Ct. R. 21.3.

Rule 22 of the Court's rules governs applications to individual Justices. As the Court's *A Reporter's Guide to Supreme Court Procedure for Applications* (available on the Court's website) explains, "[a]n application is a request for emergency action addressed to an individual Justice." Some applications involve nothing more unusual than a request for additional time for the filing of a brief. But some involve requests for truly extraordinary relief, such as a stay of execution in a capital case, or a motion to stay the effect of a court of appeals' judgment.

Such an application is addressed to the appropriate Circuit Justice (*see* § 22.4(D)), and begins: "To the Honorable [NAME], Associate Justice of the Supreme Court of the United States [or Chief Justice of the United States], and Circuit Justice for the [NAME] Circuit." The Justice receiving the application may grant it, deny it, or refer it to the full Court. S. Ct. R. 22.4, 22.5. If the Circuit Justice denies the application, it can be re-presented to each of the other Justices, *seriatim*. S. Ct. R. 22.4.

C. EXTRAORDINARY WRITS

As with all federal courts, 28 U.S.C. § 1651 (the "all writs act") empowers the Supreme Court to issue extraordinary writs. The Court's Rule 20.1 makes clear that the issuance of any kind of extraordinary writ (habeas corpus, mandamus, prohibition, and common-law certiorari) "is not a matter of right, but of discretion sparingly exercised." The general equitable standard set forth in Rule 20.1 is rigorous indeed, and reflects the reality that very few such writs are granted: "To justify the granting of any such writ, the petition must show that the writ would be in aid of the Court's appellate jurisdiction, that exceptional circumstances warrant the exercise of the Court's discretionary powers, and that adequate relief cannot be obtained in any other form or from any other court." Such petitions are to be captioned "*In re* [name of petitioner]" and prepared in the same style as a petition for certiorari. S. Ct. R. 20.2.

D. STAYS

Where a petitioner would be adversely affected by the execution or enforcement of a judgment entered by a lower court, that petitioner may move for a stay in the Supreme Court. *Cf.* § 17.4(C), *supra*. The Court's Rule 23 governs the procedure for stay applications: Such an application must "set out with particularity why the relief sought is not available from any other court or judge," and the Rule further provides that "[e]xcept in the most extraordinary circumstances, an application for a stay will not be entertained unless the relief requested was first sought in the appropriate court or courts below or from a judge or judges thereof." S. Ct. R. 23.3. The application must identify the judgment sought to be reviewed and append a copy of the lower court's (or lower-court judge's) order denying the relief in the first instance, and "set out specific reasons why a stay is justified." *Id.*

Generally, applications for stays must meet the four-part test set forth in Justice Brennan's in-chambers opinion in *Rostker v. Goldberg*, 448 U.S. 1306 (1980):

1. "[I]t must be established that there is a 'reasonable probability' that four Justices will consider the issue sufficiently meritorious to grant certiorari or to note probable jurisdiction";

2. "the applicant must persuade me that there is a fair prospect that a majority of the Court will conclude that the decision below was erroneous";

3. "there must be a demonstration that irreparable harm is likely to result from the denial of a stay"; and

4. "in a close case it may be appropriate to 'balance the equities'—to explore the relative harms to applicant and respondent, as well as the interests of the public at large."

Id. at 1308 (citations omitted). Although only four Justices' votes are required to grant certiorari, five Justices must vote to grant a stay. The Court "generally places considerable weight on the decision reached by the circuit courts in these circumstances." *Barefoot v. Estelle*, 463 U.S. 880, 896 (1983).

In some cases, the moving party may request—or the Court may grant *sua sponte*—a temporary stay in order to allow orderly briefing and consideration of the stay application, either by an individual Justice, or by the full Court. If a stay is ultimately granted, the stay order will typically make provisions for its expiration (*e.g.*, upon denial of a timely petition for certiorari or upon the Court's decision, judgment, or mandate), and may also require the movant to post security in the form of a supersedeas bond. *See* S. Ct. R. 23.4.

E. FILING, SERVICE, AND DOCUMENT-PREPARATION REQUIREMENTS

Rule 29 of the Supreme Court's Rules governs the filing and service of documents.

Filing. All documents are filed with the Clerk. S. Ct. R. 29.1. Documents that are filed in person after the business hours of the Court's Clerk's office but before midnight on the filing date may be presented to a Court security officer and stamped "received"; the document will then be forwarded to the Clerk the next business morning and considered timely filed on the date received by the security officer.

The general rule is that receipt by the Clerk's office constitutes filing. However, in deference to the fact that many counsel do not practice in the Washington, D.C. area, the rules further provide that a document is timely filed if sent to the Clerk "through the United States Postal Service by first-class mail (including express or priority mail), postage prepaid, and bears a postmark, other than a commercial postage meter label, showing that the document was mailed on or before the last day for filing." S. Ct. R. 29.2. Alternatively, if counsel uses a "third-party commercial carrier" (*e.g.*, FedEx; UPS), the document must be delivered to that carrier on or before the last day for filing, for delivery to the Clerk "within 3 calendar days" of the carrier's receipt of the package. *Id.* For inmates confined in an institution, timely filing means deposit in the institution's internal mail system on or before the filing date, accompanied by a declaration under penalty of perjury (*see* 28 U.S.C. § 1746) setting out the date of deposit and averring that first-class postage has been prepaid. S. Ct. R. 29.2. In the event that the postmark or delivery carrier's package does not clearly indicate the date of deposit, the Clerk will request a declaration from the person sending the document indicating the specifics of the filing by mail. *Id.*

Service. As with filing, service of documents may be accomplished by personal service, first-class mail, or third-party commercial carrier (for delivery within three calendar days of the carrier's receipt of the package). S. Ct. R. 29.3. If the document is prepared in booklet format (*see* S. Ct. R. 33.1), as most non-*in forma pauperis* docket petitions and briefs are, then three copies are to be served. If the document is prepared in 8½-by-11-inch-paper format (*see* S. Ct. R. 33.2), then only one copy is required. S. Ct. R. 29.3. Service is to be made on each separately represented party, not each lawyer. *Id.* "Ordinarily, service on a party must be by a manner at least as expeditious as the manner used to file the document with the Court." *Id.*

The Court's rules have recently added the requirement that all other parties must also be electronically served "at the time of filing or reasonably contemporaneously therewith." The only exceptions are (i) where the party filing the document is proceeding *pro se* and *in forma pauperis*, or (ii) where "the electronic service address of the party being served is unknown and not identifiable through reasonable efforts." *Id.*

Where the United States or any of its departments, offices, agencies, officers, or employees are to be served, service is to be made on the Solicitor General. Where a federal officer, employee, or agency with independent litigating authority is a party to the case (or is otherwise to be served), that officer, employee, or agency is to be served *in addition to* the Solicitor General. S. Ct. R. 29.4(a). In cases that call into question the constitutionality of a federal or state statute, the Solicitor General of the United States or the Attorney General of the state in question shall also be served; "the initial document filed in this Court" must also recite that the provisions of 28 U.S.C. § 2403(a) or (b)—which require the court to notify the United States, or a State, as the case may be, when the constitutionality of a federal or state statute is drawn into question—may apply, and indicate whether the lower courts certified to the U.S. or state attorney general that such an issue was presented. S. Ct. R. 29.4(b) and (c). This rule (and the notice statute, 28 U.S.C. § 2403) would apply, for example, where one private party has sued another under a federal or state statute, and the defendant has interposed a defense that the statute is unconstitutional. *See also* § 6.4, *supra*.

Proof of Service. Such proof, required by the Court's Rule 29.5, must contain (or be accompanied by) a statement indicating that "all parties required to be served have been served," and indicate the names, addresses, and telephone numbers of the counsel served, and the parties they represent. Proof can consist of (a) an acknowledgement of service signed by the party or counsel served, (b) a certificate of service reciting the facts and circumstances of service and signed by "a member of the Bar of this Court representing the party on whose behalf service is made," or (c) by a notarized affidavit (or declaration under 28 U.S.C. § 1746) from the individual making the service, when that individual is not a member of the Supreme Court Bar or otherwise duly appointed counsel. S. Ct. R. 29.5.

Corporate Disclosure. Every document filed by a nongovernmental corporation must contain a corporate disclosure statement "identifying the parent corporations and listing any publicly held company that owns 10% or more of the corporation's stock." S. Ct. R. 29.6. If there is no such company or corporation, the disclosure should so state. If a previously filed document (except for an 8½-by-11-inch paper filing prepared under Rule 33.2) has already included such a statement, that prior document can simply be cross-referenced, unless the facts have changed. S. Ct. R. 29.6. Keep in mind that the principal purpose of this disclosure statement is to allow the Justices to evaluate the necessity of recusal. *See* § 22.12(J), *infra*.

Electronic Transmission. As noted above, the Court's rules now require electronic *service* of "any document required by these Rules to be served." S. Ct. R. 29.3. Some documents must also be electronically *transmitted to the Court* at the time of filing: Electronic versions of briefs on the merits must be transmitted to the Clerk of Court and to all counsel of record at the time the brief is filed. S. Ct. R. 25.9. The same requirement applies to *amicus* briefs in cases that have been scheduled for oral argument. S. Ct. R. 37.3(a).

Preparation of Briefs and Other Papers. Rules 33 and 34 govern the preparation requirements for all documents filed in the Supreme Court. Generally, Rule 33 provides that there are two types of documents—"booklet-format" documents (S. Ct. R. 33.1) and "8½-by-11-inch paper format" documents (S. Ct. R. 33.2). Consistent with the approach of the Federal Rules of Appellate Procedure, *cf.* § 13.2(A), *supra*, the Supreme Court's recent rule changes provide word-limit requirements instead of page-limit requirements for booklet-format documents (*e.g.*, petitions for certiorari, formerly limited to 30 booklet-format pages, are now limited to 9,000 words; merits briefs, formerly limited to 50 pages, are now allowed 15,000 words). S. Ct. R. 33.1(g). As with the Federal Rules of Appellate Procedure, counsel must certify to the word count and ensure that footnotes are included in the count. S. Ct. R. 33.1(h).

Rule 33.1(g) also sets forth the required colors for the covers of booklet-format documents—*e.g.*, white for petitions for certiorari, orange for briefs in opposition to petitions for certiorari, tan for certiorari reply briefs, light blue for petitioners' opening merits briefs, light red for respondents' merits briefs, yellow for petitioners' merits reply briefs, cream for *amicus* briefs filed at the certiorari stage, light green for *amicus* briefs supporting petitioners (or neither party) at the merits stage, and dark green for *amicus* briefs supporting respondents at the merits stage.

Note that the cover colors of booklet-format briefs in the Supreme Court sometimes differ from those prescribed for appellate briefs in the courts of appeals. Merits reply briefs, for example, bear yellow covers in the Supreme Court, whereas they bear grey covers in a court of appeals.

F. EXHIBITS AND LODGING

Rule 32 deals with the unusual situations where exhibits or models—or non-record materials—need to be presented to the Court. In the case of models, diagrams, or exhibits that are part of the record evidence in a case, and that are to be inspected by the Court, those models, diagrams, or exhibits are to be "placed in the custody of the Clerk" at least two weeks before the oral argument of the case. S. Ct. R. 32.1. Counsel then has 40 days after decision in the case to remove those models, diagrams, or exhibits, or else the Clerk may destroy or otherwise dispose of them.

Rule 32.3 allows counsel to "lodge" non-record materials with the Clerk. If counsel desires to do this, he or she should set out in a letter (served on all parties) a description of the materials and the reasons why lodging would be desirable. However, the materials themselves may not be lodged unless requested by the Clerk. S. Ct. R. 32.3.

G. COMPUTATION OF TIME

The Court's Rule 30 sets forth the rules governing computation and extension of time. When the computation of time would result in a due date that is a weekend or holiday, the document or filing is due on the next day that is not a weekend, federal holiday, or day on which the Court building is closed (*e.g.*, a national day of mourning or a rare weather-related closing). S. Ct. R. 30.1.

An important provision related to applications for extensions is Rule 30.2. That rule requires applications to be filed within the time for filing (*i.e.*, out-of-time applications for extensions are inappropriate), and it further provides that, in the case of petitions for certiorari or jurisdictional statements, applications need to be filed 10 days or more before the due date, or else the application will not be granted absent a showing of "the most extraordinary circumstances." S. Ct. R. 30.2.

Extension applications for petitions for certiorari, jurisdictional statements, reply briefs on the merits, and petitions for rehearing are to be presented to an individual Justice; unlike other applications, if an extension application is denied, it may not be renewed before another Justice or before the full Court. S. Ct. R. 30.3. Any other kind of extension application may be made by letter to the Clerk and may be acted upon by the Clerk; a party aggrieved by the Clerk's action in this respect may request that the application be presented to a Justice or to the Court. S. Ct. R. 30.4.

H. REHEARING

Rule 44 of the Supreme Court Rules governs the filing of petitions for rehearing, which are rarely granted. Rule 44.1 deals with rehearings of merits decisions, while Rule 44.2 addresses rehearings of denied petitions for certiorari or extraordinary writs. In either case, a petition for rehearing is due within 25 days; the Court or a Justice may shorten or extend the time for the filing of a rehearing petition of a merits case. In either case, the petition must be accompanied by a certification from counsel that the petition is presented in good faith and not for reasons of delay; a petition for rehearing under Rule 44.2 is restricted to grounds of "intervening circumstances of a substantial or controlling effect or to other substantial grounds not previously presented," and the counsel's certification must also make that averment.

Responses are not allowed unless the Court calls for one. However, the Court will not (except in extraordinary circumstances) grant rehearing without first requesting a response. S. Ct. R. 44.3. *Amicus* briefs in support of or in opposition to rehearing are not allowed. S. Ct. R. 44.5. Multiple petitions for rehearing, or petitions for rehearing that are filed out-of-time, are forbidden. S. Ct. R. 44.4.

I. MANDATES

Supreme Court Rule 45 includes procedures for the issuance of mandates. *Cf.* § 17.4, *supra*. Rule 45.2 provides that in cases coming to the Supreme Court from state courts, the mandate issues 25 days after the date of judgment (which is entered the day the Court hands down its opinion), except that a timely petition for rehearing will delay the issuance of the mandate until the petition for rehearing is denied—at which point the mandate issues "forthwith." The Court may, of course, lengthen or shorten that 25-day time period, and in appropriate cases may order the mandate to issue forthwith.

Rule 45.3 provides that in cases coming to the Supreme Court from courts of the United States (defined in 28 U.S.C. § 451), a formal mandate does not issue unless the Court specifically directs; the clerk's office will, however, send a copy of the opinion and a certified copy of the judgment to the lower court.

Of course, just as district courts are bound to follow the judgments of federal appellate courts pursuant to the "mandate rule" (*see* § 17.4(A), *supra*), so too must lower courts (state and federal) adhere to the mandates and judgments of the U.S. Supreme Court, lest they have their actions corrected by appeal—or, if appeal is unavailable, mandamus. "When a case has been once decided by this court on appeal, and remanded to the circuit court, whatever was before this court, and disposed of by its decree, is considered as finally settled. The circuit court is bound by the decree as the law of the case, and must carry it into execution, according to the mandate." *In re Sanford Fork & Tool Co.*, 160 U.S. 247, 255 (1895).

J. RECUSAL OF JUSTICES

Section 455 of Title 28, which is the same recusal statute generally applicable to court of appeals judges (see § 16.2, *supra*), also applies to Supreme Court Justices. Justices and commentators have recognized, however, that the Supreme Court should be even more sparing in its application of the recusal statutes because the Court has only nine Justices, and decides cases with all nine. A recusal, leaving only eight Justices, raises the possibility of an equally divided court, which has the effect of affirming the lower court decision but without any precedential value. *See, e.g.*, *Lotus Dev. Corp. v. Borland*, 516 U.S. 233 (1996) (per curiam) (affirming the First Circuit's decision on an important question regarding the copyrightability of computer software by an equally divided court; Justice Stevens was recused). Unlike in the courts of appeals, which can simply assign another judge to a three-judge panel in the event of recusal, or some state supreme courts, which can assign a non-supreme-court justice to sit with the state supreme court in the event of recusal, the Supreme Court cannot assign a ninth judge (*e.g.*, from a U.S. court of appeals) to the case.

An example of the reluctance of Justices to recuse themselves is *Cheney v. U.S. District Court for the District of Columbia*, 541 U.S. 913 (2004) (Scalia, J., in chambers). There, in a case involving then-Vice President Cheney in his official capacity, the late Justice Scalia rejected a request by the Sierra Club, a respondent in the case, that he recuse himself because of his personal friendship with the Vice President (as evidenced by the fact that Justice Scalia went on a duck-hunting trip with the vice president). In rejecting the request, Justice Scalia reasoned:

> Let me respond, at the outset to Sierra Club's suggestion that I should 'resolve any doubts in favor of recusal.' That might be sound advice if I were sitting on a Court of Appeals. . . . On the Supreme Court, however, the consequence is different: The Court proceeds with eight Justices, raising the possibility that, by reason of a tie vote, it will find itself unable to resolve the significant legal issue presented by the case. . . . A rule that required members of this court to remove themselves from cases in which official actions of friends were at issue would be utterly disabling.

Id. at 915–16.

At the same time, however, a Justice will recuse himself when he or she has investment holdings in a company that is a party to the case, when a close relative might benefit financially from the decision (*e.g.*, a son or daughter is a partner in a law firm involved in the case), or when the Justice has made public comments that would bring the ability of the Justice to be impartial into doubt, whether by appearance or in actuality. *See Elk Grove Unified Sch. Dist. v. Newdow*, 540 U.S. 945 (2003) (discussed in *Cheney*, 541 U.S. at 916). Because the reasons for a recusal are rarely made public, however, there is limited precedent informing the bar of the analysis that leads to a recusal in a particular case.

PART 4

ISSUES OF ETHICS AND PROFESSIONALISM

CHAPTER 23

ETHICS AND PROFESSIONALISM IN APPELLATE PRACTICE

§ 23.1 INTRODUCTION

In various earlier chapters—most notably those dealing with the subjects of written and oral advocacy (Chapters 13 and 15, *supra*)—we have discussed some broad issues of ethics and professionalism that can arise in appellate practice. In this chapter, we touch on a few principles of ethics and professionalism that occur frequently in the context of appellate law. Of course, other issues of ethics and professionalism also occur in appellate practice; every lawyer is expected to understand the entire range of applicable rules and principles of both ethics and professionalism, and appellate lawyers are no exception to this rule.

We use the terms "ethics" and "professionalism" to define two related but distinct concepts. What we call "ethics" refers to the rules (*e.g.*, the Model Rules of Professional Conduct, or MRPC) that are enforced by the bar—largely, these are rules that require or proscribe particular conduct. What we call "professionalism" is governed more by standards than rules; they are often unwritten, they reflect a desire that law be conducted civilly, and they are "enforced" in less formal ways, such as unofficial opprobrium by fellow members of the bar. The two are not categorically separate—one might realistically think of "ethics" as referring to the minimum standard of conduct, and "professionalism" as reflecting our higher aspirations for members of the bar. Most importantly, though, the ethical and professional appellate lawyer will be a better appellate lawyer.

§ 23.2 DISCLOSURE OF CONTROLLING AUTHORITY

Most first-year law students learn that they cannot hide controlling authority from courts by failing to cite such authorities in their written briefs. Rule 3.3(a)(2) of the MRPC, entitled "Candor Toward The Tribunal," provides that "[a] lawyer shall not knowingly . . . fail to disclose to the tribunal legal authority in the controlling jurisdiction known to the lawyer to be directly adverse to the position of the client and not disclosed by opposing counsel. . . ."

The first thing to notice about this rule is that to violate it, a lawyer must "knowingly" fail to disclose adverse authority "known to the lawyer to be directly adverse to the position of the client." In turn, the Rule's knowledge standard reflects a basic difference between ethics and professionalism—an appellate lawyer with empty mind but pure heart, *e.g.*, one who simply fails to find the controlling authority and cite it, might not violate the rule as an ethical matter, but it would certainly not satisfy the expectations of the bench and bar with respect to professional competence. And, for a lawyer seeking to demonstrate excellence as an appellate lawyer and win his or her client's case, it will not be enough that the omission came about by pure oversight, or that the lawyer's opponent in court found the controlling authority and cited it.

The rule requiring disclosure of adverse controlling authority reflects a view that litigators—including appellate litigators—hold a dual trust. Yes, lawyers are fiduciaries of their clients, entrusted with zealously advocating the clients' interests in court, but they also have a parallel obligation to the court. Where the two obligations clash—where disclosure of a controlling authority would be harmful to the client but required to fulfill the lawyer's obligation to the courts, the conflict should be resolved in favor of disclosure. Of course, as a matter of professionalism—and of sound appellate practice—the better course is to identify the authority, distinguish it or call for its limiting or overruling, and if all else fails, try to preserve a challenge to the issue for review in a higher court. The appellate practitioner would prefer not to be the subject of an opinion such as *Gonzalez-Servin v. Ford Motor Co.*, 662 F.3d 931, 934 (7th Cir. 2011), in which defense counsel was described as engaging in "the ostrich-like tactic of pretending that potentially dispositive authority against a litigant's contention does not exist." (citations and internal quotation marks omitted).

Common ways for practitioners to violate this rule—or fall short of professional expectations—can be found in jurisdictional statements (*e.g.*, failing to identify the lack of finality in an appealed judgment; failing to apprise the court of events that arguably moot the dispute), misleading citations or paraphrasing of holdings (or misleadingly cropped quotations from cited cases), copying quotes from other sources (such as prior briefs or even judicial decisions) without verifying the quote from the original authority, or failing to indicate the subsequent history of a decision—either its reversal in a later stage, or a subsequent overruling (legislative or judicial) of its holding.

What constitute "directly adverse" legal authorities "in the controlling jurisdiction"? Obviously, Supreme Court decisions that are directly adverse to a client's position must be disclosed in a federal appellate court. The same rule and reasoning applies to circuit precedent (*e.g.*, a prior panel decision) within the same court. But those "binding" adverse authorities do not represent the limits of the lawyer's disclosure obligation. "Directly adverse" means more than just "legally binding." For example, in an appeal to the Fourth Circuit involving a question of Virginia law, an appellate lawyer would be required to disclose an on-point decision of the Virginia Court of Appeals. While that decision would not be "binding" on the federal appellate court in the way that a Virginia Supreme Court would be, that intermediate state appellate court decision would enter into the federal appellate court's obligation, under *Erie R. Co. v. Tompkins*, 304 U.S. 64 (1938), to make a "prediction" about how the state's supreme court would decide this unsettled question of state law. Additionally, disclosure of that decision would be necessary to aid the federal appellate court decide whether to certify the question to the Virginia Supreme Court. *See* Chapter 19, *supra.*

By contrast, in an appeal to the Second Circuit involving a construction of a federal law, there would be no obligation to cite a Fourth Circuit decision construing the federal law in a manner directly adverse to the position being advanced in the client's favor, for that would not be "legal authority in the controlling jurisdiction." But while disclosure might not be *required*, there is little doubt that it *should* be made as a matter of professionalism and good practice. After all, an experienced appellate lawyer would know that federal courts of appeals faced with interpretive questions of federal law in the first instance will look to their sibling courts' own answers. There would seem to be no good reason for a lawyer not to take the opportunity to cite the adverse, non-authoritative decision, and to address the flaws in its reasoning—especially when the opponent, and if not the opponent, then the judges and their law clerks, will inevitably find the decision.

In short, "[t]he underlying concept" of this rule "is that legal argument is a discussion seeking to determine the legal premises properly applicable to the case." MRPC § 3.3 cmt. 4. The lawyer is not required to make "a disinterested exposition of the law, but must recognize the existence of pertinent legal authorities." *Id.*

§ 23.3 SHOOT STRAIGHT WITH THE FACTS

Here, again, MRPC 3.3's command of "Candor Toward The Tribunal" guides the appellate lawyer. It provides, in MRPC 3.3(a)(1), that "[a] lawyer shall not knowingly . . . make a false statement of fact or law to a tribunal or fail to correct a false statement of material fact or law previously made to the tribunal by the lawyer." As the rule indicates, it can be violated by affirmative acts (making a "false statement of fact") or omissions (failing to correct a previous false statement of material fact, even if the initial misstatement was made innocently).

Some of the most common ways that lawyers get into trouble with factual misstatements include cropping quotations from the record (that is, providing incomplete quotations that cause the brief to reflect something different than what the record actually discloses); misquoting or mis-paraphrasing the record; making factual assertions that lack record support; and omitting material facts.

As with misrepresenting the law, the same "knowingly" standard applies to misrepresentations of fact under MRPC 3.3. Again, however, the rules set forth only a minimum standard, below which disciplinary measures may be imposed; the appellate lawyer should aspire to exceed those minimum standards. Nonetheless, the rule's requirements provide a sound guide to more professional, and superior, appellate briefs and arguments: Even absent knowing misstatements or omissions, the lawyer should aspire to present a completely accurate and reliable set of facts. To understand why this is the case, one need only consider how a skilled opponent, or the court, will respond to misleading or incorrect factual assertions when they are given the opportunity. Indeed, lawyers or law firms who make repeated appearances before a tribunal can quickly find their good names tarred (perhaps permanently). One of the authors, during his clerkship with a federal appellate judge, was informed that briefs filed by a certain law firm required extra careful attention, such that no assertion of fact or law was to be trusted without verifying the accuracy of the citation.

Of course, this duty of candor does not require the advocate to shed his or her role as an advocate. The duty of candor is not the same as a duty of objectivity or neutrality. For example, facts may be presented accurately, using techniques of narrative storytelling, in a way that furthers the interest of one's client without violating the duty of candor. There is a vast and useful academic literature on the topic of narrative storytelling in the law, much of which is summarized in J. Christopher Rideout, *Storytelling, Narrative Rationality, and Legal Persuasion*, 14 J. Legal Writing Inst. 53 (2008).

§ 23.4 TREAT COURTS AND OPPOSING COUNSEL WITH GRACE

Appellate litigation can be viewed as a triangulated discussion—the advocate is at one corner of the triangle, his or her opponent is at a second corner, and the court occupies the third. The conversations that take place between opposing counsel, and between counsel and the court, represent another area ripe for ethical and professional transgressions.

Two provisions of the MRPC have particular relevance here. One is MRPC 8.2(a), entitled "Judicial and Legal Officials," which provides that "[a] lawyer shall not make a statement that the lawyer knows to be false or with reckless disregard as to its truth or falsity concerning the qualifications or integrity of a judge, adjudicatory officer or public legal officer, or of a candidate for election or appointment to judicial or legal office." And the other is MRPC 8.4(d), entitled "Misconduct," which provides that "[i]t is professional misconduct for a lawyer to . . . engage in conduct that is prejudicial to the administration of justice."

How can a lawyer get into trouble under these provisions? One easy way is to suggest that the courts are biased or lack integrity. In *In re Wilkins*, 777 N.E.2d 714 (Ind. 2002), discussed in § 15.2(H), *supra*, local counsel signed a brief containing a footnote suggesting that the trial court had reached a conclusion without regard to the facts and law, and then had reasoned backwards to try to support that illegitimate conclusion. The local counsel was sanctioned with a brief suspension. *Id.* at 715–16, 718. While the language used in the offending footnote was mild in comparison to some of the more arch language contained in some U.S. Supreme Court dissents, that is not the yardstick for evaluating what is permissible for advocates.

The professional advocate, by contrast, avoids such *ad hominem* attacks on courts or opponents. One can allege and argue that a trial court made an error without saying or implying that the judge was dumb, lacked integrity, or was otherwise mendacious. This is bad practice besides—appellate judges and trial judges are usually familiar, and even friendly, with one another from bar associations, circuit conferences, and perhaps even from the trial judge sitting "by designation" with the appellate court as a visiting judge. In briefs and oral arguments, it is wise to avoid ascribing any kind of ill intent to one's opponent (or to a lower court), such as "Appellee's waiver argument plainly seeks to distract the court from the merits of the issue."

To avoid lapsing into the realm of the *ad hominem* with respect to one's opponents, a lawyer might usefully adopt an oral-argument strategy of referring to one's opponent as "my friend," "my colleague," or "my colleague on the other side." This strategy not only avoids ethical entanglements; it may even burnish the advocate's reputation in the eyes of the court.

An example helps to illustrate the point. In a case argued by one of the authors, representing the appellee, the counsel for appellant had opened the case by giving an aggressive argument, peppered with *ad hominem* references to the appellee that were punctuated with grand, armwaving gestures, including pointing repeatedly toward the appellee's counsel (presumably as a proxy for the appellee itself). In responding, the appellee's counsel gave a measured, reasoned argument responding to each of the points made by the appellant's counsel, prefacing each point with "My friend says that . . ." and then showing why the assertion was incorrect. As appellee's counsel prepared to leave the podium after his short argument, one of the panel members asked him, "This is an irrelevant question, but did you clerk for Judge Aldisert? Because in his writings, he advocates referring to one's opponent as his 'friend.' " This was followed by two minutes of praise for this collegial practice from all three judges on the panel, which concluded when the presiding judge—looking at the appellant's counsel—said "We could use more of that kind of professionalism around here." The testy appellant's counsel then had to deliver his rebuttal after all of that. (The appellee prevailed, unanimously.)

Recusal or reassignment motions (*see* § 17.2, *supra*) present special challenges of tact and grace, and can create difficulties of both ethics and professionalism. While it is the rare case where recusal or reassignment needs to be sought, it is enough to say here that such motions need to be supported by compelling facts, fairly presented. Overzealousness in this regard is likely to backfire doubly—not only will the request for recusal or reassignment likely be denied; but also, the advocate risks gaining a reputation, in that particular case if not later on, for unfairly attacking the judge instead of fairly seeking reversal of the judge's decisions.

§ 23.5 POSITIONAL CONFLICTS OF INTEREST

All lawyers should know of the prohibition upon conflicts of interest. *See* MRPC 1.7. While an exhaustive treatment of the topic of conflicts is best left for more general ethics treatises, there is a particular application of the conflict-of-interest rules that has repeated application to appellate practitioners—the special case of "positional conflicts."

Rule 1.7(a) generally prohibits a lawyer from representing a client if the representation would create a "concurrent conflict of interest," which exists where "the representation of one client will be directly adverse to another client," or where "there is a significant risk that the representation of one or more clients will be materially limited by the lawyer's responsibilities to another client, a former client, or a third person or by a personal interest of the lawyer."

Comment 24 to this rule expands on how this rule may bar the lawyer from certain "positional conflicts." It recognizes that "[o]rdinarily, a lawyer may take inconsistent legal positions in different tribunals at different times on behalf of different clients." However, the comment goes on to state that the significant-risk-of-material-limitation part of the rule can be violated, "for example, when a decision favoring one client will create a precedent likely to seriously weaken the position taken on behalf of the other client." Because appellate courts have dual roles—they are both case-deciders and precedent-makers—the appellate lawyer must be alert to the possibility that he or she will induce an appellate court to make a precedent that will adversely affect a position taken on behalf of another client in a different matter that will be governed by that precedent. Likewise, the lawyer should be attuned to any possibility that the interrelationship between the two cases might induce the lawyer to "soft-pedal" the arguments in one client's case in order to favor the interests of another client in a second case.

There are several important facets to the positional-conflict rule. First, it applies across institutions, not just to individual lawyers. Thus, an appellate lawyer practicing within a law firm should take steps to become aware of what other appellate cases are being handled by other lawyers in the institution, and what positions are being taken in those cases. Unlike the more ordinary conflict checks that law firms undertake to determine whether a new matter may be taken on by the institution without placing the firm in conflict with an existing client, positional conflicts are harder to identify and may arise well after the representation is commenced. No authority suggests that firms are required to track issues to avoid potential positional conflicts, however, and some jurisdictions have explicitly recognized that this is a practical impossibility. *See* Andrew Altschul, *Who Says You Can't Have It Both Ways? A Primer on Positional and Issue Conflicts*, 38 Labor & Emp. L. No. 1, at 6 (Fall 2009).

Second, conflicts problems of this sort may be ameliorated by informed consent. The comment to MRPC 1.7(a) indicates that "[i]f there is significant risk of material limitation, then absent informed consent of the affected clients, the lawyer must refuse one of the representations or withdraw from one or both matters." Assuming that this is permissible within one's particular jurisdiction (or jurisdictions, in the case of multistate practice), such a positional conflict can be avoided by creating separate teams of lawyers for each case, with an ethical screen implemented between them—again, assuming that both clients consent on full information.

Third, there may be circumstances where, regardless of client consent, the prudent measure is for the lawyer to withdraw. In *Williams v. Delaware*, 805 A.2d 880 (Del. 2002), a criminal lawyer was representing two different death-row inmates in separate appeals before the Delaware Supreme Court. In the two cases, the lawyer would have been arguing contrary positions about the weight that a jury's recommendation of death should be given by the trial judge. In *Williams*, the jury had recommended the death penalty, and the lawyer would be urging error in the court giving "great weight" to that recommendation; in another case being handled by the lawyer, *Garden*, the jury had recommended *against* the death penalty, and the lawyer had urged the Delaware Supreme Court that the trial court had erred by *failing* to give great weight to the jury's recommendation. The lawyer sought permission from the Delaware Supreme Court to withdraw from the representation of Williams, which the court granted: "Given his clients' disparate legal arguments, [the lawyer's] independent obligations to his clients may compromise the effectiveness of his assistance as appellate counsel for one or both clients, unless his motion to withdraw is granted." *Id.* at 882. The court concluded its opinion with praise for both sides' lawyers, commending both "for their recognition of and adherence to the highest standards of professional conduct." *Id.*

Issues of positional conflicts, which may arise in a wide variety of cases and factual scenarios, are explored in greater detail in articles such as Altschul, *supra*, and in bar opinions in several states and from the American Bar Association, *e.g.*, ABA Formal Opinion 93–377 (1993) (predating the current version of MRPC 1.7 and comment 24 thereto).

§ 23.6 COMPETENCE OR REFERRAL

Finally, the baseline rule of all ethics—reflected in its placement as MRPC 1.1—is competence: "A lawyer shall provide competent representation to a client. Competent representation requires the legal knowledge, skill, thoroughness and preparation reasonably necessary for the representation." Other provisions of the rules flesh out this obligation of competence. For example, MRPC 3.1 forbids lawyers from mounting frivolous proceedings (an obligation echoed in court rules like FRAP 38 and Fed.R.Civ.P. 11); MRPC 3.2 requires lawyers to make reasonable efforts to expedite litigation consistent with the interests of the client; and MRPC 4.1 requires lawyers to be truthful in their statements to others.

Of course, the whole point of this book is to aid the lawyer in becoming more competent as an appellate lawyer. Still, some of the most basic competence issues in appellate law come up where lawyers fail to know the rules of the particular appellate court in which a case is proceeding, and, in extraordinary cases, have failed to even become members of the bar of the particular appellate court. Lawyer competence is occasionally found wanting where the lawyer has failed to know or adhere to appellate deadlines—some of which are "jurisdictional" and therefore fatal to a case if they are missed. And, under the heading of "frivolous litigation," we are sometimes reminded of a quotation regularly attributed to American lawyer and statesman Elihu Root: "About half the practice of a decent lawyer is telling would-be clients that they are damned fools and should stop."

Finally, appellate practice is a specialized practice that demands competence and particular knowledge. While "[a] lawyer can provide adequate representation in a wholly novel field through necessary study," MRPC 1.1 cmt. 2; *see also id.* at cmt. 4, there should be no shame in a trial lawyer or a non-litigator recognizing that an appeal may be beyond the lawyer's competence, and that the better practice is to refer the matter to someone who has greater experience and competence, or to collaborate with another lawyer with such expertise. And in an extreme case, where the lawyer cannot realistically satisfy the Rule 1.1 standard of competence, such referral is required.

In the end, the ethical, professional appellate lawyer is a good appellate lawyer.

PART 5

THE FUTURE OF THE FEDERAL APPELLATE COURTS

CHAPTER 24

FEDERAL APPELLATE JUSTICE IN THE 21ST CENTURY

The administration of justice in the federal appellate courts has been in a state of constant change for the country's entire history. In 1819, oral argument in the famous U.S. Supreme Court case of *McCullough v. Maryland* "consumed nine days—three times that normally allowed for major cases." Jean Edward Smith, *John Marshall: Definer of a Nation* 442 (1996). Today, cases argued in the U.S. Supreme Court are allotted one hour total. And even that hour is a relative luxury: As noted above (§ 15.1, *supra*), only 50 years ago oral argument in a majority of the federal courts of appeals was "limit[ed]" to 30 minutes per side; today, the norm is 15, 10, or even fewer minutes per side—if oral argument is allowed at all.

Those changes have been driven principally by the demands of an expanding federal appellate caseload against a federal judiciary that has grown only incrementally by comparison. But other changes, too, have come with advances in technology. Indeed, because of new technologies like the Internet, and advances in computer software and hardware, it may seem as though the rate of change in other areas of federal appellate practice has been accelerating over the last 10 to 20 years. Word counts done with a computer word-processing program have largely replaced page counts for federal appellate briefs. Photos or illustrations embedded amidst the text of paper briefs are becoming more common. Electronic filings with the legal and factual authorities hyperlinked to the arguments in the briefs are increasingly becoming the norm; even video evidence may be embedded into an electronic brief. Judges—and sometimes, advocates—may appear for oral arguments remotely, via a telephonic or a closed-circuit video hookup.

Even the Supreme Court of the United States—the most tradition-steeped court in the country—requires briefs to be filed by e-mail attachment as well as in paper copy, and notifies lawyers of opinions in their cases by e-mail. In at least three cases, the Supreme Court has issued opinions referring to video evidence in the record and posted on the Court's website. *Brumfield v. Cain*, 135 S.Ct. 2269, 2284 n.1 (2015) (videotaped confession); *Kelly v. California*, 129 S.Ct. 564, 564 n.1 (2008) (Stevens, J., respecting denial of certiorari) (victim-impact video played at sentencing); *Scott v. Harris*, 127 S.Ct. 1769, 1775 n.5 (2007) (high-speed police chase).

But appellate courts now, as in the past, still depend on one thing that has not, at its core, changed: appellate advocacy. Yes, the mediums of advocacy have changed drastically—perhaps even radically—over time, but the job of the advocate is still the two-part task outlined by the great Karl Llewellyn in his final lecture: "to persuade the court that you ought to win," and "to provide the Court with the technical wherewithal"—the argument and the authorities—to write the opinion in your favor. Karl N. Llewellyn, *A Lecture on Appellate Advocacy*, 29 U.

Chi. L. Rev. 627, 638 (1962). That said, Llewellyn was speaking at a time when appellate arguments were a standard 30 minutes or more in length, and occurred in virtually every case; he declaimed that it was "the job of the brief" to provide the logic of the decision, but "[t]he job of the oral is two-fold: It's first to persuade the court that you ought to win; and second, to make them read that brief." *Id.* at 638–39. Today's advocate cannot assume that he or she will have the same opportunity for oral advocacy—it will almost certainly be shorter, if it is provided at all—and so today, "the job of the brief" may be to do *all* of the advocate's work.

In 2005, the American Academy of Appellate Lawyers issued a *Statement on the Functions and Future of Appellate Lawyers,* which was reprinted at 8 J. App. Prac. & Process 1 (2006). One overarching theme emerges from that Statement: Good appellate lawyers are an essential component of the appellate decisionmaking process because they "enhance the judicial tools for reaching good dispute resolutions and writing good precedent." *Id.* at 2 (footnote omitted).

Still, there are perpetual problems with the quality of appellate advocacy. Consider this important passage from the Academy's Statement:

> Appellate judges and experienced practitioners have been writing and teaching the same basic principles of appellate advocacy for at least fifty years. Nevertheless, appellate courts are flooded with defective briefs that violate those principles. From coast to coast and border to

> border, appellate judges consistently report that specialized appellate practitioners generally deliver useful, competent work product but that trial lawyers who do their own appeals often fail the needs of both their clients and the courts. Why? It is time to recognize that books, articles, and courses on appellate practice do not reach most trial court lawyers and general practitioners. Appellate process does not interest them, and they view continuing education in the field as not cost effective. And rightly so. It makes no economic sense to invest the time and money required to develop the writing habits, problem solving habits, technology support, and judicial information base of an appellate lawyer when one's expected appellate practice consists of infrequent efforts to revive failed cases and hold onto trial victories.

8 J. App. Prac. & Process at 12.

What are the solutions for these endemic problems? The Academy suggests that appellate practice as a specialty be better cultivated. Indeed, even now, "sophisticated clients understand that specialization leads to reduced expense, realistic evaluation, and the potential for better results." *Id.* Additionally, the Academy recommends that the courts themselves—judges and court administrators—"develop and cultivate bar organizations to help improve practice in appellate courts, relationships among practitioners, and lawyers' relationships with judges and court staffs." *Id.* at 13.

The Academy's Statement concludes with a list of specific initiatives that would assist in achieving these two goals: establishing state bar appellate specialization programs; adopting standards for admission to the federal court of appeals' bars; setting "minimum level of competence" standards for briefing and arguing cases in appellate courts; developing and improving the federal circuit bar associations; establishing and improving the links between state appellate courts and bar organizations; expanding resources in the courts by using experienced appellate lawyers as mediators; establishing appellate pro bono programs with experienced lawyers as mentors; and expanding educational and public-information programs on the appellate process. *Id.* at 13–15.

To that list we would add one more. In 1985, the Committee on Appellate Skills Training of the American Bar Association's Judicial Administration Division observed: "Trial court procedure is in all [law school] curricula. Appellate procedure is in very few." *Appellate Litigation Skills Training: The Role of the Law Schools*, 54 U. Cin. L. Rev. 129, 129 (1985). Despite the ABA Committee's thoughtful approach and its extensive list of recommendations (*id.* at 153–55), over 30 years afterward there has been only minor progress towards the goal that the Committee set as a "very minimum": "[E]ach law school should establish a basic course in the appellate process that can be taken by large numbers of students at a minimal cost." *Id.* at 153.

To be sure, more law schools, especially as of late, have established appellate "clinics." But those are frequently aimed at the most rarefied air of appellate law—practice before the Supreme Court of the United States. Education about the process and procedures in the courts where most appellate law is practiced—the federal circuit courts and the state appellate courts—remains severely under-served. As a result, many law schools' curricula reflects an unintended irony: Students spend three years of increasingly expensive legal education "learning the law" by reading appellate case opinions, yet in many instances they cannot even sign up for a course about the unique process and procedures that ultimately lead to those decisions.

We hope our contribution will help change that situation.

ADDENDUM

So much valuable information about the federal appellate courts is now available on the Internet, and particularly on the websites maintained by the individual courts. The authors have included the following list of web addresses of the federal appellate courts. Practitioners in these courts are advised to consult the court's website as it will often contain important information, such as local procedures and rules, internal operating procedures, as well as handbooks to guide the practice of law in that particular court. The authors have also included the website for the Federal Judicial Center, which is a research and education agency devoted to the federal courts.

United States Supreme Court http://www.supremecourtus.gov

United States Court of Appeals for the First Circuit http://www.ca1.uscourts.gov/

United States Court of Appeals for the Second Circuit http://www.ca2.uscourts.gov/

United States Court of Appeals for the Third Circuit http://www.ca3.uscourts.gov/

United States Court of Appeals for the Fourth Circuit http://www.ca4.uscourts.gov/

United States Court of Appeals for the Fifth Circuit http://www.ca5.uscourts.gov/

United States Court of Appeals for the Sixth Circuit http://www.ca6.uscourts.gov/

United States Court of Appeals for the Seventh Circuit http://www.ca7.uscourts.gov/

United States Court of Appeals for the Eighth Circuit http://www.ca8.uscourts.gov/

United States Court of Appeals for the Ninth Circuit http://www.ca9.uscourts.gov/

United States Court of Appeals for the Tenth Circuit http://www.ca10.uscourts.gov/

United States Court of Appeals for the Eleventh Circuit http://www.ca11.uscourts.gov/

United States Court of Appeals for the District of Columbia Circuit http://www.cadc.uscourts.gov/

United States Court of Appeals for the Federal Circuit http://www.cafc.uscourts.gov/

United States Court of Appeals for Veterans Claims http://www.vetapp.gov/

United States Court of International Trade http://www.cit.uscourts.gov/

United States Court of Appeals for the Armed Forces http://www.armfor.uscourts.gov/

United States Tax Court http://www.ustaxcourt.gov/

Federal Judicial Center http://www.fjc.gov/

INDEX

References are to Pages
